William Harry Rogers

Published in 2023 by Unicorn
an imprint of Unicorn Publishing Group
Charleston Studio
Meadow Business Centre
Lewes BN8 5RW
www.unicornpublishing.org

Text © Gregory Jones
Images © Gregory Jones, except where stated in the text

Image Credits:
Bodleian Libraries, University of Oxford: Figure 2.4, Appendix A Nos 18,
140, 142, 165, 168, 172, 233
British Library: Appendix A Nos 102, 103, 113
Cambridge University Library: Appendix A No. 134
State Library of South Australia: Figure 3.2

Gregory Jones has asserted his moral right under the Copyright, Designs and Patents Act 1988 to be
identified as the author of this work.

All rights reserved. No part of the contents of this book may be reproduced, stored in or introduced into
a retrieval system, or transmitted, in any form or by any means (electronic, mechanical, photocopying,
recording or otherwise), without the prior written permission of the copyright holder and the above
publisher of this book.

Every effort has been made to trace copyright holders and to obtain their permission for the use of
copyrighted material. The publisher apologises for any errors or omissions and would be grateful to be
notified of any corrections that should be incorporated in future reprints or editions of this book.

ISBN 978-1-911397-17-5
10 9 8 7 6 5 4 3 2 1

Designed by Felicity Price-Smith
Printed by Fine Tone Ltd

William Harry Rogers

*Victorian Book Designer
and Star of the Great Exhibition*

Gregory Jones

UNICORN

Contents

	Acknowledgements	7
ONE	Introduction	9
TWO	Life of the Artist-Designer	19
THREE	George Isaacs	37
FOUR	Two Signatures	46
FIVE	*The Builder*	50
SIX	Henry Fitzcook	63
SEVEN	The *Art Journal*	69
EIGHT	Silver	81
NINE	Sir Henry Cole	96
TEN	Queen Victoria's Cradle	106
ELEVEN	The Great Exhibition and its Successors	118
TWELVE	*Spiritual Conceits*	139
THIRTEEN	Illustrations	149
FOURTEEN	Playing Cards	161
FIFTEEN	Jewellery	168
SIXTEEN	Book Covers	174
SEVENTEEN	Contemporary Owners	196
EIGHTEEN	Patrons	202
	Appendices	
	A Gallery of Book Covers	216
	B Paris	285
	C Cover Design Re-use and Materials	291
	D Kate Rogers and Others	295
	Index of Titles for Books and Journals with WHR Covers	301
	Index	305

Acknowledgements

I FIRST ADMIRED A WILLIAM HARRY ROGERS (WHR) design three decades ago, and soon discovered that his designs were largely unrecognised and uncatalogued. However, the steady accumulation of information about his life and works, including a sprinkling of gleaming nuggets, has resulted in a much more comprehensive picture than I believed possible at the outset.

Throughout, I have received inestimable help and encouragement from my wife, Jenny Brown, and it is to her that this book is dedicated. Without her indefatigable research into the extended family of William Harry Rogers and his mid-Victorian London locations, her fact-checking trips to distant archives and ever-helpful comments on the complete draft, the book would have been very much the poorer.

Heading the list of others whom I must thank is Anthea Smith, great-great-granddaughter of William Harry Rogers, who most generously presented me with the brooch that he gave to his bride in 1847 and introduced me to the Coughtrie branch of the story. Among the antiquarian book community, I am particularly indebted to Paul Goldman and Robin de Beaumont for their support and encouragement in the early days of the project.

The staff of the Prints and Drawings Study Room at the Victoria and Albert Museum kindly arranged repeated viewings of their William Harry Rogers archive. I am also very grateful to the staff of the Bodleian Library for facilitating much use of their holdings. Assistance has also been received from the staff of the following institutions: the Robertson Davies Library at Massey College, Toronto, who arranged a viewing of the WHR items in their Ruari McLean collection; the Department of Prints and Drawings of the British Museum; the Royal Academy Library; the National Art Library at the V&A; the University of Reading Library; Cambridge University Library; the British Library; and last but not least, the very helpful State Library of South Australia and the Public Record Office Victoria, Australia.

Finally, it has been a pleasure to bring the book to fruition with Lord Strathcarron and the team at Unicorn Publishing Group.

ONE

Introduction

THE GREAT EXHIBITION OF 1851 created an explosion of interest in Britain in the design of all kinds of artefact, and especially in artistic design. The identities of the people who created such designs were, even at the time, generally unknown outside the immediate circles of the producers, though a few creators did attract contemporary attention. With the opening of the twentieth century, however, interest shifted away from the art and design of the previous century, and Victorian aesthetics remained in obloquy for half a century. An important stimulus for the gradual reversal of this neglect was provided by the Festival of Britain in 1951. Timed to celebrate the centenary of the Great Exhibition, the Festival helped to reawaken interest in its predecessor, and since that point both popular and scholarly appreciation of the art of Victorian design has increased exponentially. The present publication, however, is the first book-length treatment of the highly gifted Victorian artist-designer, much admired then and since, William Harry Rogers (1825–73).

William Harry Rogers created what are undoubtedly some of the most graceful and elegant designs of the middle decades of the nineteenth century, in his case over the thirty years from 1843 to 1873. His artworks were usually signed with a monogram of his initials WHR, and in this book he is also generally referred to by these initials (when writing, he normally signed himself as W. Harry Rogers, and was widely known simply as Harry Rogers). This publication brings together many new discoveries about WHR's life and work and provides, in effect, a catalogue raisonné for the artist. Figure 1.1 shows a photograph of William Harry Rogers in about 1860.

Our knowledge about designers during the Victorian period has been relatively slow to build, but has now achieved some impressive advances. Here there

1.1 – William Harry Rogers, *c.* 1860. Sepia-toned albumen photograph. Height 59mm.

9

is space only to mention briefly some of the other leading figures in British design who overlapped chronologically with WHR.

OTHER MAJOR VICTORIAN DESIGNERS

Augustus Welby Pugin (1812–52) has been universally recognised as a brilliant polemicist for Gothicism in architecture and an inspired designer in the same idiom.[1]

William Burges (1827–81) can be viewed as Pugin's successor Goth in architecture and design, creating a dream medieval world for the 3rd Marquess of Bute (1847–1900), reputedly the richest man in the world and, as a patron of limitless resources, the Celtic counterpart of King Ludwig II of Bavaria (1845–86).[2]

The much-chronicled leading figures of the self-declared Pre-Raphaelite Brotherhood – Dante Gabriel Rossetti (1828–82), Edward Burne-Jones (1833–98) and William Morris (1834–96) – also shared a fascination with the medieval world, and designed and produced artefacts ranging from fabrics and stained-glass windows to book covers and picture frames, as well as making notable contributions to painting.

Owen Jones (1809–74) is primarily important as a theorist of design rather than as a practitioner, a pioneer in drawing attention to the potential relevance of psychology.[3] His monument, *The Grammar of Ornament* (1856), was an eclectic compendium of patterns across time and culture.[4]

Christopher Dresser (1834–1904) was initially a protégé of Owen Jones, with a similar approach to design. He found his own voice, however, after an extensive visit to Japan in 1876–7. Among his designs for metalwork and ceramics, his use in some cases of simple geometrical forms inspired by Japanese originals proved to be prophetic of the later rise of modernist design.[5]

Finally, Lewis F. Day (1845–1910) was prolific both as a designer and as a writer on design. His work was always thoughtful and competent, if rarely inspired. It has something of an Arts and Crafts appearance, though Day did not share a commitment to handmade artefacts, and later accommodated Art Nouveau as well.[6]

WILLIAM HARRY ROGERS

The aim of this book is to provide a full portrait of another artist-designer of the period – in fact, it can be argued, *the* great artist-designer of the Victorian period – William Harry Rogers. WHR created pictures and designs in a unique, highly recognisable style which displays an extraordinary blend of deep art-historical awareness, inspired imagination and exquisite draughtsmanship. In contrast to the designers already mentioned, his beautifully composed designs incorporate strong classical influences, especially from the Italian Renaissance and from the idiosyncratic style of Grinling Gibbons (1648–1721). His work attracted great enthusiasm in the pages of the two leading contemporary journals of art and design, *The Builder* and the *Art Journal*.

WHR had a starring role at the Great Exhibition of 1851, where the cradle he designed for Queen Victoria's infant daughter, Princess Louise, was one of the sights of the

1.2 – The opening day of the Great Exhibition, 1 May 1851. Dickinson Brothers, colour lithograph after David Roberts, R.A. Height 485mm.

Chapter One – Introduction

exhibition, and his acclaimed designs were instrumental in at least four different exhibitors each being awarded the coveted Prize Medal of the exhibition. With more than six million visits recorded, the impact of the exhibition was unprecedented. Figure 1.2 illustrates how Paxton's Crystal Palace even swallowed Hyde Park's elm trees whole.

WHR was already on his way to becoming the pre-eminent designer of the Victorian book, specialising in an area where advances in technology opened up unprecedented opportunities in the borderland between art and design. During the 1850s and 1860s, the humble cloth book cover was reinvented as a major enticement for the purchase of a book. Heavy covers were lavishly blocked with designs in gold and, in the hands of WHR, were transformed into works of art.

After WHR's early death in 1873, aged forty-seven, his work retained its esteem in the closing decades of the nineteenth century. His greatest champion at this period was his fellow designer, Lewis F. Day, who was twenty years younger and outlived WHR by more than thirty years. Day possessed the critical apparatus and open-mindedness required to appreciate adequately the work of an artist-designer whose unique gift could not be pigeonholed within a particular school or movement. Day made no bones about the fact that he recognised WHR as the star of the Great Exhibition:[7]

> Among the mediocrities who designed for the 1851 Exhibition, Harry Rogers is conspicuous for the fertility and refinement of his design. ... [T]he Catalogue of the First Exhibition would be distinctly the weaker by the elimination of his contributions. There was no more graceful draughtsman working for manufacturers at that date than Harry Rogers. ... [T]here was no mistaking what he did for any one's but his.

Nearly a decade later, at the Society of Arts, Day doubled down on his admiration of WHR.[8] Day was recorded as having declared that:

> When the title page, or cover of a book, happened by exception to be ornamented with grace and distinction, it was sure to be the work of Harry Rogers.

Another admirer of WHR in the Society of Arts at that time was the architect Hugh Stannus (1840–1908), who taught at the Royal Academy. In the lengthy serialisation in 1894 of his Cantor Lectures on botany in design, Stannus mentioned only two designers. WHR received a positive endorsement, while Owen Jones received a distinct put-down on the botanic front.[9]

In 1901, as the jubilee of the Great Exhibition approached, the idea was floated by Adolphe Jonquet in 1900 of a permanent memorial for the exhibition and its progenitor, Prince Albert:[10]

> The Albert Institute of Design, ... enclosing a permanent gallery of creative art, represented by scheduled specimens of British design and manufacture executed during this period ... . Rooms of the Gallery to contain examples from the three greatest designers of the last 50 years of the 19th century. For example: Alfred Stevens, Room A, designs and works; Burne-Jones, Room B, designs and works; Harry Rogers, Room C, designs and works.

The proposed institute never materialised, despite receiving the backing of a couple of editors of art journals.[11]

In the twentieth century, the work of William Harry Rogers shared the common fate of Victorian art and design, spending the first half of the century in relative obscurity. It was only with the centenary of the Great Exhibition in 1951 that attention was drawn again to WHR, this time by the perceptive Nikolaus Pevsner.[12] WHR's cradle for Queen Victoria (see Chapter 10) was one of the few exhibits at the Great Exhibition to attract unqualified approval from Pevsner, who observed that WHR had 'designed a Cradle in a surprisingly pure Italian Renaissance style' and also pointed to WHR's 'spoons, book-clasps, encaustic tiles, frames, pipes, keys, a cradle, embroidery and a chatelaine'.

As Pevsner indicated, WHR designed many different types of artefact. Areas considered in detail include the fields of silver (Chapter 8), playing cards (Chapter 14), jewellery (Chapter 15), woodcarving and books (both inside and out). Further objects, such as a large gas-light chandelier, are to be found illustrated in Chapter 11, on the Great Exhibition and its successors. In the case of silver, the intrinsic value of the precious metal has helped to ensure the preservation of artefacts created more than 150 years ago.

DESIGNING SILVER

During the nineteenth century, the small number of traditional patterns of silver services was augmented by new designs, although these were often only minor variants of the traditional ones. But William Harry Rogers is revealed here as only the second identified creator of a new standard design of silver service, which was indeed entirely original; the only other identified creator of such a design is Thomas Stothard RA in 1811. Attribution of the design to WHR is possible because artwork for it is present in an important archive of WHR work acquired by the Victoria and Albert Museum in 1998 (this will be referred to subsequently as the WHR archive at the V&A). Other silverware is known to have been designed by WHR because it was described and illustrated in contemporary journals.

DESIGNING WOODCARVINGS

William Harry Rogers' father was the famous woodcarver, William Gibbs Rogers (1792–1875), and one of WHR's roles was chief designer at his father's firm. Their most celebrated production was the large Renaissance cradle carved in ultra-hard boxwood for Queen Victoria (as admired by Pevsner). The honey-coloured cradle has starred in displays from the Great Exhibition to the present day. WHR was the creative force for the cradle (with some input from Prince Albert), while evidence uncovered here shows that the actual execution of the cradle was carried out by several carvers employed by his father.

More generally, WHR argued in 1848 that the innate flexibility of Renaissance design meant that it was fundamentally more suited to encompassing the varied needs of the modern world than was the prevailing Gothic orthodoxy. He particularly advocated the cinquecento, the Italian Renaissance style of the early sixteenth century. In a well-known essay on 'The Exhibition as a Lesson in Taste', Ralph Wornum in 1851 came to the same conclusion, and pointed to WHR's design for the royal cradle as an embodiment of the approach.[13]

As well as being an important advocate for Renaissance design, WHR was heavily influenced by the works of the famous woodcarver Grinling Gibbons, which were carried out in what might be termed an English Baroque style. The intimate engagement of WHR with the work of Gibbons from his earliest age was a consequence of his father's own lifelong immersion in Gibbons and is clearly discernible in many of WHR's designs for book covers. Gibbons and WHR both created in their compositions the same distinctive tension between unruly individual details and balanced overall envelopes, a principle of artistic design which is delineated in this book and termed Global Symmetry and Local Asymmetry, or *GS-LA* for short.

THE BUILDER AND THE ART JOURNAL

In the 1840s, while still very young, WHR made regular appearances as both author and artist in the two leading journals in artistic and architectural circles, *The Builder* and the *Art Journal* (until the end of 1848 known as the *Art Union*). WHR's contributions to the two journals are described here in Chapters 5 and 7, respectively.

At *The Builder*, WHR was initially a protégé of the visionary architectural theorist, Alfred Bartholomew (1801–45). Starting in March 1844, when WHR was eighteen, Bartholomew commissioned a different design from WHR each week to head the journal's contents. Bartholomew sadly died on 2 January 1845, and was succeeded as editor by George Godwin (1813–88), who remained in post for more than thirty years. WHR's commissions from Godwin included providing polychrome interiors for two churches where Godwin was architect, and also designing the cover for *The Builder*, which was to remain in continuous use from 1848 until well into the twentieth century.

At the *Art Journal*, there was another long-serving editor, Samuel Carter Hall (1800–89). Two of his innovations drew heavily on WHR. First, in 1848 Hall introduced a scheme entitled 'Original Designs for Manufacturers', intended to raise the quality of design in Britain. In each issue, Hall published designs from WHR and others which manufacturers were free to use as models for their products. In 1848 alone, the journal published forty-five such designs by WHR, ranging from a hyacinth-glass to iron bannisters, and from a scent bottle to a coalscuttle.

Second, for the Great Exhibition of 1851 the *Art Journal* published a series of lavishly illustrated monthly supplements which together added up to a full monograph on the exhibition, available separately in book form. The *Art Journal Illustrated Catalogue* is a delight to look at, unlike the worthy but tedious multi-volume *Official Descriptive and Illustrated Catalogue*, and remains the outstanding printed legacy of the Great Exhibition. It undoubtedly owes much of its impact to WHR, who not only designed quite a number of the most handsome exhibits depicted but also created the designs for its impressive but refined gilt cover and for many brilliant embellishments to its pages. WHR went on to add distinction to each of the *Art Journal's* subsequent separately published catalogues for international exhibitions, ranging from Dublin 1853 to Paris 1867.

Chapter One – Introduction

THE CAMPAIGN AGAINST HENRY COLE

By the later 1840s, WHR, who was already a highly experienced creator of artistic designs and a practised writer on medieval and contemporary artefacts, had the youthful confidence to engage in a public battle with a powerful establishment figure. WHR was one of the group of people (which included the editors of *The Builder* and the *Art Journal*) who viewed with dismay a takeover bid for their world by Henry Cole, an amateur in design who nevertheless had the ear of government. Cole announced hubristically that British design needed to be reformed and that he was the person to do it. To this end, he set up Felix Summerly's Art-Manufactures to commission a few people in the fine art world, such as Richard Redgrave, to produce designs for household objects and to authorise relevant manufacturers to make the objects.

Although WHR was one of the designers commissioned by the Felix Summerly firm in 1847, he was outraged by the way that Cole was attempting to dragoon British art design as a whole in the direction of his own range of largely undistinguished products. Chapter 9 reveals that, as a result, WHR campaigned in the printed media against Felix Summerly through much of 1848. As was the norm at the time, most (though not all) of WHR's writings were anonymous, and the extent of his campaigning is brought to light here for the first time, using a new source.

WHR's campaign was successful and Cole was forced to close down his Felix Summerly venture in 1849. However, Cole swiftly repositioned himself at the centre of Prince Albert's scheme for a forthcoming large international exhibition in London of all aspects of manufacturing. The huge success of what became the Great Exhibition of 1851 ensured that for twenty years thereafter Cole was in unassailable control of all the governmental levers in the world of design and, inevitably, WHR was excluded from the publicly funded design establishment.

Fortunately, there was never any shortage of other people keen to commission designs by WHR, as described in the separate chapter on his patrons. Sometimes these were private individuals, such as the wealthy art-lover, Dudley Coutts Marjoribanks, the first Lord Tweedmouth. Others were manufacturers, and the largest single group were the publishers who valued the artistic and critical appeal of WHR's outstanding designs for the covers – and interiors – of books.

DESIGNING BOOK INTERIORS

WHR enhanced the interiors of many books over the period 1844–70, reaching a peak in the years 1858–62. The work is described here in Chapter 13, entitled *Illustrations*, though WHR was never a mere illustrator. His intricate designs more often provide a flow of elegant, semi-detached counterpoints to the text; their imaginativeness making them rewarding to study as independent creations.

In 1862 WHR had the opportunity to devise a book in its entirety – the text and its appearance, the engraved plates and the cover – and the result was his highly individual masterpiece, *Spiritual Conceits* (later re-issued as *Emblems of Christian Life*), discussed in

Chapter 12. Contemporary reviewers were enthralled. One critic asserted:[14]

> Few books like that of which we have here given the title ever come before the world. … the illustrations are from the graceful hand of Mr. Rogers himself, and leave one in doubt which most highly to estimate—the fertility of his imagination, or the facility of his execution.

Another critic piled on the superlatives:[15]

> This splendid book is a marvel of beautiful drawing and printing. … an exquisite artist … Of the illustrations regarded as drawings, it is impossible to speak too highly … matchless for forcible expression of sentiment.

Admiration of WHR's artistry has continued to the present time, and a striking thematic continuity with the Bilotti paintings of Damien Hirst was acknowledged by the incorporation of many designs from *Spiritual Conceits* into Hirst's exhibition catalogue.[16]

DESIGNING BOOK EXTERIORS

Sybille Pantazzi was the first of a series of modern writers to draw attention to WHR as a designer of book covers. She reported eighteen titles as having covers designed by William Harry Rogers, although much later Jane Brown and this author demonstrated that some of these were in fact designed by an unrelated artist, William Ralston, who signed his designs with the two letters WR rather than the three letters WHR.[17]

In the years following Pantazzi, a considerable number of other books with covers which can be identified as having been designed by WHR came to light, with a total of about sixty-five cover designs documented prior to the present work, in particular by Edmund King of the British Library.[18] Here, however, that number is eclipsed by the publication of 244 designs by WHR, a fifth of which appeared in America as well as in Britain. Figure 1.3 shows the appearance on the shelf of some of the books. The quality of these WHR designs for covers is almost invariably superb, and collectively they were unsurpassed in the nineteenth century. An early admirer was Ruskin:[19]

> On the cover of this volume the reader will find some figure outlines of the same period and character, from the floor of San Miniato at Florence. I have to thank its designer, Mr. W. Harry Rogers, for his intelligent arrangement of them, and graceful adaptation of the connecting arabesque.

Only the prolific John Leighton (1822–1912) designed more covers than WHR in the nineteenth century. His work is competent but, in comparison, mundane, relying mainly on pictorial realism and geometric patterns. Chapter 16 discusses the art of nineteenth-century books covers, juxtaposing the relatively few cover designs by Dante Gabriel Rossetti with those of WHR.

WHR's designs for covers provide a wonderful display of his ability to fascinate the viewer's eye by effortlessly reconciling apparent opposites – the classically restrained with the extravagant, the serious with the playful, the symmetric with the asymmetric. Virtuosic

Chapter One – Introduction

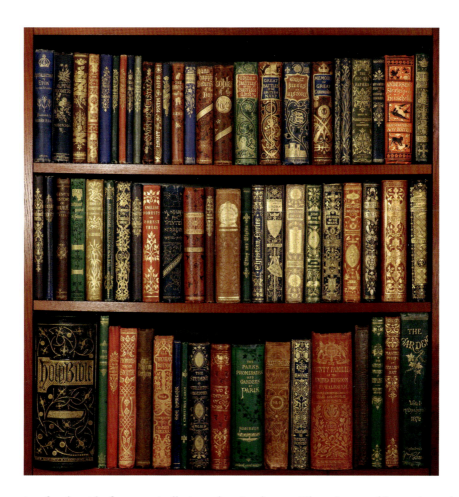

1.3 – Some book covers designed by WHR, showing their spines only. Height 840mm.

lettering for the title fits organically into the visual array. There is something unique about each design, and yet, as Lewis F. Day pointed out, they are almost all impossible to confuse with the work of any other designer. The design was usually stamped out in pure gold, which could achieve an effect described by the reviewer of one volume with a WHR cover as 'stupendously magnificent'.[20] In fact, a WHR cover could altogether upstage an author's text, as in one poetry book the same year, when the *Athenaeum* opined that WHR's design was 'perfection', while the poet's efforts were 'wearisomely foolish'.[21]

A gallery of books bearing these WHR designs is illustrated here in Appendix A. The gallery complements what we know about WHR's impressive achievements in other fields of art design, such as silverwork, by providing an almost complete picture of the core area of WHR's book design work. It thus presents an unrivalled opportunity to explore the complete arc of this artist's striking designs as they evolved over the quarter-century from 1848 to 1873.

NOTES

1. Paul Atterbury and Clive Wainwright (eds), *Pugin: A Gothic Passion* (New Haven, CT and London: Yale University Press and the Victoria and Albert Museum, 1994); Rosemary Hill, *God's Architect: Pugin and the Building of Romantic Britain* (Allen Lane, 2007).

2. J. Mordaunt Crook, *William Burges and the High Victorian Dream*, revised and enlarged edition (Frances Lincoln Ltd, 2013).

3. E.H. Gombrich, *The Sense of Order: A Study in the Psychology of Decorative Art* (Phaidon, 1979), pp. 51-5.

4. Carol A. Hrvol Flores, *Owen Jones: Design, Ornament, Architecture, and Theory in an Age in Transition* (New York: Rizzoli, 2006).

5. Michael Whiteway (ed.), *Christopher Dresser: A Design Revolution* (V&A Publications and New York: Cooper-Hewitt National Design Museum, Smithsonian Institution, 2004).

6. Joan Maria Hansen, *Lewis Foreman Day (1845–1910): Unity in Design and Industry* (Woodbridge: Antique Collectors' Club, 2007).

7. Lewis F. Day, in *British Art During Her Majesty's Reign* (J.S. Virtue, 1887), pp. 185-202; p. 189.

8. Report of 'Discussion' by the Chairman, Lewis F. Day, of 'English book illustration: 1860–1870', *Journal of the Society of Arts*, Vol. 44, 1896, pp. 455-66; p. 465.

9. Hugh Stannus, 'Artificial Foliage in Architecture', *Journal of the Society of Arts*, Vol. 42, 1894, pp. 881-91, 893-903, 905-16, 917-25 and 928-40; pp. 898, 940.

10. A. Jonquet, 'The Albert Institute of Design', *Journal of Decorative Art*, Vol. 20 June 1900, p. 172.

11. *Ibid.*, p. 151; *Artist*, Vol. 30 (January 1901), p. 50.

12. Nikolaus Pevsner, *High Victorian Design: A Study of the Exhibits of 1851* (London: Architectural Press, 1951), pp. 63, 65, 154; Nikolaus Pevsner, 'A century of industrial design and designers: 1851–1951', in *Designers in Britain 1851–1951*, Vol. 3, 1951, pp. 175-82; p. 182.

13. *The Art-Journal Illustrated Catalogue of the Industry of All Nations 1851* (George Virtue, 1851), pp. I★★★-XXII★★★.

14. *Morning Post*, 28 November 1861, p. 6.

15. *Literary Churchman*, Vol. 8, 16 January 1862, p. 35.

16. *Damien Hirst, The Bilotti Paintings*, Gagosian Gallery, 8 March–23 April 2005, 4-16.

17. Sybille Pantazzi, 'Four designers of English publishers' bindings, 1850–1880, and their signatures', *Papers of the Bibliographical Society of America*, 1961, Vol. 55, pp. 88-99; Gregory V. Jones and Jane E. Brown, 'Victorian binding designer WR: William Ralston (1841–1911), not William Harry Rogers', *The Book Collector*, 2003, Vol. 52, 171-98.

18. Edmund M.B. King, 'The book cover designs of William Harry Rogers', in *'For the love of the binding'. Studies in bookbinding history presented to Mirjam Foot* (The British Library, 2000), pp. 319-28, and *Victorian Decorated Trade Bindings 1830–1880* (The British Library and Delaware: Oak Knoll Press, 2003), pp. 204-21.

19. John Ruskin, *The Seven Lamps of Architecture* (Smith, Elder, and Co., 1849), p. 204.

20. *Herald and Genealogist*, 1865, Vol. 2, p. 362.

21. *Athenaeum*, 18 March 1865, p. 384.

TWO

Life of the Artist-Designer

When discussing the designers of exhibits in the 1851 and 1862 international exhibitions in London, Nikolaus Pevsner pointed out how little we know about the life of WHR (and his contemporaries):[1]

> … and W. H. Rogers who appears with spoons, book-clasps, … and a chatelaine (1851 and 1862). Such men would be well worth closer acquaintance. How did they live, how were they remunerated? We know little about that.

This chapter is an attempt to piece together a picture of how W.H. Rogers did live, difficult though that is for a man who was born more than a decade before Victoria came to the throne and who died too early to publish an autobiography, as some of his longer-lived contemporaries did. Only with the digital resources which have become available in the last thirty years or so has it become feasible to research in detail not only the works of an artist-designer like WHR but also the context in which they were created.

Although William Harry Rogers will usually be referred to as WHR elsewhere, the focus of this chapter on his life among his family and his friends makes it appropriate to refer to him here simply as Harry, the name by which they would have known him. Harry was born in 1825, in the wake of the great changes from rural to urban living brought about by the Industrial Revolution and the end of the Napoleonic wars. His forebears had successfully weathered the changes, and he was brought up in a London household that was imbued with both the creation and the collecting of art objects, his father becoming well-known as 'Woodcarver to Queen Victoria'. A good education and a highly individual artistic gift allowed Harry to make an early and confident entry into the adult world. His family background is sketched first, before Harry's own personal life is traced decade by decade.

FAMILY BACKGROUND

William Gibbs Rogers, Harry's father, was born in the sea-port town of Dover to William Rogers (1762/3–1839) and Sarah Rogers, née Sarah Gibbs (1757/8–1841), who had married at St Mary the Virgin in Dover on 13 April 1790. The 1794 visiting card of an uncle, 'Captain Rogers, Duchess of York, Passage Vessel, Dover', was preserved by the family.

Sarah was born in Kent, perhaps near Canterbury, and at the time of her birth there were Gibbs relatives, also with links to Canterbury, already established in the City of London, with whose descendants William Gibbs Rogers had close connections throughout his life.[2]

William Gibbs (as he will be called to avoid confusion with his son, William Harry) was the eldest of four boys and two girls, born on 10 August 1792 and baptised at the Zion Chapel in Dover. He showed precocious ability at drawing and modelling, according to his obituary in the *Art Journal*. In January 1807, when he was fourteen, a leading carver and gilder, David McLauchlan, of Printing House Square in the City of London, a stone's throw from St Paul's Cathedral, took on 'little Gibbs' as an apprentice and he soon became adept at carving with a mallet and chisel.[3] He probably lodged with his Gibbs relatives in the City, and London was to become his home for the rest of his life.

During his apprenticeship, William Gibbs was gripped by a profound interest in the woodcarvings of Grinling Gibbons. He was taken under the wing of an elderly colleague named Richard Birbeck, who, at a similarly youthful age, had worked with elderly colleagues who had worked under the direction of Gibbons himself at St Paul's Cathedral. Figure 2.1 shows one of the panels carved there by Gibbons.[4] Accompanied by Birbeck, Rogers studied the extant works of Gibbons in London, and resolved to explore similar artistic territory himself once his apprenticeship was completed. This line of direct apostolic succession back to Grinling Gibbons was in due course to provide an important influence on Harry.

2.1 – A panel carved by Grinling Gibbons for St Paul's Cathedral (above the choir stalls), as drawn by T.A. Strange. Image width 177mm.

In 1814, William Gibbs Rogers received the freedom of the City of London by presentation from David McLauchlan, who was Master of the Worshipful Company of Shipwrights 1813–14.[5] He continued to work for McLauchlan on difficult or unusual carvings for a couple more years, but then decided to move away from the firm's conventional productions to follow his own inclinations towards more sculptural carving in wood, fuelled by visits to further works of Grinling Gibbons outside London. Over the next decade he established a major reputation in this field, as signalled in 1831 by a commission from the Duke of Sussex (a younger brother of George IV and William IV) to adorn several rooms in Kensington Palace with his carvings.

About a decade after completing his apprenticeship, William Gibbs Rogers had met Mary Johnson, born *c.* 1797 in Dulwich, south of the Thames, the daughter of Martha Johnson of Camberwell. The couple were probably Gibbs cousins.[6] They married in St Giles Church, Camberwell on 28 April 1824 and began their married life at 13 Church Street, just south of Soho Square, the centre of London's famous cosmopolitan quarter.[7] William Gibbs was to remain in and around Soho Square for the rest of his working life, in a series of Soho's many spacious historic properties dating from the seventeenth and eighteenth centuries, which by this time were mainly in divided occupancy, with artists, craftspeople and tradespeople associated with the arts among the other tenants.

This was still the heyday of an object-based approach to historical study, which Rosemary Hill has identified as prevailing during the period 1789–1851.[8] English dealers (and a few collectors) ransacked France, Italy and Spain for their abundant medieval and later artefacts, which fetched considerably higher prices in Britain than on the Continent. We learn from his obituary that by the early 1830s William Gibbs' growing prosperity had enabled him to build a substantial collection of art objects, consisting principally of carvings but ranging from Limoges enamels to specimens of wrought-iron, and that 'every room in his house, at 13, Church Street, Soho, was crowded by beautiful objects'. The collection formed a selling exhibition, much visited by artists and patrons, and in particular by wealthy individuals seeking to embellish their houses. Clive Wainwright, describing Rogers as a 'celebrated woodcarver who also dealt in old carvings', quoted advice in a letter of 4 May 1842 by the architect William Burn on how a client should create atmospheric interiors in the Scottish mansion he was building:[9]

> For old oak carvings go to Messrs Pratt No. 47 New Bond Street … and for the most splendid carvings of every description to W. G. Rogers No. 18 [*sic* – actually 13] Church Street Soho where you will be charmed.

Mary and William Gibbs were to have a long and successful marriage, with five children: William Harry (b. 12 May 1825), Mary Eliza (b. 1 May 1827), Edward Thomas (b. 14 August 1830), Frederick Horace (b. 28 April 1835) and George Alfred (b. 17 October 1837). Three of Harry's younger siblings achieved distinction in their separate fields and formed with Harry an affectionate and supportive foursome: Mary Eliza as a travel writer and artist, Edward Thomas as a successful diplomat in the Ottoman lands, and George Alfred following in his father's footsteps as an artistic carver. Frederick Horace emigrated at a young age to Australia and then to California.[10]

The name Harry was not a family one and appears to have been bestowed by Mary and William Gibbs in honour of Harry Harford (1747–1827), a retired Lombard Street banker and philanthropist living in Camberwell, who had a connection with Harry's grandmother, Martha Johnson, as is evident from their two wills.[11] In 1824, in his late seventies, Harford was a witness to the Johnson-Rogers marriage, along with Mary's sister Eliza Johnson and a Gibbs cousin, Peter Gellatly, and in 1827 he spent his last months in Greenwich, where Mary Rogers probably cared for him. She gave birth to Mary Eliza Rogers, Harry's sister, in Park Row, Greenwich, adjacent to the historic naval buildings, on 1 May. On 18 June, Harford died, and a month later his will was proved.

Harry Harford's will did not list any family members but did detail two dozen legacies totalling nearly £8,000 to individuals from his childhood onwards, several of whom had been named 'Harry' or 'Harry Harford'. Martha Johnson and her three daughters were all mentioned, but her daughter Mary Rogers was singled out for by far the largest legacy, namely, £2,000 plus the residue of the estate. Her two-year-old son, Harry, had not been forgotten. A late codicil bequeathed 'my Silver Watch and two Seals one of them with my initials H.H. upon it' to Mary's husband to look after for 'William Harry Rogers till he is capable of taking care of it himself'.

HARRY IN THE 1820s AND 1830s

Throughout most of Harry's childhood, his family remained at 13 Church Street, which was then largely residential. At the western end of the street, on Dean Street, was St Anne's Church, where Harry was baptised on 10 July 1825.[12] Figure 2.2 shows on the left a contemporary engraving of Church Street and St Anne's Church, with its idiosyncratic steeple at the west end, built in 1802–03 to the design of Samuel Pepys Cockerell.[13] On the right is the same view today. No. 13 was close to the Church on the left side of the views (now rebuilt, unlike the opposite side). St Anne's Church was largely destroyed by wartime bombing in 1940, but the steeple survived and rises above the modern buildings in Dean Street built on the site of its former nave.

In 1830, when Harry was five and Mary Eliza two, the exhibits crowding the rooms of 13 Church Street included, for example:[14]

> … the singular Gothic pulpit of Martin Luther from Nuremburgh, two magnificent Gothic gates, with curious friezes of mermaids and mermen in armour, &c.

though admittedly it had been necessary to find a nearby building to accommodate

> the most splendid carved library now existing in Europe … fit for a room about 40 feet square, or gallery 160 feet in length.

To liberate space at Church Street, and also to escape the cholera and other epidemics which swept London in the 1830s, the family had a second residence in the countryside from approximately 1834 to 1840. It was six miles east of Soho, in Coborn Street, an elegant recent development outside the village of Bow. Their last two sons were baptised at Bow Church, and Harry's earliest known writings are two poems – *Love* and *Hope* – written aged twelve in Bow in 1837 and 1838. His sister Mary Eliza, the de facto family archivist, later transcribed them into a poetry album (its carved binding is shown in Figure 11.12).[15]

In the 1841 census, the Rogers family were back in Soho again, with two female servants, the sole inhabitants of 13 Church Street. By this time only the two youngest children would have been constantly at home, the others being at various stages of their formal education, with Harry's perhaps nearing completion. George Alfred, who much later wrote admiringly about his oldest brother's achievements, said that Harry had received a 'Classical education', but did not say where.[16] George Alfred himself was probably the

Chapter Two – Life of the Artist-Designer

2.2 – Left: Church Street with St Anne's Church in 1829. Image height 92mm. *Right:* Its present appearance (now Romilly Street).

George Rogers, aged thirteen, and born Middlesex, Bow, who was recorded in 1851 boarding at an exclusive private Academy, Morden Hall in Merton.

William Gibbs, a positive and engaging man, had no doubt been a supportive paterfamilias with regard to Harry's education, and he must have been delighted to find his eldest boy developing into a multi-talented and resourceful youth with his own artistic agenda, who also looked like becoming an asset to him on both his woodcarving and antiquarian fronts. With regard to carving, Harry never wielded a chisel himself but later provided beautiful designs for prestigious works made by his father's firm. With regard to antiquarian art objects, even in his late teens Harry was already able to hold his own with his father's antiquarian contemporaries and quickly became a published authority.

HARRY IN THE 1840s

In the early Victorian era, talent could make its own way without the need for formal qualifications, and by 1843 the seventeen-year-old Harry had already launched himself as a professional artist-designer (see Chapter 5), with his activities expanding throughout the decade (see Chapters 7 to 10).

Harry's address was initially 3 Great Newport Street, his father's new residence in one of the oldest streets in Soho, a couple of hundred yards from 13 Church Street.[17] It had fallen vacant on the death of Francis Deschryver, a dealer in antique furniture.[18] In 1843, the *Art Union* visited Harry's father there.[19] It admired his

> ... collection of carvings in wood, ancient and modern, in every *genre* in which carving has been attempted. Many are by Grinling Gibbons ... In the collection of Mr. Rogers are some rare and beautiful specimens of Gothic tracery, and other curiosities, dating even from the thirteenth century; also one or two small panels of grotesque design, by Giovanni da Udine, Raffaelle's *arabesquiste*.

However, between 1843 and 1847 life in Great Newport Street was disrupted by the widening of the adjacent Upper St Martin's Lane. Nos 1 and 2 disappeared, and by 1847 the Rogers' house, No. 3, had become a tavern and hotel, the family having moved to 10 Carlisle Street, Soho Square, which would be their base until the late 1850s. Another disruption in 1847 was a fire in the ancient premises at 59 Greek Street, which housed William Gibbs' carving workshop and store, losing him 'valuable frames and ancient carvings'.[20]

Harry, meanwhile, was constructing an independent existence for himself, often in the company of his great friend George Isaacs, a talented young man of the same age, whose enterprises with Harry are described in Chapter 3, and whose life has been traced by Anne Black.[21] The Rogers and Isaacs families had probably been friendly for some time, because in 1837 Harry's youngest brother, George Alfred, had been given the names of the two oldest Isaacs brothers, at that time a common way of marking a special relationship between families.

It was in company with George that Harry made what was probably his first trip abroad in 1844, when they lived in Paris for six months. Harry mused about watching the cliffs of Dover recede in a poem, *On Leaving England*, that was included in a letter sent home from '3 Rue de la Tonnellerie [transcribed as Tournellerie] près de la Rue St Honoré' and dated 30 September 1844.[22]

In Paris, Harry and George led an unconstrained social life, and this perhaps continued back in London, though their professional circumstances diverged. Harry became a prolific artist-designer and also writer, whereas George, who had a private income, was able to make further trips in search of antiquities. Socially, however, they were both to enter into alliances in circumstances which suggest that their families may have frowned upon their chosen partners. By 1847 both had left home and were lodging in neighbouring streets in St Pancras, two miles from Soho. George was at 30 George Street, off the Hampstead Road. We catch a glimpse of their informal lifestyle in a letter of 22 March 1847 from Harry to George, telling him that he had dropped by to consult George's books, and while there had enjoyed some apple pie made by Grace, who has been described as a romantic muse for George.[23]

On 8 December 1847, Harry (artist, aged twenty-two, of 22 Little George Street) married Mary Ann Lansdale (aged twenty-one, same address) at the St Pancras Registry Office in London. Mary Ann signed the marriage register with a cross and the witnesses were office staff. She was a native of Andover in Hampshire, and the 1841 census recorded her father Christopher as a hawker. However, if the marriage did indeed alienate Harry's family, the rift was soon repaired, and Harry's bridal gift to Mary Ann demonstrates that he himself felt his marriage was a solemn and pivotal moment. Figure 2.3 shows the brooch

Chapter Two – Life of the Artist-Designer

2.3 – The double-glass-sided wedding brooch which WHR gave to his bride, Mary Anne Rogers, in 1847. Height 73mm.

which he created for her, which was not only a touching love token but also announced the new way in which he would henceforward sign his artworks (see Chapter 4).

Harry and Mary Ann moved on to 3 Munster Street, near Regent's Park, where the first of their seven children was born on 15 April 1849 and named Mary Eliza (often shortened to Isa), after her aunt. Around this time Harry and another young artist, Henry Fitzcook, decided to form a professional partnership in order to smooth out their individual incomes (see Chapter 6). However, the partnership lasted for only about fifteen months before fizzling out, after which their paths do not seem to have crossed again.

George Isaacs was now no longer close at hand. He had moved out of central London, listing his father's Turnham Green villa for his membership of the British Archaeological Association for 1849 and 1850, though spending time at houses in town, including that of Harry's father.[24] On 18 September 1850, at 22 Gold Hawk Terrace, a small row of houses on the road to Turnham Green, a child named Emily Georgina Isaacs was born to George Isaacs and Marion Isaacs (formerly Lane). George precipitately sold up his possessions and before the end of 1850 he, Marion and baby Emily were embarked on a ship bound for South Australia. George received a scribbled last-minute note (dated 'Nov 28 or 29 1850') from William Gibbs Rogers, sending good wishes for the voyage from himself and the sad ladies present – 'Miss Gellatly was quite sorry about it' – and giving George the names of the Rogers cousins in Hobart.[25]

HARRY IN THE 1850s

By now, the name of W. Harry Rogers was one to conjure with in the world of artistic design. Harry invariably described himself as 'Artist' in official documentation, with sometimes an extra descriptor such as 'on wood' (i.e. to be engraved), 'illuminator', 'designer' or, once, 'painter'. He continued to use his father's premises as his own professional addresses, though it is not known to what extent he used them as workplaces. Thus, throughout Harry's membership of the British Archaeological Association, his address was listed as 'Carlisle-street, Soho-square'.[26]

The 1851 Census lists the residents of 10 Carlisle Street as William Gibbs Rogers, 'Carver in wood. Master employs 15 men', Mary his wife, Mary Eliza ('designer'), Mary A. Gellatly ('2nd Cousin') and a female servant, together with the families of two other tenants, a portrait painter and a picture restorer. The building was also known as Carlisle House and was the finest of the family's Soho locations, an impressive seventeenth-century

2.4 – Carlisle House. From the anonymous frontispiece of *Carlisle House, Carlisle Street, Soho, London* [1936]. The Bodleian Libraries, University of Oxford, G.A.Lond.4° 546.

mansion with a fashionable history and decorative interior.[27] Figure 2.4 shows its exterior.[28] The occupants since 1802 had been the family of George Simpson, a prominent picture dealer and restorer for the Royal Collection.[29] The death of Simpson's portrait painter son in 1847 meant the lofty and elegant rooms, ideal for exhibiting large carvings or holding meetings, became vacant just when William Gibbs needed them. He stayed for eight years, and both 59 Greek Street and 10 Carlisle Street must have seen intense activity in the build-up to the Great Exhibition of 1851 (see Chapter 11).

The exhibition had been constantly in the news in Britain, and also in Australia, for well over a year before it opened in May 1851, and George Isaacs would have been wryly conscious of the unique experience he was missing. As far as is known, Harry never saw his comrade again, or even corresponded with him, though the latter may reflect how preoccupied both now were by professional endeavour and family life.

In 1852, younger brothers of both George and Harry also left for Australia, much in the news since its first gold rush started the previous year. Sydney Isaacs, aged nineteen, left on the *Himalaya* on 3 July 1852 and in November the *Melbourne Argus* carried the following notice: 'GEORGE ISAACS, Esq, will find a letter from his brother, Sydney Isaacs, at the Melbourne post office.'[30] Less than a fortnight after Sydney's departure, 'Rogers Frederick H', aged seventeen, sailed for Melbourne on 15 July 1852 on the *Arundel*, en route for

Hobart, Tasmania. Here he began to farm and in 1855 married the recently arrived niece of a Tasmanian (but Dover-born) Rogers cousin, John Rogers Fraser.[31]

In the run-up to the opening of the Exhibition, Harry lost his last grandparent, the long-widowed Martha Johnson, who died in March 1851 aged eighty-four. She was the only grandparent who had lived to see him marry and, further, name his daughter after two of her own daughters, Mary and Eliza. The mourning period for her would account for the black border around a letter sent by Harry to the engraver, George Dalziel, in June 1851. Six years later, the matriarch of the extended family, Harry's great-aunt Elizabeth Gellatly from Limehouse, died aged ninety-six. The Gellatly family was close to the Rogers family, though concerned not with art but with the law, finance and shipping – Edward Gellatly, brother of Mary Ann Gellatly, gave his name to a shipping line.[32] They had been buried in Stepney Meeting House burial ground until it closed in 1853, and Elizabeth was the first Gellatly to be interred at Abney Park cemetery, an event memorialised by Harry in a long poem.[33] Abney Park, founded in 1840, was a pioneering non-denominational burial ground set in the beautiful grounds of the former Abney House in northeast London.

Harry, Mary Ann and the baby made one more short move in St Pancras, to 46 Munster Square, a more spacious area of charming terraces and central gardens, where two sons were born, Sydney and Arthur, on 15 October 1851 and 24 July 1854, respectively. However, London was more overcrowded than ever and Soho Square was only a quarter-mile from the infamous Broad Street water-pump, the source of a cholera outbreak in 1854 which killed more than 500 people in ten days. Harry and Mary Ann decided to move right out to the village of Wimbledon, at that time in rural Surrey. By 1 May 1857 they were living on the ancient Ridgeway (now Ridgway), where Emily was born on 10 November 1857. They then moved to 4 Hill Side (now Hillside), a quiet cul-de-sac off the Ridgeway, recently built on allotments at the edge of the village, with gardens at front and back and wide views across the fields and lanes of Surrey.[34] Here Kate was born on 24 August 1861.

In Wimbledon, Harry could easily take the train back into London when necessary via Wimbledon station (opened in May 1838), but a surge in his output of book illustrations at this time (see Chapter 13) may have reflected the possibility of such work being carried out largely at home. Throughout the 1850s Harry had also become increasingly sought-after as a designer of book covers, which he treated as individual, meaningful works of art, and which contributed to a steady, though not generous, income. His knowledge and enjoyment of nature is clear from his design work and also from many poems in his sister's album. Two poems sent to his sister for her birthday on May Day show just how happy he was to have escaped to Wimbledon. The 1854 poem from Regent's Park is short and pensive. The exuberant 1855 poem from the Ridgeway, Wimbledon, celebrates wild bees, flowering trees, wriggling tadpoles, happy swallows and the young villagers who have healthier complexions 'than those the Town confines'.[35]

At this time, Harry had another kindred spirit in his closest friend, Charles Henry Bennett (1828–67). Charles was a gifted and amiable man whose impoverished early career as a cartoonist and illustrator turned a corner in 1856, when he began receiving praise as a writer and illustrator of children's books. In 1856 Charles and his wife Elizabeth had named their second son Harry Rogers Bennett in Harry's honour. Harry's first son, Sydney, must have been a particular favourite of theirs, as in November 1857, Charles Bennett dedicated one of his early children's books to Sydney, who would have just had his sixth birthday.[36] Bennett's delightful dedication page was headed: 'To Sydney Rogers, a playmate of mine.' It continued:

> My Dear Syd., If you laugh heartily at the Pictures in this book, I shall not have laboured in vain … with love to all at home, Believe me to be, My dear little Boy, Your affectionate friend, Charles H. Bennett.

By 1860, the year in which his strikingly original illustrated edition of *Pilgrim's Progress* was published, with cover designed by Harry, Charles also was able to afford to move to Wimbledon, and his son George was born there in August.

Harry was not an archetypal bohemian, and was once described by Ralph Bernal as '… young Rogers, forsooth, In cravat starched and smooth …'[37] Nevertheless, both he and Charles were close friends of the bohemian Brough brothers: Robert Barnabas Brough, the coruscating social critic; John Cargill Brough, the pioneer of scientific and technical journalism; William Brough, the playwright; and, later, Lionel Brough, the actor. This eclectic group all became members – most of them founding members – of the free-wheeling artistic and literary gatherings in London public houses which evolved in 1857 into the Savage Club.[38] For years to come, this was their congenial bolt-hole from the pressures of family life and earning a living. A number of the early 'Savages' also contributed to a new illustrated literary periodical called *The Train*, launched on 1 January 1856, which saw the first appearance of Lewis Carroll, the alter ego of Charles Dodgson (1832–98). Both Harry and Charles were part of 'The Train-band', as they became known, Charles as an illustrator and Harry supplying a poem.[39]

HARRY IN THE 1860S

WHR had long emphasised the symbolic or emblematic in his art, an approach neglected at that time owing to the prevailing realism of painters and illustrators alike, who were yet to be outdone in realism by the ubiquitous camera. The arrival of Charles Bennett as a neighbour in his peaceful Wimbledon retreat in 1860 triggered plans for an ambitious collaboration in this field. One can imagine Harry and Charles striding along the surrounding farm lanes, working out the details before returning to their wives and children, who by then comprised altogether four boys and five girls aged from eleven years downwards. Their project was to combine their ideas and artistic forces to re-imagine for the nineteenth century the most famous of English emblem books, originally created in the seventeenth-century.

In their *Quarles' Emblems*, published in 1861, the two artists retained the texts for all seventy-five emblems but replaced each one's original simple woodcut with a sumptuous full-page engraving. For each one, Harry composed an extraordinary outer part incorporating a range of emblematic devices (Figure 13.5 reproduces Harry's key to these), the whole surrounding a rectangular or circular picture by Charles which vividly re-imagined the original woodcut. As an example, Figure 2.5 shows their combined emblem for 'Mundus

2.5 – An illustration by WHR (outer) and Charles Bennett (inner) for Quarles' Emblems, *1861. Height 140mm.*

Chapter Two – Life of the Artist-Designer

29

in exilium ruit' (The world rushes into banishment).[40] Charles's contribution echoes the seventeenth-century original by portraying an orb hitched to a pair of stampeding animals. Harry's dark contribution has a range of sinister creatures both real and fantastic, with the orb heading at the base for a fiery, shark-toothed gape.

After *Quarles' Emblems*, Charles reverted to writing and illustrating books for children, and he also received the ultimate accolade for a cartoonist of a staff post on *Punch*. However, he was already suffering from tuberculosis (then often recorded medically as 'phthisis'), the insidious infection that had been epidemic during his lifetime. Contemporaries who escaped it sometimes lived on into the twentieth century, and it waned later in the nineteenth century as living conditions and medical understanding improved, but it cut short the lives of many of Charles' and Harry's friends. Both of them contributed in 1867 to the Savage Club's first publication, *The Savage Club Papers*, which was sold as a benefit for a deceased Savage's family. But by the time it came out three more members, two of them listed as contributors, had succumbed to phthisis, one of whom was Charles Bennett himself, aged thirty-eight.

Harry's final period in Wimbledon was spent working on his own masterpiece, *Spiritual Conceits* (1862), whose every aspect he authored – the content and appearance of the text, the one hundred plates and the striking binding (see Chapter 12). From this settled and rewarding period in Harry's life, records exist that give glimpses of his good-natured and amicable relationship with his parents. To his mother he presented copies of both *Quarles' Emblems* and *Spiritual Conceits*, bearing inscriptions speaking of his love and gratitude, and a letter to his father in 1862 ends:[41]

> I am glad to hear you are well and jolly as usual. So am I, happily, except that a slight cold has settled in my nose … I remain
>> Your affectionate Bardolph
>> Wm Harry Rogers

In March 1862 there was also a happy event for the whole family when Harry's brother, Edward Thomas Rogers, came home from Syria to marry his Gellatly cousin, Nancy. She then returned with him to Damascus, where he was British Consul in the 1860s (his successor being the famous explorer and author, Sir Richard Burton). However, Harry's Wimbledon idyll would soon draw to a close.

Since about 1858 Harry's London base had become 21B Soho Square, the final Soho home of William Gibbs, his wife, daughter Mary Eliza and son George. The house, built in the 1790s, subsequently became part of the presbytery of the adjacent Catholic Church and is still extant, now numbered as 21A.[42] The 1861 census shows William Gibbs aged sixty-eight and still employing seven men and one boy, his wife, his daughter 'authoress' and his son 'carver in wood'; sharing the property were a piano dealer and family. Harry's daughter Isa, now twelve, was also spending some time up in town. She was not at home in Wimbledon for the census, but in Finsbury, visiting the home of a young woman from the well-known Soho Bazaar in the Square (founded as a venue for army widows and daughters to sell their handmade goods).

Despite the many and varied remunerations which came Harry's way, with five children

Chapter Two – Life of the Artist-Designer

to provide for he must have struggled sometimes to pay the bills. J.B. Groves, who was employed as a master engraver by the well-known firm of Joseph Swain, later remembered Swain engraving Harry's designs for *Spiritual Conceits*. Reminiscing about the artists with whom he had dealt, Groves remembered Harry as 'energetic' but 'always hard up'. On one occasion, Harry received a cheque from the book's publishers, Griffith and Farran, after the banks had closed, so brought it round to Mr Swain to cash. Swain did not have the cash available, so sent his boy with it to the man who made their engraving blocks, who was out. His wife, Mrs Wells, however, not only saved the day by cashing the cheque, but sent Harry's money back to Swain having neatly, if unconventionally, 'corked it up in a pickle bottle'.[43]

Harry was still very actively producing designs, especially for books, and it could have been partly to achieve greater efficiency in his daily dealings with publishers, engravers, binders and other manufacturers that Harry returned to Soho in late 1863 or early 1864. However, the major reason was undoubtedly that William Gibbs was winding down his business. By 1863 he had already vacated 21B Soho Square and was living at Stamford Cottage, New Road, Hammersmith, with his wife, Mary Eliza and George Alfred.[44] Figure 2.6 shows William Gibbs' carte-de-visite, signed by him in 1863 (for the Keele Hall caption attached to the carving, see Ralph Sneyd in Chapter 18). He retained 59 Greek Street for several more years, with a parting entry in 1865 in the Commercial list of the *London Postal Directory*:

2.6 – Carte-de-visite photograph of William Gibbs Rogers, 1863. Height 93mm.

> Rogers Wm. Gibbs, wood carver to Her Majesty the Queen (prize medal 1862), & collector of ancient works of art, 59 Greek street, Soho W.

In 1868 that last remnant of William Gibbs' Soho operation was relinquished, and he, Mary and Mary Eliza returned to their former country retreat, Coborn Street, Bow, where they were close neighbours of an old friend, Jane Saul, and her brother George, both collectors and patrons of the arts.

George Alfred Rogers now had a reputation as a woodcarver in his own right. He was also a tutor of woodcarving, which had become a fashionable hobby, and in 1864 acquired premises in Mayfair, at 33 Maddox Street, off Regent Street.[45] He moved to live there after marrying Ann Jane Burwash (Jeannie) at St Paul's, Hammersmith in 1866, and in 1867 published a popular guide to wood carving which reached its eleventh edition in 1879.[46]

31

Harry spent the rest of his life in Soho, where he had been born and bred, apart from a short spell after returning from Wimbledon. At that point the family stayed at 13 Rathbone Place, Marylebone, which now became Harry's professional address as well. It is a few minutes' walk from Soho, on the other side of Oxford Street, and is where his sixth child, Isabel, was born on 2 September 1864. His seventh and last child, and third son, was born back in Soho proper on 26 July 1867, at 3 Charles Street (now Soho Street), off the north side of Soho Square, which was to be his final abode and professional address. After having three girls in a row, this was the first opportunity for Harry and Mary Ann to reciprocate the Bennetts having named their second son Harry Rogers Bennett, and they named their new child Charles Bennett Rogers. It was a melancholy gesture, however, because Bennett had died a few months before the baby arrived. Harry campaigned personally to provide help for Elizabeth and her nine fatherless children.[47]

On 1 July 1868, the *Publishers' Circular* carried an advertisement from publishers Sampson Low for a children's book that Harry had produced, *A Bushel of Merry-thoughts*, 'Described and Ornamented by Harry Rogers, with upwards of 100 Humorous Illustrations' (see Appendix A: *174. A Bushel of Merry-thoughts 1868*). When it came out the four youngest Rogers children ranged in age from ten years down to eleven months. The inventiveness and fun of the pictures and rhymes which Harry put into the book suggest that the family might indeed have had merry times previewing his efforts. However, that autumn darker times returned as Harry and Mary Ann suffered another loss, that of their first son, Sydney – Charles Bennett's former playmate. Sydney had travelled to Damascus to join his uncle, Edward Thomas Rogers, but died at the British Consulate there a week after his seventeenth birthday, on 24 October 1868.

HARRY IN THE 1870s

After the family moves of the 1860s, Harry's physically closest relative was now his brother George Alfred, half a mile away in Maddox Street. By the time of the census in spring 1871, George had moved from No. 33 to No. 29, sharing the premises with a society florist holding the Royal Warrant, and employing four men and a boy. In the same census Harry's two oldest surviving children were no longer at home. One was Arthur, of whose whereabouts nothing further has been discovered after he was recorded at the age of six in 1861. The other was their first-born child, Mary Eliza Rogers (Isa), who Harry and Mary Ann were soon to see happily settled. She was probably the Mary E. Rogers, aged twenty-one and born in London, who was recorded by the census as a governess at Downton Castle near Ludlow. But by 30 November 1871, she had travelled to Hong Kong to marry James Billington Coughtrie at St John's Cathedral in Hong Kong, she aged twenty-two and he aged thirty-four.[48]

J.B. Coughtrie was an artist from Manchester, who had, for example, contributed a frontispiece etching of the moated Clayton Hall to a book on Droylsden near Manchester in 1859, and who went on to become an accomplished painter, at one time sharing a studio in London with prominent painter, watercolourist and illustrator, J.D. Watson, and with other professional artists.[49] Coughtrie was an enthusiastic member of the Savage Club and 'dear friend' of the loquacious Gustave Strauss, a pillar of the club who was known in his later years as the Old Bohemian. Strauss recounted in his memoirs that James, who 'was married to a daughter of the late Harry Rogers' had painted his portrait and presented it to him.[50]

Harry had known James for several years before the wedding, and when James had left for Hong Kong on 19 April 1866 he had been presented with a *liber amicorum* for which Harry had designed a cover that incorporated 'Bon Voyage' and a JBC monogram, the artwork for which is present in the WHR archive at the V&A.[51] Despite his strong artistic leanings, Coughtrie pursued the safety of a career in insurance, initially as a clerk for Holliday, Wise & Co. He became the Secretary of the China Fire Insurance Company at about the same time that he married Isa.[52]

The next year saw the death of Harry's mother at 21 Coburn Street on 21 October 1872, aged seventy-five (and eighteen months away from her golden wedding anniversary). Six weeks before his wife died, William Gibbs Rogers had secured a plot in Abney Park cemetery, in which she was buried. As a memento after her death, Mary Eliza presented her mother's friend, Jane Saul, with the copy of *Quarles' Emblems* that Harry had inscribed to his mother. While Harry and Mary Ann were in mourning for his mother, the good news would have reached them towards the end of 1872 that their daughter Isa was expecting to give birth to their first grandchild in the spring. By this point, however, Harry's own health was failing, a victim of the disease which had already killed his friend Charles Bennett.

2.7 – The Gellatly obelisk at Abney Park; WHR was buried nearby.

Harry did not live to hear the news from Hong Kong of the birth of his first grandchild, Kate Ruskin Coughtrie, on 7 March 1873.[53] The remarkable, intense and creative life of William Harry Rogers was extinguished well before its time, on 19 January 1873 at 3 Charles Street, aged forty-seven. The event was reported by George Alfred, who had been present at the death, the cause certified as phthisis pulmonalis.

Harry was buried with his mother at Abney Park. The cemetery is now also a nature reserve, and the Rogers gravestone or monument has not yet been uncovered.[54] Figure 2.7 shows the obelisk which still stands at the neighbouring Gellatly grave, however, and whose inscriptions include a commemoration of Harry's sister-in-law, Nancy Rogers, who died in Damascus in 1865.[55]

The records for the Rogers grave show also that, two years after Harry's death, it received George Alfred's only child, Harry's wife, and finally his father. The *Morning Post* announced the birth of George Alfred's son in September 1874, but Alfred Horace Gibbs Rogers lived for only four months. After Harry died, his widow Mary Ann joined the exodus from central London to newly built suburbs, moving two miles north to 23 Chalk Farm Road with their remaining children. But she was also suffering from tuberculosis and died aged forty-eight on 12 January 1875, attended at the last by Mary Eliza. Two months later, on 21 March 1875, Harry's father, William Gibbs Rogers, aged eighty-two, was recorded at inquest as 'Found dead. Syncope' (i.e. fainting) at 21 Coborn Street.

EPILOGUE

With Sydney dead, Isa married and Arthur vanished, what happened to the remaining four orphans of Harry and Mary Ann? The eldest daughter, Emily, went out to support her married sister, Isa Coughtrie, in Hong Kong. The two younger sisters, Kate and Isabel, were taken under the wing of their aunt Mary Eliza, and are seen in the 1881 census with her at 7 Southampton Street (now Conway Street), off Fitzroy Square. Appendix D describes how Harry's artistic gifts lived on through three of his daughters, tracing the careers of Kate and Isabel Rogers, together with that of Isa's oldest daughter, Kate Ruskin Coughtrie.

Harry's youngest child, Charles Bennett Rogers, was aged only seven when his mother died in January 1875. It seems likely that he too was initially taken in by his aunt Mary Eliza, or by his uncle George Alfred and aunt Jeannie. In 1879, aged twelve, he obtained a highly competitive place at the London Orphan Asylum, a charitable institution established in 1813 that had recently moved to spacious grounds in Watford in Hertfordshire, where he remained until 1882. In the list of children, his entry reads:[56]

> Rogers, Charles Bennett, born 26th July, 1867. Both parents dead. Father was an artist and author; three children unprovided for. [Born] St. Anne, Westminster.

However, it has not been possible to trace Charles Bennett Rogers after the early 1880s.

Of Harry's own siblings, Edward Thomas Rogers survived Harry by just over a decade. He received the title Rogers Bey for his distinguished service in Egypt, dying in Cairo on 10 June 1884. George Alfred Rogers died at 29 Maddox Street on 30 August 1897. Mary Eliza Rogers, maiden aunt and universal helpmeet to the family, lived on into the twentieth century, taking on the orphaned children not only of Harry but also of Edward Thomas, and dying in Surbiton on 18 February 1910.

Chapter Two – Life of the Artist-Designer

NOTES

1. Nikolaus Pevsner, 'A century of industrial design and designers: 1851–1951', in *Designers in Britain 1851–1951*, Vol. 3, 1951, pp. 175-82; p. 182.

2. Genealogical information (mainly from church records and state registration of family relationships, censuses, wills and trade directories) has been accessed via public record offices or www.ancestry.co.uk, except where otherwise indicated; the visiting card is at V&A E1138-1998.

3. *Art Journal*, 1875, pp. 206-07.

4. Reproduced from Thomas Arthur Strange (c. 1858–1906, author and publisher), *English Furniture, Decoration, Woodwork & Allied Arts* (1900), p. 15. See also David Esterly, Grinling Gibbons and the Art of Carving (V&A Publications, 1998), pp. 162-7.

5. C. Harold Ridge, *Records of the Worshipful Company of Shipwrights*, Vol. 2: 1728– 1858 (Phillimore, 1946), pp. xii, 62, 83. William Gibbs Rogers was apprenticed in January 1807; their '*Freedom book*' has been lost.

6. It is likely that Harry's maternal grandmother, Martha Johnson, was born as Martha Gibbs, sister of Elizabeth Gibbs (baptised 11 March 1766 and 16 July 1764, respectively, in Holborn). Elizabeth (born in Leather Lane, Hatton Garden) married Peter Gellatly (in Canterbury) and later their son Peter witnessed the Johnson-Rogers marriage. His daughter Mary Ann Gellatly, visiting the Rogers family on 30 March 1851 (three days after Martha's death), was entered in the census by William Gibbs Rogers as 'second cousin'. Martha's marriage to a Johnson and baptisms of her children remain untraced; it was possibly a re-marriage.

7. Church Street was renamed Romilly Street in 1937. See F.H.W. Sheppard, *The Parish of St. Anne Soho*, Survey of London: Volumes 33 and 34 (Athlone Press, 1966), Vol. 33, pp. 202-03.

8. Rosemary Hill, *Time's Witness: History in the Age of Romanticism* (Allen Lane, 2021), pp. 2, 272-84.

9. Clive Wainwright, *The Romantic Interior: The British Collector at Home 1750–1850* (New Haven, CT and London: Yale University Press, 1989), pp. 49-53; p. 60, citing Scottish Record Office MS GD 152/58/2/6.

10. There are photographs and brief biographies of William Gibbs Rogers and his family on a website curated by his descendant, Joyce Stephenson: woodcarverschildren.weebly.com

11. Harry Harford: Probate 18 July 1827. Martha Johnson: Probate 11 April 1851. Martha's will included the bequest of a dial clock to her granddaughter Mary Eliza Rogers, and half the residue to each of her two daughters, Mary Rogers and Eliza Brett.

12. Sheppard, *The Parish of St. Anne Soho*, op. cit., Vol. 33, pp. 256-77.

13. *London and its Environs in the Nineteenth Century, illustrated … by Thomas H. Shepherd* (Jones & Co., 1829), Plate 123, opposite p. 107.

14. *Morning Post*, 14 June 1830, p. [1].

15. Mary Eliza Rogers (compiler), *Gleanings from an Old Desk* (unpublished album), pp. [24]-[25].

16. *The Builder*, 1879, p. 1387.

17. Sheppard, *The Parish of St. Anne Soho*, op. cit., Vol. 34, pp. 343-6.

18. Mark Westgarth, *A Biographical Dictionary of Nineteenth Century Antique & Curiosity Dealers*, Regional Furniture Society, 2009, p. 88.

19. *Art Union*, Vol. 5, 1 September 1843, p. 248.

20. Sheppard, *The Parish of St. Anne Soho*, op. cit., Vol. 33, p. 189; *Morning Post*, 21 April 1847, p. 6.

21. Anne Black, *Pendragon: The Life of George Isaacs, Colonial Wordsmith* (Mile End, South Australia: Wakefield Press, 2020).

22. Rogers, *Gleanings from an Old Desk*, op. cit., pp. [38]-[39].

23. Bodleian Libraries MS. Eng. Misc. c. 22, fols 22r-22v; Black, *Pendragon*, op. cit., pp. 23-4.

24. Black, *Pendragon*, op. cit., p. 26.

25. Scrapbook of George Isaacs, State Library of South Australia, D Piece (Archival), D6668(Misc), p. 59. Miss Gellatly would have been Mary Ann Gellatly, eldest daughter of the family, recorded visiting Carlisle Street in 1851.

26. *Journal of the British Archaeological Association*, Vols 3-9, 1848–54.

27. Sheppard, *The Parish of St. Anne Soho*, op. cit., Vol. 33, pp. 145-7. Another Carlisle House, on the opposite side of Soho Square, was demolished in 1791: *Ibid.*, pp. 73-9.

28. The illustration is based on an anonymous photograph forming the frontispiece to *Carlisle House, Carlisle Street, Soho, London*, British Board of Film Censors [1936]. The text is signed J.B.W. by the Board's Secretary, Joseph Brooke Wilkinson. Another version of the same photograph appears as Plate 99 in Sheppard, *The Parish of St. Anne Soho*, Vol. 34, 1966, where it is described (p. xii) as taken 'in 1936. Photograph in possession of G.L.C., copyright unknown.'

See also Sian Barber, 'Wilkinson, Joseph Brooke (1870–1948)', *Oxford Dictionary of National Biography* (2015).

29. www.npg.org.uk/research/programmes/directory-of-british-picture-restorers/british-picture-restorers-1600-1950-s

30. prov.vic.gov.au, unassisted passengers lists: VPRS 947/P0000, October–November 1852; trove.nla.gov.au/newspaper: *Melbourne Argus*, 1 November 1852.

31. prov.vic.gov.au, unassisted passengers lists: VPRS 947/P0000, October–November 1852; Frederick Rogers may have farmed on land granted in 1833 to Harry Harford Ridler, brother of Martha Johnson's executor, Frederick Ridler (H.H. Ridler himself had recently returned to London).

32. George Blake, *Gellatly's 1862–1962: A Short History of the Firm* (Blackie, 1962).

33. Rogers, *Gleanings from an Old Desk, op. cit.*, pp. [4]-[5].

34. Richard Milward, *Historic Wimbledon* (Fielders, 1989), pp. 150-56.

35. Rogers, *Gleanings from an Old Desk, op. cit.*, pp. [30]-[31].

36. The book was Charles H. Bennett (editor and Illustrator), *Old Nurse's Book of Rhymes, Jungles and Ditties* (Griffith and Farran, 1858).

37. Scrapbook of George Isaacs, *op. cit.*, p. 10.

38. www.savageclub.com; Aaron Watson, *The Savage Club: A Medley of History, Anecdote and Reminiscence* (T. Fisher Unwin, 1907), pp. 16-23.

39. William Harry Rogers, 'Song', *Train* (1857), Vol. 3, p. 62. *Edmund Yates: His Recollections and Experiences*, two vols (Bentley, 1884), Vol. 1, p. 326.

40. *Quarles' Emblems, illustrated by Charles Bennett and W. Harry Rogers* (Nisbet, 1861), Book 1, Emblem 11.

41. National Art Library, Special Collections, V&A number MSL/1985/4.

42. Sheppard, *The Parish of St. Anne Soho, op. cit.*, Vol. 33, pp. 80-81.

43. British Library Add MS 88937/2/3 [1916], p. 17.

44. Rogers, *Gleanings from an Old Desk, op. cit.*, p. [71].

45. *Morning Post*, 16 July and 2 August 1864. pp. [1] and 5.

46. George Alfred Rogers, *The Art of Wood Carving* (Virtue & Co., 1867).

47. British Library, Add MS 35226, Vol. V. 1865-1868, f.290, William Harry Rogers: Letter to Dean Stanley.

48. *London and China Telegraph*, 22 January 1872, p. 58.

49. John Higson, *Historical and Descriptive Notices of Droylsden, Past and Present* (Manchester: John Higson, 1859); information provided by a great-granddaughter of Isa Coughtrie.

50. [Gustave L. M. Strauss], *Reminiscences of an Old Bohemian*, two vols (Tinsley Brothers, 1882), Vol. 2, p. 183.

51. V&A E692-1998 and E828-1998.

52. *The Chronicle & Directory for China, Japan, and the Philippines, for the year 1868* [and *1876*], Hong Kong: The 'Daily Press' Office.

53. *London and China Telegraph*, 21 April 1873, p. 255.

54. Recorded as Grave 050831.

55. Recorded as Grave 019628.

56. Surrey County Council's History Centre: London Orphan Asylum, Watford, *Annual Report 1882*, p. 71. The institution was renamed Reed's School in 1939 after its founder, and subsequently moved to Cobham, Surrey.

THREE

George Isaacs

EORGE ISAACS WAS A CONTEMPORARY of WHR and his closest friend as a young man in the 1840s, from 1843 (or earlier) until 1848, when there was a cooling, followed by a complete break in 1850.

The link between WHR and George can be traced in a number of 1840s journals, but a fuller view of their connection has become apparent only with the revelation that George maintained an extensive scrapbook, which has been in the State Library of South Australia since 1916.[1] The scrapbook is featured in a recent biography of George Isaacs by Anne Black, who is married to his great-great-great-grandson.[2] George's full name was George Samuel Isaacs and his date of birth, documented only indirectly as 5 January 1825, makes him the elder of the two friends by a few months.[3] He died aged fifty-one on 14 February 1876, slightly more than three years after WHR.

It is likely that the fathers of George and of WHR had met in the antiquarian world. George was the eldest son of a prosperous dealer in works of art, Samuel Isaacs. An 1838 illustrated trade directory showed the grand facade of his premises at 131 Regent Street, with the caption: 'S. Isaacs. Importer of Paintings, China & Curiosities'.[4] The alphabetical Street Directory on the publication's wrapper listed him as 'Issacs, S. Dealer in Jewellery and Bronzes'.

The dual interests of Samuel Isaacs in paintings and in objets d'art were reflected in a number of auction sales undertaken as he ran down his business in the mid-1840s. Two of these were held by the auctioneers Foster and Son, the first at their premises in Pall Mall on 14 February 1844, featuring:[5]

> the capital collection of pictures of the Dutch, Flemish and French schools, the entire property of Mr. Samuel Isaacs, of Regent-street, collected at a liberal expense from distinguished cabinets in England and on the continent, and to be sold in consequence of the proprietor retiring from business.

The second was held over the five days, 15–19 May 1848, in Isaacs' large house at 7 Upper Gower Street. It featured:[6]

> the very rare collection of objects of art and vertu, and all the singularly elegant furniture, cellar of 200 dozen of very choice wines, sideboard of 1,000 ounces of chased and modern plate, a fashionable brougham, and effects of Samuel Isaacs,

Esq. In attempting to describe this melange of taste and ornament, Messrs. Foster feel embarrassed by the rarity and beauty of the collection … Limoges enamels of rare quality, a collection of Raffaelle ware, among which are a few pieces matchless for form, colour, and subject; … and a vast assemblage of beautiful specimens of taste and curiosity.

After this sale, the Isaacs family downsized to an out-of-town villa in Turnham Green, near Chiswick.

Although the primary business of William Gibbs Rogers was wood-carving, he also collected and dealt in old carvings and curios. Both sons shared their fathers' antiquarian interests, and there are several records of WHR and George pursuing these in tandem. The earliest of these relates to a conversazione held by the fledgeling Institute of the Fine Arts at Willis's Great Room on 25 May 1844.[7] Both WHR and his father were substantial individual lenders of the exhibits arranged around the room, but the entry for a piece of fifteenth-century iron work concludes: 'Contributed by Mr. W. Harry Rogers, with the permission of the owner, G. Isaacs, Esq., of Claremont-terrace, Pentonville.'

THE HESPERUS

Several months before the conversazione at Willis's, WHR was already involved in a literary enterprise with George. *The Hesperus* aimed to publish work only by youthful contributors. It ran for just five issues from September 1843.[8] The publication was anonymous, with contributors identified only by their initials, but George's scrapbook contains letters by him as editor of the *Hesperus*, where he was also leading contributor ('G.I.' for prose and 'S.I.' for poetry). WHR ('R.') was the next most frequent contributor.[9] Appropriately for one who was to make a career in journalism, George's contributions fill most of each issue's twelve pages with an eclectic mixture of opinion, poetry and fiction.

WHR's contributions to the *Hesperus* were more serious. In each issue he reviewed a particular topic in art history, such as the fleur-de-lys, in the learned manner which later characterised his art history contributions to the *Art Journal* and *The Builder*. He wrote on the following topics. Issue 1: The style of the sixteenth century, pp. 3–4; Issue 2: The daisy, pp. 18-19; Issue 3: Long hair, pp. 26-8; Issue 4: Royalty of purple and vermillion [*sic*], pp. 38-40; Issue 5: The fleur-de-lys, pp. 53-5. In the first issue, WHR also discussed one of the odes of Horace, for which he produced an English version, 'Friendship'.[10]

Shortly after the conversazione of 25 May 1844, WHR and George left London in order to live in Paris for about six months. About seventeen years later, in Australia, George committed to paper a rollicking account of the visit, though its two anonymised protagonists were identified only relatively recently by Anne Black.[11]

THE PARIS MEMOIR

George's account of his time with WHR in Paris appeared in a magazine he published in South Australia in April 1861, called *Number One*, which, appropriately enough, ran for only one number. Most of the contents were written under George's pseudonym of 'A. Pendragon' (i.e. a pen drag on) from Gawler, a small town north of Adelaide. The memoir was an article entitled, 'How we fared when hard up in Paris', in which Isaacs explains that he and WHR (who he calls 'Harry R—') lived in Paris 'for about six months of the year 1844', when 'we had neither of us reached the age of twenty'. George reprinted the memoir in 1865 in book form, with minor editorial corrections – see Appendix B for a full reproduction.[12] Whether WHR was ever aware of his Australian depiction is not known.

In George's memoir, it is explained that 'Harry's income was a precarious one. He received from time to time a five-pound note from England, and made some few francs a week out of commissions from the booksellers. I had more assured resources; about £125 a year, from house property—and £100 saved from the rents of two previous years. We had, however, a common purse.'

The two of them ran through all the money they had brought to Paris for the six months in just six weeks. They 'had a taste for masquerades, dances at the Barrieres, billiards, punch, and pastry lunches', not to mention 'the little suppers of four—the excursions (also of four) to Versailles, Montmartre, and other suburban shows'. But fun only accounted for about a third of the £60 which Isaacs had brought with him. George explains that 'Harry R— was an artist; I had no profession; but shared with him an enthusiasm for art, a great passion for antique remains, and some taste for literature.' As a result, George spent the other £40 on 'my ungovernable passion for old china, silver chasings, quaint enamels, ivory carvings, and illuminated MSS'.

After a fortnight of desperate measures to stave off starvation after the money had run out, George records that 'Harry, wistfully regarding my collection of rarities' suggested a sale. 'Surprise, for a moment, struck me dumb: were the pangs of hunger driving Harry mad, that he, an artist, and an antiquary, should suggest such an outrage.' Eventually, though, George cracked and decided to pawn 'a choice gold ring, set with an antique gem'. Harry went to pledge it at the Mont de Piété for 40 or 50 francs, while George ordered a slap-up meal for them at the Café de France. But Harry arrived with neither money nor the ring, which had been impounded by an official because he was underage. George's moneyed father fortunately arrived in Paris in the nick of time, and George and Harry were able to resume their enjoyment of Parisian life.

WHR IN THE ST GERMAIN-DES-PRÉS QUARTER

It is not known how WHR 'made some few francs a week out of commissions from the booksellers'. Perhaps he drew illustrations for engraving or 'illuminated' individual customers' purchases for presentation. Nor do we know if the occasional five-pound note from England was payment for drawings or simply an allowance from his father. We do know that some drawings which he made in Paris at this time were published in *The Builder* several years later.

The memoir says that WHR and George lived in a suite of rooms on the fifth floor at 15 Rue de Bussi. The street (now Rue de Buci; then in fact Rue de Bussy) is just east of the famous church of St Germain-des-Prés on the left bank of the Seine. A 1904 monograph on the Rue de Buci, containing a ground plan of the street and a photograph of No. 15 (now demolished), shows it as a seventeenth-century townhouse with four storeys surmounted by a triangular pediment. However, at the rear it extends behind the five-storey No. 13 where the apartment occupied by WHR and George was presumably to be found, at the back and up many stairs.[13]

In the WHR archive at the V&A are twenty drawings on thin paper of objects studied by WHR in Paris, mainly in the area of St Germain-des-Prés, some of them annotated.[14] Several of the drawings were later worked up by WHR for *The Builder*. The earliest to appear, in 1848, was an engraving of a Romanesque capital surmounting a column in the church of St Germain-des-Prés itself, unchanged in its appearance to the present day.[15]

Two years later, WHR produced four articles in *The Builder* on the subject of the decorative exterior ironwork of Parisian buildings, with engraved illustrations based on some more of the drawings.[16] The ancient iron door-knockers particularly attracted WHR's attention. An example in the Louvre was later illustrated by Burty.[17] A recent walk around the area of St Germain-des-Prés reveals that several of the objects drawn by WHR are still in situ, including a few of those engraved for *The Builder*. Figure 3.1 shows two examples. In the centre is the engraving produced from WHR's drawing of a door-knocker with a lion's head boss, said to be of the Renaissance period.[18] On the left is a photograph of it now, having sadly lost the finial at the top and the strapwork to the left of its hinge. On the right is another door-knocker drawn by WHR, but not reproduced in *The Builder*, which has been preserved by the drastic means of nailing it to the door and rendering the cherub at the base almost invisible by painting over it.[19] This door faces the Seine, at the Bibliothèque Mazarine of the Institut de France (see Figure B.1 in Appendix B).

One of the Paris drawings in the WHR archive has been torn in half across its inscription.[20] When the two halves are joined up, WHR's caption to his drawing reads 'Sketch of the bannister of my own Francaise. Maison Sorbonne 13 – rough but good in idea.'[21] One could speculate that 'my own Francaise' was WHR's partner at those dinners

3.1 – Centre: Renaissance door-knocker in Paris as drawn by WHR, from *The Builder*, 1850. *Left:* Its present day appearance. *Right:* Another knocker drawn by WHR, at the Bibliothèque Mazarine.

and excursions alluded to in George Isaacs' memoir and, further, that years later it was WHR's wife or sister who tore the artwork right across the word 'Francaise'.

EARLY ARCHAEOLOGY

After Paris, WHR and George remained friendly and gave linked talks on antiquities at the fourth annual congress of the British Archaeological Association (BAA) at Warwick in July 1847. Interest in the new field was high, and the *Illustrated London News* (*ILN*) devoted three of its broadleaf pages to the meeting.[22] The *ILN* was particularly impressed by WHR, describing:[23]

> a very excellent paper, by Mr. W. Harry Rogers, on Limoges enamels, especially illustrative of the beautiful collection of these objects in Warwick Castle. Mr. Rogers traced the history of enamels from the period of Egyptian history to the 17th century, and explained the various changes and vicissitudes through which it had passed. This paper was followed by another good contribution on the same subject, by Mr. George Isaacs.

WHR's wide-ranging paper on enamelling was published by the BAA the following year.[24]

George's more specific paper on a single enamelled plate (belonging to the Rev. Henry Crowe) was also published by the BAA in the same volume.[25] This plaque bore a long and somewhat opaque Latin message inscribed at its rim, and George recounted as follows that he had turned to WHR to translate the legend from the Latin:[26]

> It has been thus rendered by Mr. W. Harry Rogers:
> 'His art was before gold and gems. He, Henry, before all as an inventor gives, while living, presents in brass to God. His life places *him* (who is equal to the Muses in intelligence, and before Mercury in oratory) on a level with the saints in fame. As a servant sent before, he fashions gifts acceptable to God. May an angel after the gifts snatch the giver to heaven! Yet should it not accelerate or excite thy grief, O England, for him to whom peace, war, activity, and rest, are alike.'

Only four years later, the British Museum received the plate as a bequest from the Rev. Crowe.[27] The BM catalogue entry notes that several different alternative translations of the Latin inscription have been offered since that of Isaacs, but WHR's authorship is not mentioned.

Following the Warwick meeting in July 1847, WHR returned to the topic of enamelling at the BAA meeting on 12 January 1848, and his talk was again printed in the BAA's journal.[28] WHR exhibited an enamelled crucifix 'kindly placed at my disposal by Messrs. Falcke, of Oxford-street' and drew attention to its monogram of 'IHI', deviating from the usual IHS or IHC, and concluded that this probably represented a simple error, perhaps influenced by the abbreviation INRI. He further observed that similar errors were widespread, ending with the example of a 'Naria' ring:

> I may close by reminding you, that upon a costly nigellum ring, exhibited at one of our meetings by Mr. George Isaacs, it was seen that the word 'Maria' commenced with an N.

Like the Rev. Crowe's enamelled plate, the Naria ring is now in the British Museum.[29] George sold his prized collection of early rings in 1850 via Thomas Crofton Croker to Lord Albert Conyngham, who was created Lord Londesborough in 1850.[30] Croker then edited a privately printed catalogue of the collection.[31] A dozen of the rings, including the Naria ring, subsequently passed to Sir Augustus Wollaston Franks, who bequeathed them to the museum in 1897.

Two of George's other rings in the Franks bequest were each set with a toad stone as an amulet.[32] They featured in a paper on toad stones which George contributed to a BAA meeting on 30 May 1849.[33] After this, neither WHR nor George contributed again to the BAA's journal, though they remained listed as BAA members until at least 1855.

DRIFTING APART

Despite their shared experiences and especially their shared interest in antiquities, WHR and George drifted apart in the late 1840s, though they were still in touch. Figure 3.2 shows an invitation to George from WHR dated 9 October 1849 (for the group to whose meeting George was invited, see Chapter 5).

WHR was starting to concentrate upon the busy professional career in London which he needed in order to support the wife he married in December 1847 and their first child, born in April 1849. Thus, when he made a business trip to Paris in 1849 he was busy recording the quinquennial Exhibition of the Works of Industry in France for the lengthy features on it which were carried in the August and September issues of the *Art Journal* (see Chapter 7), and was unlikely to have been able to linger to revisit his old haunts. George, on the other hand, continued to make leisurely trips on the Continent, mingling agreeably with other connoisseurs. His experiences in France during the period 1847–8 are described in another of his autobiographical memoirs, 'Without a passport'.[34]

George's chapter opens with him accidentally meeting 'Lord Dereham, previously the noted Sir J—b A—y … prowling about the *Bric-a-brac* shops of Paris'. The lightly disguised reference is to Lord Hastings (1797–1859), previously Sir Jacob Astley, whose family seat was at Melton Constable Hall, near Dereham in Norfolk. By helping Astley, Isaacs became embroiled in a legal dispute which prevented him travelling to France with a passport:

> I, nevertheless, made two short excursions to Paris and back without passport and without molestation; for being well-known to the landlords of the Marine Hotel at Boulogne, and the Hotel de la Bourse, Paris, at which houses I was accustomed to sojourn, I was enabled with their aid to evade the ordinary police regulations as regarded passports.

Thus encouraged, Isaacs embarked on a longer stay in the South of France. Here, however, he suffered a series of problems due to his lack of a passport, until finally he found safety just over the Sardinian border (at that time) in Nice: 'for many months my happy home'.

In 1850, the cosmopolitan life led by George came to an abrupt end. He abandoned the life of a well-connected dealer and connoisseur, and left the country for a new life in Australia, sailing for Adelaide from Gravesend on 29 November on the *Mountstuart*

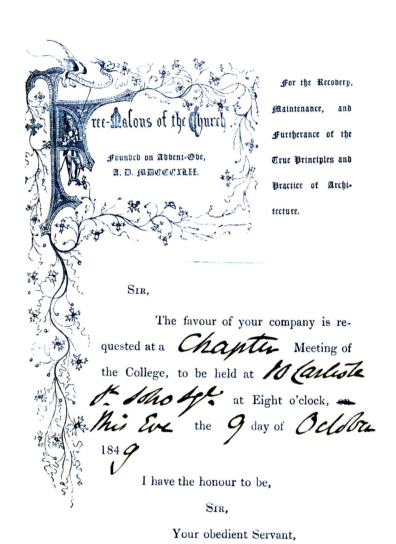

3.2 – Invitation from WHR to George Isaacs, 9 October 1849. The device of St George and the dragon was created by WHR in 1843 or 1844; it appeared in *The Builder* on 6 April 1844 (Vol. 2, p. 181). State Library of South Australia D 6668(Misc), Scrapbook of George Isaacs, p. 61.

3.3 – A chivalric design for George Isaacs, as drawn by WHR in the *Art Journal*, 1858. Width 40mm.

Elphinstone with his new-born daughter, Emily Georgina Isaacs, and her mother Marion. Marion named herself as 'Marion Isaacs formerly Lane' when she registered Emily's birth, but no trace of a marriage between George and Marion has emerged, though they were to live as though married for decades in Australia. A bitter court case with family members about his inherited properties or their disapproval of his relationship with Marion are likely to have been precipitating factors for his sudden departure. Further, by mid-century the gentleman antiquarian was starting to be eclipsed by a new professionalism.[35] Australia offered attractive new possibilities, and early gold discoveries there in the late 1840s were already fuelling emigration by people hoping to prosper in the event of a gold rush.

Before sailing, there was just time for George to sell up the treasures he had been accumulating since his Paris days with WHR six years earlier. The auctioneers, Puttick and Simpson, advertised the sale of 'Choice Works of Mediaeval Art, the Collection of Mr. George Isaacs', to be held on 12 November.[36]

One of the more striking items listed was 'a life size silver head of the 12th century, from the cathedral of Basle'. The day after the sale, the *Morning Post* reported that this 'chef, or silver gilt reliquary of the twelfth century' was one of the items that was 'acquired by the trustees' of the British Museum.[37] George's 'St Eustace Head Reliquary' counts in the present day as one of the British Museum's prize possessions, exhibited by them in 'A History of the World in 100 Objects' and many other exhibitions around the world.[38] The 'great passion for antique remains' which George shared with WHR in the 1840s was extraordinarily productive.

WHR did not forget his friend George Isaacs. In 1851, a few months after his departure, the *Art Journal* catalogue of the Great Exhibition contained a design by WHR for a key, the head of which incorporated a GI monogram.[39] Seven years later, in 1858, the *Art Journal* published, in its feature 'Original designs, as suggestions to manufacturers, etc.', a range of designs by WHR for letterheads.[40] This was

> in order to assist in rendering these headings as far as possible auxiliaries to Art, which considers nothing, however trifling and evanescent, beyond or below its reach.

Figure 3.3 shows the chivalric design which WHR produced for 'GI'. In it, WHR introduced a Latin motto which elegantly alluded to George's remarkable early discoveries:

REBUS NON VERBIS (By things not by words). Clearly WHR was unaware of the irony that in Australia George now earned a living by his pen, and that a more suitable motto for 1858 would have been VERBIS NON REBUS.

NOTES

1. Scrapbook of George Isaacs, State Library of South Australia, D Piece (Archival), D6668 (Misc).
2. Anne Black, *Pendragon: The Life of George Isaacs, Colonial Wordsmith* (Mile End, South Australia: Wakefield Press, 2020); dedication page and pp. 177-8.
3. Although mostly omitted, 'Samuel' appears, for example, on his son George Alfred's birth registration in South Australia registration in 1852. The exact date of George's twenty-first birthday was attested in an 1849 legal case – see Black, *Pendragon*, p. 210 n. 2.
4. *Tallis's London Street Views*, Part 12 [1838].
5. *The Times*, 30 January 1844, p. 12.
6. *The Times*, 13 May 1848, p. 11.
7. *Art Union*, 1844, pp. 134-6.
8. *The Hesperus: An original monthly magazine of humour, literature, and art*, No. 1 September 1843 – No. 5 January 1844 (G. Purkess, publisher).
9. Black, *Pendragon, op. cit.*, pp. 5-14, 184-5, 242 n. 28.
10. *Hesperus, op. cit.*, pp. 8-9. The Latin original was *Liber Primus: III.*
11. Anne Black, 'A colonial wordsmith: George Isaacs in Adelaide, 1860–1870', in Philip Butterss (ed.), *Adelaide: A literary city* (Adelaide: University of Adelaide Press, 2013), pp. 39-55.
12. A. Pendragon (ed.), *Number One* (Adelaide: Rigby, April, 1861), pp. 37-42; George Isaacs, *Rhyme and Prose; and, a Burlesque, and its History* (Melbourne: Clarson, Shallard, & Co., 1865), pp. 23-33.
13. P. Fromageot, *La Rue de Buci, ses maisons et ses habitants* (Firmin-Didot et Cie., 1904), opposite p. 28 and opposite p. 132.
14. V&A E693.193-1998 to E693.212-1998.
15. *The Builder*, Vol. 6, 1 April 1848, p. 163.
16. *The Builder*, Vol. 8, 1850, 5 October, p. 475; 12 October, p. 487; 16 November, p. 547; 21 December, p. 607.
17. Philippe Burty, *Chefs-d'œuvre of the Industrial Arts* (Chapman and Hall, 1869), pp. 287 and opposite.
18. *The Builder*, Vol. 8, 16 November 1850, p. 547.
19. V&A E693.196-1998.

20. The two halves are V&A E693.195-1998 and E693.195A-1998.
21. Rue de Maison Sorbonne was one of the small streets swallowed up by the expansion of the Sorbonne later in the nineteenth century. Another of the drawings, V&A E.693.207-1998, is also captioned 'rue de Maison Sorbonne'.
22. *Illustrated London News*, 24 July 1847, pp. 52-4.
23. *Ibid.*, p. 53.
24. W. Harry Rogers, 'On the history of enamelling', *Journal of the British Archaeological Association*, Vol. 3, 1848, pp. 280-96.
25. George Isaacs, 'On an enamelled plate of the twelfth century. In the possession of the Rev. Henry Crowe', *Journal of the British Archaeological Association*, Vol. 3, 1848, pp. 102-05.
26. *Ibid.*, p. 104.
27. BM number 1852,0327.1.
28. *Journal of the British Archaeological Association*, Vol. 4, 1849, pp. 58-9.
29. BM number AF.1868; thirteenth to fourteenth century.
30. Thomas Crofton Croker (1798–1854) makes a cameo appearance in Rosemary Hill, *Time's Witness: History in the Age of Romanticism* (Allen Lane, 2021), pp. 167-8.
31. *Catalogue of a collection of ancient and mediæval rings and personal ornaments formed for Lady Londesborough* (printed for private reference, 1853).
32. BM numbers AF.1025, sixteenth century; AF.1030, seventeenth century.
33. Subsequently published: *Journal of the British Archaeological Association*, Vol. 5, 1850, pp. 340-43.
34. George Isaacs, *Not for Sale; a Selection of Imaginative Pieces* (Adelaide: Sims & Elliott, City Steam Press, 1869), pp. 31-47.
35. Hill, *Time's Witness, op. cit.*, pp. 6, 269-88.
36. *Morning Chronicle*, 7 November 1850.
37. 'More purchases of mediaeval art for the British Museum', *Morning Post*, 13 November 1850.
38. BM Number 1850,1127.1.
39. *Art Journal* catalogue 1851 (Virtue), p. 321.
40. *Art Journal*, new series, Vol. 4, January 1858, p. 23.

FOUR

Two Signatures

For most of his professional life, from late 1847 until his death in 1873, William Harry Rogers signed his work with inventive variations of the same basic monogram. This consisted of a conjoined H and R which shared an upright that projected upwards, until it reached a W above, denoted in this chapter as the W/HR monogram.

However, it has not previously been noted that, prior to developing his canonical W/HR signature, for several years – 1840 until 1847 – the young WHR employed a very different monogram as his signature, denoted here as the H/RWR monogram. The failure to recognise this as an alternative signature for William Harry Rogers means that much of his earlier work has remained unidentified until now.

As will be explained, there is evidence that it was WHR's marriage in late 1847 which indirectly provided the catalyst for his change of signature from H/RWR to W/HR.

4.1 – WHR's early monogram signature, on a contribution to The Builder *in April 1844. Height 64mm.*

H/RWR MONOGRAM, 1840–47

The first, H/RWR signature of WHR did not appear in print until WHR was aged eighteen. It made the earliest of its many appearances in the pages of *The Builder* in March 1844. The editor at that time – the architect Alfred Bartholomew – published a letter from WHR illustrated by a drawing bearing a H/RWR monogram and with the letter itself signed with the same monogram. Part of another letter from WHR published the following month is reproduced as Figure 4.1.[1] The arrangement of the letters in this early monogram was not an obvious one. At its core was the letter H, with the letter W entwined around its uprights below its crossbar. Conjoined to the W's rightmost upright was a letter R and, for symmetry, conjoined to its leftmost upright was a mirror-reversed R.

The same monogram had earlier been used by WHR to sign unpublished artwork from 1840 onwards. Examples

Chapter Four – Two Signatures

exist in the V&A collections, but not in the WHR archive which it acquired in 1998.[2] Instead, these early WHR artworks reside in an archive of his father's papers acquired approximately twenty years earlier.[3]

The earliest artwork known to carry the H/RWR monogram is an ink drawing of a seated figure.[4] Within a framing ink line the monogram AH is accompanied by another monogram, H/RWR. Outside the framing ink line but inside a second, wider border are written 'Arnd. Houbraken fecit.' and 'WHRogers delin.' Outside the second border are written Houbraken's dates (1660–1719) and the date of WHR's drawing, namely, 24 December 1840. At this time, WHR was aged fifteen. The date, and its presence in the W.G. Rogers archive, together suggest that WHR might have made the drawing as a Christmas gift to his father. Only a few weeks later another drawing was signed H/RWR below the image, and inscribed on the verso with W.H. Rogers, 8 February 1841.[5]

Returning to *The Builder* of 1844, WHR designed a range of very large initial letters, signed with his H/RWR monogram, to be used to start off each week's editorial by Albert Bartholomew.[6] Figure 4.2 illustrates one of these imaginative compositions, full of fantastical creatures. Alfred Bartholomew died after editing *The Builder* for only one year but, some years later, his successor as editor, George Godwin, enterprisingly borrowed many of the 1844 WHR capitals for his own 1850 book, by which time their H/RWR signatures were anachronistic.[7]

The year after its 1844 appearances in *The Builder*, the H/RWR monogram started to appear also in the *Art Union* (later re-named as the *Art Journal*).[8]

The earliest known book to include the H/RWR monogram, Lambert's *Church Needlework*, was published just a couple of months after the monogram's first appearance in *The Builder*.[9] It accompanied an engraving described as 'Fald-stool [i.e. prie-dieu or kneeler], from a design of Mr. W.H. Rogers'.

The last known sighting of the H/RWR monogram is in *The Builder* in April 1847, attached to three drawings of Renaissance capitals in Rouen.[10] At this point, WHR seems for a few months to have stopped using a monogram at all, so that illustrations of his father's carving in June and July 1847, though presumably by WHR, are unsigned.[11]

4.2 – WHR enlivened *The Builder* in June 1844 with a surreal construction that included his early monogram on a shield. Height 133mm.

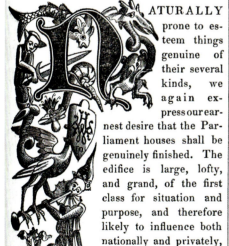

W/HR MONOGRAM, 1847–73

In autumn 1847, WHR introduced the new monogram, denoted here as W/HR, in which a conjoined HR was linked

47

4.3 –
Left: WHR's monogram from the reversible wedding brooch he gave to Mary Ann Rogers, 1847.
Right: His painting of the Archangel Michael on the other side of the brooch.
Height 59mm.

by a ligature to a W above. This monogram had the advantage of improved transparency, being readily parsed visually to convey an association with the artist W. Harry Rogers. Nevertheless, it must have been a wrench for WHR to abandon his longstanding H/RWR monogram. The catalyst appears to have been WHR's impending marriage to Mary Ann Lansdale on 8 December 1847.

WHR decided to construct a jewel-like brooch to present to his bride (illustrated as Figure 4.3). Its design was to be based on their two monograms. This posed the question, however, of what the monogram for Mary Ann Rogers would look like. WHR tried out a range of possibilities. We know this because of an apparently unpromising survival in the WHR archive at the V&A, namely a plain and ragged cloth binding which has entirely lost its contents.[12] The reason why WHR retained this wreck through thick and thin is provided by a set of doodle-like pencillings on its rear endpaper, which are in fact a series of trial MAR monograms.

First of all, on the left-hand side of the endpaper, WHR drew half a dozen different MAR monograms which bore no relation to his own current monogram. But it then must have occurred to him that it would be symbolic for the MAR monogram to have the same structure as his own. Thus he next drew five monograms to the right of the first group, each of which echoed his H/RWR monogram by virtue of enclosing the letters MA (in various arrangements) with an R on the right and a reverse-R on the left. He was evidently not satisfied with any of this second group of monograms either, but finally – eureka! – the answer came to him. He squeezed in two more monograms on the extreme right of the endpaper, which did share a common structure but had a simplicity and elegance his youthful monogram had lacked. Mary Ann Rogers would have a monogram consisting of a conjoined AR linked to an M above – and William Harry Rogers would have a matching monogram consisting of a conjoined HR linked to a W above. Figure 4.3 shows WHR's resulting jewel-like miniature painting of them, removed from the wedding brooch. The two new monograms, W/HR and M/AR, are rendered strikingly in black on white, with the year, 1847, less prominently arranged around them. The brooch was reversible, and also shown is its other side.

The W/HR monogram which WHR thus arrived at was the signature which was to appear on hundreds of his designs over the next quarter-century. While all instances of the W/HR signature share the same basic structure, most of them are uniquely constructed from elaborated letters which makes each such instance an artistic delight. Some examples of the new monogram signature dating from October 1847 onwards are present on artwork in one of the albums of the WHR archive at the V&A.[13] Three weeks after WHR's marriage, the new W/HR monogram made its appearance in print, starting with the New Year 1848 issue of *The Builder*.[14]

Finally, one curious variant of the W/HR signature should be described. Shortly after devising the monogram for the wedding brooch, WHR tried swapping its upper and lower parts, putting HR above and W below, contrary to the natural flow of the name William Harry Rogers. This inverted variant was used to sign a drawing by WHR of his father's carvings which appeared in the *Art Union* and was then reproduced in *The Builder*, both in November 1847.[15] But there were to be no further outings for this eccentric variant.

NOTES

1. *The Builder*, 1844, Vol. 2, 2 March, p. 103; 13 April, p. 193.

2. The William Harry Rogers archive is catalogued as E650-1998 to E1150-1998.

3. The William Gibbs Rogers archive is catalogued as E1661-1979 to E1727-1979.

4. V&A E1668-1979. The drawing is based on part of an Arnold Houbraken engraving, which previously has been given the title 'Two figures in a classical landscape'.

5. V&A E1664-1979, entitled 'Mask from an Italian Chest of the 16th Century'.

6. *The Builder*, 2 March 1844–29 June 1844.

7. George Godwin, *Buildings & Monuments, Modern and Mediaeval*, Office of 'The Builder', 1850.

8. *Art Union*, Vol. 7, 1845, November, p. 340. Also Vol. 8, 1846, January, p. 22.

9. Miss Lambert, *Church Needlework … Illustrated by Engravings* (John Murray, 1844), pp. xvi, 154.

10. *The Builder*, Vol. 5, 17 April 1847, p. 182.

11. *Art Union*, June 1847, p. 211; July 1847, p. 244.

12. V&A E1136-1998.

13. Earliest uses are on the artworks E693.53-1998, inscribed October 1847; E693.84-1998, inscribed 16 November 1847; and E693.112-1998, inscribed 15 December 1847.

14. *The Builder*, Number 256, 1 January 1848; cover and pp. 3 and 7.

15. *Art Union*, 1 November 1847, p. 388; *The Builder*, 5 November 1847, p. 567.

FIVE

The Builder

THE BUILDER AND THE ART JOURNAL were the two journals which dominated the world of design in Britain, including its hinterlands of architecture and art, from the early 1840s to the late 1870s. WHR was heavily involved with both (for the *Art Journal*, see Chapter 7).

Together, the present accounts of *The Builder* and the *Art Journal* (originally called the *Art Union*) illustrate the considerable range and sophistication of the field of art design in Britain in the 1840s. They call into question whether calls for design reform that emerged towards the end of the decade, most notably from Henry Cole (discussed in Chapter 9), had any valid basis or were merely careerist manoeuvring.

WHR was a fixture at *The Builder* at various times during the 1840s, right from its very beginning at the start of 1843. His appearances in it were threefold, involving first his creation of artistic designs for the journal itself; secondly, his writing and illustration of articles on design; and thirdly his involvement in an idealistic group of architects and artists founded by Alfred Bartholomew. These three threads often intertwined and thus are dealt with concurrently in the year-by-year account which follows.

1 8 4 3

An initial, trial issue of a journal called *The Builder* was brought out on 31 December 1842. The editor was Joseph Hansom (1803–82), the architect who became famous as the progenitor of the Hansom cab. The role of architect was becoming increasingly professionalised, and Hansom aimed to moderate this tendency by producing a journal which could be read with profit equally by architects and by practical builders.[1] As it turned out, although the response from the architects was favourable the journal turned out to have less appeal for the builders.[2]

After the trial issue, *The Builder* commenced its regular weekly publication with the issue of 18 February 1843. WHR, then aged seventeen, appeared in this very first regular issue. The context of his appearance was the launch of a new Architectural College, to whose membership it was reported that he had been elected on 14 February 1843 as the College's illuminator. At the same time, 'A beautiful Illuminated Election Diploma was ordered to be adopted,' which presumably referred to the adoption of artwork already prepared by WHR and may have incorporated the device shown in Figure 3.2.[3]

The report also lists the twenty-three people who had set up the College on Advent Eve 1842 (i.e. 26 November 1842). One of them was WHR's father, William Gibbs Rogers, who was appointed as the College's [Grinling] Gibbons Carver. Two others whose paths were to cross with WHR's in the future were the ceramist Walter Chamberlain of Worcester (1795–1868) and the architect Robert William Billings (1813–74). A fourth member of the group was the architect Alfred Bartholomew (1801–45), who was the founder and Honorary Secretary of the College.

Bartholomew was an architectural theorist who saw the creation of *The Builder* and of his Architectural College as twin beacons which would guide the future path of architectural practice in Britain.[4] The objectives of the college were defined at the outset as follows:[5]

> the rediscovery of the ancient principles of architecture; the sanction of good principles of building, and the condemnation of bad ones; the exercise of scientific and experienced judgment in the choice and use of the most proper materials; the infusion, maintenance, and advancement of science throughout architecture; and, eventually, by developing the powers of the College upon a just and beneficial footing, to reform the whole practice of architecture.

The name chosen for the college was Freemasons of the Church. This was not an obvious choice, since neither freemasonry nor the church were easily discerned in the society's aims. The 'freemasons' part of the name must have been intended to evoke a continuity with medieval builders. The epithet 'of the Church' seems to have been intended to differentiate the members from the larger, better-known group known simply as 'freemasons' (i.e. participants in organised freemasonry), perhaps by evoking a continuity of interest in the building of churches. The choice of name drew criticism at the time. Thus, the *Spectator* journal wrote very positively about the society in its Fine Arts column, except in this regard:[6]

> Our young friends have taken perhaps a foolish name, in calling themselves 'Freemasons of the Church.' They have run counter to two strong classes of prejudice,—first, the prejudice (it may deserve a better name) of those who consider 'freemasonry,' nowadays, a childish mysticism, affording a mere cloak for convivial meetings, which have little to distinguish them from other merry-makings; secondly, to the strong religious feeling of those who consider the Church of the present day as a body ready to grasp, were it possible, at Papal power and dominion over the consciences as well as the pockets of men. Setting aside the name, however, (which in its very faults indicates a hearty zeal,) we have great hopes of this society, and we look upon it as an indisputable proof of the advance of a sound opinion on matters of taste in this country.

Thus although intended to evoke a group aiming to revive the ideals of those who built medieval churches, the name misfired, being open to misinterpretation as a Church-oriented group within the body of freemasonry as generally understood.

WHR and his father exemplified the distinction. As far as is known, neither of them was ever a freemason in the normal modern sense. In particular, neither WHR nor his father has been found in the Membership Registers of the United Grand Lodge of England.[7]

1 8 4 4

At the end of the first year of *The Builder*, a change of editors was announced in its pages.[8] It was Alfred Bartholomew who took over from Joseph Hansom for the 1844 volume, and as might be expected he gave his aspiring architectural college, the Freemasons of the Church, a relatively high profile in the journal. Most relevantly for the present account, Bartholomew commissioned a series of conspicuous contributions to the journal from the college's illuminator, WHR, who was still aged only eighteen when Bartholomew took over.

For each issue from 2 March 1844, as soon as Bartholomew had written the editorial which commenced the issue, he commissioned WHR to take the first letter of his editorial and produce an elaborate design for it, somewhat in the style of an illuminated manuscript. WHR presumably had to make his design almost immediately, given that it still had to be engraved before the journal went to press. Despite this, WHR succeeded in considerably enlivening the appearance of the journal each week. An example has been illustrated as Figure 4.2. The arrangement continued with a new design for each of the eighteen weeks from 2 March to 29 June 1844. All designs except those for 23 March and 8 June were signed with WHR's early monogram (which can be denoted as H/RWR).[9] After 29 June 1844, the existing WHR designs were recycled for the remainder of the year.

WHR and his friend George Isaacs were on good terms with the indefatigable collector Ralph Bernal (1783–1854). WHR's stream of letter-designs might well have been in Bernal's mind when, in the course of some undated, humorous verse addressed to Isaacs, he included an amusing couplet about WHR:[10]

> Who imprisons in fetters,
> all the alphabet letters.

WHR's relations with Bernal and his collection are described further here in Chapter 7 which deals with the *Art Journal*, where they are grouped under the year 1849.

At the same time as WHR commenced his weekly designs for *The Builder* in 1844, he also started contributing short illustrated articles. The first two were published as letters (one of them has been illustrated as Figure 4.1) and dealt with old stone carvings on English churches.[11]

WHR's third article was trailed on 4 May by a report from a meeting of the Freemasons of the Church which stated that WHR had exhibited there a specimen of ancient wrought-iron, and added that *The Builder* would be publishing an engraving of it.[12] A fortnight later, the illustration duly appeared, signed with WHR's monogram and described as the 'extraordinary specimen of iron-work found at Norwich'.[13] Another fortnight further and the current owner of the ironwork was identified, noting that after being found in Norwich it had been purchased from an antiquary there by Mr. G. Isaacs of Claremont Terrace, Pentonville.[14] This was the first time that we see WHR and his friend George Isaacs named together in print.

Shortly afterwards, WHR and George left for their prolonged visit to Paris, as described in Chapter 3 (and Appendix B). The departure for Paris forced WHR to end, on 29 June, his sequence of just-in-time weekly designs for Bartholomew's editorials in *The Builder*, and he made no further appearance in the journal during the second half of 1844.

1 8 4 5 – 6

At the end of 1844 there was a change of editor at *The Builder* for the second time in only two years, when Alfred Bartholomew died after a short illness on 2 January 1845.[15]

Bartholomew was succeeded as editor of *The Builder* by the architect, George Godwin (1813–88) who, in contrast to his two predecessors, was destined to remain in that post for thirty-eight years, until 1883. Godwin continued to print regular reports in *The Builder* of the meetings of the Freemasons of the Church, but the enterprise was not a personal interest of his.

Bartholomew was succeeded in his other role as Honorary Secretary of the Freemasons of the Church by another architectural theorist, W.P. Griffith (William Pettit Griffith, 1815–84), who was elected on 11 March.[16] However, whatever chance there had been of realising Bartholomew's original vision – that the Architectural College of the Freemasons of the Church should become a major educational institution – probably disappeared with his demise.[17] Although the association continued to adopt the rhetoric of a college of architecture, it functioned in practice as a learned society and campaigning group, with a number of influential members. At the same 11 March 1845 meeting which elected Griffith as Honorary Secretary, 'Benjamin D'Israeli, Esq., M.P.' was elected as a Vice-President.

For WHR personally, as a protégé of Alfred Bartholomew, the early death must have been a blow. In the ensuing couple of years we see little of WHR in *The Builder*, except for the text of an address he made to the Freemasons of the Church on 'Illuminated books in their connection with architecture'.[18] He was to return to this topic in the pages of *The Builder* in 1848.

1 8 4 7

Relations between WHR and George Godwin seem to have become considerably closer at the start of 1847. *The Builder* reported an auspicious meeting of the Freemasons of the Church on 12 January 1847. The report began by noting that the meeting 'was held in the Society's new rooms, No. 10, Carlisle-street, Soho-square', that is, in the impressive new premises of the Rogers family. Next, it reported that 'Mr. George Godwin, F.R.S.' was unanimously elected as an honorary fellow. Finally, the report printed a detailed account of WHR's address to the meeting, 'observations upon the antiquities of the University of Cambridge'.[19]

A few months later, WHR published an article in *The Builder* on 'Capitals of the Renaissance Period', which concerned columns and pilasters in Rouen and included three illustrations signed with his monogram.[20] Towards the end of the year, under the heading 'Modern carvings', *The Builder* reprinted two illustrations by WHR which had already appeared in the *Art Union*, one of an altar-rail 'recently executed in oak by Mr. W. G. Rogers, from the design of his son'.[21] In the following week appeared WHR's final contribution for 1847. Headed 'Architectural details from Leicester', the signed article and its page and more of illustrations focused on St Mary's Church, and in particular a large carved oak screen which 'has been lying for years in a state of uselessness in an obscure corner of the nave'.[22]

1 8 4 8

The following year, 1848, was the year of peak visibility for WHR in *The Builder*. His eye-catching design for the journal's masthead on its front cover – part of the advertising pages which surrounded its editorial pages – had its first outing on the 1 January 1848 issue, and could not have been missed by any contemporary reader (though the advertising pages were sadly often discarded in bound-up volumes). It was the first of the designs which WHR was to make for the covers of hundreds of different publications. It was also the first appearance in public of his new monogram, W/HR, which he was to use for the rest of his life. WHR's masthead for *The Builder* remained in unbroken weekly use until well into the twentieth century.

In the same issue appeared two articles by WHR. The first discussed Gothic armrests from Milton Church near Cambridge and Astley Church in Warwickshire, the illustrations signed with his new monogram. The second continued his Leicester exploration with an article on St Margaret's Church, focusing on the ancient ironwork on a door near its tower.[23]

WHR published a stream of other illustrated articles in similar vein during 1848, and these are merely listed here:

> Carved armrests from Winchester Cathedral, 5 February, p. 67
> A capital from St Germain-des-Prés, Paris, 1 April, p. 163
> Carved wood friezes from Rouen and Wiltshire, 8 April, pp. 175-6
> Stall-ends at Landbeach Church, Cambridgeshire, 27 May, p. 259
> Ironwork on a chest in the Stowe sale, 9 September, p. 439.

WHR also published two longer theses in *The Builder* in 1848. The first of these analysed what could be gleaned about the history of architecture from illuminated manuscripts, and was much augmented from his brief summary which had appeared in *The Builder* on 15 November 1845. In fact, the contents had to be spread over two issues of *The Builder*, each with a whole-page plate.[24] Figure 5.1 shows the first of these plates.[25] It is conceivable that WHR's construction of these learned and attractive plates caught the eye of John Ruskin (1819–1900) and led him to invite WHR to design the striking cover for his celebrated book *The Seven Lamps of Architecture*, which appeared in May 1849.

In the following month, July 1848, WHR published a significant article, arguing for the adoption of a renewed Renaissance style, though not 'a servile copy of its Italian precursor of the sixteenth century'.[26] Quickly spurning the standard 'Louis Quatorze' of his time, he also pointed to the unsuitability of the Gothic beyond its ecclesiastical heartland:

Chapter Five – The Builder

5.1 – A page of illustrations by WHR for his articles on architecture in ancient manuscripts (here, up to about the year 1200) in *The Builder* in May and June 1848. Height 280mm.

> Many attempts have been made to render the Gothic style the vehicle for imparting beauty to our manufactures. But none have been attended with success, for that style is so limited to particular proportions and geometrical arrangements, that in many cases either its principles must be violated, or convenience sacrificed to its absolute demands.

Instead, WHR argued for the inherent flexibility of the Renaissance style, asserting that

> the accessory decorations are by far the principal features of the style … Here unbridled fancy roves through a succession of forms selected from both kingdoms, disposed with the most exquisite balance,

and arguing cogently that:

> It is the freedom from specified limitations and restrictions, whether in form or in proportion, which makes the style of the Renaissance so suitable for modern employment in architecture and decorative art.

The article was also important for another reason, because in it WHR took a public side-swipe at Henry Cole, the civil service administrator who was attempting to impose himself on the world of art manufacture in Britain. This aspect of the article is highlighted in Chapter 9.

In October, *The Builder* flagged up an event which bore directly on WHR, because it led to him being elected as the third (and final) Honorary Secretary of the Freemasons of the Church, following Alfred Bartholomew and W.P. Griffith. The event was the resignation of the secretaryship by Griffith, who had held it for over three years. In its report of the resignation, *The Builder* commented sympathetically on the demanding nature of this unpaid post:[27]

> The society meeting once a fortnight during the whole year, the labour of the office must have been very considerable.

WHR delivered an inaugural address as the new Honorary Secretary at the 'last meeting for 1848' of the Freemasons of the Church. However, this was announced not in *The Builder* but in the *Art Journal*.[28] It was a strategic choice by WHR, who hoped to broaden the association's appeal beyond the relatively narrow confines of the architectural audience of *The Builder* by embracing also the artists and manufacturers who subscribed to the *Art Journal*:

> The Society … is one of high importance as an engine which, to be permanently useful, requires only to be better known. And we take this opportunity of referring to the advantages it offers in bringing artists and manufacturers in conjunction with architects, frequently a class of men otherwise inaccessible, and in extending information from the most acknowledged sources upon subjects relative to those Arts in which architecture is concerned.

The logic of WHR's strategy was clear, because architecture in Britain was now well-

Chapter Five – The Builder

supplied with successful professional bodies (most notably, the Royal Institute of British Architects, founded in 1834 with royal charter in 1837, together with the Architectural Association, founded only in 1847). Hence, if the Freemasons of the Church were to gain a new, distinctive constituency, they would have to re-orient their mission away from the crowded institutional field of architecture itself and into the less populated areas which adjoined architecture.

One final feature of the *Art Journal* article was its report that whereas the final meeting for 1848 had been 'held at the residence of the Secretary, 10, Carlisle Street, Soho Square … all future business of the College will be conducted at 49, Great Marlborough Street'.

1 8 4 9

The Builder reported the first meeting of the year of the Freemasons of the Church on 9 January, including accounts of the artefacts exhibited by WHR and by George Isaacs.[29]

Shortly afterwards appeared WHR's only article in *The Builder* in 1849. It chimed with his advocacy of a renewed Renaissance style, because it described a book cover carved in Renaissance style that had appeared in the recent sale of the Duke of Buckingham's possessions at Stowe.[30] Figure 5.2 shows the cover, as drawn by WHR.

WHR continued to feature in reports in *The Builder* of the meetings of the Freemasons of the Church during the year.[31] By the time of the October meeting, a surviving invitation (reproduced as Figure 3.2) shows that the venue had reverted to 10 Carlisle Street.

5.2 – A book cover in carved oak from the Stowe sale, drawn by WHR, from The Builder in February 1849. Image height 212mm.

WHR's sensible attempt to revitalise the society by diversifying the membership towards artists and manufacturers may have been actively opposed by other leading members. Certainly an uncompromising reversion to the purely architectural aspirations of the society was manifest in a full-page appeal which appeared in *The Builder* at the end of 1849. WHR's name was conspicuously missing, and instead the appeal appeared above the name of the architect G.R. French.[32] The founder of the Freemasons of the Church, Alfred Bartholomew, has attracted criticism for his lack of realism.[33] George Russell French (1803–81), however, took the prize for naivety with his public offer of

> holding out an invitation to the profession in its different branches to join the College of the Freemasons of the Church … that the elder Institute of British Architects, the younger Architectural Association, and that still more recently-established society, for the laudable purpose of publishing architectural works, may one and all … consent to make common cause with the Freemasons of the Church, in whose name I am privileged to state that on their side every just concession will be made

> ... and if it be asked why do not its members rather fuse into other societies, than expect to be joined by those whose date is older, or whose numbers are greater than their own, the reply is simply this,—that, without casting the slightest disrespect upon any other society, or doubting its usefulness, it is their conscientious belief that only in their own body is to be found a well-digested code of laws for every occasion ...

In an editorial accompaniment, *The Builder* itself felt obliged to give French's proposal short thrift:,

> At the request of the committee of this society we give insertion to this appeal ... It is necessary, however, that we should say, we do not participate in the belief that the Royal Institute of British Architects is at all likely to 'fuse' into the Freemasons of the Church: this is of course out of the question.

ST MARY THE VIRGIN, WARE

A month earlier, *The Builder* reported in September on the first of two churches whose interiors were enhanced by WHR with polychrome decorative designs. This was St Mary's, the parish church of the town of Ware in Hertfordshire.[34] George Godwin stated that he had been engaged to carry out an internal restoration of the fabric of the church, and had invited WHR to decorate it. To avoid reviewing his own work in *The Builder*, Godwin reprinted, as the main body of the article, a review of St Mary's Ware which had recently been published in the *Ecclesiologist*. This commented on WHR's polychrome interior as follows:[35]

5.3 – Two elements of WHR's polychrome interior at St Mary's Ware as photographed in or before 1914. *Left*: The Creed. *Right*: The Lord's Prayer. Image heights 14mm.

> The most striking feature in the restoration is the quantity of polychrome which has been applied. The spandrils of the nave arches, ten in number, are filled with flower-pots, from which grow lilies, each bearing a scroll, with one of the beatitudes inscribed upon it. The commandments are painted, where they are ordered, on two tablets on each side of the chancel-arch. The Creed and the Lord's Prayer are on the eastern wall, flanking the east window. The bosses of the nave and chancel-roofs are coloured and gilt, and the architectural portions of the roof of the Lady Chapel are emblazoned.

Returning to the Ware restoration in *The Builder* the following May, Godwin provided an engraving of the resulting appearance of the southeast section of the interior. However, this provided only a very sketchy indication of WHR's designs for the Lord's Prayer to the right of the east window, and a nearby Commandments tablet.[36]

WHR's designs were still clearly visible in the earlier part of the twentieth century. A postcard of the interior of St Mary's Ware posted in August 1914 bore a distant, blurred but tantalising monochrome photograph of them (neither the photographer nor the publisher were named). Figure 5.3 shows two details from the photograph, the Creed and the Lord's Prayer, positioned to the left and right, respectively, of the east window. They adopted the style of illuminated manuscripts, with the Creed commencing with a twelve-line 'I' and a chequered top line 'BELIEVE', and the Lord's Prayer commencing with a four-line 'O' and emphatic top line 'UR FATHER', both concluding with a chequered 'AMEN' at lower right. Both designs were surmounted by elaborate spires, and enclosed on their other three sides by spirally ribboned poles.

Sadly, WHR's interior at Ware is no longer visible, having been painted over in the 1960s. A modern history of the Ware church described how the WHR interior appeared originally, but continued:[37]

> By 1962, however, the walls of the church were so dirty it was very hard to distinguish these paintings and they were lost when the walls were repainted. More recently it has been possible to trace the outline of the decorations on the eastern wall and the Chancel arch.

1 8 5 0

Towards the end of 1850, WHR published a short series of articles gleaned from his time in Paris in 1844. The new articles all dealt with Parisian ironwork, already discussed in Chapter 3, and had illustrations signed by WHR. They comprised:

Knockers, 5 October, p. 475
Gate protectors, 12 October, p. 487
Knockers, 16 November, p. 547
Knockers, 21 December, p. 607.

With regard to the Freemasons of the Church, after French's ill-judged appeal in *The Builder* in December 1849 they made only one more appearance in the pages of their erstwhile house-journal, when *The Builder* briefly reported the proceedings of their meeting of 12 March 1850.[38]

A much fuller account had already been provided in the *Morning Post* newspaper.[39] The main purpose of the meeting was to express support for the forthcoming 'Great Industrial Exposition of 1851'. G.R. French was obliged to move the first motion, 'That in the opinion of this college the objects of the intended exposition, &c., in 1851, are especially deserving of the support of all societies connected with science and art.' French observed somewhat grumpily:

> In proposing the first resolution he felt that the initiative was imposed upon him rather by virtue of his office of grand master than from his ability best to present the subject to the members.

WHR, the secretary, on the other hand proposed with convincing enthusiasm the second motion, regarding the inclusion of medieval artefacts:

> That in the opinion of this college a most judicious step has been taken by the Society of Arts in projecting an exposition of objects of ancient and mediæval art, as this will afford a good lesson to manufacturers intending to compete at the great exposition of 1851.

The middle part of WHR's address evinced the same stance toward medieval artefacts as John Ruskin adopted toward medieval buildings:

> Another important point in connection with an exposition of mediæval art was, that it would draw the attention of manufacturers of our own age to the question of design, for, although many of the works of the middle ages were rudely executed, incorrectly engraved, they were all beautiful, and they were beautiful despite the badness of the execution, because they were designed by the hand of a master. (Cheers.)

However, as exemplified by the March 1850 meeting itself, the forthcoming Great Exhibition was increasingly monopolising the attention of all those who would be concerned with it, and this seems likely to have been a factor in the Freemasons of the Church reaching the end of the road not long afterwards. WHR was correctly listed as their Honorary Secretary in an 1850 almanack.[40] However, although the identical entry appeared also in the almanacks for 1851 and 1852, no evidence has been found that the society was in fact still functioning after 1850.

ST MARY THE BOLTONS, BROMPTON

A second church whose interior was enhanced by WHR was St Mary's West Brompton (now known as St Mary The Boltons, in Brompton, London). In 1850, *The Builder* described how the church had been newly erected according to the design of George Godwin.[41] Money was short, and the spire would not be added until 1855. The *Ecclesiologist* found fault with Godwin's layout of the church, and hence this time Godwin unsurprisingly published his own account of the church rather than reprinting the review in the *Ecclesiologist*, as he had done for St Mary's Ware.[42]

In his article, Godwin praised WHR's contribution to the interior, which appears to have shared some features with the Ware church but to have been less extensive owing to financial constraints:

> The coloured decorations, necessarily limited at present, are confined mainly to the east end, and comprise the Lord's Prayer and Belief illuminated under painted canopies on each side of the east window; the Commandments under

5.4 – Part of WHR's polychrome interior at St Mary The Boltons, formerly known as St Mary's West Brompton, engraved in *The Builder* in October 1850. Image height 255mm.

similar canopies on the east wall of the nave (on either side of the arch); a rich diaper, red and gold, [original footnote: I.H.C., lily and cross alternately] under east window, forming reredos of altar; and a diaper at back of sedilia, with the pelican and *Agnus Dei*; the whole exceedingly well done by Mr. W.H. Rogers.

Godwin provided an engraving which showed WHR's 'rich diaper' along the east wall and his other diaper under the canopy of the sedilia. Figure 5.4 reproduces the engraving, with the east wall diaper on the left (the engraver forgot to reverse the rendering of 'ihc') and the sedilia diaper on the right.

As with St Mary's Ware, WHR's designs at St Mary The Boltons are sadly no longer visible. According to a history of the church, it suffered war damage in 1940 and its fabric deteriorated for several years afterwards. Major alterations were then made in 1952, and these included whitewashing the walls.[43]

POST 1850

After 1850, WHR stopped making contributions to *The Builder*, almost certainly because of his increasing commitments elsewhere rather than as a result of any falling out with George Godwin. Evidence of the continuing good relations between Godwin and WHR is that in 1853 Godwin commissioned WHR to design a letterhead for his journal correspondence.

5.5 – Letterhead for 1853, commissioned by George Godwin from WHR for use at *The Builder*. Width 84mm.

Figure 5.5 displays an example of the WHR letterhead, on a letter of 22 October 1853 from Godwin to his contributor, Henry Mogford, seeking an illustration of the building that would house the forthcoming 1855 Paris Exhibition. Godwin was enabled to print a sectional view of the Paris building the following July.[44]

NOTES

1. For a discussion of Hansom's intentions for *The Builder*, see Brian Hanson, *Architects and the 'Building World' from Chambers to Ruskin* (Cambridge University Press, 2003), pp. 103-10.
2. Michael Brooks, '*The Builder* in the 1840s: The making of a magazine, the shaping of a profession', *Victorian Periodicals Review*, 1981, pp. 14, 86-93.
3. *The Builder*, Vol. 1, 18 February 1843, pp. 23-4.
4. For a full account of Bartholomew's place in the history of architecture, see Hanson, *Architects and the 'Building World' from Chambers to Ruskin*, pp. 110-20.
5. *The Builder*, Vol. 1, 18 February 1843, p. 23.
6. *Spectator*, 1847, p. 594.
7. Consulted via www.ancestry.co.uk
   In contrast, at a relatively late date WHR's brother, Edward Thomas Rogers, does appear in the registers, affiliated to two Cairo lodges in Egypt: *Bulwer* from 1869 and *Star of the East* from 1871.
8. *The Builder*, Vol. 1, 30 December 1843, p. 561.
9. Proof copies of eight of the designs are in the V&A Rogers archive, E851-1998 pp. 11-12.
10. Scrapbook of George Isaacs, State Library of South Australia, D Piece (Archival) D6668(Misc), p. 10. Also transcribed by Anne Black, *Pendragon: The Life of George Isaacs, Colonial Wordsmith* (Mile End, South Australia: Wakefield Press, 2020), pp. 28-9, 215 n. 60.
11. *The Builder*, 2 March 1844, p. 103 and 13 April 1844, p. 193.
12. *The Builder*, 4 May 1844, p. 224.
13. *The Builder*, 18 May 1844, p. 253.
14. *The Builder*, 1 June 1844, p. 282.
15. Bartholomew's obituary was published in *The Builder*, Vol. 3, 18 January 1845, p. 29.
16. *The Builder*, Vol. 3, 15 March 1845, p. 125.
17. Hanson, *Architects and the 'Building World' from Chambers to Ruskin, op. cit.*, pp. 120-21.
18. *The Builder*, Vol. 3, 15 November 1845, p. 550.
19. *The Builder*, Vol. 5, 16 January 1847, p. 25.
20. *The Builder*, Vol. 5, 17 April 1847, p. 182.
21. *The Builder*, Vol. 5, 27 November 1847, p. 567.

22. *The Builder*, Vol. 5, 4 December 1847, pp. 578-9.
23. *The Builder*, Vol. 6, 1 January 1848, pp. 3 and 7-8.
24. *The Builder*, Vol. 6, 1848: 20 May, pp. 245-7, and 3 June, pp. 269-71.
25. *Ibid.*, p. 246.
26. W.H. Rogers, 'On the style of the Renaissance and its adoption in England', *The Builder*, Vol. 6, 29 July 1848, pp. 362-3.
27. *The Builder*, Vol. 6, 7 October 1848, p. 485.
28. W. Harry Rogers, Hon. Sec. The Freemasons of the Church, *Art Journal*, Vol. 1, 1 January 1849, p. 34.
29. *The Builder*, Vol. 7, 20 January 1849, p. 32.
30. *The Builder*, Vol. 7, 24 February 1849, p. 91.
31. *The Builder*, Vol. 7, 24 March, p. 142 (meeting of 13 May, 'held at Great Marlborough-street'); 1 2 May, p. 226 (meeting of 8 May); and 20 October, p. 501 (meeting of 9 October)
32. G.R. French, 'Union is strength. The architectural societies', *The Builder*, Vol. 7, 15 December 1849, p. 592. Elsewhere, its author George Russell French was styled as the society's Grand Master.
33. Hanson, *Architects and the 'Building World' from Chambers to Ruskin, op. cit.*, p. 116.
34. *The Builder*, Vol. 7, 8 September 1849, pp. 426-7.
35. *Ecclesiologist*, Vol. 10 (= new series Vol. 7), August 1849, pp. 75-7.
36. *The Builder*, Vol. 8, 11 May 1850, pp. 222-3.
37. Dorothy Palmer, *St. Mary the Virgin, Ware, Hertfordshire: History and guide* (privately printed, 1980), p. 12.
38. *The Builder*, Vol. 8, 16 March 1850, p. 130.
39. *Morning Post*, 13 March 1850, p. 5.
40. R.W. Buss (ed.), *The Almanack of the Fine Arts for the Year 1850* (George Rowney and Co., 1850), p. 148.
41. *The Builder*, Vol. 8, 19 October 1850, pp. 498-9.
42. *Ecclesiologist*, Vol. 11 (= new series Vol. 8), October 1850, p. 195.
43. Arthur Tait, *St Mary The Boltons* (Parochial Church Council of St Mary with St Peter, 2004), pp. 25, 29.
44. *The Builder*, Vol. 12, 22 July 1854, p. 389.

SIX

Henry Fitzcook

FOLLOWING HIS MARRIAGE ON 8 December 1847, the twenty-two-year-old WHR had to think about securing an income which was more reliable than that of the solitary hand-to-mouth freelancer. The solution which he embarked upon on 23 February 1848 (as he revealed in a letter dated 25 July 1848 to his friend George Isaacs) was to enter into a professional partnership with another young artist, so that their pooled earnings would smooth out the ups and downs of their individual incomes.[1] The partner was Henry Fitzcook, who was just five months older than WHR. Promisingly, Fitzcook had already had a painting hung at the 1846 Royal Academy exhibition.[2]

However, by the time that WHR wrote to George Isaacs, he was already rueful about his partnership of just five months' standing. WHR explained that soon after entering into the partnership, Fitzcook had quarrelled with Mr G. Stiff, proprietor of the *London Journal*, for whom he had been working. He sued Stiff for £12 10s owed to him but lost in the Sheriff's Court, so WHR not only lost his half of the *London Journal* fees but also, adding insult to injury, had to pay out his half of Fitzcook's £4 costs.

BRIEF BIOGRAPHY

Henry Fitzcook was born on 25 November 1824, the son of Maria Louisa and Edmund Cook, a law stationer, of Hermes Street, Pentonville, and when baptised on 2 January 1825 at St James Church, Pentonville, was given the name Henry Fitz-Edmund Cook.[3] By the time of WHR's letter of 25 July 1848 he had dropped the 'Edmund' and was calling himself Henry Fitz-Cook, or just Henry Fitzcook, but WHR referred to him familiarly as 'Harry Cook', suggesting that he had already known him for a while.

In 1841, Henry was the oldest of five children living with their parents in Carey Street, near the Strand. In 1851, with Henry now listed as 'Artist' aged twenty-six years, the family were all still together in New Ormond Street, Bloomsbury. But by the 1861 census, Henry was living separately in nearby Bloomsbury Square with his wife, Rosina Sophia Thornton, born in 1827 in the village of Worth, near Dover. She married Henry in Kent towards the end of 1862. By 1871 the couple were living in Pentonville Road, and thereafter they made the larger move to Hastings in Sussex, where they were recorded in the 1881 and 1891 censuses, prior to Henry's death there on 18 November 1898, when he left an estate of only £65.

WHR IN PARTNERSHIP WITH HENRY FITZCOOK

Henry Fitzcook appeared alongside WHR in the *Art Union* at the beginning of 1848, in the first of their series of 'Original Designs for Manufacturers'.[4] In this issue, a dozen designs were shown, spread over four pages. On both the first and second pages, the lead design was from WHR, with Fitzcook also contributing two designs. In the months to come, WHR continued to dominate the 'Original Designs for Manufacturers' but with Fitzcook continuing to be highly visible.

Evidence of the partnership between WHR and Fitzcook was first apparent a couple of months later, when one of the 'Original Designs for Manufacturers' (for poker, tongs and rake) was captioned 'Design for a set of fire-irons. The upper parts by H. Fitz-Cook, the lower by W. Harry Rogers.'[5] This design is shown in Figure 6.1. Unfortunately, Fitzcook's figures of Vulcan, Pluto and Charon seem rather clumsy above WHR's suave cinquecento lines. It can be seen also that Fitzcook's monogram was composed of a C and its mirror image, enclosing a small H and F, suggesting that it was devised when the artist's surname was still simply 'Cook'; it was poorly planned because the letters H and F in engravings were often too small to be legible.

Since January 1848, WHR had been providing the design for a large capital letter at the start of each issue of the *Art Union*. The large capital 'S' for the June 1848 issue bore another sign of the new partnership, displaying the monograms of both WHR and Fitzcook.[6]

Another joint design by WHR and Fitzcook appeared in October 1848, captioned as 'Design for a lucifer matchbox'.[7] Six months later appeared:[8]

> Design for a cruet stand. The framework of this design is by W.H. Rogers, the figure by H. Fitz-Cook. The artists have here worked harmoniously together, and have produced a very elegant object.

The following month, on 1 May 1849, appeared 'Design for a candelabrum', credited to both WHR and Fitzcook.[9] This seems to be the last appearance of a joint WHR-Fitzcook design within the *Art Union* scheme of 'Original Designs for Manufacturers', though the scheme itself continued intermittently until July 1850.

Apart from the *Art Union* designs, only one other item has been noticed as bearing the monograms of both WHR and Fitzcook. This was a vignette contributed to a small charitable publication by Anna Maria Hall in 1848.[10] Later that year, she re-used the vignette in a commercial publication.[11] Thus the evidence indicates that the partnership which WHR and Fitzcook commenced in February 1848 did not continue much, if at all,

6.1 – Fitzcook's figures atop WHR's designs for a set of fire-irons in the *Art Union*, May 1848. Height 129mm.

beyond April 1849, having lasted little over a year.

Fitzcook did not in general design book covers, but one design is known from late 1849. Its lettering and scrolling seem to show the influence of WHR, whether or not the partnership had formally dissolved by that point. The cover was for Washington Irving's titles in George Routledge's early series in paper-covered boards entitled *The Popular Library*, whose first titles were advertised in January 1850.[12] In his signature (in the front cover's lower margin), Fitzcook added 'ook' to his usual monogram, so as to complete 'Cook'. The series cover was illustrated in Ruari McLean's book on paper covers, though he did not identify the designer.[13]

POST-PARTNERSHIP ILLUSTRATIONS

Henry Fitzcook was keen to pursue a career as a painter. In 1853, the *Illustrated London News* noticed his painting entitled 'Beware!' at the British Institution.[14] Shortly afterwards, Fitzcook's work exhibited at the Society of British Artists was mentioned positively in the same newspaper.[15]

6.2 – Cover for Fitzcook's All About Shakespeare [1864]. Height 189mm.

Fitzcook worked also as a freelance illustrator, for example contributing a large engraving to the same newspaper in 1856 entitled 'The Common Hall on corporation reform, in Guildhall'.[16] His association with the *Illustrated London News* probably came to an abrupt end in 1861, however, after he unsuccessfully sued the estate of Herbert Ingram, the deceased proprietor, for payment for an engraving.[17] Another pot-boiler commission was to provide several illustrations for the Bernal catalogue which Henry Bohn published in 1857.[18]

In 1858, the *Art Journal* revived for one year only its feature of 'Original Designs for Manufacturers', in which Fitzcook participated, though it was stated in the May issue that he had given up designing for manufacturers.[19]

In 1864, two books were entirely illustrated by Fitzcook. The first was a slim volume that cashed in on the Shakespeare tercentenary that year. Figure 6.2 shows its card cover, signed by Fitzcook, though unusually both the cover and the title page credited the engraver ahead of the artist.[20] The second volume was a new edition of Bunyan's *Holy War*, with forceful plates and engraved title page (re-issued in 1869 with added colour).[21]

INNOVATIONS

Fitzcook had an enterprising side to him and was interested in new technical developments. Three instances may be given.

1. Papier-mâché furniture: Jennens & Bettridge, manufacturers of papier-mâché articles, included a Fitzcook design in their display at the Great Exhibition:[22] 'The "day dreamer,"— an easy chair, designed by H. Fitz Cook, and manufactured in papier-mâché, by the exhibitors.' A century later, Nikolaus Pevsner described the chair both as representative of its period (in terms of its name, its appearance and its figurative mouldings) and as forward-looking (in terms of its novel material).[23]

2. Graphotype: Fitzcook's most important involvement with technical innovation came in the mid-1860s. Graphotype was a method of obviating the need at that time for an engraver to intervene between an artist's drawing and its reproduction. Instead, the artist drew on a specially prepared surface, from which a metallic printing block could be created mechanically. Although Fitzcook did not discover the process, he was instrumental in promoting its use. In December 1865, he gave a paper to the Society of Arts entitled, 'On the graphotype, a process for producing from drawings blocks for surface-printing'.[24] The following year, he was one of the artists contributing graphotype illustrations to a book entitled *Twigs for Nests*.[25]

Also in 1866, Fitzcook superintended the publication of another book, with more ambitious pictures. This was an illustrated edition of *Divine and Moral Songs for Children*.[26] On the title page, the name of Holman Hunt was set in larger type than that of the other names that followed (including J.D. Watson and G. du Maurier). Fitzcook himself contributed twelve illustrations and the other fifteen artists contributed one each. The *Athenaeum* was encouraging about the illustrations, despite some reservations, and presumed that:[27]

> future results may become more valuable in Art than those which are before us here.

Buoyed up by the involvement in graphotype of the prominent artist, William Holman Hunt (1827–1910), Fitzcook decided to float a company which would exploit the graphotype process by taking over the company of Edward Roper, which held the patent. Fitzcook was to be Managing Director and Holman Hunt one of the other directors, while Edward Roper would become General Manager. 'The Graphotyping Company, Limited' was set up with 10,000 shares at £10 each, and in March 1866 a public offering of the shares was made.[28] Holman Hunt, however, pulled out at the last moment and a revised prospectus had to include a letter from him, explaining that he would be absent abroad.[29]

The graphotype enterprise subsequently turned out badly for Fitzcook. The following year, 'Fitzcook v. The Graphotyping Company (Limited)' was listed to be heard at the Court of Common Pleas, Westminster, on 29 November 1867.[30] The implication that Fitzcook had parted company with graphotyping was borne out by his failure to use it in a book he illustrated the following year.

3. Magic lantern: Fitzcook's 1868 book was a new illustrated edition of William Cowper's *John Gilpin*, with his drawings reproduced by traditional engraving.[31] The gilt-blocked cloth cover was also designed by Fitzcook, who signed it with a new version of his monogram: the reverse-C and the C were unchanged, but instead of containing a small H and F they were both straddled by a large F, de-emphasising at last the old C for Cook.

Chapter Six – Henry Fitzcook

6.3 – Magic lantern slide with John Gilpin illustration by Fitzcook [1868]. Height 82mm.

Fitzcook's new idea for technical innovation was to issue his *John Gilpin* not only as a book but also as a set of magic lantern slides. Figure 6.3 shows an example. Each slide was inscribed with the text 'John Gilpin. Illustrated by H. Fitz Cook. By permission of Messrs. Longman & Co'.

However, a set of magic lantern slides must have provided only small consolation to Fitzcook for his dashed hopes of developing the graphotype process. It is noticeable that he had brought at least three separate court actions within a score of years – against the *London Journal* in 1848, against the *Illustrated London News* in 1861, and now against the Graphotyping Company in 1867 – which suggests either that he was consistently unlucky or else that he was not very good at navigating the commercial world. Either way, it seems likely that WHR's short-lived professional partnership with Fitzcook was ill-fated from the start.

NOTES

1. Scrapbook of George Isaacs, State Library of South Australia, D Piece (Archival) D6668(Misc), p. 60.
2. The painting illustrated a scene from Robert Southey's *Thalaba the Destroyer*, 1801. See Algernon Graves, *The Royal Academy of Arts: A Complete Dictionary of Contributors … to 1904*, Vol. 3 (Henry Graves and George Bell, 1905), p. 121. Fitzcook exhibited altogether at four Royal Academy exhibitions, spanning more than half a century: 1846, 1858, 1871 and 1898.
3. Records of Fitzcook's life were found at www.ancestry.co.uk
4. *Art Union*, Vol. 10, 1 January 1848, pp. 11-14.
5. *Art Union*, Vol. 10, 1 May 1848, p. 147.
6. *Art Union*, Vol. 10, 1 June 1848, p. 165.
7. *Art Union*, Vol. 10, 1 October 1848, p. 295.
8. *Art Union*, Vol. 10, 1 April 1849, p. 127.
9. *Art Union*, Vol. 10, 1 May 1849, p. 152.
10. Mrs S.C. Hall, *The Old Governess, a Story*, For the benefit of the Asylum for Aged and Decayed Governesses [1848], p. 41.
11. Mrs S.C. Hall (ed.), *The Drawing Room Table Book* (George Virtue [1848]), final page.
12. *Athenaeum*, 19 January 1850, p. 85.
13. Ruari McLean, *Victorian Publishers' Book-bindings in Paper* (Gordon Fraser, 1983), p. 62.
14. *Illustrated London News*, 26 February 1853, p. 164. Fitzcook was to exhibit only one other painting at the British Institution, in 1864, according to Algernon Graves, *The British Institution 1806–1867: A Complete Dictionary of Contributors* (George Bell and Algernon Graves, 1908), pp. 190-91.
15. *Illustrated London News*, 9 April 1853, p. 272. Over the years, Fitzcook contributed a total of nine paintings to the Society of British Artists and twelve to the other London galleries, according to

Algernon Graves, *A Dictionary of Artists who have Exhibited Works in the Principal London Exhibitions from 1760 to 1893*, new edition (Henry Graves, 1895), p. 99.
16. *Illustrated London News*, 26 April 1856, p. 421.
17. *Glasgow Daily Herald*, 28 September 1861, p. 2.
18. Henry G. Bohn, *A Guide to the Knowledge of Pottery, Porcelain, and other Objects of Vertu. Comprising an Illustrated Catalogue of the Bernal Collection* (Bohn, 1857); illustrations opposite pp. 133, 163, 195, 211 and 426.
19. *Art Journal* (1858), new series, Vol. 4, May 1858, p. 146; July 1858, p. 211.
20. *All About Shakespeare, profusely illustrated with wood engravings by Thomas Gilks, drawn by H. Fitzcook* (Henry Lea, [1864]).
21. John Bunyan, *The Holy War* (Nisbet, 1864).
22. *Official Descriptive and Illustrated Catalogue of the Great Exhibition of the Works of Industry of all Nations* (Spicer Brothers, 1851), Class 26, Exhibitor 187; p. 748 and Plate 30.
23. Nikolaus Pevsner, *High Victorian Design: A Study of the Exhibits of 1851* (London: Architectural Press, 1951), pp. 39-40.
24. *Athenaeum*, 16 December 1865, p. 849.
25. *Twigs for Nests* (Nisbet, 1866).
26. Isaac Watts, *Divine and Moral Songs for Children. Illustrated in the New Graphotype Engraving Process by W. Holman Hunt, … Under the Superintendence of H. Fitzcook* (Nisbet [1866]).
27. *Athenaeum*, 15 December 1866, p. 801.
28. Advertisement in *The Times*, 20 March 1866, p. 4.
29. Advertisement in *The Times*, 27 April 1866, p. 4.
30. *Daily News*, 29 November 1867, p. 6.
31. *The Diverting History of John Gilpin. Illustrated by H. Fitz-Cook and engraved by J.C. Whymper* (Longmans, Green and Co. [1868]).

SEVEN

The Art Journal

OUNDED IN 1839 (AS THE *ART UNION*), for its first forty years the *Art Journal* reigned unchallenged as the leading British journal devoted to all forms of art. WHR's major contributions to the *Art Journal* were made in the period 1845–50, and were concurrent with his contributions to the more specialist journal *The Builder* (see Chapter 5), except that they commenced two years later. In the last three years of this period, 1848 to 1850, WHR was ubiquitous in the *Art Journal*, which included more than sixty of his artistic designs for manufacturers. (At the time, the official titles were *The Art-Union* and *The Art-Journal*, but in accordance with modern usage the hyphens and definite articles are generally omitted here.)

After 1850, WHR confined himself at the *Art Journal* to lavish contributions to the catalogues which the journal issued periodically for twenty years to memorialise the series of international exhibitions which commenced with the Great Exhibition of 1851. Each of these catalogues was first published as a series of supplements to the regular monthly issues of the *Art Journal*, which were then gathered up and issued separately in book form. These *Art Journal* catalogues are considered separately in Chapter 11.

WHR's earliest contributions were made while the journal was still called the *Art Union*. The name *Art Journal* was introduced from 1849, at which time the format of the journal was enlarged and its complement of engraved illustrations much increased. Before that, there had been ten volumes of the *Art Union*, from 1839 to 1848, so the first two years of the *Art Journal* – 1849 and 1850 – were initially numbered Volumes 11 and 12 to signal continuity between the two titles. The following year, however, the publishers decided to rationalise the *Art Journal* sequence, numbering 1851 as Volume 3 rather than 13, and retrospectively re-numbering 1849 and 1850 as Volumes 1 and 2 (which are the volume numbers used here).

The editor of the *Art Journal* (and its predecessor *Art Union*) was Samuel Carter Hall, usually known as S.C. (or Carter) Hall. He was married to Anna Maria Hall, also known as Mrs S.C. Hall, a successful author. Both Mr and Mrs S.C. Hall were devotees of WHR's work and are considered in more detail in Chapter 18, on WHR's patrons.

As with *The Builder*, WHR's appearances in the *Art Union* and the *Art Journal* are considered here chronologically.

1844

WHR features in the *Art Union* for the first time in 1844, in its report of a new body set up with the aim of providing a venue for the arts that was less exclusive than the Royal Academy. This was to be the Institute of the Fine Arts and Art-Unions.[1] It had held a conversazione on 25 May, with art objects displayed around Willis's Great Room for the benefit of the 300 people attending. Leading the contributors to the display was WHR's father, William Gibbs Rogers, whose carvings had been praised by the journal in the previous year.[2] WHR himself contributed three objects to the display, including the wrought-iron canopy he had illustrated in *The Builder* of 18 May 1844.

The account of WHR's contributions concluded by describing a fascinating collaboration between WHR and the ceramist Walter Chamberlain of Worcester, a founder Freemason of the Church. It appears that Chamberlain was attempting to recreate the appearance of old Limoges enamel in ceramics, and that WHR (who did not reach the age of nineteen until May 1844) was acting as his designer:[3]

> Though last, not least, in our list is 'A Design by Mr. W.H. Rogers for an Ornamental Tazza in the style of the Limoges Enamel of the Sixteenth Century', which is now being attempted to be restored by Mr. Walter Chamberlain, of Worcester. The subjects in the four medallions are —'Cupid riding on a Dolphin,' 'Mercury playing with a Cock,' 'Bacchus with a Goat,' and 'Hercules strangling the Serpents.'

Sadly, the Chamberlain-WHR project appears not to have come to fruition. However, in 1852 the Chamberlain firm was taken over by Kerr and Binns, who ten years later were to provide the basis of the famous Worcester Royal Porcelain Company.[4] A dozen years after the Chamberlain-WHR attempt, Kerr and Binns finally succeeded in launching a much-admired range of 'porcelains in the style of Limoges enamels', and presented such a tazza to Queen Victoria.[5]

Finally, it should be mentioned that the *Art Union* provided extensive, illustrated coverage of the Tenth Exposition of the Industrial Arts of France, held in Paris this year.[6] There is no evidence that WHR contributed to this account, but it is noteworthy as the prototype for future *Art Journal* catalogues of international exhibitions.

1845

This year the *Art Union* published its first illustration by WHR.[7] The whole-page plate, signed with the monogram that WHR used until 1847, depicted a wooden overdoor containing two blank ovals for portraits, which WHR had presumably designed and which had been carved by his father.

The works of William Gibbs Rogers had been highly praised in the preceding issue of the journal.[8] However, that article had also raised an issue (only to dismiss it) of the extent to which carvings attributed to William Gibbs Rogers came solely from his own hands, as opposed to those of the carvers whom he employed:

There has been some silly and unmeaning carping relative to Mr. Rogers—assertions that because he does not, any more than the sculptor, finish the figure entirely from the block, but employs assistants, he is not to be considered the worker.

The article also quoted William Gibbs Rogers himself, implicitly explaining his need to employ other carvers:

I have created, by my own industry during the last twenty years, a *large* business, and have been rewarded by liberal patronage from almost every capital in Europe, as well as in my own country.

Mutterings about the extent to which carvings produced by the firm of William Gibbs Rogers were actually carved by the master himself were to rumble on in the following years, reaching a crescendo in the context of the Queen's cradle. Chapter 10 here includes previously overlooked but compelling evidence as to who did what in the course of executing WHR's design for the Queen's cradle.

1 8 4 6

As in the previous year, the *Art Union* carried an illustration of wood-carving designed by WHR (and signed with his monogram), of brackets in seventeenth-century Venetian style, carved by his father.[9] The brackets formed part of the contribution by his father to the Exposition of British Industrial Art held in Manchester, which the *Art Union* treated to an entire Supplementary Number in January 1846.[10]

1 8 4 7

In June 1847 the *Art Union* devoted a whole page to WHR's designs for carvings in early Renaissance style, referred to as the 'Italian' style (the word 'Renaissance' was not mentioned), the text making clear their radical nature:[11]

The Italian style of ornament is one eminently suited to purposes of wood-carving, and the perfection to which it was carried in the sixteenth century is testified by many a gorgeous interior among the palaces of Italy, and … owed its existence mainly to the discovery of the baths of Adrian and other antique remains towards the close of the fifteenth century … The style flourished not more than fifty years without corruption … Since then, (if we except the productions of France, which have always some impure characteristic), no imitations of that style have been attempted, except by Mr. Rogers, and his son, Mr. W. Harry Rogers (his principal designer), and of their success—at all events as far as it relates to their designs—our readers will be enabled to judge, from the specimens we shall occasionally lay before them.

It was reported that Queen Victoria and Prince Albert had acquired two boxwood brackets from a set emblematic of the four seasons:

> Mr. Rogers has had the honour of submitting them to her Majesty, when his Royal Highness Prince Albert paid the artist the compliment of retaining two of them, Spring and Autumn.

The following month, the *Art Union* continued the theme by illustrating a Rogers carving which this time was stated explicitly to be in the Renaissance style.[12] The depiction was of a boxwood spoon of a type 'presented last year to H.R.H., the Prince of Wales, on the 9th of November'.

A few months later, however, the *Art Union* occupied a whole page with William Gibbs Rogers wood-carvings designed by WHR in differing Gothic styles.[13] One illustration was of a Rogers altar rail in the Early English style 'from the design of his son'. The other illustration, signed with a WHR monogram, showed an elaborate canopy in the Perpendicular style. The illustrations received the accolade of being immediately reproduced by *The Builder*.[14] In the following issue of the *Art Union*, WHR's versatility was further demonstrated when a hat-trick of English Gothic design was achieved with the illustration of Rogers carvings in the Decorated style.[15]

1848

In this year appeared a series of decorated capital letters by WHR which were used to commence the editorial matter in each issue of the journal for several years following. The first to be deployed was the letter O at the start of the January 1848 issue.[16] The capitals were generally unsigned, but proofs of them are in the WHR archive at the V&A.[17] This year, WHR had entered into the short-lived design partnership with Henry Fitzcook described in Chapter 6, and the capital S which appeared first in June 1848 bore the monograms of both WHR and Fitzcook.[18]

January 1848 was also the start of two years in which almost every issue of the journal was packed with WHR designs, because it saw the commencement of the journal's series of 'Original Designs for Manufacturers'. WHR dominated this for nineteen successive months (January 1848 – July 1849). There was a range of contributors to the series (including Fitzcook) but WHR's designs were the most prominent, usually spread over two or even three pages of each issue. The scheme was described at its outset as follows:[19]

> Original Designs for Manufacturers.
> The designs, engraved and described under this head, are made expressly for publication in the Art-Union:—they have been purchased for this Journal, and are free to all Manufacturers, who may copy any of them, entire, or in parts. … Hitherto, we have been satisfied to FOLLOW the manufacturer whom we shall now aim to LEAD; … believing that beauty is not only of as easy attainment as deformity, but that the one may be produced as cheaply as the other … Our great object will be to promote intercourse between the ARTIST and the MANUFACTURER.

Chapter Seven – The Art Journal

7.1 – Two botanic designs by WHR in the *Art Union*. *Left*: Convolvulus encircling a vase, May 1848. Height 113mm. *Right:* Wild strawberry spreading along a fabric, August 1848. Height 97mm.

During 1848, WHR published a total of forty-five 'Original Designs for Manufacturers' in the *Art Union*, covering the following artefacts:

> Egg cup; Hand-screen and handles.[20]
> Two Door-scrapers; Tea-caddy spoon.[21]
> Wash-hand jug; Jug; Sugar-tongs; Coal-scuttle.[22] (The sugar tongs are described further in Chapter 8.)
> Scent bottle; Fender.[23]
> Pepper box; Hyacinth-glass; Knocker; Set of Fire-irons (jointly with Henry Fitzcook), illustrated here as Figure 6.1.[24]
> Knife-rest; Iron railings; Iron scraper; Two Wine-glasses; Child's mug; Marmalade pot.[25]
> Gas bracket; Iron banisters; Prie-Dieu chair.[26]
> Set of Fire-irons; Silver jug; Card-case; Taper candlestick; Hair-brush; Two Muslins.[27]
> Two Pairs of scissors.[28]
> Key; Paper knife; Knife; Dinner knife; Match-box (jointly with Henry Fitzcook).[29]
> Drawing-room chair; Tea-tray.[30]
> Scent-bottle; Encaustic tiles; Silk; Wine-tray.[31]

This wide-ranging array of designs included some exquisite botanically based compositions. Figure 7.1 shows two of these. On the left, the design for a hyacinth-glass shows a vase of ground glass entwined by a convolvulus in polished glass. On the right, the design for a muslin for dressmaking is based on the wild strawberry.[32]

7.2 – Masthead by WHR for the newly named *Art Journal* in 1849. Width 190mm.

Nearly half a century later, the architect Hugh Stannus (1840–1908), who taught at the Royal Academy, gave a highly detailed set of Cantor Lectures on the use of foliage in design.[33] It is remarkable that the only person mentioned during the course of the lectures was 'the late Mr. W.H. Rogers', who was said to have used petiole-articulation extensively, for example in the *Art Journal*, in the twin forms of vermiculate-tendrils and of stalk-leaves.[34] In his closing words, Stannus did mention 'the late Mr. Owen Jones', but only in the course of withholding from him the credit for producing 'a "Grammar of Ornament" from Nature', asserting that Owen Jones's work of that name 'is rather a Polyglot Dictionary of Historic Decoration'.[35]

The 1848 volume of the *Art Union* had a number of other elements relating to WHR. The least important was the illustration of a lead cloth mark which he contributed to the serialisation of Mrs. S.C. Hall's *Pilgrimages to English Shrines*, although two years later he did design the cover for the published volume.[36]

Of greater significance was news in June of a commission from Queen Victoria and Prince Albert to William Gibbs Rogers for a royal cradle, which WHR was to design (though he was not mentioned in the initial announcement). In May a whole page had been devoted to William Gibbs Rogers, with illustrations bearing WHR's monogram.[37] The next issue carried a brief announcement:[38] 'Mr. Rogers, the distinguished carver in wood, has, we understand, been commanded to execute a cot for the infant Princess.' Three months later, the details were firmed up:[39]

> We have already noticed the fact of Mr. Rogers having been appointed by Her Majesty to carve in *boxwood* the cradle for Her Royal Highness the Princess Louisa [usually known as Louise], and expressed our gratification that a work of such importance, and to be executed in so costly a material, has been placed in the hands of an artist who stands at the summit of his profession, and is eminently capable of doing what has not been done since the glorious period of the Renaissance in Italy. The style to be used is the Italian, slightly modified by a reference to some of the cradles forming accessories to early German pictures. Out of the numerous designs which Mr. Rogers has successively submitted to the inspection of Her Majesty, every alteration or suggestion in return has been for the better with regard both to elegance and propriety of purpose.

The further progress of the royal cradle, and WHR's central role in its creation, are traced in Chapter 10.

Finally, in yet another important contribution to the 1848 *Art Union*, WHR launched a blistering and initially anonymous attack on Henry Cole and his attempt to impose himself on the world of design. Details of WHR's campaign against Cole are provided in Chapter 9.

1 8 4 9

For its eleventh volume in 1849, the name of the journal was changed from the *Art Union* to the *Art Journal*, and later re-numbered as Volume 1. WHR designed a header for the new journal name, together with its proud declaration, 'Dedicated by command to His Royal Highness the Prince Albert', as shown in Figure 7.2. The header was printed at the top of the second page of the unnumbered *Art Journal* advertising pages, which were wrapped around the numbered editorial pages of each issue, and universally discarded if bound up into a volume.

7.3 –
Left: Illustration by WHR of a plate belonging to Ralph Bernal, in the *Art Journal* for March 1849.
Right: Its re-use in a Christmas annual, twenty years later. Image height 105mm.

In January, WHR commenced a detailed article on majolica, under the title 'On Raffaelle-ware'. He published a second instalment in March, longer and with his own copious illustrations.[40] WHR's most striking image, shown here on the left of Figure 7.3, depicted a plate belonging to his friend, the connoisseur Ralph Bernal.[41] A droll couplet by Bernal about WHR has already been given in Chapter 5, for the year 1844. The plate, and in particular WHR's representation of it, had a notable afterlife.

WHR's illustration was used subsequently as the frontispiece of Fairholt's dictionary of art in 1854, and later was included in Marryat's volume on ceramics, before being cannibalised two decades later for the Christmas number of the journal *Once a Week*, in the form shown on the right of Figure 7.3.[42]

Bernal died in 1854 and his vast collection was dispersed at auction. The WHR plate was catalogued as Lot 1856 and sold to the British Museum for £42.[43] It is salutary that WHR's drawing provides a clearer representation of the plate than does an excellent modern colour photograph on the British Museum (BM) website, because it incorporates WHR's understanding of the original ceramist's intentions. For example, the drawing conveys in the plate's white annulus what the BM catalogue entry describes as 'interlaced designs in bianco sopra bianco' which, understandably, are barely visible in the photograph.

Bernal's collections were of superb quality and considered so definitive that eventually the catalogue of the dispersal sale was published separately as a guide to ceramics.[44] Before the sale, there had been talk of preserving the collection intact for the nation. WHR, however, expressed a more original and prescient view. In an early analogue of arguing for the return of the Elgin Marbles to Greece, WHR wrote to the *Daily News* to propose the return to France of a particular treasure in the Bernal collection, as the first in a rolling programme of mutual cultural restitution:[45]

> … there is one lot, the extraordinary magic crystal of Lothaire, which I should like purchased by our government either to be presented to the French nation, or exchanged for some valuable relic having a higher historical interest for England than for France. Such objects abound in the museums of our ally. This would be the beginning of a plan for getting (as far as antiquities go) 'the right thing in the right place'.

As WHR feared, however, after selling for £267 at the Bernal auction, this extraordinary Carolingian engraved crystal did indeed remain in England, at the British Museum.[46]

Elsewhere in the January issue, it was reported that, late in 1848, WHR had become the Honorary Secretary of the Freemasons of the Church, as already noted in Chapter 5.[47]

From January to July, the flow of 'Original Designs for Manufacturers' continued, and included seventeen further WHR designs, as follows:

> Rose, shamrock and thistle pattern; Carriage-door handle; Decanter stopper; Key-handle.[48]
> Finger-glass; Fire-grate and fender.[49]
> Tea-kettle and stand.[50]
> Book-covers; Cruet stand (jointly with Henry Fitzcook).[51]
> Candelabrum (jointly with Henry Fitzcook); Caddy spoon; Key; Buckle.[52]
> Two Ice-plates; Salt-spoon and sugar-sifter; Tea-caddy spoon.[53]
> Three Umbrella handles.[54]

The elegant equine design for a carriage door handle from the January 1849 issue is shown here as Figure 7.4. The *Art Journal* reported a few months later that the handle had just been made and exhibited at the Annual Exhibition of the Society of Arts:[55]

> Mr. Penny, of Union Street, Middlesex Hospital, has contributed a very prettily executed carriage door-handle, in metal gilt, from a design by W.H. Rogers, published in the *Art-Journal*, representing a group of three sea-horses.

Chapter Seven – The Art Journal

7.4 – Sea-horses carriage door handle design by WHR in the *Art Journal*, January 1849. Width 121mm.

There was also one other appearance by WHR in the 1849 'Original Designs for Manufacturers', for which his identity appears to have been deliberately disguised.[56] A whole page was occupied by extensive designs for an etui, with views of the work-case and of several matching sewing items, some of them bearing lettering. The elegance and individuality of the drawing and of the lettering point strongly to WHR, but the published attribution was: 'By G.G. (12, Conduit Street, West, Hyde Park).' The attribution of the page to WHR on stylistic grounds is however confirmed by the discovery that proof copies of its various images can be found in the WHR archive at the V&A.[57] Further, the published attribution appears to be an accommodation address at Mr Dovey, the fruiterer. WHR was already dominating the March 1849 issue of the *Art Journal* with two pages of illustrations for his article on majolica (pp. 80–82), followed by an original design on p. 83, so it might have been felt that another whole page of illustrations under his own name on p. 84 ran the risk of the *Art Journal* appearing to be a WHR monoculture.

After July 1849, 'Original Designs for Manufacturers' made way for lengthy illustrated reports from two exhibitions, held in Paris (August and September issues) and in Birmingham (October issue). WHR drew exhibits from both. The feature on 'Original Designs for Manufacturers' was restarted in December 1849, but for the first time WHR did not participate in the scheme that month.

The Paris exhibition was the five-yearly Exhibition of the Works of Industry in France, held on the Champs-Élysées.[58] WHR drew a number of the illustrations in the *Art Journal*, identifiable by their superior appearance. He signed only one of them, depicting a bronze by M. Matifat of Rue de la Perle.[59] However, the proofs of several others are present in the WHR archive at the V&A, and these include the first two illustrations in the journal's account.[60] Consistent with WHR's developing interest in book covers, these drawings are of bookbindings (by M. Buchet of Rue Montholon and by M. Marius Michel of Rue Salle-au-Comte). Another example with an extant WHR proof is a silver tazza top (by M. Denière).[61]

Finally, for the Birmingham exhibition it was stated explicitly that WHR attended it as an artist on behalf of the *Art Journal*.[62] In the following paragraph it was noted that the pace had been hectic for producing 'this largely Illustrated Report; the whole of which has been produced in somewhat less than a month—collected, drawn, engraved and printed'. The only pictures in the report that bear WHR's monogram are those displayed in the whole-page treatment of his father's carvings.[63]

1850

The year started with an illustrated article by WHR entitled 'On transitions of style'.[64] WHR argued that it would be fruitful to take forms typical of Gothic panelling but to populate them with Italian (i.e. Renaissance) motifs, as had occurred historically in some transitional sixteenth-century chapels. As examples, he provided nine roundels which each deployed stylised foliage (Italian) in accordance with varied patterns of symmetry (Gothic). WHR probably got the idea of using roundels from a book published the previous year by R.W. Billings (1812–74), one of the original Freemasons of the Church, which showed how Gothic tracery could be built up from simple geometric elements in a large (he asserted 'infinite') number of different ways.[65] A letter from Billings duly appeared in the next issue arguing that his book should have been mentioned.[66]

The feature on 'Original Designs for Manufacturers' resumed in February and continued in a desultory way for only a few odd issues. WHR contributed four designs, taking his total number for the whole run up to sixty-six designs in the period 1848–50. His 1850 designs were as follows:

> Pickle-fork.[67]
> Finger-plate; Door-scraper.[68]
> Drawer handles.[69]

This July selection of 'Original Designs for Manufacturers' was the final one of the series, and included a well-earned tribute to WHR:

> We know of no designer whose taste in this description of artistic matters is purer than that of Mr. Rogers; many of the best examples which have adorned our pages have emanated from his pencil.

On a different tack, the productions of the émigré French goldsmith, M. Morel, had created a stir in London. As described in Chapter 15 (and illustrated in Figure 15.1), WHR was commissioned to provide four pages of drawings to illustrate Morel's approach:[70]

> … we now offer to our readers a set of carefully executed illustrations from the pencil of Mr. W. Harry Rogers, and we believe they will not only prove interesting to most persons from their beauty and novelty, but by showing to the British manufacturer what the French are able to produce, will be really useful in explaining somewhat of the attitude which the art will assume in the great Exhibition of 1851.

Finally, the Queen's cradle which WHR had designed was unveiled in a heavily illustrated four-page spread, as discussed in more detail in Chapter 10.[71]

FROM 1851

By 1850 WHR had made a considerable name for himself as a leading figure in both the theory and practice of designing art objects, his reputation bolstered by his contributions to the *Art Journal* and *The Builder*. At that point, however, WHR decided to make a strategic change in his activities. He became a full-time independent designer, and rationed his appearances in journals to the lavish supplements which the *Art Journal* published as permanent records of several major international exhibitions, to be discussed in Chapter 11.

Apart from the *Art Journal* catalogues, WHR therefore made minimal contributions to the *Art Journal* from 1851. In 1851 itself, his 'Finis' design appeared on the last page of the journal.[72] It had, however, been cannibalised from the *Art Journal* catalogue of the 1851 Exhibition.

It only remains to note that in 1858 the *Art Journal* made a short-lived attempt to revive its 'Original Designs for Manufacturers' feature in a couple of its issues. WHR contributed to both, firstly with designs for Letterheads, including designs for his friends Charles Bennett and the emigrant George Isaacs (illustrated in Figure 3.3).[73] Then in March he contributed designs for a Toasting-fork and for three Playing-cards (illustrated in Figure 14.1).[74] But the feature did not continue after this, despite the *Art Journal* paying there another glowing tribute to WHR:

> This page contains four engravings from designs by Mr. W. Harry Rogers (Wimbledon). The artist has established a reputation for large acquaintance with a special class of Art; and perhaps he is surpassed by no one in thorough knowledge of 'the Italian:' it is very general in its applicability, and his information thus conveyed may be useful to many orders of manufacturers. We shall not do justice to Mr. Rogers, however, if we thus limit his powers: he is familiar with nearly every branch of Art, a resort to which may be serviceable to the fabricant; and, moreover, he is acquainted with the capabilities of the producer to avail himself of the 'teaching' of the designer.

NOTES

1. *Art Union*, Vol. 6, June 1844, pp. 134–6.
2. *Art Union*, Vol. 5, September 1843, p. 248.
3. *Art Union*, Vol. 6, June 1844, p. 135.
4. Geoffrey A. Godden, *Chamberlain-Worcester Porcelain 1788–1852* (Barrie & Jenkins, 1982), p. 148.
5. 'The works of Messrs. Kerr and Binns, of Worcester, in the Ceramic Court at the Crystal Palace', *Art Journal*, January 1857, p. 28; Godden, *Chamberlain-Worcester Porcelain, op. cit.*, p. 171.
6. *Art Union*, Vol. 6, August and September 1844, pp. 225-270.
7. *Art Union*, Vol. 7, November 1845, pp. 340–41.
8. *Art Union*, Vol. 7, October 1845, p. 322.
9. *Art Union*, Vol. 8, January 1846, pp. 36-7.
10. *Ibid.*, pp. 23-54.
11. *Art Union*, Vol. 9, June 1847, p. 211.
12. *Art Union*, Vol. 9, July 1847, p. 244.
13. *Art Union*, Vol. 9, November 1847, p. 388.
14. *The Builder*, Vol. 5, 27 November 1847, p. 567.
15. *Art Union*, Vol. 9, December 1847, p. 401.
16. *Art Union*, Vol. 10, January 1848, p. 3.
17. V&A E851-1998 p. 64.
18. *Art Union*, Vol. 10, June 1848, p. 165.
19. *Art Union*, Vol. 10, January 1848, p. 11.
20. *Ibid.*, pp. 11-12.
21. *Art Union*, Vol. 10, February 1848, pp. 54-5.
22. *Art Union*, Vol. 10, March 1848, p. 74.
23. *Art Union*, Vol. 10, April 1848, pp. 105, 107.
24. *Art Union*, Vol. 10, May 1848, pp. 146-7.
25. *Art Union*, Vol. 10, June 1848, pp. 187-9.
26. *Art Union*, Vol. 10, July 1848, pp. 217-18.
27. *Art Union*, Vol. 10, August 1848, pp. 241-3.
28. *Art Union*, Vol. 10, September 1848, pp. 273-4.
29. *Art Union*, Vol. 10, October 1848, pp. 294–5.
30. *Art Union*, Vol. 10, November, p. 322.
31. *Art Union*, Vol. 10, December 1848, pp. 355-6.
32. *Art Union*, Vol. 10, May and August 1848, pp. 146 and 243.
33. Hugh Stannus, 'Artificial Foliage in Architecture', *Journal of the Society of Arts*, Vol. 42, 1894, pp. 881-91, 893-903, 905-16, 917-25 and 928-40.
34. *Ibid.*, p. 898; also pp. 910 and 931.
35. *Ibid.*, p. 940.
36. *Art Union*, Vol. 10, April 1848, p. 121.
37. *Art Union*, Vol. 10, May 1848, p. 148.
38. *Art Union*, Vol. 10, June 1848, p. 202.
39. *Art Union*, Vol. 10, September 1848, p. 287.
40. *Art Journal* Vol. 1, January 1849, p. 25; March 1849, pp. 80-82.
41. *Ibid.*, p. 82.
42. F.W. Fairholt, *A Dictionary of Terms in Art* (Virtue, Hall, & Virtue [1854]); Joseph Marryat, *A History of Pottery and Porcelain, Mediaeval and Modern*, second edition (John Murray, 1857), p. 76; *Oranges and Lemons*, the Christmas number of *Once a Week*, 25 December 1869, p. 96.
43. BM 1855,1201.63, catalogued as probably made in Pesaro in 1490–1510.
44. Henry G. Bohn, *A Guide to the Knowledge of Pottery, Porcelain, and other Objects of Vertu. Comprising an Illustrated Catalogue of the Bernal Collection* (Bohn, 1857).
45. Wm. Harry Rogers, 'The Bernal collection', *Daily News*, 16 March 1855, p. 5.
46. Bohn, Lot 1295, p. 130; BM 1855,1201.5.
47. *Art Journal*, Vol. 1, January 1849, p. 34.
48. *Ibid.*, pp. 26-8.
49. *Art Journal*, Vol. 1, February 1849, pp. 62, 64.
50. *Art Journal*, Vol. 1, March 1849, p. 83.
51. *Art Journal*, Vol. 1, April 1849, pp. 126-7.
52. *Art Journal*, Vol. 1, May 1849, pp. 152-4.
53. *Art Journal*, Vol. 1, June 1849, pp. 190-91.
54. *Art Journal*, Vol. 1, July 1849, p. 222.
55. *Art Journal*, Vol. 1, April 1849, p. 106; the exhibition commenced on 7 March.
56. *Art Journal*, Vol. 1, March 1849, p. 84.
57. V&A E766-1998, E767-1998, E790-1998, E806-1998 and E822-1998.
58. *Art Journal*, Vol. 1, August 1849, p. 233.
59. *Art Journal*, Vol. 1, September 1849, p. 278.
60. *Art Journal*, Vol. 1, August 1849, p. 235; V&A E740-1998 and E752-1998.
61. *Art Journal*, Vol. 1, August 1849, p. 238; V&A E769-1998.
62. *Art Journal*, Vol. 1, October 1849, p. 293.
63. *Ibid.*, p. 305.
64. *Art Journal*, Vol. 2, January 1850, pp. 25-6.
65. Robert William Billings, *The Infinity of Geometric Design Exemplified* (Edinburgh and London: William Blackwood and the author, 1849).
66. *Art Journal*, Vol. 2, February 1850, pp. 63-4.
67. *Ibid.*, p. 50.
68. *Art Journal*, Vol. 2, March 1850, p. 87.
69. *Art Journal*, Vol. 2, July 1850, p. 226.
70. *Art Journal*, Vol. 2, September 1850, pp. 289-92.
71. *Art Journal*, Vol. 2, August 1850, pp. 241-4.
72. *Art Journal*, Vol. 3, December 1851, p. 328.
73. *Art Journal*, new series, Vol. 4, January 1858, p. 23.
74. *Art Journal*, new series, Vol. 4, March 1858, p. 90.

EIGHT

Silver

In the second half of the 1840s and the first half of the 1850s, a range of items of silverware appeared which can be identified as having been designed by WHR. British silver at the time was stamped with hallmarks which included a year mark and a maker's mark. The maker's mark generally gave no clue as to the identity of the person who designed the piece of silver (or of the person or persons who actually made it, for that matter), but instead signified only the owner of the firm under whose auspices the silverware was made. A range of other evidence, however, serves to identify WHR as the artist who designed a number of silver items, including the silver table service known as Ornamental Elizabethan.

As recounted later in this chapter, WHR designed Ornamental Elizabethan for the leading tableware silversmiths Francis Higgins (maker's mark FH), who were acting on behalf of Hunt & Roskell, the successors of the famous silversmith, Paul Storr. Francis Higgins, in fact, made most of the silver items known to have been designed by WHR. However, the first such item to be considered was made not by Higgins but by Benjamin Smith (maker's mark BS), who was acting on behalf of Henry Cole. In Chapter 9, WHR is identified as the leading force in a successful campaign to derail Cole's more general manufacturing ambitions. But here we focus on the silver design which Cole had commissioned from WHR a year or two previously.

TEA PLANT CADDY SPOON, 1847

Henry Cole was not a designer but an administrator and entrepreneur. He wrote under the nom-de-plume of Felix Summerly, and founded a firm, Summerly's Art-Manufactures, which was to be devoted to the manufacture of household artefacts of artistic merit, 'entrusted only to the most eminent British Manufacturers'.[1] The firm had a brief but influential life in the period 1846 to 1849.[2] Most of the artefacts were designed by either the painter Richard Redgrave ARA (later RA), the artist H.J. Townsend or the sculptor John Bell, but there was a scattering of designs by other artists, including one by WHR, namely, a caddy spoon.

Henry Cole was a master of publicity, and the products of Summerly's Art-Manufactures are much better documented than other artefacts of the period.[3] The main section of his

December 1847 Summerly catalogue was headed 'Just Ready', and its final item (whose designer was not given) was listed briefly as:

> A TEA CADDY SPOON, in Silver, executed by B. Smith, 12, Duke Street, Lincoln's Inn.

The caddy spoon's maker was the high-end silversmith, Benjamin Smith (born 1818), who had taken over the silversmith firm of his father (of the same name).[4] His bankruptcy in 1850 was followed shortly by his death.

Cole ramped up the publicity further at the Free Exhibition of British Manufactures which was staged by the Society of Arts at their premises in John Street, Adelphi, during March and April 1848. He did not endear himself to other exhibitors, as Shirley Bury noted:[5]

> In March 1848 Cole organized the second annual exhibition of British Manufactures for the Society of Arts and rashly gave a disproportionately generous showing to the Summerly wares.

The Summerly exhibits were accompanied by a whole-page advertisement in the *Athenaeum* which listed the entire display.[6] In a typical ploy, Cole gave the WHR caddy spoon a second launch by flagging it up as one of the firm's articles that was 'entirely new and made public in this Exhibition for the first time', with a fuller version of the 1847 catalogue entry:

> TEA CADDY SPOON, ornamented with the common Tea plant, designed by W.H. Rogers, made in Silver, by B. Smith for Summerly's Art-Manufactures; exhibited by Chamberlains.

The exhibition was covered by the *Illustrated London News*, who picked out the WHR design for illustration.[7] Their engraving is shown on the left of Figure 8.1. It can be seen that the caddy spoon's bowl is plain, but its handle is pierced and takes the form of naturalistic twigs of the tea plant, *Camellia sinensis*, complete with its leaves and flowers. Although silver caddy spoons were made in a variety of shapes and sizes in Britain in the nineteenth century, this one appears to be unique in its combination of, firstly, massiveness in both the bowl and the handle (the handle's width is of a similar order to its length) and, secondly, a severe, undecorated bowl allied to a sculptural, pierced handle. The *Art Union* commented that the caddy spoon 'made by Smith, from a design by W.H. Rogers, is an adaptation of the tea plant, a work of small pretension, but exceedingly graceful'.[8]

The *Athenaeum* advertisement listed twenty-six London firms who would supply Summerly's products. Of these, fifteen firms supplied only limited areas of

8.1 – Tea plant caddy spoon designed by WHR for Felix Summerly's Art-Manufactures. *Left:* The silver original, from the *Illustrated London News*, 1848. Image height 55mm. *Right:* The silver-plated version. Length 97mm.

product. The designated exhibitor of the WHR caddy spoon, Chamberlains, of 155 New Bond Street, was one of the remaining eleven firms who could supply Summerly's products across the board.[9] Chamberlains was the producer of the well-known Worcester porcelain, and the New Bond Street premises was its London showrooms, though a shortage of funds had forced it to sell the freehold in 1845.[10] It was logical for a firm whose products included tea services to have been named as the exhibitor of a tea caddy spoon at the Society of Arts. The *Athenaeum* advertisement also named Cole's main agent as Joseph Cundall, of 12 Old Bond Street, the publisher and bookseller who was shortly to become an important artistic patron for WHR.

The advertisement in the *Athenaeum* was too tasteful to enter upon the matter of what Summerly's articles might cost, but later that year, the *Express* had no such qualms, advertising:[11]

> Presents for Weddings, Birth-days, and all Festivals. Felix Summerly's Art-Manufactures, designed by the most eminent English artists, executed by the first English manufacturers, and sold by all respectable dealers in town and country.
> … A TEA-CADDY SPOON, in plated metal, 2s. 6d.; in silver, £3 10s. …

However, when the advertisement was repeated less than a fortnight later, the advertised price of the silver spoon had plunged to about a third of its previous level:[12]

> … A TEA-CADDY SPOON, in plated metal, 2s. 6d.; in silver, 24s. …

Perhaps £3 10s had been the original price of the silver caddy spoon when announced in December 1847, but whoever placed the first advertisement in December 1848 had overlooked that in the meantime the price had been slashed to £1 4s to achieve sales. All the Summerly artefacts and their prices were also listed decades later in Henry Cole's memoir.[13] However, the memoir had been completed after Cole's death by two of his children.[14] For this reason perhaps, the memoir did not resolve the discrepancy between the two silver prices when it described the WHR caddy spoon:[15]

> A TEA CADDY SPOON, the ornament formed of the common tea plant. Designed by H.G. Rogers [*sic*], made by B. Smith, London. In Plated Metal, 2s. 6d., in Silver, at various prices. S.K.M.

The initials 'S.K.M', which concluded many of the entries, represented 'specimens which may be seen in the South Kensington Museum'.[16] However, that claim is questionable, because Bury asserted that Cole did not acquire any of his original specimens for the museum which he himself founded:[17]

> One tangible proof of Cole's disappointment with Summerly was his failure to purchase any of the articles for the collections of the new Museum of Manufactures in 1852. It was only later that he realized the importance of the experiment and commissioned some re-issues, which is why most of the Summerly wares in the Victoria and Albert Museum were made in the eighteen-fifties and 'sixties.

Certainly there is no sign of a Summerly caddy spoon in the V&A today, and indeed no specimen at all has been located of the Summerly caddy spoon executed in silver by Benjamin Smith.

An important development manifested in both the *Express* advertisements of December 1848 and the Cole memoir of 1884, however, is that the WHR caddy spoon was no longer said to be available only in solid silver, but had also become available more cheaply 'in plated metal'. By 1848, the form of production often referred to as 'Old Sheffield Plate' had been rendered obsolete by the introduction of electrical plating, still in use today. At the time, the alloy which was most commonly used as the substrate to be covered electrically by a thin layer of silver was an alloy of tin called Britannia metal (known then also as white metal).[18]

In the Cole memoir, WHR's caddy spoon is included in a group of three objects with the heading 'Britannia metal and white metal'.[19] The other two articles were a Camellia teapot designed by Richard Redgrave, available (like the WHR caddy spoon) in silver or plated metal, 'executed by Dixon and Sons, Sheffield'; and a salt cellar and spoon, designed by John Bell, available only unplated, 'manufactured in white metal by Broadhead and Atkins [*sic* – actually, Atkin], Sheffield'. For the WHR caddy spoon, no manufacturer's name was given by Cole.

The discovery of an actual example of the silver-plated caddy spoon, shown on the right of Figure 8.1, allows the manufacturer to be identified. On its lower side it is marked with 'B & A', for Broadhead and Atkin.[20] Thus, Henry Cole must have commissioned Broadhead and Atkin to make the Britannia-metal WHR caddy spoon alongside the John Bell salt cellar and spoon. Broadhead and Atkin will then have electroplated the caddy spoon themselves, having taken out a licence for silver-plating from the patent-holders, Elkington, in September 1845.[21]

The firm of Broadhead and Atkin was a partnership between Roger Broadhead and Henry Atkin which had originated in 1834. Following their production of the 1848 WHR caddy spoon, they were exhibitors at the Great Exhibition of 1851, showing 'Silver plate. Electro-silver plate. Britannia metal goods. Mounted jugs, &c'.[22] However, their partnership did not long survive the Great Exhibition, dissolving in 1853.[23]

Comparison of the two images in Figure 8.1 shows that although the design of the silver-plated WHR caddy spoon has been slightly modified from that of the solid silver original, it has preserved all its distinctive features, namely, massiveness in bowl and handle, an undecorated bowl allied with a pierced handle and a handle elaborately modelled as naturalistic twigs of *Camellia sinensis*, with leaves and three flowers. The most obvious difference is that the silver-plated handle has been truncated, by removal from the design of the leaves beyond the three flowers, perhaps to increase robustness or perhaps as an economy measure. The silver-plated caddy spoon is finely modelled on both sides and thus must have been cast (rather than stamped or spun) in Britannia metal before it was electroplated.[24]

Asa Briggs picked out the electroplated WHR caddy spoon for commendation without (as far as is known) having seen either the spoon or a depiction of it, solely from its description in Cole's memoir:[25]

Chapter Eight – Silver

> There was imagination … in a tea-caddy spoon made out of Britannia Metal, the ornament of which was more appropriately said to be 'formed of the common tea plant'.

Finally, there is a possibility that WHR created a tea plant caddy spoon first for Francis Higgins, rather than Summerly. Higgins produced a tea plant silver caddy spoon with a simpler, unpierced handle – a parcel-gilt example is hallmarked for 1858–9 – which matches the tea plant teaspoons which he had been making since 1846–7. In view of WHR's association with Higgins (described next) it is conceivable that WHR was also responsible for this earlier design and modified it for Summerly. However, there is no direct evidence for this theory.

FRANCIS HIGGINS

Francis Higgins executed a number of WHR designs in silver. He was born in about 1792 and died in 1880.[26] He was apprenticed in 1805, first entered his mark at the London Assay Office in 1817, and from 1837 until 1869 occupied premises in 40 Kirby Street, Hatton Garden. His speciality was the production of flatware, in particular silver knives, forks and spoons. The quality of the firm's work was unsurpassed, and only rivalled by two other leading London firms, Chawner & Co and Henry Holland.

The father of our Francis Higgins was also a silversmith and also called Francis Higgins, allowing the Francis Higgins firm to trace its origin back to 1782. Our Francis Higgins had a son in 1818, who likewise was called Francis and became a silversmith. In 1868, this Francis Higgins junior became a partner in his father's firm, which accordingly became known as Francis Higgins & Son.

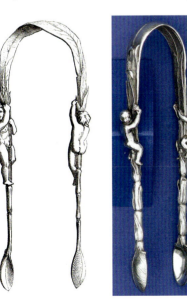

8.2 – Climbing Boys sugar tongs. *Left:* Engraving of WHR's design, 1848. Image height 110mm. *Right:* Silver executed by Francis Higgins. Length 134mm.

By the late 1840s, our Francis Higgins had become interested in artistic flatware, as opposed to producing only the well-established standard designs such as those known as Old English, Fiddle and King's. In 1848 he gained an entrée to the wider world of refined artistic taste when his silverware was reviewed enthusiastically in the pages of S.C. Hall's *Art Union* (soon to be re-named as the *Art Journal*). The trigger for this review was Higgins' manufacture of a design by WHR which had been published in the *Art Union* a few months earlier and may be termed the Climbing Boys sugar tongs.

CLIMBING BOYS SUGAR TONGS, 1848

The left-hand side of Figure 8.2 shows an engraving which appeared in the *Art Union*, accompanied by the following text:[27]

> DESIGNS BY W. HARRY ROGERS. … Our next design is for a pair of SUGAR-TONGS, in which

two boys are represented picking sugar from the cane. The semi-circular handle is formed by two leaves of the plant, which cross each other; the knots in the stems give support to the figures.

A few months later, there appeared in the same journal a laudatory article on Francis Higgins which revealed that he had put the WHR design for sugar tongs into production:[28]

> SILVER MANUFACTURES. —The indications of improved taste among our manufacturers are constantly occurring to us … . In no objects of general use has this improvement been more marked than in ordinary silver articles, spoons, knife, and fork handles, of which we have recently seen some specimens by Mr. Higgins, of Hatton Garden, remarkable for their elegant simplicity, or elaborate and rich workmanship; manufactured too at a price which brings them within the reach of a class not absolutely wealthy. Instead of recurring to fiddles, and such matters whereon to base his designs, the party in question has had recourse to the beautiful forms of nature … . He has also executed a pair of sugar-tongs, after the design by Mr. Rogers, which appeared in our Journal some three months back [*sic* – in fact, six]: these are exceedingly rich, and by no means costly, considering the weight of metal and the delicate workmanship required to produce them.

The right-hand side of Figure 8.2 shows the 'exceedingly rich' Climbing Boys sugar tongs as actually executed by the firm of Francis Higgins (this example was hallmarked in 1855–6). It can be seen that WHR's original design was adapted slightly to encompass thicker arms for the tongs, doubtless due to the practical experience of Higgins. To provide the greater thickness, the plants being climbed have been changed from sugar-cane to an alternative source of sweetness: banana. A less obvious change can be seen in the depiction of the boys' hair. In WHR's original design, the boys appear to be the conventional putti of western art. In the artefact as executed, on the other hand, the boys' hair appears to be tightly curled, presumably intended to suggest that they possess an African heritage – which raises the uncomfortable question of whether the boys' activity might represent labour under a coercive colonial regime rather than a manifestation of youthful high spirits.

ORNAMENTAL ELIZABETHAN, 1850

Ornamental Elizabethan is the name given to a design for silver tableware which was registered by Francis Higgins in 1852. The designer has been unknown, but was in fact WHR. Identification is possible because his original artwork for Ornamental Elizabethan (teaspoon, fork and spoon, and knife) is present in the WHR archive at the V&A.[29]

It has been asserted that Ornamental Elizabethan 'was produced by Francis Higgins for Hunt & Roskell'.[30] Certainly one set of Ornamental Elizabethan fork, spoon and knife, hallmarked for 1855–6 (in affluent circles of the period, a recognised gift for a child's baptism) has been seen in its original box which is gilt-stamped 'Hunt & Roskell, Late Storr

Chapter Eight – Silver

& Mortimer, Jewellers & Goldsmiths to the Queen and Royal Family, 156 New Bond Street'.

Hunt & Roskell was the successor firm to that of the celebrated silversmith Paul Storr (baptised 1770, died 1844).[31] Storr's firm had descended via his nephew John Samuel Hunt.[32] The box illustrates that Hunt and Roskell, in addition to creating their own works in silver, also retailed items from other top-end silversmiths, especially from Francis Higgins. At this period, Hunt & Roskell employed eighty to one hundred staff in its workshops at Harrison Street and no fewer than thirty-five staff in its retail premises at New Bond Street.[33]

Ornamental Elizabethan was available over the entire range of tableware. Figure 8.3 illustrates Ornamental Elizabethan pieces which could have been found in a wealthy household. In the lower half of the photograph are the seven items comprising a place setting (a standard service of silverware comprises twelve such place settings, or eighty-four items in all). From the left, the seven items are teaspoon, dessert fork, dessert knife, dessert

8.3 – Silver pieces in the Ornamental Elizabethan pattern designed by WHR. Length of ladle 331mm.

spoon, table fork, table knife and tablespoon. In the upper half are five additional items which might be required. From the top, these comprise a basting spoon, a soup ladle, a caddy spoon, a salt spoon and grape shears.

Apart from WHR, only one other designer of a pre-twentieth-century pattern of silver service is known. This is the painter Thomas Stothard, RA (1755–1834), who was identified as such in the biography published in 1851 by the author Anna Eliza Bray – Stothard was the father of her first husband.[34] Bray stated that Stothard designed 'boar-hunt silver-handled knives', for which his designs were translated into three-dimensional models by the sculptor Sir Francis Chantrey, and 'Bacchanals … intended for the handles of knives and forks'. She also stated that 'the Stag Hunt was designed by him for plate'. These three designs have been identified with a group of rare silver patterns all depicting vigorous action and known nowadays as, respectively, Boar Hunt and Mask, Bacchanalian and Stag Hunt.[35] They were first produced for the crown jewellers Rundell, Bridge & Rundell in 1811–12, at a period when their manufacturing was actually being carried out by the firm of Paul Storr. Storr's firm thus provides a direct link between the two known designers of silver services before the twentieth century, Thomas Stothard and WHR.

Later in the nineteenth century, WHR's slightly younger contemporary, the architect and designer William Burges (1827–81) also designed a number of items of silver tableware, such as sugar tongs (1869), a dessert service (1880) and gem-set cutlery (1871, 1879).[36] However, these were generally one-off items, often for his own use or for that of his patron, the 3rd Marquess of Bute.

Developing a new pattern of service intended for widespread use was a major undertaking for a silversmith, and Francis Higgins took legal steps to protect WHR's design. On 21 December 1852, Higgins registered the design under the Ornamental Designs Act 1842. Such was the importance attached by Higgins to the WHR design, it turned out to be the only design that he ever registered. Registration provided Higgins with three years' copyright in the pattern. The protection could be signalled on objects by a registration mark in the form of a diamond, and is to be found on most items of Ornamental Elizabethan design which were hallmarked from 1852–3 to 1855–6.

However, despite the apparent clarity provided by the registration process, it turned out to give rise to misunderstandings which have persisted to the present day with regard to both the naming and the dating of the WHR design.

First, with regard to naming, the original document which registered the Ornamental Elizabethan design is revealing.[37] It was submitted on behalf of Francis Higgins by Robertson Brooman & Co., Registration Agents. It is apparent from the document that the name 'Ornamental Elizabethan' applied to the WHR design arose as a misreading. At that period, copyright in a design could be obtained either with regard to its appearance, under the Ornamental Designs Act 1842, or with regard to its function, under the Utility Designs Act 1843. Robertson Brooman & Co.'s document is headed as follows (the layout and the use of italic versus roman lettering reproduce the original):

Ornamental.
Elizabethan Pattern.

Thus it is clear that what Robertson Brooman & Co. did was to register a pattern named 'Elizabethan' under the Ornamental Designs Act (rather than under the Utility Designs Act). But a subsequent misreading of the registration document, presumably by staff either at Francis Higgins or at Hunt & Roskell, led to the pattern being named 'Ornamental Elizabethan' instead. It is conceivable, however, that the misreading was deliberate, because an unrelated pattern which has also been called 'Elizabethan' was first produced in about 1850, perhaps by Chawner & Co.[38] Thus 'Ornamental' could have been deliberately appropriated for 'Elizabethan' by Higgins to differentiate his own pattern.

The second misunderstanding which the registration process has given rise to concerns the date of introduction of the Ornamental Elizabethan design. The earliest date-mark seen on ordinary pieces of Ornamental Elizabethan is Gothic R, which was in use from 29 May 1852 to 28 May 1853, and hence is consistent with the design being introduced in the months following its registration on 21 December 1852, as might be expected.[39] However, two exotic pieces of Ornamental Elizabethan have been seen which bear earlier date-marks.

8.4 – Silver-gilt Ornamental Elizabethan fork encrusted with agates. Length 184mm.

Figure 8.4 shows a fork in the Ornamental Elizabethan pattern, but with six of its domed silver surfaces replaced by cabochon agates. On the upper side of the handle, in order from the bowl, the agates are brown, blue-grey, and brown and white (the largest); underneath, the colours are the same except the largest agate is white and grey. The date mark is Gothic Q, which was in use from 29 May 1851 to 28 May 1852. That is, this exotic fork was made and hallmarked at least six months before the design was registered.

The earliest sighting of Ornamental Elizabethan is pushed back a further year for an exotic spoon whose sale has been archived on the internet by a dealer. This had similar decoration except with different stones (the two stones nearest the bowl were agates, followed by two coral cabochons and finally two citrines). This spoon was date-marked Gothic P, for 29 May 1850 to 28 May 1851.

It is possible that the exotic fork and spoon were made by Francis Higgins specifically for his display at the Great Exhibition, which was opened by Queen Victoria on 1 May 1851 and closed by Prince Albert on 15 October 1851. However, the chronology does not match entirely, because the fork was not hallmarked until after 29 May 1851, after the opening of the Great Exhibition. Furthermore, Ornamental Elizabethan was not included in the two-page spread on Higgins' designs which appeared in the *Art Journal* catalogue of the 1851 Great Exhibition. Exhibiting Ornamental Elizabethan might also have been inadvisable if Higgins was contemplating subsequently registering the design. In 1853, post-registration, Ornamental Elizabethan was indeed illustrated in the account of the works of Francis Higgins that was included in the *Art Journal* catalogue of the follow-up exhibition held in Dublin.[40]

Ornamental Elizabethan has been classified by Ian Pickford as a rare pattern:[41] 'Odd examples may be found; building a service would be very difficult.' Nevertheless, the pattern was still being employed by the Francis Higgins firm at the end of the nineteenth century. One example of an Ornamental Elizabethan dessert service with date-marks 1896–7 and 1897–8 was probably retailed by the luxury firm Asprey, because the lock on its box is marked 'Leuchars London', and the box-makers Leuchars had been absorbed by Asprey in 1888.

Machine-made flatware predominated in Sheffield after 1840, but in London handmade flatware remained the rule.[42] Hammering a bar of silver into the three-dimensional shape of a spoon or fork was a highly skilled process, especially with regard to the bowl or tines. The decoration of the handle was produced by a steel die in two pieces, an upper and a lower half, each with a reverse impression of their intended patterns. The blank silver would be inserted between the two halves of the die, which would then be hammered together in order to force the silver into the desired designs (later, a screw press came into use for this). Cutting these dies was skilled work, and had to be repeated a number of times to produce dies for the range of differently sized handles within a service.

Could an Ornamental Elizabethan service still be produced today? This is most unlikely. First, the specialist skills of making silver tableware by hand have largely been lost. Second, the dies themselves were almost certainly destroyed about eighty years ago. Francis Higgins & Son Ltd were wound up in 1940, by which time they possessed not only their own range of dies but also the dies they had inherited from a number of other leading nineteenth-century silversmiths. Nevertheless, J.W. Potter, who sorted the stock at the time, was quoted by Culme as stating, 'Only the popular spoon and fork dies were purchased by the Goldsmiths & Silversmiths Co Ltd. Literally hundreds were sent for scrap for the war effort.'[43] The dies for Ornamental Elizabethan were doubtless among those consigned to the furnace.

CARTOUCHE AND SPIRAL, 1846

Francis Higgins made a number of other graceful pieces of tableware from the late-1840s onwards, either in the naturalistic mode of WHR's tea plant caddy spoon or in the abstract and historicist mode of his Ornamental Elizabethan. It is difficult not to believe that some at least of these other pieces derive from the pencil of WHR. Attribution of naturalistic designs to WHR is relatively hazardous, however, because this genre had been around since the Regency period, though Higgins took it to new heights for tableware. A similar view with regard to naturalism has previously been expressed by Culme:[44]

> It is tempting to attribute some of Higgins's other designs of this period to W.H. Rogers, but without further evidence this remains impossible. Besides, the type of naturalism favoured by the firm, successfully shown at the Great Exhibition and at the Dublin Exhibition of 1853, was not new; Higgins may simply have been working in one of the current styles first made popular by Rundell, Bridge & Rundell some twenty years before.

Chapter Eight – Silver

8.5 – Silver Cartouche and Spiral set. Length of knife 190mm.

In considering the wider output of Francis Higgins at this period, therefore, naturalistic designs will be placed to one side and attention will be focused on abstract or historicist designs where a more specific link to WHR is present.

Heading such designs is what may be called the Cartouche and Spiral pattern. Figure 8.5 shows a baptismal set hallmarked for 1846-7, which is the earliest date encountered for this pattern. This hallmark was used from 29 May 1846, when WHR (born 12 May 1825) was aged only twenty-one, but was already an experienced artist-designer. The pattern formed part of the display by Higgins at the Great Exhibition. The *Art Journal* catalogue illustrated the knife's handle and described it as 'of silver, with ornaments of a conventional character … distinguished by considerable elegance'.[45]

What singles out the Cartouche and Spiral design for special attention is that a knife in this design is present in the archive of WHR artwork acquired by the V&A in 1998.[46] It is in fact the only component of the archive which is not paper-based. The knife is hallmarked 1873–4 (i.e. 29 May 1873 to 28 May 1874) so postdates WHR (who died on 19 January 1873), but only by about four to sixteen months. The probable compiler of the WHR archive was his sister, Mary Eliza Rogers, who shared WHR's artistic interests and, after WHR's death, helped to care for his children. It is difficult to believe that Mary Eliza, herself a designer, would have added a silver Cartouche and Spiral knife to the WHR archive for any reason other than that she knew it to have been designed by her late brother. It might even have held a special significance for her when curating the archive, if it were WHR's first design to be executed in silver.

CHARITY, OR RICH FIGURE, 1853

This design has been described by Ian Pickford as:[47]

> Rich Figure: A rare pattern of the second half of the nineteenth century, which appears in the Francis Higgins Pattern Book and was made by him for Hunt & Roskell.

As with Ornamental Elizabethan, however, the name by which the pattern came to be known has differed from its original form.

The left side of Figure 8.6 reproduces an engraving of the pattern, which was given pride of place in the article on Francis Higgins' silverware in the *Art Journal* catalogue of the Dublin Exhibition in 1853.[48] The accompanying text makes it clear that the original name of the design was 'Charity':

> The productions in silver of Mr. F. Higgins are far above the ordinary cast of

similar works; his establishment is limited, as we believe, almost, if not quite, exclusively to the manufacture of knives, forks, and spoons; the opportunities we have had, on more than one occasion, of carefully examining what it sends forth, satisfy us of the really artistic and mechanical skill bestowed upon design and execution. The engravings on this page afford our readers the means of judging how far we are correct in our commendation of the art of design; the workmanship of these beautiful objects is in no degree inferior. The large spoon, which the manufacturer calls the 'charity spoon,' from the emblematical figures introduced into it, is very elegant.

Charity is symbolised in this design by the classical iconography of a female figure with breasts exposed and two babies, also holding a dove aloft in each hand. It is difficult to

8.6 – Charity, or Rich Figure design. *Left:* Displayed at the Dublin Exhibition 1853. Image height 235mm. *Centre:* Silver-gilt spoon executed by Francis Higgins. Length 80mm. *Right:* Design by WHR for a metal handle, the *Art Union*, January 1848. Height 132mm.

imagine anyone other than WHR personifying Charity in this historicist manner on silver tableware. Further, the figure is strikingly similar to one which WHR published as part of his design for another handle (of a hand-screen), as shown on the right side of Figure 8.6. This design had appeared as part of the first batch ever of 'Original Designs for Manufacturers' offered by the *Art Union* (see Chapter 7), which noted:[49]

> the design for a handle is intended for metal, and a suitable lightness has therefore been imparted to it.

In terms of the design itself, the looped decoration below Charity's feet possesses *GS-LA* (global symmetry, local asymmetry), a WHR hallmark. Finally, WHR is known to have created an iconographically related depiction of Charity for one of the wood-carvings in the church of St Michael Cornhill.[50] Overall, it is safe to attribute the Charity design to WHR.

By the 1870s, the original WHR design had been subtly revised in a more conventional direction by Higgins, as can be seen in the spoon shown in the centre of Figure 8.6, which is hallmarked for 1880. The drapery has been revised and now leaves only one breast bare, while the regularity of the looped decoration has been increased.

Several other designs for Francis Higgins which were illustrated in the *Art Journal* catalogues for the Exhibitions of 1851 and 1853 are likely to have been created by WHR, but firm evidence is lacking. Francis Higgins was not included in the coverage of the *Art Journal* catalogue for the London International Exhibition of 1862, but the WHR–Higgins combination was in fact present in at least one exhibit, as follows.

MIDDLESEX HOSPITAL
RECORD OF BENEFACTIONS, 1854

To commemorate their benefactors, Middlesex Hospital decided to inscribe their names in a volume with a suitably impressive binding constructed from silver-mounted carved wood. Francis Higgins provided the silverwork (e.g. clasps bearing an MH monogram), William Gibbs Rogers provided the wood-carving and WHR designed both contributions.

Figure 8.7 shows the engraving of the Middlesex Hospital volume which appeared in the *Illustrated London News* coverage of the International Exhibition of 1862, and which is signed with WHR's monogram.[51] His artwork for the carved oak front cover of the volume is still extant in the WHR archive at the V&A.[52] The description in the accompanying text was as follows:[53]

> This large and handsome volume, in which are recorded the names of all benefactors to Middlesex Hospital, from its foundation to the present day, is formed of several hundred sheets of vellum. The back and sides are of rich morocco, the former embroidered with patterns in gold thread, and the latter decorated with panels of English oak, elaborately carved in the Wrennian style by Mr. W.G. Rogers, of Soho-square. The clasps and corners are the production of Mr. Higgins, the silversmith, of Kirby-street, Hatton-garden; and the design for the whole work was furnished by Mr. Harry Rogers.

Although exhibited in 1862, the Middlesex Hospital volume must have been created in 1854 or earlier, because it was described in a book which appeared at the end of that year.[54] John Timbs noted that the Middlesex Hospital was established in 1745 and enlarged and improved in 1848. He continued:

> In the Council-room is a large vellum Benefaction-book, wherein are beautifully written the names of the Benefactors to the Hospital, from its foundation. The binding is elaborately carved oak, by W.G. Rogers; and the clasps, corners, and bosses, are rich ormoulu [sic]. This sumptuous volume is protected by an ornamental iron stand.[55]

The present location of the Middlesex Hospital volume, and indeed whether it is still extant, are not known. After merging with University College Hospital, Middlesex Hospital was closed in 2005 and demolished, its records being inherited by University College London Hospitals NHS Foundation Trust.

In the next chapter, we provide a fuller consideration of WHR's relations with the impresario who commissioned an early silver design from him, Henry Cole.

8.7 – Middlesex Hospital Record of Benefactions, 1854, from the *Illustrated London News*, 1862. Image width 148mm.

NOTES

1. *Fifty Years of Public Work of Sir Henry Cole*, two vols (George Bell, 1884), Vol. 2, p. 180.
2. Shirley Bury, 'Felix Summerly's Art Manufactures', *Apollo*, January 1967, pp. 28–33.
3. *Art-manufactures. Collected by Felix Summerly, Shewing the Union of Fine-art with Manufacture*, sixth edition, December 1847.
4. John Culme, *The Directory of Gold and Silversmiths*,

Jewellers & Allied Traders 1838–1914, Vol. 1: The Biographies (Woodbridge: Antique Collectors' Club, 1987), p. 424.

5. Bury, 'Felix Summerly's Art Manufactures', *op. cit.*, p. 30.

6. *Athenaeum*, 18 March 1848, p. 304.

7. *Illustrated London News*, 25 March 1848, p. 204.

8. *Art Union*, Vol. 10, April 1848, p. 127.

9. WHR's collaboration with Walter Chamberlain in 1844 has been described in Chapter 7.

10. Geoffrey A. Godden, *Chamberlain-Worcester Porcelain 1788–1852* (Barrie & Jenkins, 1982), p. 145.

11. *Express* (of London), Monday 4 December 1848, front page.

12. *Express* (of London), Saturday 16 December 1848, front page.

13. Cole, *Fifty Years*, *op. cit.*, pp. 178-94.

14. Bury, 'Felix Summerly's Art Manufactures', *op. cit.*, p. 28.

15. Cole, *Fifty Years*, *op. cit.*, p. 191.

16. Cole, *Fifty Years*, *op. cit.*, p. 180.

17. Bury, 'Felix Summerly's Art Manufactures', *op. cit.*, p. 33.

18. Britannia metal consisted of tin with approximately 5-10% antimony and 1-2% copper, according to Frederick Bradbury, *History of Old Sheffield Plate* (Macmillan, 1912), p. 496.

19. Cole, *Fifty Years*, *op. cit.*, pp. 191-2.

20. Three adjoining marks on the caddy spoon comprise a Gothic 'B', probably for Britannia, an 'S' for Sheffield and (part of) eight crossed arrows, a trademark of Broadhead and Atkin.

21. Shirley Bury, *Victorian Electroplate* (Hamlyn, for Country Life Books), 1971, p. 33.

22. *Official descriptive and illustrated catalogue of the Great Exhibition of the Works of Industry of all Nations* (Spicer Bothers, 1851), p. 680. Atkin was listed as Atkins, probably the origin of the same error in the Henry Cole memoir.

23. See hawleysheffieldknives.com/index.php?kel=616

24. Bury, *Victorian Electroplate*, *op. cit.*, p. 22.

25. The Lord Briggs of Lewes, 'Metals and the imagination in the industrial revolution: The Chester Beatty Lecture', *Journal of the Royal Society of Arts*, 1980, Vol. 128, pp. 662-75; p. 667.

26. For this and the further details about Higgins, see Culme, *Directory of Gold and Silversmiths*, pp. 229-31.

27. *Art Union*, March 1848, p. 74.

28. *Art Union*, September 1848, p. 287.

29. V&A E.693:135-1998, E.693:136-1998 and E.693:137-1998, respectively.

30. Ian Pickford, *Silver Flatware: English, Irish and Scottish 1660–1980* (Woodbridge, Suffolk: Antique Collectors' Club, 1983), p. 147.

31. John Culme, revised, 'Paul Storr (bap. 1770, d. 1844)', *Oxford Dictionary of National Biography* (2004).

32. Culme, *Directory of Gold and Silversmiths*, *op. cit.*, pp. 245-6.

33. *Ibid.*, p 245.

34. Mrs Bray, *Life of Thomas Stothard, R.A., with personal reminiscences* (John Murray, 1851), p. 162.

35. Pickford, *Silver Flatware*, *op. cit.*, pp. 127-9.

36. J. Mordaunt Crook, *William Burges and the High Victorian Dream*, revised and enlarged edition (Frances Lincoln Ltd, 2013), pp. 22, 283, 313.

37. National Archives, BT 43/8/88449.

38. Pickford, *Silver Flatware*, *op. cit.*, p. 92.

39. For the origin of the annual changeover date of 29 May, see Charles James Jackson, *English Goldsmiths and their Marks* (Macmillan, 1905), pp. 59-60.

40. *Art Journal*, 1851 catalogue, pp. 26-27; *Art Journal*, 1853 catalogue, p. 9. For full catalogue titles, see Chapter 11.

41. Pickford, *Silver Flatware*, *op. cit.*, p. 147.

42. *Ibid.*, pp. 22-5.

43. Culme, *Directory of Gold and Silversmiths*, *op. cit.*, p. 230.

44. *Ibid.*, p. 230.

45. *Art Journal*, 1851 catalogue, p. 27.

46. V&A E.1150-1998.

47. Pickford, *Silver Flatware*, *op. cit.*, pp. 148-9.

48. *Art Journal*, 1853 catalogue, p. 9.

49. *Art Union*, Vol. 10, January 1848, p. 12.

50. A photograph of the Charity carving is present in an album of WHR designs that was assembled by his brother, George Alfred Rogers. The same photograph is present in: *Some Account of the Wood Carvings of Saint Michael's Church, Cornhill* (printed for George Alfred Rogers [1860]).

51. Middlesex Hospital record of benefactions in the International Exhibition, *Illustrated London News*, 16 August 1862, pp. 195-6.

52. V&A E693.132-1998.

53. *Illustrated London News*, 1862, p. 195.

54. John Timbs, *The Curiosities of London* (Bogue, 1855), p. 385. This was advertised in the *Athenaeum* on 16 December 1854 as due to appear on 1 January 1855.

55. Timbs's description of the metalwork as ormolu implies that he assumed it was composed of gilt bronze, whereas in reality the metal was silver-gilt.

NINE

Sir Henry Cole

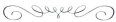

By the start of 1848 the newly married, twenty-two-year-old WHR had established himself both as an important voice in art journalism and as a gifted designer. At the two dominant art journals, the *Art Union* (shortly to become the *Art Journal*) and *The Builder*, he was a highly regarded protégé of both their long-term editors, namely, Samuel Carter Hall and George Goodwin, respectively. He had received the accolade from would-be design guru Henry Cole of being invited to design for his firm, Felix Summerly's Art-Manufactures. Later in the year he would become the Honorary Secretary of the band of architecture and design enthusiasts called the College of Freemasons of the Church (who, despite their name, were not affiliated either to the Church or to freemasonry in the conventional sense of the word). He was even shortly to embark on a commission from Queen Victoria herself, along with Prince Albert, of designing the extraordinary cradle which his father's firm was to carve for their daughter, Princess Louise.

With everything going for him, WHR appeared destined to become a pillar of the art and design establishment in the not-too-distant future. However, this destiny was not to be fulfilled, although WHR carried on for another quarter-century as a brilliant artist-designer. That establishment instead became populated by people who, even if less gifted, could be relied upon to toe the party line set by the energetic and opinionated Henry Cole (1808–82). Cole eventually became so dominant in the art and design world that in latter years he regularly attracted the nursery-rhyme epithet 'Old King Cole', applied to him as early as 1862.[1] Figure 9.1 reproduces his portrayal in *Vanity Fair* in 1871.

But that was in the future. In 1848 Cole was widely viewed as a cuckoo in the art and design nest, feathers having been ruffled particularly by the franchise business he had set up under the name Summerly's Art-Manufactures. WHR decided that he should be the one to raise a commotion about this interloper. What happened, however, was that WHR won the battle but lost the war. He succeeded

9.1 – Henry Cole, as portrayed in *Vanity Fair*, 19 August 1871. Width 191mm.

in forcing Cole to close down Summerly's Art-Manufactures, but not in preventing Cole's inexorable rise within the administrative establishment of British art and design. And as tends to happen for a songbird up against a cuckoo, it was WHR who was heaved out of this particular nest.

COLE AND DESIGN

Under his commercial pseudonym of Felix Summerly, the Civil Service administrator Henry Cole had been broadcasting his view that design in Britain was terrible and that he was the man to redeem it. Shirley Bury has traced 'how strenuously he had manoeuvred to acquire the reputation as an authority on industrial design'.[2] As someone who was steeped in the study of design and highly gifted at its practice, WHR must have been irritated by Cole's self-aggrandising ways. At the time, however, the continued presence of Cole in WHR's world was by no means assured. Cole's campaigning about design was the third cause which he had taken up in the 1840s, and the two earlier campaigns (about postage stamps and about railways) had both been relatively short-lived. In the case of design, however, Henry Cole never went away.

Cole's key move was to take control of the Society for the Encouragement of Arts, Manufactures and Commerce (founded in 1754), becoming a member of its council soon after joining it in 1846.[3] This hitherto sleepy establishment, usually called simply the Society of Arts (Royal Society of Arts from 1908) provided Cole with access to an administrative ace of trumps in the person of their president, because since 1843 this had been the progressively inclined Prince Albert. Cole immediately grasped that if he took on the role of organising exhibitions for the society, it would provide him with an important means of controlling the agenda for art and manufacturing. One item on his agenda was to use the exhibitions to provide a platform for marketing his own Felix Summerly range of designer objects. But it was with a second item that Cole struck gold.

What became known as the Great Exhibition of 1851 was launched from the Society of Arts platform. Cole played the central role in implementing Prince Albert's vision of holding in London a large international exhibition to embrace all aspects of industry. The Great Exhibition turned out to be a huge popular success, and has remained a key reference point in many accounts of the nineteenth century as a whole. Thereafter, Cole (eventually Sir Henry Cole) was untouchable by his critics. He maintained an iron grip on the organisation of the official world of design, including the Government School of Design and the South Kensington Museum (from which the Victoria and Albert Museum was spun off at the end of the nineteenth century).

WHR'S CAMPAIGN AGAINST COLE

Why exactly did WHR decide to take on Henry Cole in 1848? He gave an account of his active campaigning against Cole to his friend George Isaacs (see Chapter 3). This was in a long letter of 25 July 1848, which Isaacs took with him when he emigrated to South Australia in 1850.[4] In the letter, WHR ascribed the origin of his campaign only to 'a quarrel' which he had had with Felix Summerly. The nature of this original quarrel is unclear, though one might speculate that it had something to do with the design which WHR had provided in late 1847 for Cole's Felix Summerly business. For example, did Cole consult WHR before arranging (as described in Chapter 8) that his design should be manufactured, not only in its original form by a leading London silversmith but also in modified form by a Sheffield silver-plater?

The original quarrel between WHR and Henry Cole was aggravated by the exhibition of British Manufactures and Decorative Art, organised by Henry Cole on behalf of the Society of Arts, and held at their rooms in March 1848. Though many prizes for exhibitors had been advertised by the society, in the event very few materialised. In his letter to Isaacs, WHR recounted that he and his professional partner, Henry Fitzcook, had submitted about twenty designs which they felt should have won a clutch of prizes. Instead, however, they did not receive a single one, only a token two-guinea merit award for a design for a gas chandelier by Fitzcook.[5] WHR attributed the withholding of the rightful prizes unequivocally to Henry Cole.

WHR'S OPENING SHOT

In retaliation, WHR had immediately published a 'severe article' in the *Art Union*, he told Isaacs. This must have been the very lengthy, anonymous review of the exhibition which the journal published in April 1848.[6] The review was scathing about the Society of Arts in general and Henry Cole in particular. It stated of the Society of Arts that:[7]

> of late years, its approaches to senility have been somewhat more than suspected; when suddenly it casts off the semblance of decay, and assumes in its stead the character of juvenile enthusiasm—perhaps approaching impetuosity. … These undertakings must be acknowledged to be highly meritorious; … the whole, or any of these objects are, however, beyond the ability of any association of gentlemen to effect. It requires far more extended means and authoritative influence than can be wielded by a Society which has just emerged from an idle patronage of Art by a yearly parade of silver palettes and medals to the young scions of their households for 'trifles' of no conceivable value.

Turning from the general to the particular, the review continued:[8]

> … we fear a suspicion or misunderstanding may arise in the minds of many as to the genuineness of the Exhibition as a display of specimens of British Manufactures, when it looks so strangely like a display of Felix Summerly's series of Art Manufactures—accompanied by some others.

Nor did the review hold back about the standard of design of Summerly's wares themselves. Figure 9.2 shows the Britannia metal teapot entitled the Camellia by Cole, which the *Illustrated London News* depicted, noting that it was surmounted in Parian by 'a Chinese Faëry, examining the Tea-plant'.[9] The *Art Union* review remarked scathingly:[10]

9.2 – Camellia teapot, designed by Richard Redgrave for Felix Summerly, from the *Illustrated London News*, 1848. Image width 53mm.

The shape of the object, which however is the composition of R. Redgrave, A.R.A, is far from pleasing. The outline reminds us of a hanging pear, which is not of itself particularly graceful, but less so when supplied with spout and handle.

The author of this unfortunate design, Richard Redgrave (1804–88), was an early and long-term Cole loyalist who had joined the staff of the Government School of Design in 1847.[11]

WHR's damning review of the exhibition certainly stung Cole. According to WHR's letter to Isaacs, it caused Cole to threaten S.C. Hall, editor of the *Art Union*, with prosecution for libel, though in due course Cole dropped the threat.

WHR'S CAMPAIGN BROADENS

Undeterred by Cole's threat, WHR explained to Isaacs that he was continuing his anti-Cole campaign, and had already done so with a 'sarcastic letter' in *The Builder* and another item in the *Lady's Newspaper*.

WHR's letter in *The Builder*, signed by 'An Artist', had appeared at the end of April.[12] One of the targets at which he took aim was a much-publicised tea set, designed by Cole himself, with which the Felix Summerly range of manufactured articles had been launched. WHR indicated that the prize it had received at an earlier Society of Arts exhibition was an inside job by Cole:[13]

> Three years ago this Society of Arts rewarded, by the gift of medals, &c., some designs for articles of tea-service, by a gentleman who presented the designs under an assumed name; and it is for others to judge if they were cognizant of the matter, or in a condition of blissful ignorance of the real truth. The affair itself proved of very little consequence in results, for after plentifully foretelling that from the peeress to the washerwoman tea would thenceforth only be drunk out of the society's pot, it has vanished from the crockery shops into oblivious security.

Unlike *The Builder*, the *Lady's Newspaper* was a declared Cole supporter. But WHR told George Isaacs that he had risked its editor's wrath by inserting an article containing an anti-Cole section while the editor was away. The article was anonymous, but accompanied by an illustration which was signed with his WHR monogram. The relevant section referred disparagingly to:[14]

> the joint manufactures of Mr. Minton and Felix Summerly, the adopted works of the latter gentleman being attempts, though seldom successful, to combine good manufacture with good design.

The editor later made amends to Cole at the earliest opportunity. When discussing another exhibition at the Society of Arts, attention was drawn to 'one of its most active members,

Henry Cole, Esq., a gentleman well known for his enthusiasm and taste in all matters relating to art'.[15]

WHR REVEALS HIS IDENTITY

WHR's campaign against Cole had hitherto been anonymous, primarily because most articles in most journals were unsigned at the time. But at this point WHR put his name to an attack.

In his letter of 25 July 1848 to George Isaacs, WHR said that he had further material to use against Cole, but had not yet decided how to deploy it. He also separately mentioned that he had just received from George Godwin the proofs for correction of an article he had written on the Renaissance, to be published in *The Builder*. In the event, when this article was published in the issue of 29 July it included an attack on Cole, probably inserted by WHR only at this stage of correcting proofs. The article was a signed one, so by this point, if not earlier, WHR will have crossed the Rubicon of an open attack on Cole.

During the course of the article, WHR publicly ridiculed Cole's self-appointed role as the reformer of artistic design.[16] He argued that artistic styles develop in an organic way and cannot:[17]

> be effected by individual caprice or the probably well-intended efforts of a particular clique. From a conviction of the truth of this fact, confirmed as it is by every thing which can be brought to bear upon the subject, we smile at the dreams of those French enthusiasts who desired that the reign of each of their sovereigns should represent a fresh school of architecture and decorative art, and more recently at the still prouder pretensions of Felix Summerly.

At the same time, the veil of anonymity was also effectively lifted in another attack on Cole in the *Art Union*. An article in the issue of 1 August accused Cole of deception in advertising a Felix Summerly carved-wood bread platter as having been 'completed' by Joseph Rodgers, a metal-working firm that Cole dealt with in Sheffield. The article pointed out that Rodgers had nothing to do with wood-carving, and that the actual carvers were known to be the unrelated firm of Philips and Wynne. The article added that carved-wood bread platters had been made for years by 'Mr W.G. Rogers, the celebrated wood-carver', and accused Felix Summerly of seeking to capitalise on the reputation of Rogers by attaching the spurious name of Rodgers to his own product.[18] It would have been unlikely for the genial W.G. Rogers to have written the article himself (in the third person), and Cole would have realised that it must instead have been his son, WHR, who was responsible for it.

A couple of months later, in the October 1848 issue of the *Art Union*, WHR had more fun at Cole's expense in the anonymous text accompanying an elaborate match-box design signed by Henry Fitzcook and himself, taking the opportunity to reprise his own mockery of the 'Crusader's Altar Tomb' matchbox previously exhibited by Felix Summerly at the Society of Arts.[19] This time he wrote:[20]

Chapter Nine – Sir Henry Cole

> Some time back we had occasion to express our opinion upon a match-box, which appeared as a candidate for public favour at the Exhibition of the Society of Arts. That match-box presented the design of a Crusader's altar-tomb, thereby offering about as unintelligible an allusion to its purpose as the most obscure metaphysician could have required, and as ludicrous a connexion as the most comic genius could have invented.

There were further denunciations of the Felix Summerly operation in 1848, for which the general anonymity of the journals at the time has meant that it is not known whether or not they emanated from WHR. Thus Felix Summerly was mocked in *Punch* and elsewhere in *The Builder*, while the *Art Union* published further complaints about the handling of the Society of Arts exhibition.[21] It is already clear, however, that it was WHR who conducted the most fierce and prolonged campaign against Cole and his alter ego, Felix Summerly.

THE EFFECT OF WHR'S CAMPAIGN ON COLE

9.3 – The popular Dorothea, made for Summerly by Minton in Parian, after John Bell's 1838 marble original. Height 360mm.

WHR won his battle against Cole's much-vaunted Felix Summerly design operation, which Cole soon began quietly to drop. Confirming this, Shirley Bury (who did not know that WHR was the author) identified WHR's review of Cole's Society of Arts exhibition in the April 1848 issue of the *Art Union* as the beginning of the end for Felix Summerly.[22] At the same time, she vindicated the central plank of WHR's critique by concluding that the 'basic weakness' of the Summerly scheme was the ignorance of Cole and his artists in matters of design. Figure 9.3 shows the only Summerly product, Dorothea, which sold sufficiently well to make a profit, and Bury also pointed to the irony that Dorothea was not in fact an original design for manufacture, but instead a reduced copy of an existing sculpture.

Stirred up by WHR's campaign, mutterings against Cole surfaced even in his stronghold, the Society of Arts, at a meeting on 22 November 1848.[23] Indeed, eventually Cole's powers at the Society of Arts were curtailed by a change in the bylaws on 4 March 1850, provoking Cole and his group briefly to resign from the society's council.[24]

At around this time, Cole was also losing ground in his attempt to grab control of education in design. In November 1849, the distinguished Ralph Wornum (1812–77, subsequently Keeper of the National Gallery), who worked for the Government Schools of Design, publicly joined the anti-Cole campaign. He wrote to the *Art Journal* to oppose Cole's campaign to create a post of administrative supremo for himself. Wornum poured ridicule upon an already rejected report which, though ostensibly independent of Cole, in reality had his fingerprints all over it:[25]

> The upshot of all this sifting appears to be, that the Schools of Design will never be of any use to the community until a 'well

paid' deputy-president be appointed to control the whole working machinery of the Schools. This is the scheme of Mr. Henry Cole; and the chief feature of this rejected report is its constant bearing on the evidence of this witness, from which, indeed, it makes long extracts, and evinces altogether an irresistible propensity to father its most hostile paragraphs.

By 1851, however, the idea of toppling Cole switched from being a possibility to being unthinkable, and in this sense WHR won the battle of Felix Summerly but he and others such as Wornum lost the war of Cole's Aggrandisement. Cole's integral role in organising the huge popular success that was the Great Exhibition of 1851 gained for him not only the Companionship of the Order of the Bath but also an unchallengeable position within government administration. For more than twenty years he continued to steamroller any opposition within his own domain. This brought significant achievements to his name but must also have antagonised a lot of people, and Cole was not advanced to KCB until 1875. *Vanity Fair* put it tactfully[26]:

> The peculiarity of Mr. Cole's career is that he has always succeeded in compassing his objects in the face of the most fierce and unsparing opposition. He appears to have a strange power of bending all men and things to his purpose.

As already mentioned, WHR told George Isaacs that in 1848 Cole had threatened to prosecute for libel WHR's patron, S.C. Hall, the editor of the *Art Journal*. Cole had not followed through on that threat. In 1851, however, Cole found a more subtle way to undermine Hall, participating in a train of events which led to Hall's partial ruin and the forced sale of his majority holding in the ownership of the *Art Journal*.

S.C. HALL AND THE TWO 1851 CATALOGUES

By 1851, the year of the Great Exhibition, the *Art Journal* had a record unrivalled in the UK for providing extensive, illustrated records of major exhibitions of art manufactures. The exhibitions it had covered in detail included the 1844 Paris Tenth Exposition of the Industrial Arts of France, the 1846 Manchester Exposition of British Industrial Art, the 1849 Paris Eleventh Exposition of the Productions of Industry, Agriculture and Manufacture in France, and the 1849 Birmingham Exhibition of Manufactures and Art.[27] Commissioned by S.C. Hall, WHR had participated prominently in the coverage of the two 1849 exhibitions, and to a lesser extent in that of the 1846 exhibition, as documented here in Chapter 7.

In view of the unparalleled experience of the *Art Journal* in recording large exhibitions, Hall had high hopes that it would be given a clear run for what was planned to be its largest ever catalogue (with extensive contributions from WHR), devoted to the 1851 London Exhibition of the Industry of All Nations. However, this was not to be, and Hall was left embittered by the decision to produce a rival, official catalogue. He blamed the exhibition's Executive Committee, and no doubt had in mind Henry Cole in particular, since Cole was the member of the Executive Committee who was involved with the official catalogue.[28] More than thirty years later, Hall was still outraged by Cole's spoiler operation:[29]

Not long after my announcement of the Illustrated Catalogue I contemplated issuing with the *Art Journal,* the 'executive' of the Exhibition advertised for a rival to it; that is to say, they sought to obtain a sum of money for the privilege of publishing an officially recognised catalogue, and accordingly issued proposals for tenders. I declined to be among the applicants, and the right that I had reason to hope would have been secured to me in acknowledgement of my past labours was purchased by Messrs. Spicer and Clowes, for the sum of £2,000.★ [Original footnote: ★It was understood that they lost £2,000 by the speculation, and the £2,000 they had paid for the privilege was in consequence returned to them out of the surplus that remained when the doors of the Exhibition had been finally closed, and all expenses met.] Their Illustrated Catalogue was, however, badly done; for they could bring to the work neither the experience nor the resources that I possessed.

Had the sole right of issuing an Illustrated Catalogue remained in my hands, it is my belief that the venture I embarked upon would have 'paid.' … From May to December, 1851, double numbers of the *Art Journal* were issued, price five shillings each, and the public paid that year for the *Art Journal* a sum exceeding £72,000. Large, however, as were the receipts, the expenses were still larger. I was then the principal proprietor of the work; but the consequence of a 'loss' arising out of the publication of the Art Journal Illustrated Catalogue was the sale of my shares to my co-proprietors—men of business and calculating habits—and I became, from 1851, only the paid Editor of the work.

THE EFFECT OF WHR'S CAMPAIGN ON WHR

WHR's campaign against Henry Cole reveals him as someone prepared to take a stand against what he perceived as unfairness and ignorance. The verdict of history is surely that WHR was right and Cole was wrong. It can be argued that Cole's forceful and dogmatic approach went on actively to hinder the flourishing of design in Britain. Certainly, Sir Ernst Gombrich endorsed Charles Dickens's views about 'the type of reformers, such as Henry Cole, he regarded as self-important meddlers'.[30]

From a purely pragmatic point of view, however, the campaign against Cole also revealed WHR's lack of experience, in neglecting to think through what might be the longer-term consequences for himself of attacking such a well-established figure. In this context, it must be remembered that in April 1848 WHR was still only twenty-two years old.

For WHR, the legacy of his attempt to derail the Cole juggernaut was to be his permanent exclusion from the art and design establishment of which Cole shortly became the accepted arbiter. One would not necessarily expect to see any evidence of direct intervention by Cole in WHR's career, because all that was needed was a studied neglect of WHR in the circles which Cole influenced. However, a decade later, direct sabotage by Cole probably can be identified in connection with the 1862 International Exhibition in London, when Cole was at the peak of his powers.

THE CANCELLED COVER
OF THE 1862 OFFICIAL CATALOGUE

Cole was the éminence grise of the 1862 International Exhibition in London, fighting almost single-handedly for its existence but refusing initially to accept any official position in its organisation, to avoid attracting criticism.[31] By April 1861, however, Cole had agreed to 'take charge' of several core aspects of the exhibition, including its catalogue, while insisting still on being listed officially only as a mere consulting officer.[32] As covert supremo of the 1862 official catalogue, Cole turned out to be in the frame when WHR suffered a setback over the 1862 official catalogue, just as he had been when S.C. Hall suffered his more major setback over the 1851 official catalogue.

The main official publication for the International Exhibition of 1862 was the multi-volume *Illustrated Catalogue*, and the person appointed as its official superintendent was the high-end publisher Joseph Cundall. In the late 1840s, Cundall's bookshop in Old Bond Street had acted as the principal retail outlet for Cole's range of Felix Summerly artefacts. But Cundall was also a great admirer of the work of WHR and, as described in Chapter 18, commissioned designs by him regularly from 1853 until the end of WHR's life. Further, Cundall would have been aware that WHR had been a lynchpin for the *Art Journal* of not only their London 1851 exhibition volume but also their Dublin 1853 and Paris 1855 exhibition volumes, so might enjoy a fresh challenge with the official publication for London 1862. At Cundall's invitation, therefore, WHR this time switched from the *Art Journal* catalogue to producing designs for both the interior and the exterior of the official *Illustrated Catalogue*.

The interior of the *Illustrated Catalogue* as published was duly enlivened by WHR, as were the illustrated paper wrappers which clothed the work's issue in parts. Surprisingly, however, the most high-profile part of WHR's work was never put into production. This was his elegant design for the gilt stamping of the cloth-bound volumes in which the completed version of the catalogue was to appear, which featured symbols of industry, of art and of the different continents. Instead, the covers of the published volumes have an anonymous, incoherent design in which a swirl of mythological figures on the front bears no relation to a pair of rectilinear tridents on the spine.

We know about the cancelled WHR cover design only because it still exists in the archive of WHR's work acquired in 1998 by the Victoria and Albert Museum, ironically the successor of Cole's own South Kensington Museum. The WHR artworks in the archive (which descended through his family) consist largely of preliminary sketches which WHR had retained, because his finished designs would have almost always ended up in the possession of the commissioners or executants of the designs. Consistent with this, the archive does indeed possess a preliminary sketch by WHR for the *Illustrated Catalogue* gilt cover.[33] Unusually, however, the archive also possesses the final, fully worked-up artwork for the gilt cover, proudly lettered in the lower-left margin 'W. HARRY ROGERS. INVT. 1862'.[34] Clearly this had been rejected and returned to the artist.

It seems impossible to imagine that the rejection of WHR's finished artwork for the cover of the *Illustrated Catalogue* volumes was the work of Joseph Cundall, WHR's long-term admirer and patron, even though it was Cundall who was officially the superintendent of the catalogue. Instead, what surely must have happened is that Cundall's undeclared boss, Henry Cole, was horrified when he discovered that the public, official face of his own 1862 exhibition was to be provided by his old adversary, and stepped in to countermand Cundall's intended use of WHR's cover design, resulting in its return to the artist and the cobbling together of a replacement.

NOTES

1. Elizabeth Bonython and Anthony Burton, *The Great Exhibitor: The Life and Work of Henry Cole* (V&A Publications, 2003), p. 208.
2. Shirley Bury, 'Felix Summerly's Art Manufactures', *Apollo*, January 1967, pp. 28-33; p. 28.
3. Bonython and Burton, *The Great Exhibitor, op. cit.*, pp. 99–100.
4. Scrapbook of George Isaacs, State Library of South Australia, D Piece (Archival) D6668(Misc), p. 60.
5. *Art Union*, 1 July 1848, p. 216; illustrated 1 December 1848, p. 355.
6. Society of Arts, 'Exposition of British Manufactures', *Art Union*, 1 April 1848, Vol. 10, pp. 125-9.
7. *Ibid.*, p. 125.
8. *Ibid.*, p. 126.
9. *Illustrated London News*, 25 March 1848, pp. 203-04.
10. Society of Arts, 'Exposition of British Manufactures', *op. cit.*, p. 127.
11. Anthony Burton, 'Richard Redgrave as art educator, museum official and design theorist', in Susan P. Casteras and Ronald Parkinson (eds), *Richard Redgrave 1804–1888* (Yale University Press, 1988), pp. 48–70; p. 49.
12. 'The mystery of art-manufacture. "All not gold that glitters"', *The Builder*, Vol. 6, 29 April 1848, pp. 213-14.
13. *Ibid.*, p. 213.
14. 'Reopening of the Royal Polytechnic Institution, Thursday, April 20', *Lady's Newspaper*, 22 April 1848, p. 334.
15. 'Exhibition of the pictures, drawings, sketches, &c., of William Mulready, R.A., at the Society of Arts, Adelphi', *Lady's Newspaper*, 10 June 1848, p. 466.
16. W.H. Rogers, 'On the style of the Renaissance

and its adoption in England', *The Builder*, Vol. 6, 29 July 1848, pp. 362-3.
17. *Ibid.*, p. 362.
18. 'An illustrated prospectus', *Art Union*, 1 August 1848, Vol. 10, pp. 258-9.
19. *Art Union*, 1 April 1848, Vol. 10, p. 128.
20. *Art Union*, 1 October 1848, Vol. 10, p. 295.
21. 'Punch's milk jug', *Punch*, 10 June 1848, p. 238; 'Felix Summerly's trusses', *The Builder*, Vol. 6, 1 April 1848, p. 163; '"A Subscriber", The Society of Arts and Felix Summerly', *Art Union*, 1 June 1848, Vol. 10, p. 201; '"A Manufacturer", Felix Summerly's art-manufacture', *Art Union*, 1 September 1848, Vol. 10, p. 279.
22. Bury, 'Felix Summerly's Art Manufactures', *op. cit.*, p. 32.
23. Bonython and Burton, *The Great Exhibitor, op. cit.*, p. 101.
24. *Ibid.*, p. 102.
25. *Art Journal*, Vol. 1, November 1849, p. 349.
26. 'Men of the day', No. 29, *Vanity Fair*, 19 August 1871 [no pagination].
27. *Art Union*, Vol. 6, 1844, pp. 225-70; *Art Union*, Vol. 8, 1846, pp. 23-54; *Art Journal* Vol. 1, 1849, pp. 233-86; *Art Journal*, Vol. 1, 1849, pp. 293-321.
28. Bonython and Burton, *The Great Exhibitor, op. cit.*, pp. 138-9.
29. S.C. Hall. *Retrospect of a Long Life: From 1815 to 1883*, two volumes (Richard Bentley & Son, 1883), Vol. 1, pp. 379-80.
30. E.H. Gombrich, *The Sense of Order: A Study in the Psychology of Decorative Art* (Phaidon, 1979), p. 35.
31. Bonython and Burton, *The Great Exhibitor, op. cit.*, pp. 201-02.
32. *Ibid.*, p. 205.
33. V&A E694.140-1998.
34. V&A E668-1998.

TEN

Queen Victoria's Cradle

ONE OF THE MUST-SEES AT the Great Exhibition, along with the massive Koh-i-Noor diamond, was another of Queen Victoria's new possessions, her cradle carved in boxwood. The cradle had been years in the making, partly because the extremely hard wood of the box tree made it slow work to carve, but mainly because the small size of the box tree made it difficult to source the desired large pieces of wood. The honey-coloured cradle starred again in a more recent exhibition, stationed at the entrance to the Queen's Gallery at Buckingham Palace.[1]

To whom should the creation of this cradle be credited? It is concluded here that the primary author of the cradle was William Harry Rogers, who created its remarkable design. Secondary credit goes to two other Williams, William Gibbs Rogers and William Perry. William Gibbs Rogers, WHR's father and eminent wood-carver, has been the name most frequently associated with the cradle, both at the time it was made and subsequently.[2] However, although it was undoubtedly his workshop which produced the cradle, it is clear from the hitherto unnoticed contemporary testimony reviewed here that he did not personally carve the cradle. Instead, the carving was done by a group of his employees, of whom the most prominent (and the only one identifiable by name) was the relatively little-known William Perry.

Here we first consider WHR's creation of the cradle's design, and then uncover the evidence as to who executed his design.

THE CRADLE'S DESIGN

In the early 1850s, the cradle was depicted by several different publications, mainly as engravings. However, its most glamorous depiction came as a large coloured lithograph in Matthew Digby Wyatt's work illustrating highlights of the Great Exhibition, which is reproduced as Figure 10.1.[3]

An early photograph of the cradle was included in the deluxe four-volume issue of the *Reports of the Juries*, copies of which were presented to dignitaries for their services to the Great Exhibition.[4] The photograph has been reproduced in a recent book, where it is attributed to Claude-Marie Ferrier, and has also been displayed by the Art Gallery of Ontario.[5]

The official catalogue of the Great Exhibition featured the cradle prominently in its

Chapter Ten – Queen Victoria's Cradle

10.1 – Cradle designed by WHR for Queen Victoria and carved in boxwood, from Digby Wyatt's The Industrial Arts of the Nineteenth Century: Choicest Specimens at the Great Exhibition. *Image width 320mm. Actual length 910mm.*

account of Class 30 of the Exhibition, the Fine Art Court. The brief introduction for this class by Robert Ellis said of wood-carving that:[6]

> attention will be drawn … particularly to the Royal Cradle, exhibited by Her Majesty the Queen, carved in boxwood.

The catalogue also included two engraved views of the cradle.[7]

Other contemporary engravings of the cradle abounded, for example in *Tallis's Crystal Palace* and in the *Illustrated Exhibitor*.[8] The *Illustrated Exhibitor* got a bit carried away and captioned their picture as the 'Prince of Wales's Cot', despite the Prince of Wales (later Edward VII, born 9 November 1841) already being aged six when the cradle was commissioned and eight when it was delivered. Appropriately enough, the cradle was even illustrated in children's literature, in one of *Aunt Mavor's Picture Books for Little Readers*.[9] The accompanying text was charming:

> The wood of the box-tree is harder than any other, yet Mr. Rogers has carved it into this cradle, made for the Queen. It is covered with beautiful figures and emblems of sleep, and shews how hard Mr. Rogers must have toiled, to make so pretty a piece of work out of so hard a material.

The most comprehensive account of the cradle, however, had been provided a year before the Great Exhibition, in the 1850 *Art Journal*.[10] For this, WHR had supplied the *Art Journal* with three pages of pictures, including three drawings of the cradle's overall appearance, and

107

ten drawings of its details. Only the final engraving was signed with WHR's monogram but the monogram was accompanied, unusually for WHR, by 'INVENIT'. WHR clearly wished to emphasise that it was he who had authored the cradle.

The article in the 1850 *Art Journal* explained that the cradle had taken a relatively long time to create. When first announced, the cradle had been intended for Queen Victoria's sixth baby, Princess Louise (later Duchess of Argyll), who was born on 18 March 1848.[11] But by the time the cradle was ready, it was occupied instead by Victoria's seventh baby, Prince Arthur (later Duke of Connaught and Strathearn), who was born on 1 May 1850.[12] The 1850 *Art Journal* article's introductory page of text first explained the long period which it had taken to complete the cradle:[13]

> The cradle is carved in the finest Turkey box-wood, and has been in hand nearly two years, delays having been occasioned by various circumstances, but principally by the difficulty of procuring wood of high quality and sufficient size, to render as few joints as possible necessary.

The introduction ended by emphasising the historical significance of the work:

> In conclusion we would only say, that we believe the cradle in question to constitute one of the most important examples of the art of wood-carving ever executed in this country, reflecting equal credit both on manipulator and designer.

In between its editorial commencement and conclusion, the *Art Journal* included 'some remarks by the designer of the cradle, Mr. W. Harry Rogers'. Within this lengthy passage, WHR explained the updated Renaissance style which he had adopted:

> the Italian style of ornament of the sixteenth century … may be said to have reached its greatest perfection towards 1520 … but it appears to require some modifications to reduce it to the wants and tastes of the present day. … I have thought it expedient to divest the style of those 'monsters and hydras and chimeras dire' which form so prominent a feature in most productions of the sixteenth century, as the fashion of the day now requires that in matters of ornament no objects should be introduced unless having a positive meaning to pourtray. The flowers also throughout the cradle have been drawn and carved from nature, instead of being executed with the conventional treatment they would have received three centuries ago.

WHR went on to interpret each of the elements of the cradle. His incorporation of Nox and Somnus was to provoke controversy, as described later. In Roman mythology, Nox personified the night, and her son Somnus personified sleep.

Figure 10.2 shows details from WHR's drawings.[14] Its upper part reproduces that part of the engraving of WHR's drawing of the cradle's principal front, which includes Nox. The text which described this element was as follows:

Chapter Ten – Queen Victoria's Cradle

10.2 – Upper: Head of Nox on a bat's wings. *Lower:* Head of Somnus. From the *Art Journal*, 1850. Image heights 48mm.

The point of juncture between the heraldic panel and the exterior of the rocker is occupied by a luxuriant garland of poppies, more prominently executed than other parts of the work; beneath it is the head of Nox represented as a beautiful female with closed eyes, supported upon bat's wings and surrounded by seven stars.

The lower part of Figure 10.2 shows the corresponding location at the other end of the cradle, where there was a similar element, described as:

a bold head of 'Somnus' with closed eyes.

109

RESPONSE OF QUEEN VICTORIA

The design of the cradle had been arrived at in consultation with the Queen and Prince Albert themselves. Figure 10.3 reproduces a later photograph of the royal couple, a carte-de-visite albumen print by John Edwin Mayall (unsigned), taken at Buckingham Palace in February 1861.[15] According to the 1850 *Art Journal*:

> The shape of the cradle … was suggested by Her Majesty, partly in consideration of those representations of cradles which generally appear of this form in early Italian and Flemish pictures.

Queen Victoria's suggestion was perhaps transmitted via Prince Albert, who certainly had a hands-on involvement with the cradle's design. This emerged in the context of the large exhibition of loaned artworks which opened at Alton Towers on 10 July 1865 and was successful in raising the funds needed to complete the Wedgwood Memorial Institute at Burslem.[16]

The cradle was one of the stars at Alton Towers:[17]

> Among the carvings, her Majesty the Queen most kindly contributes the exquisitely-carved boxwood cradle by Mr. Rogers, from Windsor Castle; Miss Burdett Coutts also sends some examples of Mr. Rogers's work.

10.3 – Queen Victoria and Prince Albert. Photograph by John Edwin Mayall, 1861. Height 84mm.

To commemorate the occasion, William Gibbs Rogers had a document printed to list these and his other contributions, among which Item 6 was 'Three working drawings of the boxwood cradle, showing the Prince Consort's valuable suggestions.'[18]

Certainly Queen Victoria was delighted by the cradle. When it had arrived at Osborne House, she confided to her journal that it:[19]

> is really a 'chef d'œuvre',—finer than anything of the kind, either antique or modern.

The following year, on a visit from Buckingham Palace, she was pleased to spot her cradle at the Great Exhibition:[20]

> The Fine Arts Court, containing wood carving, of every kind and sort, was most beautiful. Amongst it was our beautiful cradle.

RESPONSE OF JOHN HENRY NEWMAN

Despite the royal endorsement of, and indeed participation in, the cradle's design, it was denounced, on religious rather than artistic grounds, by no less a figure than John Henry Newman (1801–90), who had famously been received into the Roman Catholic church in 1845, and ordained priest in 1847 (and later was made a cardinal in 1879 and canonised in

2019). Newman deprecated the cradle's use of mythological imagery in the course of his more general argument for a Catholic approach that should pervade all aspects of society:[21]

> Just as a heathen phraseology is now in esteem, and 'hymeneals' are spoken of, and the trump of fame, and the trident of Britannia, and a royal cradle is ornamented with figures of Nox and Somnus; so in a Catholic age or country the Blessed Saints will be invoked by virtuous and vicious, in every undertaking, and will have their place in every room of palace or of cottage.

Thirty years later, John Henry Newman's intervention was recalled in the *Magazine of Art* by WHR's brother, George Alfred Rogers, during his account of the Exhibition of Fine Arts held in the Albert Hall in 1880, at which the cradle was exhibited.[22] Having noted that the cradle was 'a centre of attraction' at the Great Exhibition of 1851, he continued:[23]

> In that year Dr. Newman (now the Cardinal) preached a sermon denouncing the introduction of heathen emblems in a cradle which was to be used by the Royal Family of England, Nox and Somnus being represented in the principal panels. The anathema did not, however, cause them to be removed. Visitors to the State Apartments at Windsor Castle can see this choice work, for it is very seldom away; in fact, since 1851 it has only been removed three times for the purposes of exhibition—viz., to the Wedgwood Institution at Alton Towers, to the Bethnal Green Museum, and to the Royal Albert Hall.

At the Great Exhibition of 1851 itself, no reservations were expressed about the cradle's iconography. The cradle, and in particular its design, was highlighted in the citation for the award to W.G. Rogers of a Prize Medal:[24]

> A cradle executed in box-wood for Her Majesty the Queen Victoria, and richly ornamented with carved reliefs; … These works show an extraordinary dexterity in the treatment of the material, and the ornaments of the cradle are in excellent taste. Prize Medal.

WHO CARVED THE CRADLE?

Although it is clear that WHR was the author of the cradle, the question of who actually executed WHR's design enters murky waters. Both at the time and subsequently, the carving of the cradle has customarily been attributed to William Gibbs Rogers in person. However, William Gibbs Rogers ran a substantial wood-carving firm, as indicated by the occupation recorded for him (aged fifty-eight years) in the 1851 Census, 'Carver in Wood. Master employing 15 men'. For much of the work produced by his firm, carving by William Gibbs Rogers in person will necessarily have been quite limited.

For a piece intended for royalty or for exhibition, the situation could have been different and William Gibbs Rogers might have wished to have hands-on control. However, boxwood is so hard and fine-grained that it was normally used at that time for printing blocks, on which a sharp burin was used to engrave two-dimensional (rather than three-dimensional) images. In the case of the cradle, carving an extraordinarily large volume of boxwood must have been physically intensely demanding, in terms both of time and effort. It was in this context that a claim was made by a considerably younger carver, William Perry, that it was actually he who had made the most important contribution to carving the cradle, rather than William Gibbs Rogers himself. Although Perry made his claim public at the Great Exhibition, it appears to have been generally overlooked, despite being later reported – and indeed exaggerated – by a third wood-carver exhibitor, Thomas Wilkinson Wallis.

WILLIAM PERRY

William Perry (1819–84) was a cabinet-maker's son, born in Taunton, Somerset, where he was working as a carver at the time of both the 1841 and 1851 Censuses.[25] In 1851, he had five children, all but one born in Taunton. The fourth one, daughter Hannah, aged four, was born in London, Middlesex. These entries suggest that William Perry, though based in Taunton, had lived in London in the late 1840s with his family, and thus are consistent with his having worked for William Gibbs Rogers for a period that included the years in which the cradle was carved, namely, 1848–50.

Subsequently, Perry and his family moved back to London for good, where they are to be found at various address in the Censuses of 1861 to 1881. Perry prospered as a wood-carver, with a high-point being his work relating to the tree known as Herne's Oak, in the Home Park of Windsor Castle. This tree had been identified with one mentioned in Shakespeare's *The Merry Wives of Windsor*, but was blown down in 1863. Perry carved a range of objects from its salvaged wood, and subsequently published a book defending the identification of the blown-over tree with the one mentioned by Shakespeare.[26]

Some copies of the book had wooden covers carved by Perry from Herne's Oak.[27] Inside the book, he described two other objects he had carved from Herne's Oak. First, 'By the Queen's commands I executed a bust of Shakspeare for Her Majesty.'[28] Second, he carved a casket to hold two Shakespeare volumes (one of them a First Folio), 'a portion being most graciously given by Her Majesty Queen Victoria to Miss Burdett Coutts, for the purpose of encasing volumes which are—"Not for an age, but for all time".'[29]

It was in 1851 that William Perry made his claim about the cradle at the Great Exhibition, where he exhibited in his own right a vase he had carved in boxwood.[30] Nearby were the exhibits of William Gibbs Rogers and Thomas Wilkinson Wallis.[31] The cradle was exhibited in the Fine Art Court by Queen Victoria.[32] Perry made his claim about the cradle at the end of a three-page pamphlet which he had had privately printed about the vase that was his own exhibit at the Great Exhibition:[33]

> William Perry was the Executor of the most important parts of the carving in her Majesty's Cradle, which has attracted so much admiration.

THOMAS WILKINSON WALLIS

Thomas Wilkinson Wallis (1821–1903) was a wood-carver from Louth in Lincolnshire, whose work displayed much virtuosity in the minute realism of its representations of foliage and – his speciality – dead birds suspended by their claws. Figure 10.4 illustrates

Chapter Ten – Queen Victoria's Cradle

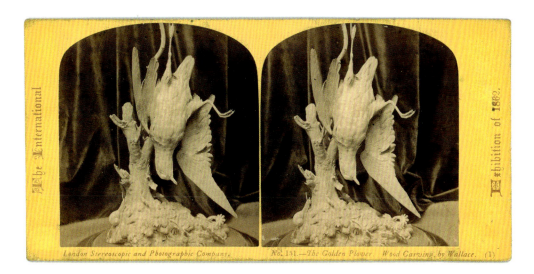

10.4 – Carving of a dead golden plover by Thomas Wilkinson Wallis, one of a set of stereo photographs of exhibits at the 1862 Exhibition in London. Card width 173mm.

one of his carvings. Wallis and William Gibbs Rogers were the only two UK recipients of Prize Medals for wood-carving in Section 30 of the Great Exhibition, but in most other respects they were polar opposites. Wallis worked mainly on his own whereas Rogers ran a large workshop; Wallis was almost unknown prior to 1850, whereas Rogers had a long-established reputation; Wallis was prickly, whereas Rogers was urbane, which seemed only to irritate Wallis further.

Wallis continued carving after the Great Exhibition, but decided in 1870 to train for a new career as a surveyor and in 1873 was appointed as an inspector under the Local Health Act, producing no more of his distinctive carvings after this date. He blamed his abandonment of carving on damage he had suffered to his eyes when viewing an eclipse of the sun in 1858.[34] In 1873, *The Builder* briefly noted a pamphlet which Wallis had sent them:[35]

> 'A Few Thoughts on Sanitary Questions, by T.W. Wallis,' Sanitary Engineer (Larder, Louth), interest us mainly because they are the work of one who some years ago made himself worthily known by the production of some admirable carvings of dead game, for which medals were justly awarded him. Mr. Wallis has changed his profession, and we are sorry for it. The letters here put together doubtless woke up some of the good people of Louth and its neighbourhood, and will do good elsewhere. Nevertheless, we regret his loss in the practice of an art the difficulties of which he had mastered.

GEORGE ALFRED ROGERS, ELICITED BY WALLIS

It was only in 1879 that Wallis put his thoughts on the Great Exhibition of 1851 into print. This was triggered by a letter in *The Builder* from George Alfred Rogers, the son and successor as carver of William Gibbs Rogers, who had died in 1875. George Alfred Rogers had originally responded to a reader's worries about 'the want of wood-carving talent in

113

England' by explaining that a more precise formulation would be:[36]

> not that 'good work cannot be done in England,' but that 'one man cannot do it.' In fact, there are three required,—the master, the artistic designer, and the wood-carver. The first buys, and for years stores, the wood till in good condition. He provides light and suitable premises for work, and also that peace of mind brought by regular wages. The second, is a man of cultivated artistic attainments, and generally one who has had opportunities in early life of gaining that information and knowledge which are required in designing harmoniously. Now comes the third, the wood-carver, who carries the work out under the control of the two first, and success is gained. … I may mention that the best work done in this country is seldom exhibited publicly, and the critics have, therefore, little opportunity of judging what is being done, the commissions having to be delivered directly they are finished.

A fortnight later, Wallis published a rejoinder under the lugubrious heading of 'A voice from the dead'.[37] In his letter, he held himself out as a living proof of the possibility of success for solitary endeavour in wood-carving, at least for exhibition pieces:

> For many years I exclusively followed wood-carving, doing my own special individual work, and employing first-class London carvers to do my ordinary trade carving; but every work I exhibited in London, Paris, Manchester, &c., was the product of my own pocket, brains, and fingers, and thus '*one man did do it.*' Mr. Rogers's theory (and practice?) that it takes 'three men' to produce wood-carving seems puerile in the extreme to me. Perhaps it may be true as illustrating the cradle in which he has been nursed, and which the necessities of London life impose upon men who are engaged in the manufacture of goods Society is willing to buy.

After this mention of a metaphorical cradle, Wallis moved on to the actual cradle:

> This recalls a scene in the Fine Arts Court, Exhibition of 1851. Mr. A. Rogers's father, Mr. W.G. Rogers, was a man of good taste and clever business habits; this, together with his cheery geniality and admiration of Gibbons's carving, did very much to promote or direct the public taste to wood-carving. He was dubbed the 'Queen's Carver,'—a cradle carved in box-wood was exhibited as proof. This was, I believe, a triple product: Mr W.G. Rogers was the capitalist, his son Harry was the designer, and the actual carving was done by Mr. Perry, of Taunton; a fact which he then and there publicly declared in writing.

Finally, Wallis described how he had proceeded:

> My method of proceeding with these models was as follows:—Having obtained the dead birds,—one, two, or three, as the case might be,—I suspended them by the leg, or legs, then arranged them so as to form a well-balanced mass as a whole. When my eye was satisfied, I secured the wings, &c., so as to retain their

position … The rest depended upon the dexterity of my fingers being able to represent what the eye could see.

The following week, Rogers, in his mild and slightly humorous way, pointed out the flaws in Wallis's arguments:[38]

> I submit that to tie up some dead canaries, and pin out a wing on one side, and ruffle some feathers on the other, and then to 'represent what the eye could see,' does not show that the executant is a designer, however faithfully and delicately the subject may be copied. … Mr. Wallis, in fact, all through his letter, confirms my statement. He says he pursued his own individual work, but employed the best London men to do the other styles of carving. Again, he acknowledges that London life renders the triple method necessary.

With regard to the cradle, George Alfred Rogers implicitly conceded that William Gibbs Rogers did not carve the cradle himself, but he did not credit its carving to William Perry either:

> The Royal Cradle was designed by my brother, and the carving was executed by several of my father's trained hands, not by *one*, as Mr. Wallis states. I have all the details of time and expenditure to refer to, apart from my own knowledge of the way the work was carried out.

As Rogers indicated, Wallis had undoubtedly exaggerated the role of Perry. In 1851, Perry himself had only claimed to have been one of the carvers of the cradle. Thus with regard to the question 'Who carved the cradle?' the answer which we have arrived at is that it was not William Gibbs Rogers in person, but was instead a group of the carvers he employed, among whom William Perry is likely to have been the most prominent. Rogers also took the opportunity to put Wallis right about his father's character and motivation:

> He was a man of rare artistic genius and quick imagination, and a master-carver of the first order. Scarcely a man of business, however; for he spent his fortune in the pure and simple effort to advance his art, collecting specimens of ancient and modern art-work from all parts of Europe long before there was a South Kensington Museum in which to study, and keeping young men employed through years without the chance, or even the wish, for gain, and training them as he so well knew how to do.

Finally, George Alfred Rogers concluded by paying a detailed and intimate tribute to WHR:

> With regard to my late brother, Mr. Harry Rogers, I may, without chance of denial, say that he was one of the best, if not the best, ornamental designer England has produced this century. His knowledge of architecture and architectural ornament of every style, his studies here and in Continental cities, and not the least his Classical education, combined to produce an artistic designer to whom

I looked up with the greatest pride, and to whose teachings I owe what talent in design I possess.

Reverting to the actual carving of the cradle, the last word was to be had by the dogged Wallis, when he printed a blow-by-blow account of his life twenty years later, in 1899.[39] This time, Wallis's narrative of the cradle at the Great Exhibition implicitly accepted the account of George Alfred Rogers that William Perry had not in fact carved the cradle on his own, but made the new assertion that, back in 1851, Perry had augmented his claim by 'adding that he had executed others of Mr. Rogers's best works, and, as this was never contradicted, its truth may be accepted'. On this occasion, however, George Alfred Rogers was unable to refute Wallis's assertion, having died in 1897.

NOTES

1. Jonathan Marsden (ed.), *Victoria & Albert: Art & Love* (Royal Collection Publications, 2010), illustrated pp. 247-8. The original cost was listed as a substantial £330; Leah Kharibian, *Passionate Patrons: Victoria & Albert and the Arts* (Royal Collection Publications, 2010), illustrated p. 50.

2. Thus, when the cradle was displayed in September 2021 at the wide-ranging exhibition, *Grinling Gibbons: Centuries in the Making*, at Compton Verney Art Gallery, there was no mention of WHR in the cradle's wall caption, only of William Gibbs Rogers.

3. M. Digby Wyatt, *The Industrial Arts of the Nineteenth Century: Choicest Specimens at the Great Exhibition*, two volumes (Day & Son, 1851–3), Plate 130.

4. *Exhibition of the Works of Industry of All Nations, 1851. Reports of the Juries*, in four volumes. Vol. 4: Reports—Classes 29, 30 (Spicer Brothers, 1852), p. 1554.

5. Anthony Hamber, *Photography and the 1851 Great Exhibition* (New Castle, DE: Oak Knoll Press, and London: V&A Publishing, 2018), p. 319; ago.ca/collection/object/2007/1940.4.28

6. *Official Descriptive and Illustrated Catalogue of the Great Exhibition of the Works of Industry of all Nations* (Spicer Brothers, 1851), p. 820.

7. Plate 121, opposite p. 824. Its upper engraving appears to be the source, not cited by the author, of Figure 39 in Nikolaus Pevsner, *High Victorian Design: A Study of the Exhibits of 1851* (London: Architectural Press, 1951), p. 65.

8. *Tallis's History and Description of the Crystal Palace and the Exhibition of the World's Industry in 1851* (John Tallis and Co. [1852]), plate with two views, opposite p. 204; *The Illustrated Exhibitor … the principal objects in the Great Exhibition of the Industry of All Nations, 1851* (John Cassell [1851]), pp. 102, 104.

9. *Uncle Nimrod's First Visit to the Exhibition* (George Routledge & Co. [1852]), p. 7.

10. *Art Journal*, August 1850, Vol. 2, pp. 241-4.

11. *Art Union*, Vol. 10, September 1848, p. 287.

12. George Alfred Rogers, *Memorial of the Exhibition of Wood Carving Held at the Royal Albert Hall, 1880* (privately printed, 1881), p. 5.

13. *Art Journal*, August 1850, Vol. 2, p. 241.

14. *Ibid.*, pp. 242-3.

15. The National Portrait Gallery has a very similar image in two forms, one signed and one unsigned, NPG x26101 and NPG x26102, respectively.

16. *Art Journal*, 1865, p. 252.

17. *Ibid.*, p. 274; nowadays the cradle is usually on display at Kensington Palace rather than Windsor Castle.

18. *An Illustrated List of the Wood and Ivory Carvings, by W. G. Rogers. Contributed to the art collection at Alton Towers, in Aid of the Funds for Completing the Erection of The Wedgwood Institution* (privately printed, [1865]), p. 5.

19. Queen Victoria's Journals, www. queenvictoriasjournals.org, 4 June 1850, Vol. 29, p. [160].

20. *Ibid.*, 14 May 1851, Vol. 31, p. [242].

21. John Henry Newman, *Lectures on certain difficulties felt by Anglicans in submitting to the Catholic Church* (Burns & Lambert, 1850), Lecture IX, p. 231.

22. He had co-convened the extensive wood-carving section and subsequently described it: George Alfred Rogers, 'Wood-carving.—I. & II.', *Magazine of Art*, Vol. 4, 1881, pp. 120-24 and 226-32.

23. *Ibid.*, p. 227.

24. *Reports of the Juries* (1852), *op. cit.*, p. 694.

25. In the 1851 Census he was living at 22 Bridge Street, Taunton, with his wife Hannah, three sons and two daughters.

26. W. Perry, *A Treatise on the Identity of Herne's Oak, Shewing the Maiden tree to have been the Real One* (L. Booth, 1867).

27. Earlier, some copies of the Rogers' family production, Beeton's *Shakspeare Memorial*, 1864, had been similarly embellished.

28. Perry, *A treatise, op. cit.*, p. x.

29. *Ibid.*, unpaginated appendix.

30. Exhibitor 101 in Class 30's Fine Art Court. The vase is illustrated in the *Art Journal* catalogue, p. 166.

31. Exhibitors 74 and 89, respectively, in Class 30.

32. Exhibitor 353 in Class 30. Entries for the four Class 30 exhibitors are listed here: *Official descriptive and illustrated catalogue of the Great Exhibition*, pp. 824-6 and 842.

33. *Description of the Taunton Allegorical Vase. Designed and Executed by William Perry, an Amateur Carver* (printed by W. Bragg & Son, Herald Office, Taunton; May 1851), p. 3.

34. *Autobiography of Thomas Wilkinson Wallis, sculptor in wood, and extracts from his sixty years' journal* (Louth: J. W. Goulding & Son, Printers, 1899), pp. 145, 170, 178, 236.

35. *The Builder*, Vol. 31, 25 January 1873, p. 74.

36. George Alfred Rogers 'Wood-carving', *The Builder*, Vol. 37, 22 November 1879, p. 1300.

37. T. W. Wallis, 'Wood carving: A voice from the dead', *The Builder*, Vol. 37, 6 December 1879, pp. 1354-55.

38. George Alfred Rogers, 'School of wood-carving', *The Builder*, Vol. 37, 13 December 1879, p. 1387.

39. *Autobiography of Thomas Wilkinson Wallis, op. cit.*, p. 97.

ELEVEN

The Great Exhibition and its Successors

THE GREAT EXHIBITION OF THE Works of Industry of All Nations that was held in London's Hyde Park in 1851 swept aside all precedent in the scale of its exhibits, in the daring of Paxton's Crystal Palace for housing them and by reaching an audience to be numbered in millions. It provided an indelible exclamation mark in the nation's cultural history. Naturally, it also triggered an avalanche of commemorative imagery, from the paintings commissioned by Prince Albert (Figure 1.2 showed one of the Dickinson prints based on those paintings) right down to notepaper headed with a finely engraved view of the Crystal Palace, as shown in Figure 11.1.

11.1 – The Crystal Palace, built to house the Great Exhibition of 1851. Engraved as a letterhead on notepaper. Image width 120mm.

The Great Exhibition has already been touched upon at several points in this book. Chapter 1 saw Lewis F. Day, when reviewing the past half-century of design for Queen Victoria's jubilee in 1887, pick out WHR's unique fertility and refinement in design there. Chapter 8 discussed the silver by WHR exhibited by Francis Higgins at the Great Exhibition, at its first successor exhibition in Dublin in 1853, and at the second London exhibition in 1862. Chapter 10 recorded WHR's cradle for Queen Victoria as a leading attraction in 1851.

It also emerged in Chapter 9 that the *Art Journal* produced an extraordinarily successful record of the Great Exhibition, though undermined financially by Henry Cole's manoeuvring. The journal devoted the equivalent of six entire issues to its illustrated catalogue of the Great Exhibition, issuing them as bound-in supplements within double issues of the journal from May to October 1851, and then issuing the catalogue in more convenient form as a single volume. The resulting *Art Journal* catalogue has remained the best record of the exhibition that we have. Its richly presented, illustration-packed pages captured the spectacle in a way that completely eluded the dreary listings of the official catalogue.

The *Art Journal* catalogue of the Great Exhibition also provided the formula for our most vivid records of four subsequent blockbuster exhibitions in the 1850s and 1860s, namely those of Dublin in 1853, Paris in 1855, London again in 1862 and Paris again in 1867. In each case, the *Art Journal* published an impressive, illustrated catalogue, firstly as monthly supplements and then, on completion, as a separate volume.

There is no better place to see how WHR lit up the Great Exhibition and its successor exhibitions than in the pages of the five *Art Journal* catalogues. He did so in two separate ways. First, and most obviously, WHR was the designer of some of the most artistic exhibits which were illustrated in the catalogues. Secondly, the contents of the volumes themselves were presented by WHR with exquisite artistic flair. Both types of contribution will be described here for each exhibition.

After twenty years of giant art-manufacturing exhibitions, enthusiasm for them palled in Britain. Henry Cole, however, continued to take a proprietary interest in their organisation and started a new series of annual exhibitions in London in 1871. The *Art Journal* dutifully published some catalogue supplements in 1871 and 1872, but interest in an annual event was limited and no separate catalogue volume was produced. The editor of the *Art Journal* blamed the decline on his old bête noire, Henry Cole.[1] The 1872 exhibition had been loss-making, and after two more years of losses in 1873 and 1874, the annual exhibitions of the newly retired Henry Cole were quietly abandoned. The Prince of Wales himself seems to have knocked them on the head, telling Cole in 1874 that 'Exhibitions are over & Museums take their place.'[2]

Here we consider in turn each of the canonical exhibitions from 1851 to 1872, as refracted through its *Art Journal* catalogue. The titles of the catalogue volumes varied unpredictably (e.g. the titles of the catalogues for the Dublin 1853 and Paris 1855 exhibitions did not mention the *Art Journal*, and the title of the catalogue for the Paris 1867 exhibition did not mention Paris). Therefore the title of the relevant catalogue is spelled out for each exhibition before discussing, first, WHR's exhibits and, second, his artistic enhancements of the volume itself.

LONDON, 1851

TITLE

The Art-Journal Illustrated Catalogue of the Industry of All Nations 1851 (George Virtue [1851]).[3]

EXHIBITS

The number of exhibitors displaying artefacts designed by WHR stretched into double figures, and his designs were instrumental in four of them being awarded the coveted Prize Medal of the exhibition. These designs are noted in the order in which they were illustrated in the volume.

11.2 – Salt cellar centrepiece designed by WHR for the Great Exhibition, with stamp of W.G. Rogers on the base. Width 141mm.

(a) Wood carvings by W.G. Rogers:[4] The catalogue featured a lavish spread on the carvings of William Gibbs Rogers, illustrating and describing them over three full pages, following a brief introduction:[5]

> Mr. Rogers's fame, as is well known, rests mainly on his imitation and extension of the style adopted by his great forerunner in wood-carving, Grinling Gibbons; but he has recently diversified his labours by adding to the works of the character described, such as may be truly called the *bijoux* of the art, consisting of small and delicately finished objects, chiefly in box-wood, and in the Italian style. From among these minute performances, executed with the co-operation of his son W. Harry Rogers, as designer, we have principally selected the illustrations of our great carver's contributions to the Exhibition.

Figure 11.2 shows one of these Renaissance carvings in boxwood, a bijou stablemate of the Queen's cradle. It was illustrated on the first page of the spread, a hexagonal salt cellar for use as a table centrepiece (at that time, accompanied by a carved spoon). It was described thus in the Official Catalogue:[6]

> Boxwood salt-cellar, enriched with columns, and sunk panels, with spoon; designed by W. Harry Rogers for the Exhibition.

It is because the centrepiece was designed for the Great Exhibition that one of its panels displays *1851*; the other five panels display Raphaelesque grotesques. Extending the fantasy, the surrounding colonnade is designed as six rough-hewn tree trunks and the feet are bunches of grapes.[7]

Only with the third and final page of the spread did the catalogue reach one of the exhibition's star attractions:[8]

> In the centre of the page is the celebrated box-wood cradle, executed for her Majesty the Queen, and with the details of which our readers are already familiar.

As described in Chapter 10, the *Art Journal* had already splashed a comprehensive account of the cradle over no fewer than four of its pages in August 1850, so the subscribers did not need to be reminded of its virtues. Other contemporary journals and books were not encumbered in this way in their response to the cradle, which appealed to art-lovers and royal-watchers alike, and was featured enthusiastically in both august and unpretentious publications.

W.G. Rogers was awarded the Prize Medal of the exhibition for his display. One jury cited 'the beautiful cradle and other objects by Mr. Rogers', the main jury for Class 30 *Sculpture and Works of Plastic Art* asserted that 'the ornaments of the cradle are in excellent taste', while the *Supplementary Report on Design* by Richard Redgrave referred to the 'well-composed design by his son, W. Harry Rogers'.[9]

(b) Fair linen cloth by Gilbert French of Bolton.[10] The illustration was signed by WHR with his monogram, presumably as designer.

(c) Silver by Higgins.[11] WHR was not mentioned, but he designed for Francis Higgins and there is evidence that the Cartouche and Spiral design illustrated, at least, was his (see Chapter 8).

11.3 – Album designed by WHR and made for J.S. Evans, from the *Art Journal* catalogue of the Great Exhibition, 1851. Image height 112mm.

(d) Two album covers made by J.W. Evans for his father, J.S. Evans, a specialist purveyor of top-end albums.[12] For the first album, it was explained that 'The interior of each cover is of white vellum, elegantly tooled in gold, from a pattern by Mr. W. Harry Rogers.' WHR's cover for the second album was described in detail:

> The second is a royal quarto, of brown Russia, inlaid with black kid, a novel process as applied to rich workmanship, though not unusual in simple bookbinding. The design, in harmony with the colours of the materials employed, is in the Etruscan style, and is from a drawing by Mr. Rogers. A vase occupies the centre, and the borders and corners are composed of Archaic foliage, in which the honeysuckle is prominent.

(The use of kid in simple bookbinding referred to the use of morocco lettering-pieces on leatherbound spines.) Figure 11.3 reproduces WHR's striking design for the

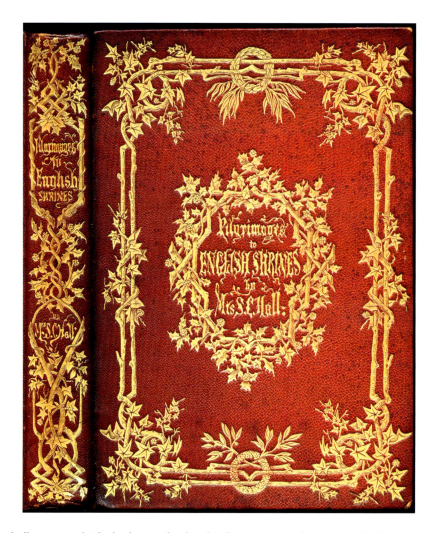

11.4 – *Pilgrimages to English Shrines*, 1850, the cover designed by WHR in Knüttel style, executed here in red morocco by W. Bone. Height 225mm.

second album, in which the brown leather has been rendered as white. J.S. Evans received the Prize Medal of the Exhibition, the second medal linked to WHR's designs.[13] The Jury highlighted the album illustrated here: 'An album in the Etruscan style, black kid laid upon a brown ground, the edges of the leaves ornamented to correspond.'

(e) Bridle by Mr J. Penny.[14] 'He calls it the "Prince of Wales's Bridle", having made it with a view to its being adopted by his Royal Highness. … The design of the harness, altogether and in detail, is by Mr. W. Harry Rogers.' Mr Penny received an Honourable Mention from the Jury for the 'state pony bridle, designed by W.H. Rogers, made by W. Langdon'.[15]

(f) Embroidered altar-cloth by T. Harrison.[16] 'A flowing pattern of trefoil and gothic pine-apples forms an elegant border to the cloth … The design for the embroidery is the work of Mr. W. Harry Rogers.' T. Harrison received an Honourable Mention from the Jury 'for altar-cloth, and cushions of crimson Genoa velvet, embroidered in gold'.[17]

(g) Book cover by Bone and Son.[18] The designs for a book's spine and side were

Chapter Eleven – The Great Exhibition and its Successors

11.5 –
Chatelain-head designed by WHR and made in steel by Walter Thornhill, from the *Art Journal* catalogue of the Great Exhibition, 1851. Image height 79mm.

illustrated and described: 'They are designed by Mr. W. Harry Rogers, and cannot fail of being admired for the lightness and elegance of the composition.' Though not mentioned in the *Art Journal* catalogue, the designs had been created for *Pilgrimages to English Shrines*, 1850, by Mrs S.C. Hall, which is shown in Figure 11.4. Bone and Son received a Prize Medal of the Exhibition for their 'cloth bookbinding', the third medal linked to WHR's designs.[19]

The idiom of WHR's design was noted in Wornum's Prize Essay (which is considered later in this chapter). Wornum referred to,[20] 'The German interlacing of stems and leaves … known as the Knüttel style.' More recently, Pevsner quoted Wornum and noted that the Knüttel style originated with Dürer.[21] Buchanan-Brown has labelled it the 'stick' style of 'rustic trellising', pointing out its technical suitability for early wood-cuts and tracing its subsequent revival in the engravings of German Romantics.[22]

This WHR design, as mediated by the *Art Journal* catalogue, created a sensation in the US. Prominent publishers in New York (George P. Putnam and Charles Scribner), in Boston (Phillips, Sampson & Co. and Wentworth & Co.) and in Philadelphia (Willis P. Hazard) all scrambled to put it on their own books during the early 1850s.

(h) Chatelain-head by Walter Thornhill.[23] Figure 11.5 reproduces the engraving of this sculpted disk.

> It is entirely produced by hand, in hard steel, chiefly by means of minute files. The principal portions are flat, perforated and engraved, but a slight projection is given to the more important ornaments or emblems introduced. The design which is by Mr. W. Harry Rogers, is in the Italian style.

Around a monogram of the initials of Victoria and Albert are six medallions with the heraldic crests of Prince Albert, the instigator of the Great Exhibition. Clockwise from the bottom left, these are: for Saxony, a coronet surmounted by a plumed hat; for Thuringia, a coronet surmounted by buffalo horns; for (Counts of the) Mark, a bull's head; for Meissen, a bearded man; for Jülich, a griffin; and for Berg, peacock's feathers. Walter Thornhill was awarded a Prize Medal of the Exhibition, the fourth medal linked to WHR's designs.[24]

(i) Bible cover, carved in boxwood by W.G. Rogers for the publisher, Nisbet.[25] Both the front and back were illustrated. The back cover, with matching field and border, was 'carved by Mr Rogers and designed by his son'. The front cover retained the same border (signed there with WHR's monogram), with its pictorial field apparently signed with John Gilbert's monogram (though Gilbert was not mentioned).

(j) Key bearing a monogram for GI, that is, WHR's recently emigrated friend George Isaacs.[26] The text commented extensively on WHR:

123

The merits of Mr. W. Harry Rogers as a designer we have long recognised, and have repeatedly availed ourselves of his talents in connection with our Journal; we were, therefore, pleased to see in the Exhibition a large number of ornamental works, manufactured from the designs he has furnished to the producers, as well as many subjects from his pencil applicable to future manufactures. Whatever Mr. Rogers puts forth is characterised by the purest taste, a taste which is fostered by an intimate acquaintance with the best works of the medieval ages. We introduce here a design for a Key, in the Italian style; other illustrations from his hand will be found on the last page of our Catalogue.

(k) Two caddy spoons. This was the final page of the catalogue proper, and the text again singled out WHR, citing several further exhibits he had designed which (apart from the royal cradle) they had not described earlier:[27]

From the designs exhibited by Mr. W. Harry Rogers we select three specimens exhibiting much ability in their composition, and an intimate knowledge of the peculiarities of the Italian style of the sixteenth century, in which some of his happiest efforts appear, and to which few have given so much attention and study. There is the great advantage in the designs by this artist, of thorough applicability to the uses of the workman and the necessities of the fabric he employs. We engrave two copies of a Spoon for a tea-caddy intended to be carved in box-wood, and another, the centre one, of a similar character. The remaining designs for manufacturers by this artists are for bookclasps, encaustic tiles, pipes, gold spoons, keys, a crozier, and a royal cradle. We may add, the head and tail-pieces which decorate our present Catalogue, are from the pencil of Mr. Rogers; they manifest his fertility of invention and the suitability of his designs.

Engravings were provided of the upper and lower sides of a boxwood spoon, and of the upper side of a spoon with perforated bowl. The spoon with the perforated bowl had been illustrated previously.[28] At least one specimen of each of the two designs is known to have survived; that with the perforated bowl is made of ivory.[29]

In addition to WHR's own designs, he also illustrated two of the foreign exhibits, as follows.

(l) Painting on glass by Kellner of Nuremberg.[30] The illustration is signed by WHR with his monogram. M. S. Kellner of Nuremberg was awarded a Prize Medal of the Exhibition for this 'copy in painted glass'.[31]

(m) Carved book cover by Madame Gruel of Paris.[32] The illustration is signed by WHR with his monogram. The illustration of a companion book cover by Madame Gruel is unsigned.[33] The Jury gave Madame Gruel of Paris an Honourable Mention, but expressed disappointment that she and other Parisian book-binders had not sent more of their works to the exhibition.[34]

ARTISTIC ENHANCEMENTS

The book is a cornucopia of WHR embellishments, which appear at almost all significant points of the volume, and provide it with an exceptionally rich artistic character. It seems

Chapter Eleven – The Great Exhibition and its Successors

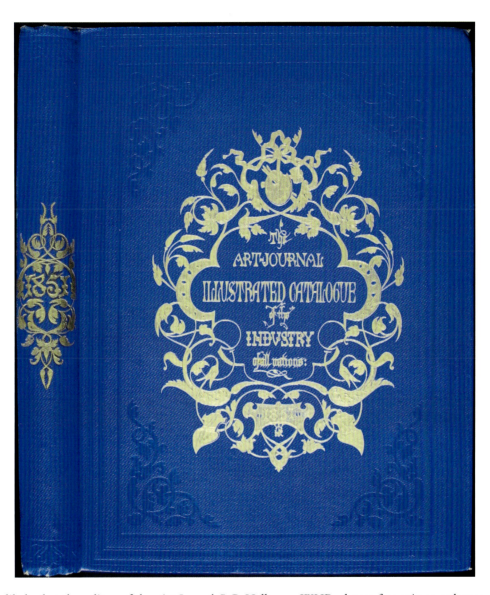

11.6 – Cover for the 1851 *Art Journal* catalogue, designed by WHR. Cloth blocked in gilt by W. Bone. Height 338mm.

likely that the editor of the *Art Journal*, S.C. Hall, gave WHR almost free rein to enhance the volume.

The book's cover is itself a striking WHR design. Figure 11.6 shows its spine and front cover, whose Renaissance-inspired gilt frame surrounds characteristically inventive and harmonious lettering, the whole gilt ensemble being unusually extensive for its time.

Inside, on the verso of the engraved title page is a design by WHR for 'The industry of all nations 1851'. Next comes an anonymous dedication page, but after that the whole riot of artistic enhancement was created by WHR. The preface starts with his monogram for the word INDUSTRY linked to an A for Albert. Then comes his Table of Contents,

125

ending with his flags of the nations. The final preliminaries are occupied by an essay on the History of the Exhibition, which starts with his flag-laden capital and ends with his sunburst for 1851. The catalogue proper follows, starting with an elaborate WHR title for the exhibition, and concluding with his design for an interpenetrating 'Finis' and '1851'.

Only after that do we meet what may be viewed as the most inventive of WHR's enlivenings of the book's interior. There are five separately paginated essays, each of which is endowed by WHR with an emblematic title, a large initial capital and a concluding design.[35] The five suites of designs exhibit impressive gracefulness and originality. Figure 11.7 gathers together WHR's designs for the five titles only: 'The Harmony of Colours as exemplified in the Exhibition', 'On the Vegetable World as contributing to the Great Exhibition'; 'The Science of the Exhibition'; 'The Machinery of the Exhibition'; and 'The Exhibition as a Lesson in Taste'.

For the first essay title, 'The Harmony of Colours', a letter dated 13 June 1851 survives from WHR to George Dalziel (1815–1902), founder of the Dalziel Brothers firm of engravers. The letter dealt with the tricky issue of how best to convey a rainbow without having access to colour. It appears that WHR had originally pencilled the rainbow as a series of long concentric semicircles, but was now suggesting that it would be easier to engrave as an arrangement of short horizontal lines – which is how Dalziel did in fact engrave the vignette. In July 1851, the Dalziels archived their final proof of this design.[36] It duly appeared in the *Art Journal* double-number for 1 August 1851, from which it was subsequently gathered up into the *Art Journal* catalogue book.[37]

WORNUM'S PRIZE ESSAY

Finally, as previously noted, the last section of the 1851 *Art Journal* catalogue consisted of an essay on 'The Exhibition as a Lesson in Taste', for which Ralph Wornum had been awarded a prize of 100 guineas by the *Art Journal*.[38] Wornum echoed a view that WHR had expressed previously, namely that the Renaissance style was ideally suited for design work:[39]

> We have ventured to assert, that the best specimens of ornamental design, as a class, are of the Renaissance, but that the great bulk of the specimens are of the Louis Quatorze varieties.

Wornum divided the general Renaissance class of designs into several components of varying merit, and handed the palm unequivocally to what he termed the 'pure Cinquecento' and reserving the unqualified term 'Renaissance' for the debased 'mixed Cinquecento':[40]

> There are, accordingly, four Italian styles of the revival—the Trecento, the Quattrocentro, the pure Cinquecento, and the mixed Cinquecento, or Renaissance; there is one French style of the period—the Renaissance, the same as the mixed cinquecento of Italy; and there is one English style—the Elizabethan, which is the English Renaissance.

Wornum continued that the pure cinquecento

> elaborated to the utmost the most conspicuous characteristics of Greek and Roman Art, especially the acanthus scroll, and the grotesque arabesques,

Chapter Eleven – The Great Exhibition and its Successors

11.7 – Five titles for essays designed by WHR, from the *Art Journal* catalogue of the Great Exhibition, 1851. Heights 98-103mm.

127

> abounding with monstrous combinations of human, animal, and vegetable forms, in the same figure or scroll-work; but always characterised, whatever the materials, by an extreme beauty of line: every natural form, and every conventional or ornamental form of antiquity, is admissible in the pure Cinquecento; ... The Cinquecento is considered the culminating style in Ornamental Art, as presenting the most perfect forms, and the most pleasing varieties; Nature and Art vieing with each other in their efforts to attract and gratify the eye.

Wornum then pointed to some meritorious exhibits of the prevalent Renaissance (i.e. mixed cinquecento) style submitted from across Europe, putting WHR's designing at the head of the home contribution, and noting that his cradle design, exceptionally, was in almost pure cinquecento style:[41]

> Of English specimens may be mentioned her Majesty's cradle by Rogers, though this specimen also borders closely on the pure Cinquecento.

After noting the impure nature of most of his examples, he continued to extol[42]

> the Cinquecento in its purity, of which however the Exhibition also affords a few fine specimens, some of which we may mention here for the sake of clearly separating these two styles. Her Majesty's cradle, as already observed, for the general character of its ornaments belongs to this style.

Wornum then proceeded to review the exhibits in detail, once again picking out:[43]

> the Cradle exhibited by her Majesty, carved by Mr. Rogers, from a design by his son; and a case containing some elegant Renaissance specimens by the same carver. ... However, much of the superiority of the cradle, as also of a Cinquecento bracket and canopy, is owing purely to the excellence of the design, and it is another illustration of the paramount value of taste, with which no mere mechanical skill can ever come into competition.

It is not known how well WHR knew Ralph Wornum, but they were united by something else besides their informed respect for renaissance design. As described in Chapter 9, both WHR and Wornum in the late 1840s had publicly – but ultimately unsuccessfully – denounced Henry Cole's bid to seize power over the field of art design.

DUBLIN, 1853

TITLE
The Exhibition of Art-industry in Dublin (Virtue & Co., 1853).

EXHIBITS
The section on exhibits was considerably shorter than in the 1851 volume. Nevertheless, several exhibits designed by WHR were illustrated in the catalogue, as follows.
(a) Wood carvings by W.G. Rogers.[44] Of the four works which were illustrated, two

Chapter Eleven – The Great Exhibition and its Successors

11.8 – Bracket in boxwood incorporating a carved monogram for WHR as designer, from the Art Journal *catalogue of the Dublin Exhibition, 1853. Image height 88mm.*

were unusual in incorporating a WHR monogram into their design (rather than adding it alongside a drawing). These were a cup and a 'very elaborate Elizabethan Bracket', both in boxwood. Figure 11.8 shows the engraving of the bracket. It seems that WHR, who had started to incorporate his monogram into the design of book covers, was extending the practice to other objects.

It can be verified that, for the bracket at least, the WHR monogram really is present in the carving, not merely added to a drawing. The bracket was later in the possession of Charles Handley-Read (1916–71), the pioneer collector of nineteenth-century art, and thus figured in the 1972 posthumous exhibition of the Handley-Read collection. The catalogue of the 1972 exhibition misinterpreted the carved monogram and listed WHR as not only designer but also carver, while a more accurate attribution of the work was formulated but dismissed as unlikely:[45]

It is possible but unlikely that the signature refers to W. Harry Rogers' part as designer of the bracket, and that it was in fact executed by his father.

In the same year, 1972, the bracket was purchased by the V&A Museum, whose catalogue notes that its original price in 1853 was £21.[46]

(b) Silver by F. Higgins.[47] As with the 1851 Exhibition catalogue, WHR was not mentioned in connection with Francis Higgins, but he is known to have designed some of the work illustrated, as detailed in Chapter 8.

(c) Bridle and two knife-rests in silver by Mr Penny, all 'from designs furnished by Mr. W. Harry Rogers'. The bridle was probably from the same suite of equine equipment as was illustrated in the 1851 Exhibition catalogue.[48] This time, two other components of it were illustrated.

(d) Two specimens of Glass ornamentation by The Ladies' Guild.[49] It was explained that the guild was intended to provide employment suitable for gentlewomen. For the Glass and the following Missal, 'The designs are all from the pencil of Mr. W. Harry Rogers.'

(e) Missal cover by Richardsons of Derby. This design for (presumably) a leatherbound *Missale Romanum* is signed with a WHR monogram. Original artwork for the binding is in the WHR archive at the V&A.[50]

ARTISTIC ENHANCEMENTS

The first page encountered is WHR's engraved title page, with Irish harp and shamrocks. A Dedication page to Prince Albert follows next, and is WHR's only contribution to the book's preliminary pages which has no Irish resonance. There was a good reason for this, because the design was a modified re-use of WHR's Dedication page in the *Vernon Gallery*, 1850 (another spin-off from the *Art Journal*). Robert Vernon's arms have been replaced by those of Prince Albert, but complete removal of Vernon's motto, 'Vernon Semper Viret', which scrolled around a pair of urns, proved more difficult and a ghostly *Vernon Semper* is still visible on Albert's right-hand urn.

There then followed a series of WHR designs with Irish allusions, for the start and end of the Introduction and the start of the Table of Contents.

The illustrations of exhibits commence on the next page, signalled by an elaborate WHR header for 'Exhibition of art-industry in Dublin 1853' and concluding with his design for 'Finis' and '1853'.

PARIS, 1855

TITLE
The Exhibition of Art-industry in Paris, 1855 (London: Virtue & Co.; Paris: Stassin & Xavier [1855]).

EXHIBITS
The section on exhibits was shorter even than that for Dublin, 1853. WHR's only stated contribution was an extraordinary 7ft 6in stand with a glass dome for displaying stereoscopes made by A. Claudet, carved in boxwood by W.G. Rogers. Its appearance was the outcome of a collaboration between WHR and the architect Charles Barry:[51]

> in every part it is richly embellished in the purest Italian style … The design, which is of architectural character, was supplied by Mr. Charles Barry, and the details are from the pencil of Mr. W. Harry Rogers.

WHR's collaborator appears not to have been Charles Barry (1795–1860) who designed the Houses of Parliament, because he had been knighted in 1852. It would instead have been his eldest son, Charles Barry (1823–1900), of a similar age to WHR, who followed his father in becoming a well-known architect.

ARTISTIC ENHANCEMENTS
The first page encountered is again an engraved title page designed by WHR. It is reproduced in Figure 11.9. The design features N E for Napoleon III and Eugénie, and (continuing clockwise) symbols of music, science, art, and architecture. There is artwork for the title page in the WHR archive at the V&A, which unusually includes a description by WHR of its different components.[52] These include the garland for Napoleon, which is encrusted with a chain of very small eagles as

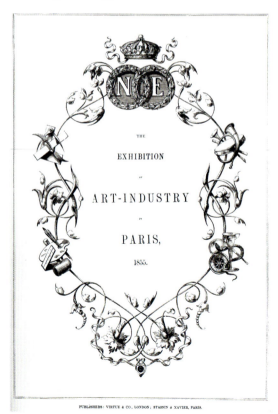

11.9 – Title page of the *Art Journal* catalogue of the Paris Exhibition, 1855, designed by WHR. Height 285mm.

in the collar of the Légion d'honneur (the eagles are upright on the right of the garland and downward on the left), and the garland for Eugénie, composed of the foliage of the orange tree in an allusion to her birth in southern Spain (upright on the left and downward on the right).

The next page bears a design, also by WHR, which combines a monogram for Napoleon and Eugénie with another one for Victoria and Albert. The essay that follows starts with an initial by WHR.

After the introductory essay, the commencement of illustrations of exhibits is signalled by an elaborate WHR header for 'Paris the exhibition of 1855'. This features a playful classical galley at the top, with N on the crow's nest, an eagle on the sail and a dolphin-like extension to its bow for ramming.

LONDON, 1862

TITLE

The Art-Journal Illustrated Catalogue of the International Exhibition 1862 (London & New York: James S. Virtue, 1862).

EXHIBITS

After the relatively slim catalogues for Dublin 1853 and Paris 1855, the Exhibits section for London 1862 was almost as large as that for London 1851. Designs by WHR were featured at several points, as follows.

(a) Carvings by William Gibbs Rogers.[53] The writer blended the names of W.H. Rogers (designer) and W.G. Rogers (carver), producing 'Mr. H. G. Rogers'.[54] Illustrations included 'a frame of the severer style of decoration, known to *virtuosi* by the style and title of *cinquecento*', and concluded as follows:

> The two remaining subjects are both productions in box-wood, which Mr. Rogers executed for Miss Burdett Coutts. The ornamental composition containing the words—'A thing of beauty is a joy for ever,' forms the central portion of an elaborate frame, destined to hold that lady's testimonial from the 'Manchester Exhibition of Art-Treasures.' The page terminates with a circular *encadrement* in the most exquisite style of the period of the Medicis. Although of diminutive size, it is a perfect *bijou* of wood carving. The terminal boys in the centre support a shield.

Artwork for the first of these, the centrepiece for a frame, is in the WHR archive at the V&A.[55] The Burdett Coutts frame as a whole is discussed in Chapter 18: Patrons.

As mentioned for the 1851 Exhibition, the 1862 display also included the hexagonal salt cellar table centrepiece (Figure 11.2). Though not mentioned in the *Art Journal* catalogue, it was depicted in Waring's *Masterpieces*.[56]

(b) Chandelier by Harrow and Son. Figure 11.10 shows the catalogue's depiction of a metal chandelier carrying eight gas lamps, with a range of emblematic features. The

W.G. Rogers firm supplied the design, undoubtedly created by WHR, and carved wooden models for the metalworking to follow. A full description of the chandelier is to be found in a contemporary newspaper.[57] This clarifies the *Art Journal* catalogue's depiction, and demonstrates how widely WHR could apply an emblematic approach. The design incorporates both dragons breathing fire and salamanders as the personification of fire (considered as one of the four elements):

> Messrs. Harrow and Son, of Portland-street, show an eight-light chandelier for gas in brass, from models designed and carved by W.G. Rogers. This chandelier is constructed in the form of an ancient grillier or fire-pot; the upper bar consists of inverted friezes richly wrought. They are divided by heads of dragons, from whose wide open mouths issue fire and lightly poised gas jets. At the bottom there is a very bold boss, composed of two large salamanders struggling and fighting with animated fury, and wildly intertwining their pliant bodies; their feet grasp the lower ring or bar of the suspended fire-pot, and thus form its base. The eight chain bands are united to an open coronet above, and are in keeping with the character of the whole.

(c) Carvings by George Alfred Rogers.[58] A carving of the sacred monogram IHS was designed by WHR. The *Art Journal* writer's confusion over the Rogers family continued by mistaking George Alfred Rogers, who was aged twenty-four at the time, for his father: 'Mr. Rogers has occupied the high position he holds during, we believe, nearly half a century.'

(d) Table Glass by Dobson and Pearce. The connection with WHR is only conjectural. The works of Dobson and Pearce of St James's Street in London were extraordinarily admired at this time:

> To the contributions of Messrs. Dobson and Pearce the palm of supremacy has been universally awarded. … The famous Tazza, here engraved, has perhaps found more general admiration than any other work in the Exhibition. We have selected … three of the Claret Jugs; they are exquisite examples of the art, in form, design, and cutting.

Two of the illustrated claret-jugs are stylistically alien to WHR but the third, featuring a cartouche enclosing water-lilies, could have been designed by WHR. The connection with WHR is provided only by a remark made about WHR after his death:

> A design for the ornamentation of a claret-jug, shown in the Exhibition of 1862, gained for him great commendation.

The *Illustrated London News* also illustrated three of the exhibited Dobson and Pearce 'ewers', comprising the water-lilies claret jug already referred to and two new jugs, one

11.10 – A chandelier for eight gas lamps, designed by WHR, from the *Art Journal* catalogue of the London Exhibition, 1862. Image height 120mm.

of which could also have been designed by WHR.[59] The description said that the latter ewer 'is rich and energetic in the composition of its ornament, and is full of well-designed grotesque shapes'. However, any attribution of Dobson and Pearce glass to WHR remains speculative at present.

(e) Bookbindings by Bone. Four front covers made by W. Bone and Son were illustrated, of which the top-left one was signed by WHR. A proof of that cover, blocked in gilt on red silk (and with no title), is present in the WHR archive at the V&A.[60] However, no book on which the cover design was actually used has yet been discovered.

(f) Artwork for Dudley Coutts Marjoribanks. This comprised a set of ink drawings by WHR, elaborately hand-bound by M.M. Holloway according to a Grolieresque design by WHR, and described here further in Chapter 18. It was not included in the *Art Journal* catalogue, but Figure 11.11 reproduces the chromolithographic illustration of the binding in Waring's *Masterpieces*.[61]

As in 1851, WHR's designs gained Medals of the Exhibition for a clutch of exhibitors, including W.G. Rogers, W. Bone and M.M. Holloway.[62]

ARTISTIC ENHANCEMENT

For this exhibition, WHR had been signed up by Joseph Cundall to enhance the official catalogue, and hence was not available to contribute anything to the appearance of the *Art Journal* catalogue. The publishers, however, re-cycled WHR's Table of Contents design from the 1851 Exhibition, though they discreetly removed its WHR monogram.

PARIS, 1867

TITLE
The Illustrated Catalogue of the Universal Exhibition published with the Art Journal (London & New York: Virtue and Co. [1868]).

EXHIBITS

(a) Casket by J.W. Benson for presentation to Prince Alfred, carved in oak by W.G. Rogers and encrusted in gold and enamel.[63] WHR is not mentioned and, if he had anything to do with the design, it would probably only have been for its fluid details rather than its squat outline.

(b) Five Picture-frames by Charles Rowley of Manchester.[64] 'Mr. Rowley has invoked the assistance of true artists; these frames are from the designs of Mr. Muckley (head-master of the Manchester School), Mr. Harry Rogers, and Mr. J. Whitehead.'

(c) Carvings in Wood by Mr. G.A. Rogers.[65] He 'has succeeded his venerable father, W.G. Rogers … There is much of the pure feeling of the father in the productions of the son'. A factor in the continuity between father and son will have been provided by WHR designing for both. Six of the frames and brackets were included in an album of WHR designs subsequently compiled by George Alfred Rogers himself. The text of the *Art Journal* catalogue said, 'They are designed as well as carved by Mr. Rogers' but, as for William Gibbs Rogers earlier, WHR's designs for the family firm were often not separately credited.

William Harry Rogers – Victorian Book Designer and Star of the Great Exhibition

Chapter Eleven – The Great Exhibition and its Successors

ARTISTIC ENHANCEMENTS

An anonymous engraved title page is followed by WHR's engraved dedication page, which features a Napoleonic bee. The design is more closely symmetric than usual for WHR, but even here the left and right sides are not mirror images (as they might at first sight appear to be), instead differing in shading and in twining patterns.

The next page, also by WHR, bears a design combining a monogram for 1867 with the scrolling motto 'To all nations unity peace and concord'.

LONDON, 1871

Paris 1867 was the last of the five separately published *Art Journal* catalogues. For London 1871 and 1872, the catalogues were printed only as supplements to issues of the *Art Journal*, albeit with their own separate page numbering.[66] Each set of supplements could be bound up in book form by the owner if desired, but was not separately issued in publisher's cloth.

It was claimed in the regular pages of the *Art Journal* that their 1871 catalogue was the eighth in the journal's history:[67]

> The chief feature of the Art-Journal during the past year has been the Illustrated Catalogue of the leading contents of the International Exhibition - the eighth thus reported since the year 1844.

The six catalogues from 1851 to 1871 are considered in the present chapter. The further two reports referred to were those for the Paris exhibitions of 1844 and 1849. Neither account of these earlier exhibitions was paginated separately, however, and hence these accounts can be considered as normal components of the *Art Journal*.

Of the exhibits illustrated in 1871, none is known to have been designed by WHR. Nevertheless, as usual WHR provided the heading on the first page of the catalogue. It is unsigned but artwork for it is present in the V&A's WHR archive.[68]

The catalogue concluded on its p. 88 with an anonymous design for 'End of the First Division 1871'. This terminology was the result of the intention to hold annual continuations or 'divisions' of the London exhibition. However, only for the 1872 'International Exhibition: Second Division' did this reach the stage of yielding another *Art Journal* illustrated catalogue.

LONDON, 1872

11.11 – Binding designed by WHR and executed by M.M. Holloway for Dudley Coutts Marjoribanks. 1862 London Exhibition. From Waring's Masterpieces, 1863. Height of image 197mm.

WHR designed several of the illustrated exhibits, as follows.

(a) Jewels by Howell and James.[69] WHR was one of the group of designers of this jewellery, though not mentioned in this text. His designs are considered separately in Chapter 15.

(b) Wood carvings by G. Alfred Rogers.[70] Those illustrated included a Gothic bracket design by WHR, and also a book cover carved in boxwood that was designed by Mary Eliza Rogers, their sister. 'On one side of this cover is carved a branch of Spina Christi; on the reverse, a Syrian fig-leaf.' Figure 11.12 shows this album of poetry.

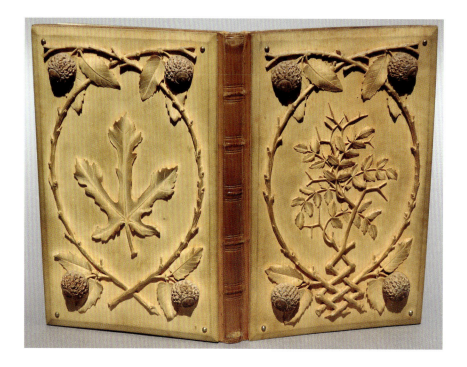

11.12 – Cover panels designed by Mary Eliza Rogers, WHR's sister, and carved in boxwood by his brother, George Alfred Rogers. 1872 London Exhibition. Height 196mm.

(c) Casket carved in oak by G.A. Rogers and 'designed by Mr. H. Rogers', to contain an illuminated address by the Ludgate Hill Committee to the Prince of Wales. There is artwork for the casket in the V&A's WHR archive.[71]

By the time the exhibition opened in May 1872, it seems that WHR's health was already declining, and he contributed no artistic enhancements to this catalogue.

CONCLUSION

For the Great Exhibition, WHR's fine designs for multiple prize-winning exhibits were complemented in the *Art Journal* catalogue volume by his outstandingly creative artistic enhancements, which together made it by far the most vivid printed record of the exhibition. After his starring role in the Great Exhibition, WHR's contributions to the later international exhibitions were in general more low-key. Several factors may have been responsible for this, such as a disenchantment with the exhibition process or greater anonymity among designers. Certainly a decline in WHR's personal prominence at the exhibitions was mirrored by a decline in the profile of the exhibitions themselves, which never succeeded in recapturing the epoch-defining excitement of the Great Exhibition of 1851.

Chapter Eleven – The Great Exhibition and its Successors

NOTES

1. *Art Journal*, new series, Vol. 11, September 1872, p. 241.
2. Elizabeth Bonython and Anthony Burton, *The Great Exhibitor: The Life and Work of Henry Cole* (V&A Publications, 2003), pp. 264-5.
3. The engraved title page omits 'of the'.
4. *The Art-Journal Illustrated Catalogue of the Industry of All Nations 1851* (George Virtue, [1851]), pp. 8-10.
5. *Ibid.*, p. 8.
6. *Official Descriptive and Illustrated Catalogue of the Great Exhibition of the Works of Industry of all Nations* (Spicer Brothers, 1851), p. 824. The spoon is no longer present.
7. This centrepiece was displayed also at the 1862 London Exhibition, when a chromolithograph of it was published by J.B. Waring, *Masterpieces of Industrial Art & Sculpture at the International Exhibition, 1862*, three volumes (Day, 1863), Plate 128.
8. *The Art-Journal Illustrated Catalogue of the Industry of All Nations 1851, op. cit.*, p. 10.
9. *Exhibition of the Works of Industry of All Nations, 1851. Reports of the Juries*, in four volumes. Vol. 4: Reports – Classes 29, 30 (Spicer Brothers, 1852), pp. 546, 694, 723.
10. *The Art-Journal Illustrated Catalogue of the Industry of All Nations 1851, op. cit.*, p. 18.
11. *Ibid.*, pp. 26-7.
12. *Ibid.*, p. 21.
13. *Reports of the Juries* (1852), *op. cit.*, pp. 424, 452.
14. *The Art-Journal Illustrated Catalogue of the Industry of All Nations 1851, op. cit.*, p. 38.
15. *Reports of the Juries* (1852), *op. cit.*, p. 395.
16. *The Art-Journal Illustrated Catalogue of the Industry of All Nations 1851, op. cit.*, p. 39.
17. *Reports of the Juries* (1852), *op. cit.*, p. 470.
18. *The Art-Journal Illustrated Catalogue of the Industry of All Nations 1851, op. cit.*, p. 39.
19. *Reports of the Juries* (1852), *op. cit.*, p. 451.
20. *The Art-Journal Illustrated Catalogue of the Industry of All Nations 1851, op. cit.*, p. iv★★★.
21. Nikolaus Pevsner, *High Victorian Design: A Study of the Exhibits of 1851* (London: Architectural Press, 1951), p. 77.
22. John Buchanan-Brown, *Early Victorian Illustrated Books: Britain, France and Germany 1820–1860* (London: The British Library and New Castle, DE: Oak Knoll Press), pp. 99-100.
23. *The Art-Journal Illustrated Catalogue of the Industry of All Nations 1851, op. cit.*, p. 40.

24. *Reports of the Juries* (1852), *op. cit.*, p. 489.
25. *The Art-Journal Illustrated Catalogue of the Industry of All Nations 1851, op. cit.*, pp. 121 and 269.
26. *Ibid.*, p. 321.
27. *Ibid.*, p. 328.
28. *Art Union*, Vol. 10, February 1848, p. 55.
29. The Society of Caddy Spoon Collectors, *Members' Newsletter*, 2009 and 2010.
30. *The Art-Journal Illustrated Catalogue of the Industry of All Nations 1851, op. cit.*, p. 7.
31. *Reports of the Juries* (1852), *op. cit.*, p. 686.
32. *The Art-Journal Illustrated Catalogue of the Industry of All Nations 1851, op. cit.*, p. 123.
33. *Ibid.*, p. 150.
34. *Reports of the Juries* (1852), *op. cit.*, pp. 425, 454.
35. The five essays commence with pp. I★, I‡, I†, I★★ and I★★★ (the numbers' suffixes derived from the catalogue's original publication in monthly installments, partly rearranged when subsequently bound up).
36. British Museum, Prints and Drawings, 1913,0415.164; Dalziel Vol. 2, No. 1222.
37. *Art Journal*, Vol. 3, 1 August 1851, new series, No. 32, p. I‡.
38. The full title was: Ralph Nicholson Wornum, 'An essay on ornamental art as displayed in the industrial exhibition in Hyde Park, in which the different styles are compared with a view to the improvement of taste in home manufactures', *Art Journal* catalogue, 1851, pp. I★★★-XXII★★★.
39. W.H. Rogers, 'On the style of the Renaissance and its adoption in England', *The Builder*, Vol. 6, 29 July 1848, pp. 362-3; Wornum, p. v★★★.
40. Wornum, 'An essay …', *op. cit.*, p. iv★★★.
41. *Ibid.*, p. vi★★★.
42. *Ibid.*, p. vi★★★.
43. *Ibid.*, p. xiii★★★.
44. *The Exhibition of Art-industry in Dublin* (Virtue & Co., 1853), p. 1.
45. *Victorian and Edwardian Decorative Art: The Handley-Read Collection* (Royal Academy of Arts, 1972), Item A8, p. 15.
46. V&A W.28-1972.
47. *The Exhibition of Art-industry in Dublin, op. cit.*, p. 9.
48. *Ibid.*, p. 43; 1851 catalogue, p. 38.
49. *Ibid.*, p. 51.
50. *Ibid.*, p. 51; V&A E1140-1998.
51. *The Exhibition of Art-industry in Paris, 1855*. London: Virtue & Co.; Paris: Stassin & Xavier, [1855], p. 1.

52. V&A E694.6–1998, artwork dated 19 April 1855.
53. *The Art-Journal Illustrated Catalogue of the International Exhibition 1862* (London and New York: James S. Virtue, 1862), p. 13.
54. This was probably the source of misnaming WHR as 'H.G. Rogers' in Henry Cole's posthumously edited memoirs: *Fifty Years of Public Work of Sir Henry Cole*, two vols (Bell, 1884), Vol. 2, p. 191.
55. V&A E693.165–1998.
56. J.B. Waring, *Masterpieces, op. cit.*, Plate 128 (misnumbered in the plate as 154).
57. *The Art-Journal Illustrated Catalogue of the International Exhibition 1862, op. cit.*, p. 156; *Morning Post*, 16 September 1862, p. 2.
58. *Ibid.*, p. 196.
59. *Ibid.*, p. 212; *Publishers' Circular*, 1 February 1873, p. 72; *Illustrated London News*, 6 September 1862, pp. 269, 272 and 274.
60. *Ibid.*, p. 224; V&A E693.168–1998.

61. J.B. Waring, *Masterpieces, op. cit.*, Plate 206.
62. *Reports of the Juries on the Subjects in the Thirty-six Classes into which the Exhibition was Divided.* Printed for the Society of Arts (1863), Class 28, p.12; Class 30, p. 3.
63. *The Illustrated Catalogue of the Universal Exhibition Published with the Art Journal* (London and New York: Virtue and Co., [1868]), p. 13, with four engravings.
64. *Ibid.*, p. 47.
65. *Ibid.*, p. 48.
66. *Art Journal*, new series, Vol. 10, 1871; Vol. 11, 1872.
67. *Art Journal*, new series, Vol. 10, 1871, p. 277.
68. V&A E694.17–1998.
69. *The Art Journal Catalogue of the International Exhibition: Second Division* (Virtue & Co, 1872), pp. 5 & 50.
70. *Ibid.*, p. 10.
71. *Ibid.*, p. 55; V&A E694.46–1998.

TWELVE

Spiritual Conceits

IN THE YEARS FOLLOWING THE Great Exhibition, WHR's known designs are to be found most often on the covers and in the interiors of books and other publications. His stream of book cover designs was particularly impressive. The cover designs are reviewed in Chapter 16 and illustrated in Appendix A. WHR's designs for the interiors of books are reviewed in Chapter 13. In the present chapter, however, we focus on a single book.

Spiritual Conceits is WHR's most complete work in book form, the only one in which he had a free hand in devising the striking whole-page plates, selecting the accompanying texts and having them printed in dramatic black-letter with red initials, and encasing the whole in a lavish cover. Figure 12.1 illustrates the title page.[1] The book provides the most extensive and striking development of WHR's exploration of the emblem. Intangible concepts (or 'conceits', as WHR archaically termed them) are here represented by means of a visual language that juxtaposes pictorially both abstract and concrete elements in novel arrangements able to convey an extensive range of meanings.

As a livre d'artiste, *Spiritual Conceits* has no obvious peer in the High Victorian period. The *Moxon Tennyson* (1857), is usually thought of as the most epoch-defining illustrated work of the period.[2] Even for that volume, however, its impact was typically compromised by diluting its minority of striking images by Dante Gabriel Rossetti and his friends with a majority of more conventional illustrations by establishment artists, complemented by indifferent typography.[3] More eclectic still, *Parables from Nature* (1865, with WHR cover design) named on its title page no fewer than sixteen illustrators, ranging from animal specialists (Harrison Weir, 1824–1906 and Joseph Wolf, 1820–99) to Pre-Raphaelites (William Holman Hunt, 1827–1910 and Edward Burne-Jones, 1833–98) and prolific contributors to the periodicals (John Gilbert, 1817–97 and Charles Keene, 1823–91). Inside such a book, there was clearly little chance of achieving a coherent artistic effect. Of course, there were also some books that were illustrated by a single artist, of which one of the most impressive is Millais' *Parables*.[4] Even here, however, there is little sense of the artist's stamp upon the book as a whole. It was put together by the Dalziels, who included thirty-three parables, of which only nineteen were illustrated; most of Millais' twenty illustrations ('The Ten Virgins' had two illustrations) had appeared previously in the magazine *Good Words*. Another notable single-illustrator work was *Moral Emblems*. However, despite its 1860 date and John Leighton illustrations, this was

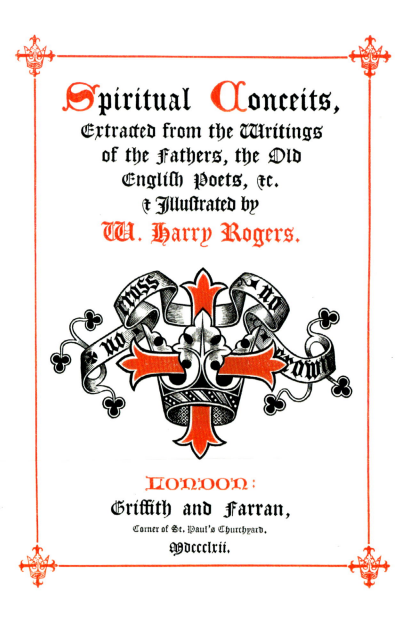

essentially a seventeenth-century book, since the Dutch of Jacob Cats was translated into English by Richard Pigot and 'the original designs of Adrian Van de Venne, in a few instances only, have been deviated from'.[5]

Spiritual Conceits was different, not only in the way that every aspect of it reflected a single mind, but also in WHR's eschewal of painterly convention. The refinement of WHR's masterful, non-painterly black line was not to be seen again until the 1890s,

12.1 – Title page of *Spiritual Conceits*, 1862. Height 196mm.

in the work of Aubrey Beardsley (1872–98).[6] WHR's art was realised flawlessly by his engraver and printer, to both of whom he paid fine whole-page visual tributes. The engraver was Joseph Swain, acknowledged on the title page verso, and the printer was Charles Whittingham at the Chiswick Press, acknowledged in the colophon.

The book is constructed as one hundred double-page openings, with WHR's title and an evocative passage (or two) on the left page, and WHR's visual representation on the right page. Below each visual representation, there is also a much briefer biblical verse (or sometimes two) relevant to that concept. These verses were probably added at a late stage of the book's production, because they do not map directly onto the iconography. Indeed, there is evidence that they were often separately suggested by WHR's mother, Mary Rogers. WHR expressed his thanks 'for her great help in the selection of biblical extracts' in the copy of the book which he presented to her.

THE CONCEPTS

WHR grouped his hundred concepts into eight categories: 1. The Dual Character of all Things, 2. Past, Present, Future, 3. Preparations for Futurity, 4. Vices, 5. Virtues, 6. Facts, 7. Reflections, and 8. Results.[7] He did not state the numbers of concepts in the different categories, but they can readily be determined.[8]

The following are three examples drawn from WHR's one hundred concepts. First, Figure 12.2 represents *Anger*.[9] It accompanies an exhortation of St John Chrysostom (*c.* 349–407) to turn anger into gentleness:

> It were good to be silent, good to have no communications with any man in act or word, until we were able to charm the wild beast that is within us. The wild beast, I say, for indeed is it not worse than the attack of any wild beast when wrath and lust make war upon us? Well then do thou first tame thy lion, and so lead him about, not for the purpose of receiving money, but that thou mayest acquire a gain to which there is none equal. For there is nothing equal to gentleness, which both to those that possess it and to those who are its objects is exceeding useful.

Second, Figure 12.3 represents *Hypocrisy*.[10] It accompanies (i) a sonnet by William Drummond of Hawthornden (1585–1649) and (ii) an apothegm by Francis Quarles (*c.* 1592–1644):

(i)   As are those apples pleasant to the eye,
But full of smoke within, what used to grow
Near that strange lake where God poured from the sky
Huge showers of flame worse flames to overthrow,
Such are their works that with a glaring show
Of humble holiness in virtue's dye
Would colour mischief, which within they glow
With coals of sin, tho' none the smoke descry;

Bad [text has 'But'] is that angel that erst fell from Heaven
But not so bad as he, nor in worse case,
Who hides a traiterous mind with smiling face,
And with a dove's white feathers clothes a raven;
Each sin some colour has it to adorn,
Hypocrisy Almighty God doth scorn.
(ii)   It is a serpent most when most it seems a dove.

Third and finally, Figure 12.4 represents *The Future*.[11] It accompanies the poetry of John Norris (1657–1712):

It must be done, my soul, but 'tis a strange,
A dismal and mysterious change,
When thou shalt leave this tenement of clay
And to an unknown somewhere wing away,
When time shall be eternity, and thou
Shalt be thou know'st not what, and live thou know'st not how.

12.2 – Spiritual Conceits: Anger. Height 110mm.

12.3 – Spiritual Conceits: Hypocrisy. Height 140mm.

Chapter Twelve – Spiritual Conceits

RECEPTION OF *SPIRITUAL CONCEITS*

12.4 – Spiritual Conceits: The Future. Height 90mm.

Almost without exception, contemporary reviewers admired *Spiritual Conceits*. The book was published on 23 November 1861, and the plaudits rolled in. The *Morning Post* fully appreciated its historic standing:[12]

> Few books like that of which we have here given the title ever come before the world. Rare old Francis Quarles has … monopolised the domain of 'Emblems' for some two centuries and a half … but … we shall be much surprised if the public do not admit that there is room for two emblematical works in the field of English moral and religious literature. … The selections have been made by Mr. Rogers … and the illustrations are from the graceful hand of Mr. Rogers himself, and leave one in doubt which most highly to estimate—the fertility of his imagination, or the facility of his execution.

WHR's selection of texts, as well as his artwork, was praised also by the *Examiner*.[13]

There is more thought in this beautiful Christmas book than is seen at a glance. … It is evident that much careful and wholesome thought has been given to the preparation of this book; and the wise selection and arrangement of the passages illustrated will entitle Mr Harry Rogers almost to as much praise as his pictures. … Mr Harry Rogers is known as perhaps our best designer of the traceries of delicate book ornament. He has exchanged here the delicacy of his touch for a broader style, learnt in the school of Albert Durer, but he retains all his taste as a designer. Apart from its meaning, nearly every drawing pleases the eye as a choice ornament by the arrangement of its lines and shadows. … One word more of praise is due to the book, … it is by far the most complete and beautiful specimen of modern black-letter we have ever seen.

The *Art Journal* echoed the praise for WHR's artwork, but cautioned that it might be above many people's heads:[14]

A book so full of deep thought, and beautiful, yet quaint artist-work as this is cannot be, though it ought to be, popular … In this age of hurry and bustle, the generality of men have, or fancy they have, no time for thinking beyond the demands of their daily avocations; … pictures are bought, and hung, and valued, because they are ornaments, but to understand them is no part of the owner's care; the same homage is not paid to books unless they can commend themselves without trouble. … There is, however, a class of persons, and a large class too, who seek both in books and pictures something beyond a momentary gratification: by this class more especially 'Spiritual Conceits' will be appreciated.

The *Daily News* did not beat about the bush, commencing simply, 'This is a sumptuous volume.'[15]

At this point, a dissenting voice was provided by the *Athenaeum*, which did not formally review *Spiritual Conceits* but instead attacked it in its section entitled 'Our Weekly Gossip'.[16] The root of its objection to the book appeared to be religious in nature:

The slow directness of the old pietist fancy loved an emblem and suspected a parable, forgetting who used the last. Such things pleased the people in old days, doubtless from an impression the emblem-dealing Church of Rome made upon the popular mind, and remaining even unsuspected, certainly unobliterated, for many years after the Reformation.

As the first-quoted review mentioned, the book appeared to many contemporaries as a work of 'moral and religious literature'. In the present day, concepts such as anger and hypocrisy are widely considered within the framework of psychological science, but this discipline was only in its infancy in the 1860s. A religious dimension to the book was implied by WHR's summary of the sources of his texts:[17]

The fathers of the Church, the noblest divines of the Middle Ages, and the old English poets.

WHR AND RELIGION

In his adult life, WHR appears not to have been very religious, at least in terms of conventional Church of England or Nonconformist observance (his father had a Nonconformist baptism and some other relatives were staunch Nonconformists). He was baptised into the Church of England as a baby on 10 July 1825 at St Anne's Church, Soho. However, his marriage to Mary Ann Lansdale on 8 December 1847 was conducted not in a church but at St Pancras Register Office. They were both buried (as were WHR's parents) in Abney Park, at that time the leading non-denominational cemetery in London. Furthermore, none of their seven children appears to have been baptised as an infant.

The first child of WHR and Mary Ann Rogers, Mary Eliza Rogers, was born on 15 April 1849 but not baptised at St Anne's Church, Soho, until aged eleven, on 12 June 1860. No other baptism of their six other children during the parents' lifetimes has been traced. That this was a deliberate choice of the parents and not a matter of defective baptism records can be clearly demonstrated for their two youngest daughters, Kate (born 24 August 1861) and Isabel (born 2 September 1864). WHR died on 9 January 1873 and his widow died on 12 January 1875. At that latter point, the two girls went into the care of their aunt, Mary Eliza Rogers. A mere twelve days later, on 24 January 1875, they were both baptised (aged thirteen and ten, respectively) at Holy Trinity Church, Haverstock Hill, Camden. They and their subsequent artistic achievements are discussed in Appendix D.

WHR's avoidance of religious observance suggests he may have been more interested in spirituality than in organised religion as such, and this is consistent with the title which he gave to his book, *Spiritual Conceits*. The second word of his title, however, proved to be problematic, as pointed out by the *Art Journal* at the end of its review of the book. Even in 1861, the dominant connotation for *conceit* was of arrogance, rather than the older connotation intended by WHR, of imaginative thought. A similar point was made at the outset of an ecstatic review of *Spiritual Conceits* which appeared in the *Literary Churchman*.[18]

> This splendid book is a marvel of beautiful drawing and printing. Its author has chosen an unfortunate title, which conveys no clear idea of the contents, aim, or character of the book, and renders the friendly office of the reviewer necessary before the public—and especially that large portion of it which lives in country houses remote from booksellers, and buys books without first seeing them— can understand what it is. Mr. Rogers appears to be a reader of early Christian literature, and an exquisite artist. … Of the illustrations regarded as drawings, it is impossible to speak too highly … as a whole they are matchless for forcible expression of sentiment.

EMBLEMS OF CHRISTIAN LIFE

When a new issue of the book was called for in 1870, WHR duly replaced its title with a phrase taken from the opening sentence of his introductory 'To the Reader', namely,

Emblems of Christian Life.[19] A separate four-page prospectus for the new edition included enthusiastic reviews of the book by not only the *Literary Churchman* but also the *English Churchman*, suggesting that organised religion was thought to provide an important part of the audience for the book.[20] The book continued to be kept in print for a further twenty years, with Griffith, Farran, Okeden & Welsh (as they had become) only remaindering their stock in 1889 because of moving to new premises.[21]

The sustained demand for *Emblems of Christian Life* was consistent with the attention which continued to be paid to *Quarles' Emblems* and its new illustrations by WHR and Charles Bennett. Nisbet had published the work in 1861, and demand remained sufficiently strong for them to re-issue it in 1886, as described in Chapter 13.

THE LONGER VIEW OF *SPIRITUAL CONCEITS*

In 1881, the poet and writer Austin Dobson (1840–1921) published a survey of 'modern English illustrated books'. He included *Spiritual Conceits* within his selection of 'a few of the books most prominent for merit or originality'.[22] Subsequently, the sometime editor of *The Studio*, Gleeson White (1851–98) published a wide-ranging and eclectic volume which became a standard work on English illustration in the 1860s.[23] White viewed *Spiritual Conceits* as interestingly anomalous because its pictures were a matter of 'design' rather than of 'illustration' in the conventional sense of that period; he noted also 'the laudatory criticism it received'. 'Illustration' in this context was implicitly confined to realist depictions of scenes in the accompanying text, and thus *Spiritual Conceits* was excluded altogether from later surveys of illustration in this period by Reid and by Goldman.[24]

Moving away from conventional illustration, Höltgen has identified the prominent place of *Spiritual Conceits* and its companion *Quarles' Emblems* in a Victorian emblematic revival.[25] He also drew attention to, for example, the Pre-Raphaelites' 'combination of realism and symbolism, which sometimes approaches emblematic concreteness', analysing in particular the context in which Holman Hunt's *The Light of the World* (versions from 1851 onwards) was able to achieve its fame.[26]

Leaving aside art-historical classifications, the images which WHR created for *Spiritual Conceits* are sufficiently striking and powerful to stand on their own. Three admirers may be mentioned here. First was Ruari McLean. He reproduced one of the book's plates in the first edition of his classic *Victorian Book Design*.[27] In his 'enlarged and revised' second edition, McLean characterised *Spiritual Conceits* suitably as an 'extraordinary book' and this time reproduced two other pages from it.[28]

A second enthusiast was John (Jock) Murray VI (1909–93), a member of the publishing dynasty. A memorial book edited by his son, John G. Murray, revealed his father's fascination with *Emblems of Christian Life* and his deployment of it on some of the books he published, citing John Betjeman's *First and Last Loves*.[29] The son's book also reproduced no fewer than twelve of WHR's plates from *Emblems of Christian Life*. It seems quite likely that it was John Betjeman himself who introduced Jock Murray to *Emblems of Christian Life*, given that Betjeman (1906–84, Poet Laureate from 1972–84) was a pioneer advocate of Victorian architecture and art, and a lifelong book collector.[30] Be that as it may, Betjeman's *First and Last Loves* in fact omitted to mention WHR at all, even though the half-title, the title page, and the dustjacket's front, back and spine all borrowed from him, instead stating on the jacket: 'Fully illustrated including drawings by JOHN PIPER who has also designed the jacket'. At least two later Murray books, however, did acknowledge their borrowings from WHR's *Emblems of Christian Life*.[31]

Finally, the influential contemporary artist Damien Hirst (b. 1965) must be mentioned. His *Bilotti Paintings* were inspired by the four Evangelists, and incorporate what appear to be actual butterflies into the paintings. The butterfly is also frequently present in WHR's work in *Spiritual Conceits* and in *Quarles' Emblems*, where it is explicitly identified with *anima*, the soul or spirit. It is therefore a graceful gesture that an illustrated book devoted to the exhibition of the *Bilotti Paintings* in 2005 should commence with thirteen plates from *Spiritual Conceits*, each of which (for example, *The Future*, Figure 12.4 here) has one or more butterflies depicted within it.[32] As already noted, unlike so many of his contemporaries WHR did not produce 'illustrations' in the limited sense of realist depictions of scenes in the accompanying text. Instead, his work is better construed as an independent and lasting contribution to fine art.

NOTES

1. *Spiritual Conceits, extracted from the writings of the fathers, the old English poets, &c. & illustrated by W. Harry Rogers* (Griffith and Farran, 1862).
2. Alfred Tennyson, *Poems* (Edward Moxon, 1857).
3. The work of the establishment artists has also been shown to repay close study: Simon Cooke, *The Moxon Tennyson: A Landmark in Victorian Illustration* (Athens, OH: Ohio University Press, 2021).
4. *The Parables of Our Lord and Saviour Jesus Christ: With pictures by John Everett Millais* (Routledge, Warne, and Routledge, 1864).
5. *Moral emblems with aphorisms, adages, and proverbs, of all ages and nations, from Jacob Cats and Robert Farlie. With illustrations freely rendered, from designs found in their works, by John Leighton, F.S.A. The whole translated and edited, with additions, by Richard Pigot* (Longman, Green, Longman, and Roberts, 1860); p. xii.
6. Linda Gertner Zatlin, *Aubrey Beardsley: A catalogue raisonné*, two vols (New Haven, CT: Yale University Press, [2016]).
7. *Spiritual Conceits*, 'To the Reader', *op. cit.*, third unnumbered page.
8. Category [1] has ten concepts, pp. 2-21; [2] has four, pp. 22-29; [3] has seven, pp. 30-43; [4] has sixteen, pp. 44-75; [5] has thirteen, pp. 76-101; [6] has eight, pp. 102-17; [7] has thirty-three, pp. 118-83; and [8] has nine, pp. 184-201.
9. *Spiritual Conceits*, *op. cit.*, pp. 38-39, among Preparations for Futurity.
10. *Ibid.*, pp. 50-51, among Vices.
11. *Ibid.*, pp. 28-29, among Past, Present, Future.
12. *Morning Post*, 28 November 1861, p. 6.
13. *Examiner*, 30 November 1861, p. 6.
14. *Art Journal*, new series, Vol. 7, 1 December 1861, p. 376.
15. *Daily News*, 2 December 1861, p. 2.
16. *Athenaeum*, 21 December 1861, p. 850.
17. *Spiritual Conceits*, 'To the Reader', *op. cit.*, second page.
18. *Literary Churchman*, Vol. 8, 16 January 1862, p. 35.
19. Only the title page (now undated) was changed in the book's contents, with *Spiritual Conceits* retained on p. 1.
20. John Johnson Collection at the Bodleian Library.
21. *Athenaeum*, 4 May 1889, p. 556.
22. Austin Dobson, 'Illustrated books', in Andrew Lang (ed.), *The Library, with a Chapter on Modern English Illustrated Books by Austin Dobson* (Macmillan, 1881), pp. 122-78; pp. 148, 150.
23. Gleeson White, *English Illustration: 'The sixties': 1855–70* (Constable, 1897), p. 116.
24. Forrest Reid, *Illustrators of the Sixties* (Faber & Gwyer Limited, 1928); Paul Goldman, *Victorian Illustration: The Pre-Raphaelites, the Idyllic School and the High Victorians* (Scolar Press, 1996).
25. Karl Josef Höltgen, *Aspects of the Emblem: Studies in the English Emblem Tradition and the European Context, with a Foreword by Sir Roy Strong* (Kassel, Germany: Edition Reichenberger, 1986). The last of Höltgen's four component essays is 'The Victorian emblematic revival', pp. 141-96; WHR occupies pp. 165-9.
26. *Ibid.*, pp. 178-83.
27. Ruari McLean, *Victorian Book Design & Colour Printing* (Faber & Faber, 1963), p. 70.
28. Second edition, 1972, p. 168.
29. John G. Murray, *A Gentleman Publisher's Commonplace Book* (John Murray, 1996), pp. [91]-[103]; John Betjeman, *First and Last Loves* (John Murray, 1952).
30. Timothy Mowl, *Stylistic Cold Wars: Betjeman versus Pevsner* (John Murray, 2000); Kingsley Amis, revised by M. Clare Loughlin-Chow, 'Betjeman, Sir John (1906–1984)', in the *Oxford Dictionary of National Biography* (2017).
31. Peter Quennell (ed.), *Byronic Thoughts* (John Murray, 1960), p. x; John Betjeman, *Uncollected Poems* (John Murray, 1982). p. [vii].
32. *Damien Hirst, The Bilotti Paintings*, Gagosian Gallery, 8 March–23 April 2005, pp. 4-16; p. 3 was by Norman Rosenthal.

THIRTEEN

Illustrations

IN THIS CHAPTER WHR's DESIGNS for the visual contents of publications are considered. *Illustrations* is the ordinary word for such contributions and thus has been used for the title of this chapter, even though the word does have a connotation – not appropriate for WHR – of realist depiction.[1] The aim is to signpost here all publications with WHR illustrations, except for those already examined in earlier chapters. For each publication, an indication is provided of the nature of WHR's work within it.

It is worth noting that all the published illustrations were drawn by WHR in pencil or pen and then translated by skilled engravers into engravings on boxwood blocks, from which the images could be printed on to paper. The boxwood blocks were extremely robust, and in consequence some WHR designs were recycled by publishers or by printers throughout the remainder of the nineteenth century. An example, originating with the *Art Journal*, has already been shown in Figure 7.3. Such re-uses are rarely noted in this chapter, which instead focuses only on the first use of each design.

Publications are listed here in chronological order. There was a great flowering of WHR's illustrations in the five years from 1858 to 1862, and thus they are grouped here into three periods: *Early* (1844–57), *Main* (1858–62) and *Late* (1863–70). Two symbols are used, separately or together, to flag up certain entries:

⋆A publication which contains particularly extensive designs by WHR.

†A publication whose *exterior* was also designed by WHR and hence is illustrated here in Appendix A.

EARLY (1844–57)

(1) Miss Lambert, *Church Needlework* (John Murray, 1844). There is a single drawing by WHR, of a prie-dieu, on p. 154.

(2) †Mrs. S.C. Hall (ed.), *The Drawing Room Table Book* (Virtue [1848]). The Contents list the 'Illustrated Title Page; designed by W. Harry Rogers'. The final page has a drawing bearing the monograms of both WHR and Henry Fitzcook, whose short-lived business partnership commenced in 1848 (this drawing also appeared in the next title).

(3) Mrs. S.C. Hall, *The Old Governess, a Story*, For the benefit of the Asylum for Aged

and Decayed Governesses [1848]. The author thanked '… Fairholt, Weir, Fitzcook and W. Harry Rogers (to the latter for the very Elegant Title Page,) for the Drawings …'.

(4) The *Lady's Newspaper*, with which is incorporated the *Pictorial Times*. Over the course of nine issues of this weekly newspaper in 1848, WHR appears to have both written and illustrated (and occasionally signed with his monogram) lengthy reports from Stowe, where the Duke of Buckingham's possessions went under the hammer.[2] One illustration is by Henry Fitzcook (p. 280), briefly WHR's financial partner.

(5) †S.C. Hall (ed.), *The Vernon Gallery of British Art*, the first series [of four] (Virtue, 1850). WHR contributed several large initials and an engraved dedication page directed to the eponymous Robert Vernon.

(6) ★†S.C. Hall (ed.), *The Royal Gallery of Art Ancient and Modern*, Part 1 (of 48) (London: Colnaghi; Manchester: Agnew, 1854–5). This contained several designs signed by WHR, namely, an engraved title page and a dedication page (both whole-page), the start and end of the introduction, and a large capital. The engraved title page has been reproduced in modern times, though without mentioning WHR.[3]

(7) †*Sabbath Bells Chimed by the Poets* (Bell & Daldy, 1856). The verso of the title page carries WHR's JC monogram for Joseph Cundall within a floral wreath, all hand-coloured. Figure 13.1 illustrates this. McLean observed that, with its mixture of hand-colouring and printed colour, 'it is a very pretty book indeed'. He also placed the monogram on the title page of his monograph on Cundall.[4]

13.1 – Device for Joseph Cundall by WHR, from *Sabbath Bells Chimed by the Poets*, 1856. Height 39mm.

13.2 – Title by WHR for Gray's *Elegy Written in a Country Churchyard*, 1858. Width 76mm.

MAIN (1858–62)

(8) ★†*The Poetical Works of Thomas Gray* (Sampson Low [1858]). The engraved title page and all the other embellishments are by WHR. His graceful designs chime perfectly with

Gray's graceful lines. Figure 13.2 shows the design for Gray's best-known poem, *Elegy Written in a Country Churchyard*.[5]

Gray's *Poetical Works* is a small book, but it is a close cousin of three larger gift books – typically these were illustrated editions of poetical works – which WHR adorned in the same year, and are listed next.

(9) ★*The Poetical Works of Edgar Allan Poe* (Sampson Low, 1858; also New York: Redfield). This book and the next one were both assembled by Joseph Cundall, credited in the preliminaries here for 'superintendence'. WHR's embellishments employ a suitably macabre palette.

(10) *Poems and Songs by Robert Burns* (Bell and Daldy; Edinburgh: Menzies, 1858). WHR contributed the delicate floral and foliar drawings.

(11) ★*Poetry and Pictures from Thomas Moore* (Longman, Brown, Green, 1858). WHR again provided the graceful embellishments, which occasionally deploy the shamrock in recognition of Moore's Irishness.

(12) ★Edward McDermott, *The Merrie Days of England* (Kent, 1859). This gift book is a little larger than the three books from the previous year, and the embellishments by WHR are also correspondingly larger. They often include a strapwork element consistent with the book's intended evocation of England in former days, such as the Elizabethan or Jacobean periods.

(13) ★†*The Home Treasury of Old Story Books* (Sampson Low, 1859). Also: E.V.B. *Child's Play* (Sampson Low, 1859). This pair of books superintended by Joseph Cundall both use a set of decorated capital letters devised by WHR, with matching page decoration.[6] Each letter is depicted as entwined in ribbon and resting on flowering tendrils, against a stippled background, and the head-pieces employ the same motifs.

(14) ★†*The Marriage Service. Illustrated by W. Harry Rogers* (Routledge, Warne and Routledge [1859]). This book is printed in gold throughout. Most of each page is devoted to WHR's emblematical design for the relevant part of the marriage service. Figure 13.3 shows the page that deals with exchanging vows. On a branch of a may tree, one songbird is declaiming to another. Halfway down, a moth is being drawn to the flame. Below that, a winged arrow engages

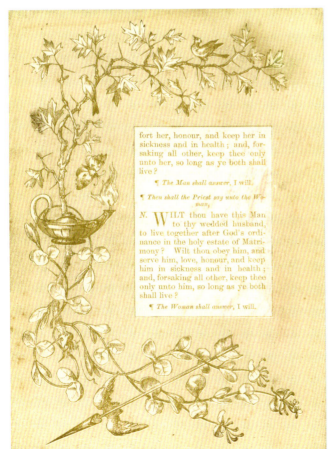

13.3 – Exchanging vows, by WHR, in *The Marriage Service*, 1859. Height 145mm.

13.4 – A page from Part F of Barclay's Monograms, 1860, by WHR. Clockwise from upper left: HF, ITDF, MEF. Height 215mm.

with tendrils of honeysuckle. At the base of the may tree there is a small WHR monogram, the tail of its R also playfully becoming a tendril which reaches almost to the arrow.

(15) *Once a Week*, Vol. 1, 1859. The same decoration by WHR occurred in the preliminaries for each volume of this journal's first series, 1859–65; another decoration appeared only in Vol. 1, and a title illustration in Vol. 5.[7]

(16) ★†William Shakspeare, *The Most excellent Historie of the Merchant of Venice* (Sampson Low, 1860). 'The emblematical devices and ornaments were designed by Harry Rogers,' p. vii. It is another Cundall book.

(17) ★*Monograms by G. Barclay, assisted by [three monograms: TF, WHR, IB] and others* [1860]. This was a part-work in which each part dealt with a particular surname initial, and provided examples of monograms combining that letter with various forename initials, with up to twenty monograms on each of several pages. At this period, monograms were frequently employed to personalise items such as stationery and silverware. Figure 13.4 reproduces a page by WHR with unusually elaborate designs.

(18) *The Children's Pilgrim's Progress* (Bell and Daldy, 1860). This was another Cundall production, whose large title page ornament is signed WHR.

(19) †Louise Chandler, *Evaline, Madelon, and Other Poems* (Bumpus, 1861). (The cover of this book re-used an existing WHR cover design, listed in Appendix A as *72. Pastoral Poems, 1858*.) The book contains several designs by WHR, probably donated by him since it was a charitable production for the Sisters' Memorial Fund, which established a Hospital for the Paralysed and Epileptic.

(20) ★†*Quarles' Emblems. Illustrated by Charles Bennett and W. Harry Rogers* (James Nisbet and Co., 1861). This re-imagining of the famous emblem book of Francis Quarles (1592–1644) was an extensive collaboration between WHR and his friend, Charles Bennett, packed with eighty full-page engravings. On each page, WHR drew the outer design and Bennett drew the inner picture, transcending the relatively crude sketches published centuries earlier.

Figure 13.5 shows the frontispiece of the book, in which WHR provided a glossary for some of his emblematical language. The following list proceeds clockwise from the mid-left part of the outer design. In each case, WHR's Latin term is first translated into its English equivalent, and then its emblem is described:

TERRA	Earth	Orb with terrestrial markings
MVNDVS	Universe	Orb without terrestrial markings
LIBIDO	Lust	Cockerel
VANITAS	Pride	Peacock
AMOR	Love	Heart
COELVM	Heaven	Armillary sphere
STVLTITIA	Folly	Jester's cap
MORS	Death	Skull
MALVM	Evil	Serpent
ANIMA	Soul	Butterfly

Chapter Thirteen – Illustrations

13.5 – The frontispiece of Quarles' Emblems, 1861, with WHR's emblematical glossary. Height 160mm.

Despite the accomplishments of both artists, the effects of their yoked illustrations sometimes seem no more than the sum of the two parts. WHR may have felt the same, because the following year he produced *Spiritual Conceits* on his own, as described in Chapter 12. Decades later, Lewis F. Day discussed the *Quarles' Emblems* volume, and was emphatic in highlighting 'Harry Rogers, who was responsible for what was best in the book'.[8]

After the premature deaths of both Bennett and WHR, their illustrations were reproduced in full in 1881 in the final volume of Alexander Grosart's complete edition of the works of *Quarles*. Grosart enthused:[9]

> I have been enabled (at considerable cost) to furnish the very remarkable new illustrations of Bennett and Rogers ... none will differ from me in affirming that in the new 'Emblems'—skilfully incorporating as they do the earlier—of Bennett and Rogers, that it is our privilege to furnish in these works, the thing has been done imperishably.

Grosart also clarified who had been charging him so much:[10]

> For the illustrations of the 'Emblems' by Charles H. Bennett and W. Harry Rogers, I am indebted to an arrangement with their proprietor, the late James Watson, Esq., of Messrs. James Nisbet and Company.

Prompted by Grosart's initiative, Nisbet re-issued the book themselves in 1886, the new contents unchanged (apart from the date) from those of a quarter-century earlier.

(21) *The Boy's Book of Ballads* (Bell and Daldy, 1861). The book has been attributed to Cundall.[11] The decorations and capital letters are by WHR, some bearing his monogram. There are proofs in the WHR archive at the V&A.[12]

(22) †*The Chemist and Druggist* (1861). When this monthly journal was re-designed in January 1861, it featured 'tasteful emblematic illustrations which figure as headings to the several departments of the Journal.'[13] They comprised *Reviews* (pair of spectacles); *Trade Report* (notebook); *The Month* (crescent moon); *Correspondence* (quill); *Notes and Queries* (padlock and key); *Patents* (scroll with seal); and *Notes of Novelties* (moth). Though unsigned, a proof is in the WHR V&A archive.[14]

(23) †*The Grocer*, 1862. For this weekly rather than monthly periodical, WHR added a heading for *The Week* (a ribbon with the days of the week) to those borrowed from the *Chemist and Druggist*. It also is present in the WHR archive at the V&A.[15]

(24) ★*The International Exhibition of 1862. The illustrated catalogue of the Industrial Department* [four volumes] (Her Majesty's Commissioners [1862]). Designs by WHR were used liberally in these volumes. They included a version of the British coat of arms that appeared on the title page of each volume (and also on the part-issue covers). For its unexpected reappearance, see Figure 14.6.

The Catalogue section proper was preceded by a History section in twelve chapters, which were given gravitas by capital letters that each incorporated a royal crown; proofs of these are in the V&A WHR archive.[16]

(25) *International Exhibition 1862. Official catalogue of the fine art department* (Her Majesty's Commissioners [1862]). This paperback included a separately paginated *Fine Arts Catalogue*

Advertiser, which carried a rare foray into advertising by WHR (p. 6), shown in Figure 13.6. Two scrolls (signed at lower right) itemised the range of Puttick and Simpson's auctions. The charge for occupying a full page like this was £50, with a guaranteed edition size of 250,000 copies.[17]

13.6 – Advertising scrolls by WHR for Puttick and Simpson in the 1862 official Fine Arts Catalogue Advertiser. *Height 107mm.*

LATE (1863–70)

(26) *The Boy's Own Magazine* [new series], Vol. 2 (S.O. Beeton [1863]). The frame for the Victoria Cross Gallery on p. 416 was signed by WHR.

(27) *Beeton's Christmas Annual*, fifth season (S.O. Beeton [1864]). The heading on p. [3] for this annual's main story, 'Number seven. The story of somebody's son, in seven parts', was signed by WHR.

(28) †*The Wine Trade Review* (Henry S. Simpson, 1864). WHR devised a new set of emblematical section headings for this periodical, all signed, comprising: *Trade Report* (ledger); *The Month* (signs of the zodiac); *Correspondence* (quills and ink-pot); and *Wine Duties Paid* (crown resting on a vine).

(29) ★†[Lady Augusta Noel], *Effie's Friends; or, chronicles of the woods and shore. Illustrated by W. Harry Rogers* (James Nisbet & Co., 1864). WHR provided chapter headings and endings for four stories about birds – swallows, peacocks, seagulls and sparrows. He also designed an engraved title page and a device on the printed title page which names him as the illustrator of this book.

(30) ★†[Mary Eliza Rogers], *Shakspeare Memorial* (S.O. Beeton, 1864). In addition to the large engraved title page which duplicates the cover design (for the paper-covered issue), WHR provided eight full-page frames in the Elizabethan style.[18]

(31) [J. Hain Friswell], *The Gentle Life* (Sampson Low, 1864). The engraved title page for this Victorian bestseller was designed by WHR. A proof in the WHR archive at the V&A includes a signature, removed in the published version. Two years later, Hain Friswell wrote to a newspaper to accuse James Blackwood of having just published a deliberate imitation:[19]

> The publisher and author of 'The Gentle Philosopher' have taken a similar title, and have also copied the design of the title page by Mr. Harry Rogers.

(32) ★ J.G. Edgar, *Cressy and Poictiers* (S.O. Beeton, 1865). WHR contributed several handsome, signed designs.[20]

(33) † *The Young Englishwoman* (S.O. Beeton, 1865). A musical section was issued for this periodical, headed by an elaborate WHR design. Figure 13.7 shows the heading for Vol. 3, 1866.

13.7 – Heading by WHR for the music supplement to Beeton's *Young Englishwoman*, 1866. Width 183mm.

(34) † Eugene Rimmel, *The Book of Perfumes* (Chapman & Hall, 1865). The title page bore a device simplified from the front cover, signed WHR. It surfaced the following year in two other places: on the printed title page of the French translation of Rimmel's book and in an advertisement for Rimmel's perfumes.[21]

(35) † J.G. Edgar, *Runnymede and Lincoln Fair* (S.O. Beeton, [1866]). The title page indicates 'heraldic' embellishments by WHR.

(36) *Beeton's Musical Album for 1866* (S.O. Beeton, 1866). The engraved title page was signed by WHR; a proof of it is in the V&A WHR archive.[22]

(37) *Beeton's Annual; a book for the young* (Frederick Warne & Co., 1866). WHR contributed three designs, a decorated title at the start, a parody coat-of-arms and a closing Amen.[23]

(38) James Greenwood, *Reminiscences of a raven* (Frederick Warne and Co., 1866). The title page has a device, signed by WHR, for 'S.O. Beeton's Books.'

(39) ★ *Lyra consolationis* (James Nisbet & Co., 1866). The designs within this book are by WHR (except for the engraved title page, signed PJ). Figure 13.8 shows the drop-head title on p. [1], signed WHR. Artwork for this is in the V&A WHR archive, along with proofs for ten of the book's many other designs (mostly unsigned).[24]

Uniquely, WHR drew only in outline, with no filled spaces. The outcome appears underpowered relative to his other work, and the experiment was not repeated.

(40) † *Psalms and Hymns for Divine Worship* (Nisbet, 1866). The title page bears a device, signed WHR, which is essentially the same as the unsigned gilt device on the cover.

(41) † Andrew Halliday (ed.), *The Savage-Club Papers* (Tinsley, 1867). WHR designed the engraved title page (and the device at the start of the text) for the original volume, 1867, which was used also for the second series, 1868, and then transferred to the cover of the yellowback issue.

(42) † *Excelsior Reader*. Also: *Excelsior Arithmetic* (Murby [1868]). The engraved title page designed by WHR in 1868 was later used on the card covers of some of Murby's titles.

(43) ★† *A Bushel of Merry-thoughts by Wilhelm Busch. Described and ornamented by Harry Rogers* (Sampson Low, 1868).

13.8 – Heading by WHR for *Lyra consolationis*, 1866, an experiment in leaving outlines unfilled. Width 74mm.

Cover designs for each of the four component stories, when published separately, were supplied by WHR, and these doubled as engraved title pages. In addition, WHR provided explanatory verses for the stories and additional designs. Figure 13.9 shows WHR's design 'Look before you leap' for the story *Cat and Mouse*, in which a cat chasing a mouse gets its head jammed in an old boot.

13.9 – 'Look before you leap' by WHR, in *Cat and Mouse,* from *A Bushel of Merry-thoughts,* 1868. Width 182mm.

Chapter Thirteen – Illustrations

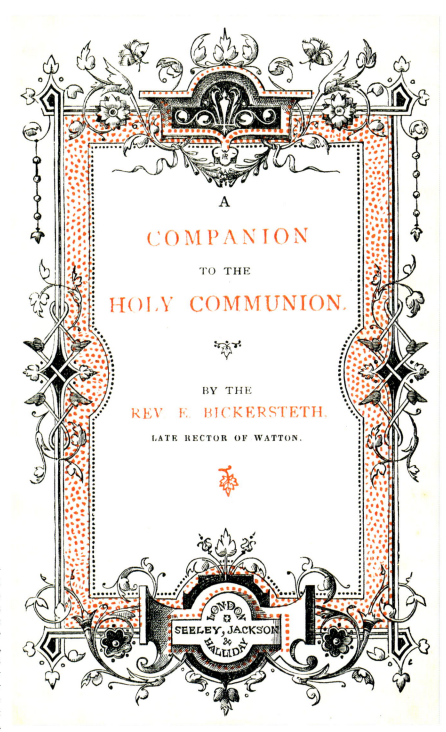

13.10 – Engraved title page to Bickersteth's *A Companion to the Holy Communion*, 1869, with WHR's monogram for once placed near the top of the design. Height 102mm.

(44) Rev. E. Bickersteth, *A Companion to the Holy Communion*, 38th edition (Seeley, Jackson, & Halliday, 1869). This book was issued with a variety of options, such as different types of cover. From the 38th to the 43rd edition, some copies had an added engraved title page by WHR. Figure 13.10 shows the engraved title page, which is unique among WHR's designs in placing his monogram near the top (just above the first word, 'A'), instead of the base.

(45) G. Barclay (ed.), *Thirty varieties of the monogram JB … Dedicated to the Right Hon. John Bright*. Barclay [1869]. Thirteen of the monograms are listed as by WHR.

(46) S.O. Beeton (ed.), *Beeton's Great Book of Poetry* (Ward, Lock, & Tyler [1870]). The first page of the main text consists of a signed WHR design for 'The Book of Poetry'.

During the final years of his life, in the 1870s, WHR moved away from a concern with the visual contents of publications, but continued to produce his characteristically artistic designs in other areas, as described in the following chapters.

NOTES

1. Alternative terms, such as *graphic art*, would be possible, but have their own misleading connotations.

2. *The Lady's Newspaper*, Vol. 4, 19 August to 14 October 1848: pp. 149-50, 160-61, 195-6, 200-01, 236, 240, 276, 280, 300.

3. Jonathan Marsden (ed.), *Victoria & Albert: Art & Love* (Royal Collection Publications, 2010), p. 46.

4. Ruari McLean, *Victorian Book Design and Colour Printing* (second edition, Faber & Faber, 1972), p. 148; Ruari McLean, *Joseph Cundall: A Victorian Publisher* (Pinner: Private Libraries Association, 1976). McLean mentioned (p. 36) that the monogram 'seems to have first appeared in The Pleasures of Hope … in 1855', but it has not been found there in a number of copies examined.

5. *The Poetical Works of Thomas Gray* (Sampson Low [1858]), p. [53].

6. Proofs are in the WHR V&A Archive, E851-1998, p. 53.

7. *Once a Week*, Vol. 1, pp. iv and 470; 'Compensation', Vol. 5, p. 329.

8. Report of 'Discussion' by the Chairman, Lewis F. Day, of 'English book illustration: 1860–1870', *Journal of the Society of Arts*, Vol. 44, 1896, pp. 455-66; p. 465.

9. Rev. Alexander B. Grosart, *The Complete Works in Prose and Verse of Francis Quarles*, in three volumes (privately printed, 1880–81), Vol. 1, pp. lxv-lxvi & lxxiv; Vol. 3, pp. 105-84.

10. *Ibid.*, Vol. 3, p. 104.

11. McLean, *Cundall, op. cit.*, p. 85.

12. V&A E851-1998, p [6].

13. *Chemist and Druggist*, Vol. 2, 15 January 1861, p. 4.

14. V&A E851-1998, p. [10].

15. V&A E851-1998, p. [64].

16. John Hollingshead, *A Concise History of the International Exhibition of 1862*, in Volume 1; V&A E851-1998, p. [51].

17. *Ibid.*, p. 126.

18. [Mary Eliza Rogers], *Shakspeare memorial* (S.O. Beeton, 1864), pp. [28-29], [32-33], [36-37] and [40-41].

19. V&A E851-1998, p. [75]; The *Pall Mall Gazette*, 23 June 1866.

20. J.G. Edgar, *Cressy and Poictiers* (S.O. Beeton, 1865), pp. 81, 146, 161, 170, 179, 189, 193.

21. Eugène Rimmel, *Le livre des parfums* (Paris: E. Dentu [*c.* 1866]); *Chemist and Druggist*, 15 December 1866, p. [6].

22. V&A E1135.29-1998.

23. *Beeton's Annual; a book for the young* (Frederick Warne & Co., 1866), pp. [1], 317, 491.

24. V&A E694.61-1998; E1135.40-1998 to E1135.49-1998.

FOURTEEN

Playing Cards

TWO AREAS OF DESIGN IN WHICH WHR was most active in the 1870s, in the final years of his life, are considered next – cards and, in the following chapter, jewellery. A small but interesting part of WHR's output was concerned with playing cards, and more generally with the area of stationery.

In 1858, WHR contributed three designs for card-backs to the *Art Journal*.[1] The accompanying text credited De La Rue with the introduction of card-back designs:

> Until of late years the backs of playing-cards were invariably plain, and we imagine we are indebted to Messrs. De La Rue for an introduction that brings Art in a novel form to our tables.

At De La Rue, playing card backs was one of their areas of design that had in practice been devolved to the well-known figure of Owen Jones. In modern times, many of his designs have been illustrated.[2] Undaunted by the involvement of Owen Jones, however, the *Art Journal* levelled some justified criticism at the De La Rue designs:

> But the designs they furnish are, for the most part, unsuited to the object, consisting often of large flowers which cover only portions of the surface, and are by no means either appropriate or refined.

Figure 14.1 reproduces the three WHR designs for card-backs published by the *Art Journal* as a corrective to the De La Rue designs. From left to right, they were described as Grolier work, a border of Indian decoration around a native plant and Italian foliage.

When WHR came to think of designing playing cards for a specific manufacturer, he turned to the firm of Charles Goodall, having presumably made himself persona non grata at De La Rue. Goodall and De La Rue were for many years the two major British makers of playing cards. Two different WHR designs for a Goodall & Son Ace of Spades exist in the WHR archive at the V&A, but neither appears to have been put into production.[3] Instead, WHR turned to a more niche manufacturer of playing cards, as follows.

RENAISSANCE PLAYING CARD

WHR was associated with two firms that operated independently but were linked in

terms of ownership. These were the playing card manufacturers Joseph Hunt & Sons and the paper-makers Fourdrinier, Hunt & Co. Although they maintained separate presences in Britain, they were to be found bracketed together abroad, in the pages of the *Publishers' Weekly* of New York in 1874. There, the New York branch of the London publishers Cassell, Petter & Galpin announced:[4]

14.1 – Designs for playing cards by WHR, described as *(left to right)* Grolier, Indian and Italian; from the *Art Journal*, 1858. Height of images 97mm.

> that they have been appointed sole agents in the United States for the Stationery of Fourdrinier, Hunt & Sons [*sic* – for Co.], London, and for the celebrated Playing Cards of Joseph Hunt & Sons.

A fortnight later, Cassell, Petter & Galpin listed in considerable detail, alongside their own books, the Joseph Hunt playing cards and the Fourdrinier, Hunt writing papers.[5] For playing cards, they listed for example Joseph Hunt's *130 Robin*, *135 Love-Birds* and *136 Wren* playing card packs, each at $15 per dozen. Figure 14.2 shows a card from each of these packs, with the pictorial card-back in each case signed by the popular Victorian animal artist, Harrison Weir. For writing papers, they listed a considerable number of combinations of paper size and paper quality, as considered later.

In 1871, WHR designed a splendid pack for Joseph Hunt & Sons which is shown in Figure 14.3. This was Hunt's *126 Renaissance* design (or perhaps their *123 Italian* design). The design featured a striking pair of elongated griffins (a griffin being a lion with an eagle's beak and wings).

Unlike Harrison Weir's birds, the WHR design was not advertised in the 1874 *Publishers' Weekly* in New York. However, all four of these designs had first appeared together in the UK three years previously, listed in the same advertisement.[6] The manufacturer proudly claimed there that

Chapter Fourteen – Playing Cards

> … the services of some of the leading Decorative Artists having been secured, these Cards are now unsurpassed either for elegance and variety of design or perfectness of manufacture.

The editorial pages in the previous month's issue had welcomed the new Joseph Hunt designs,[7] 'some of the specimens possessing unusual artistic excellence'.

Two other contemporary critics were more specific in their praise. First, Llewellynn Jewitt edited the *Reliquary* and included a lengthy article on playing cards that was extremely enthusiastic about Hunt's designs:[8]

> Some of the new patterns for the present season, of this firm, are more beautiful and more pure in design than any we have seen … the Arabesques, the Renaissance, the Italian, the Japanese, and other patterns, are as exquisite as exquisite can be. … It is not too much to say that some of the specialities of the season, of Messrs. Hunt's production, are such perfect pictures that they deserve framing for preservation.

Second, the quarterly *Book-buyer's Guide* reviewed Joseph Hunt's new *Book of Patterns*, and thought that the WHR design was irresistible:[9]

> The designs, however, are so various that every taste may be gratified. The Italian and Renaissance styles will, we think be generally preferred. Messrs. Hunt and Sons' book should be inspected. The only danger is that the inspectors will be too well pleased to resist the desire to invest in a few packs. They might invest their money worse in other matters.

14.2 – Three pictorial playing cards signed by Harrison Weir, for Joseph Hunt & Sons. *Left to right:* Robin, Love-Birds and Wren. The outer pair are dated 1870. Height of images 95mm.

163

It is a pity that it has not been possible to trace any surviving copy of the Joseph Hunt *Book of Patterns*, since it might well contain further designs by WHR. The WHR archive at the V&A contains several other designs for card-backs which it is possible were put into production.

At this point, it is relevant to enquire how WHR can be identified as the designer of the Renaissance card-back, given that the image is not signed. The answer is that there is a detailed sketch of the design in the WHR archive at the V&A.[10] In the sketch, a WHR monogram is enclosed by the small circle situated centrally about a quarter of the way up the design, though this did not appear on the card as manufactured.

Only a partial pack of these WHR playing cards with the V&A design has been located, and it does not include an Ace of Spades, traditionally the only card in a pack to bear the maker's name. One therefore might also wonder how the maker of the WHR playing cards can be identified. Identification is possible because the precise iconography of each of the twelve court-cards in a pack varied with the maker and the period. Figure 14.4 shows on its left the Queen of Clubs pattern which occurs on the other side of a WHR Renaissance card, and is known to have been used only by Joseph Hunt & Sons in the period *c.* 1865–*c.* 1875.[11] By a remarkable coincidence, the lithographic stone used for printing the black key image of this particular set of court cards has survived, perhaps uniquely.[12] Figure 14.4 shows on its right the Ace of Spades used by Joseph Hunt & Sons at that time (though it comes from another pack).

14.3 – Renaissance playing card design by WHR for Joseph Hunt & Sons, 1871. Height 95mm.

PILGRIMAGES PLAYING CARD

Reynolds & Sons was another minor manufacturer of playing cards, but less ambitious than Joseph Hunt & Sons. In about 1880, and doubtless without permission, it borrowed a WHR design of thirty years earlier as the frame for a playing-card back. This is shown in Figure 14.5, together with its Ace of Spades.

The frame is a simplified copy of the WHR design for the cover of *Pilgrimages to English Shrines* (1850) that appeared in the *Art Journal* catalogue of the Great Exhibition (see Figure 11.4). Shoehorned inside the WHR frame is an unrelated palm motif, which appears to be based on a silk design by Gabain of Berlin in the same catalogue.[13]

Chapter Fourteen – Playing Cards

*14.4 –
Left:* Queen of Clubs from a Renaissance pack. *Right:* A matching Ace of Spades. Height 95mm.

*14.5 –
Left:* An 1850 WHR design adapted in about 1880 for the outer part of a playing card by Reynolds & Sons. *Right:* Its Ace of Spades. Height 94mm.

165

SOVEREIGNS OF ENGLAND

This was a card game produced by the leading game manufacturer, John Jaques and Son. An advertisement on p. 3 of *The Times* for 29 October 1870 listed it as one of their 'New winter games', price 1s. In addition to thirty-six cards each showing a king or queen, it included 'The Game Card' which displayed the Royal Arms, printed in colours. The same Royal Arms were engraved on the box which held the cards, as shown in Figure 14.6. The engraving bore the monograms of WHR as designer and Edmund Evans (EE) as engraver.

The engraving of the Royal Arms was not newly made for the game, however. It was recycled from the blocks used for the *Official Illustrated Catalogue* for the International Exhibition of 1862, having appeared (surrounded by foliage) on the paper wrappers of the issue in parts, and on the title pages of the issue in cloth-bound volumes.

14.6 – The Sovereigns of England game, showing its design signed by WHR.
Left: Original box, 1870.
Right: Modified maker's name, c. 1900.
Below: The Game Card.
Card width 92mm.

Chapter Fourteen – Playing Cards

FOURDRINIER, HUNT

At the start of the nineteenth century, the Fourdriniers were wholesale stationers in London who developed the first paper-making machine. In 1809 they had had to bring in additional finance from, among others, a member of the Hunt family of playing card makers, eventually becoming Fourdrinier, Hunt & Co.[14]

In Fourdrinier, Hunt's previously-mentioned 1874 advertisement in New York, it listed its wide range of writing papers which were sold 'In 5 quire pkts. handsome wrap'.[15] *Large Post* paper was available in three grades of their *Fourdrinier* brand, while *Small Post* paper was available both in two grades of *Fourdrinier* and in two grades of their cheaper brand *Sherborne* (so called because for many years Fourdrinier, Hunt had premises at 12 Sherborne Lane).

It appears that WHR was invited by Fourdrinier, Hunt to design the 'handsome wraps' for these packets of differing sizes and grades, amounting to five *Fourdrinier* and two *Sherborne* types. Unfortunately, no extant wrapper has been traced for any of them. However, the WHR archive at the V&A contains extensive artwork: three *Fourdrinier* covers and two *Sherborne* covers, plus a *Sherborne* side-strip.[16] On timing, the first two *Fourdrinier* artworks listed here are inscribed by WHR with his final address in Charles Street, and thus it seems quite likely that the Fourdrinier, Hunt commission was linked to his 1871 playing card commission for Joseph Hunt & Sons.

Finally, it is noteworthy that the *Fourdrinier* and *Sherborne* artworks are scattered over two different albums, E693 and E694, in the WHR archive at the V&A. This strongly suggests that these albums were compiled from unsorted WHR material after the death of the artist. The compiler was probably WHR's sister, Mary Eliza Rogers, protecting her brother's legacy on behalf of his orphaned children.

NOTES

1. Original designs, as suggestions to manufacturers, etc, *Art Journal*, new series, Vol. 4, March 1858, p. 90.
2. Michael Cooper and Ken Lodge, 'Owen Jones (1809–1874): Architect, decorative artist & designer of playing cards', *Playing-Card*, 2006, Vol. 34, No. 3, pp. 181-92.
3. V&A E693.119-1998, E693.121-1998.
4. *Publishers' Weekly*, 7 February 1874, p. 145.
5. *Publishers' Weekly*, 21 February 1874, p. 201.
6. *Stationer & Fancy Trades' Register*, 5 September 1871, p. 201.
7. *Ibid.*, p. 72.
8. Art at the card table, *Reliquary*, Vol. 12, 1871–2, pp. 178-80; p. 179.
9. *Book-buyer's Guide*, No. 7, September 1871, pp. 12-13.
10. V&A E693.123-1998.
11. Ken Lodge, *The Standard English Pattern*, second

revised and enlarged edition (Norwich: privately printed, 2016), pp. 119-24; Michael H. Goodall, *Joseph Hunt & Sons* (Woking: privately printed, 1997), pp. 12-17.
12. The key stone is illustrated (and described by Ken Lodge) in Mike Goodall, Sue Gosling and Keith Bonnick, 'Playing-cards of the Cuming Museum: English Pattern cards and artefacts', *Playing-Card*, 2003, Vol. 31, No. 6, pp. 253-61; see pp. 254-6.
13. *Art Journal* catalogue (Virtue, 1851), pp. 39 and 55.
14. Goodall, *Joseph Hunt, op. cit.*, pp. 6-11.
15. *Publishers' Weekly*, 21 February 1874, p. 201.
16. Fourdrinier: V&A E693.117-1998, E693.118-1998 and E693.150-1998. Sherborne: E694.35-1998 and E694.102-1998. Sherborne side-strip: E694.4-1998.

FIFTEEN

Jewellery

IT COMES AS NO SURPRISE THAT, as an artist with a special gift for designing the graceful and elegant, WHR was interested in the creation of jewellery. The first practical expression of this interest came in 1847 when he designed a striking brooch to present to his bride, Mary Ann Lansdale, shown as Figure 2.3.

Three years later, WHR came into direct contact with the highest echelons of contemporary jewellery when he produced four pages of illustrations in the *Art Journal* of the works of Jean-Valentin Morel, a leading French jeweller.[1] Morel had been goldsmith to Louis Philippe in Paris, but moved to London after Louis Philippe lost the French throne in 1848. WHR's drawing was perfectly adapted to capturing the lusciousness of Morel's jewellery. As an example, Figure 15.1 reproduces p. 291 of the *Art Journal* article. This page has also been reproduced by Shirley Bury, though she did not mention that the images were drawn by WHR.[2]

Despite WHR's evident interest in jewellery, he does not appear to have been explicitly credited with designing jewellery that was put into production until much later, for Howell & James.[3]

Howell & James was a large store in Regent Street. Shirley Bury was amusing about their aspirations at the 1862 London Exhibition:[4]

> Howell James & Company optimistically describe themselves as 'Goldsmiths, silversmiths, etc.' rather than (as they were) vendors with an eye to fashion.

A decade later, Howell & James made a more determined bid to break into the top flight of jewellers by commissioning five well-known artists and architects to design jewellery for them to show at the London 1872 Exhibition. The five were WHR, John Leighton, Lewis F. Day, Charles Eastlake and Sir Matthew Digby Wyatt. The designs that they submitted fell into two categories that sat awkwardly with each other. The designs of WHR, Leighton and Day were oriented towards the emblematic, but those of Eastlake and Wyatt were oriented toward the antique and geometrical, so the collection as a whole lacked coherence.

Some circumstantial evidence suggests that WHR took the lead with Howell & James on the emblematic front. First, an essay by WHR entitled 'Emblematical Art as applied to jewellery' is present in the WHR archive at the V&A.[5] This is a manuscript copy sent

15.1 – Drawings by WHR of jewels by Jean-Valentin Morel, in the *Art Journal*, 1850. Image height 275mm.

in 1871 (postmark) to the artist J.B. Coughtrie, who became WHR's son-in-law in that year. WHR may have been soliciting comments on an article intended for a Howell James booklet. The same archive also holds WHR's artwork for a title page design for the same title.[6] In addition, there is a proof in the same archive of a paper cover designed by WHR for 'Howell James & Co. Goldsmiths, Jewellers &c to the Queen and the Prince and Princess of Wales', which could have been intended for a booklet to be distributed to favoured visitors at the 1872 exhibition.[7]

15.2 – Three lockets designed by WHR for Howell & James. *Left:* Betrothal. *Centre:* Bridal (with modern colouring). *Right:* Bridesmaid's. 1872 London Exhibition. Image heights 55-65 mm.

By the time of the exhibition in 1872, however, WHR's health was declining, and he is less prominent in some reports of the Howell & James jewellery than would otherwise have been the case. Nevertheless, a number of items of jewellery designed by WHR and exhibited by Howell & James at the London 1872 Exhibition can be identified – four lockets and a bracelet. No surviving examples have been located, but all except one were illustrated at the time. Figure 15.2 shows three of the lockets.

BETROTHAL LOCKET

On the left of Figure 15.2 is a betrothal locket designed by WHR which appeared in the *Art Journal* illustrated catalogue of the London 1872 exhibition, though with no mention of its designer.[8]

Attribution of the betrothal locket to WHR is made possible by cross-reference to another journal. It was one of four WHR exhibits described in some detail in a short-lived journal entitled *The Ladies*.[9] This journal said of the Howell & James jewellery as a whole:

> The 'Emblematical Jewellery' contained in this case is its most noteworthy feature. We have here a whole series of works designed not merely as things of beauty, but for the purpose of expressing at the same time a graceful idea. … Among the

emblematical jewellery which strikes us as having especial merit are …

For 'Harry Rogers', the first of the items then listed was:

the betrothal locket, by Mr. Rogers, two hearts, one in pearl the other in turquoise, united by a love-knot.

Clearly this is the same Howell & James item as was illustrated by the *Art Journal*.

BRIDAL LOCKET

The Ladies followed its description of the WHR betrothal locket with a description of his bridal locket:

the bridal locket, by the same designer, with marriage bells and the torch of Hymen, surrounded by a wedding-ring.

The *Art Journal* did not provide an engraving of this locket, but a photograph of it was provided in another journal, *Art Pictorial and Industrial*, and this is shown in the centre of Figure 15.2. This monthly journal reproduced photographs using the heliotype process, a recently-invented variety of the collotype process, and ran two articles on the Howell & James jewellery. The first article appeared before the Exhibition opened.[10] The second article appeared two months later, and included an illustration of the WHR bridal locket.[11] Its text, however, overlooked the surrounding wedding ring and misidentified the locket as intended for a bridesmaid rather than a bride:

The oval bridesmaid's locket, with wedding bells, hymeneal torch and bow, is by Mr. Harry Rogers.

The real bridesmaid's locket is considered next.

BRIDESMAID'S LOCKET

The bridesmaid's locket by WHR is shown on the right of Figure 15.2 and, like the bridal locket, includes the torch of Hymen, the Greek god of wedding ceremonies, in this case alongside a wreath of orange blossom. As with WHR's betrothal locket, this engraving appeared without labelling in the account of the Howell & James jewellery in the *Art Journal* catalogue.[12]

LILY LOCKET

One further WHR locket was described by *The Ladies*:

the locket with the lily, the emblem of purity, by Mr. Rogers.

However, no illustration of this locket has been found.

MARRIAGE BRACELET

Finally, Figure 15.3 shows an engraving of WHR's marriage bracelet which also appeared without labelling in the *Art Journal* illustrated catalogue.[13] Again, the bracelet can be identified because of its detailed description in *The Ladies*:

> There is one other emblematical bracelet which we should mention. It is by Mr. Rogers, and embodies an exceedingly pretty fancy—fairy marriage bells ringing from a spray of orange blossoms.

WHR AND LEWIS F. DAY

It is pleasing that WHR was spared long enough to see his jewellery designs put into production for the 1872 exhibition. At first sight, it is surprising that the *Art Journal* supplement for the London 1872 exhibition published engravings of WHR's designs without crediting him. A likely explanation is that, owing to illness, WHR was not much in evidence by the time that the exhibition opened in May 1872. It would be sad if this meant that he did not get to meet one of the four other Howell & James designers, Lewis F. Day.

Lewis F. Day was aged twenty-seven at the time of the exhibition, and had commenced his long and successful career as an independent designer only in 1869. Cementing his link with Howell & James, a year after the exhibition he married the sister of one of their directors.[14] In later years, Day affirmed on more than one occasion that he had always been a great admirer of WHR's works. It is therefore to be hoped that the paths of WHR and of Lewis F. Day did in fact cross when they both designed jewellery for the Howell & James display at the 1872 International Exhibition in London.

15.3 – Marriage bracelet designed by WHR for Howell & James, from the *Art Journal* catalogue of the 1872 Exhibition. Image width 57mm.

Chapter Fifteen – Jewellery

NOTES

1. *Art Journal*, Vol. 2, September 1850, pp. 289-92; WHR was identified on p. 289.
2. Shirley Bury, *Jewellery 1789–1910*, two vols (Woodbridge: Antique Collectors' Club, 1991), Vol. 1, p. 395.
3. The firm had started as Howell & James in 1819, but by 1832 its official name was Howell, James & Co. However, it was still widely known as Howell & James, and this was later officially re-adopted, in the form of Howell & James Ltd in 1884. 'Howell & James' is used here, following the example of Joan Maria Hansen, 'Howell & James of London: Retailing the Aesthetic Movement', *Journal of the Decorative Arts Society*, 2010, No. 34, pp. 20-41; pp. 21-2, 38.
4. Bury, *Jewellery, op. cit.*, Vol. 2, p. 457.
5. V&A E1137-1998.
6. V&A E694.62-1998.
7. V&A E824-1998; a proof 'Price-list' heading seems to belong typographically with the cover,

V&A E694.172-1998.
8. *The Art Journal Catalogue of the International Exhibition: Second Division* (Virtue & Co, 1872), p. 5.
9. *The Ladies: A Journal of the Court Fashion and Society*. The Howell & James jewellery is described on the first page of its 18 May 1872 supplement.
10. *Art Pictorial and Industrial*, Vol. 3, May 1872, p. 78; the illustration opposite p. 78 was reproduced by Bury, *Jewellery, op. cit.*, Vol. 2, p. 452.
11. *Art Pictorial and Industrial*, new series, Vol. 1, July 1872, pp. 7-8; heliotype opposite p. 7.
12. *The Art Journal Catalogue of the International Exhibition: Second Division, op. cit.*, p. 50.
13. *Ibid.*, p. 5.
14. Joan Maria Hansen, *Lewis Foreman Day (1845– 1910): Unity in Design and Industry* (Woodbridge: Antique Collectors' Club, 2007), pp. 20-22.

SIXTEEN

Book Covers

ALTHOUGH WHR DESIGNED MANY TYPES of artefacts, the objects as executed rarely carried his signature. The covers of his books are the exception, because almost all of those designed by WHR can be identified by his monogram signature. Consequently, it is his book cover designs which demonstrate most readily WHR's unlimited ability to create designs that draw and hold the eye; each design unique, yet each recognisably from the same hand. In this chapter, an account of WHR's peerless designs is preceded by a brief sketch of the general history of book cover design in the nineteenth century. Several book covers created by other designers are illustrated in this chapter, but all known by the author to have been created by WHR are gathered together and illustrated in Appendix A.

BOOK COVER DESIGN IN THE NINETEENTH CENTURY

From the 1820s, the traditional process of hand-binding copies of a title individually in leather began to be supplanted by the process of covering a whole edition of the title uniformly in identical cases covered with specialised sized bookcloth. Soon the bookcloth was also usually embossed with a fine grain, such as that of morocco (popular from the 1830s onwards). As well as employing a relatively inexpensive material, cloth casing had a major advantage in preparation time over traditional binding because the two processes of making the book cover and sewing the book contents could be carried out independently. The result was that books became more affordable, bringing in large new readerships.

The process of decorating these cloth covers with designs stamped out of sheets of gold leaf, using small custom-engraved brass blocks, was introduced in 1832.[1] The designs engraved on the brasses were initially modest, such as a shield or rectangle around the title on the spine, harking back to the use of hand tools to stamp small gilt decorations on leather. Soon, small gilt pictures were introduced, together with formulaic scrolls in gilt or without it ('in blind'). By the 1840s the brasses were getting larger and were starting to be used on the front cover as well as the spine of the book, but the designs themselves were still prosaic. Signs of an increase in artistic calibre were however starting to appear.

Chapter Sixteen – Book Covers

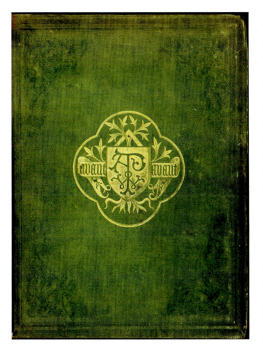

A.W.N. PUGIN

A notable exception to the nondescript results of the first decade of gilt blocking on cloth was a cover designed by Augustus Welby Northmore Pugin (1812–52) for one of his own books, *True Principles*.[2] Figure 16.1 shows the front cover of *True Principles*, which was quarter-bound (i.e. spine only) in leather. On the cloth-bound front Pugin boldly placed centre-stage his own AWP monogram and motto in a harmonious composition of shield, scroll and foliage.[3] Soon after, Pugin designed a similarly striking gold-blocked cover for another of his own books, *Glossary of ecclesiastical ornament* (Henry Bohn, 1844).

In their combination of invention and elegance, Pugin's designs for his own book covers, though few, provide the only real precedents for WHR's designs. It was not so much that the designers shared a particular vocabulary of design – WHR's influences were to be found primarily in classicism, rather than Pugin's gothic – but more that the designs of both combined imaginativeness with surefooted virtuosity in execution. Wainwright likewise has asserted that Pugin's *True Principles* and *Glossary* covers must have been 'the inspiration' for WHR's design for Ruskin's *Seven Lamps of Architecture* (1849) 'although it in no way copies a Pugin design'.[4] WHR did indeed display his admiration for Pugin publicly at the 1862 International Exhibition in London by exhibiting a design by Pugin for a portrait frame.[5]

16.1 – The cover of *True Principles*, 1841, designed by A.W.N. Pugin. Height 263mm.

OWEN JONES AND NOEL HUMPHREYS

It was in the second half of the 1840s, when WHR was entering his twenties, that a number of artists became increasingly interested in the burgeoning opportunities afforded by book covers. Two of the earliest were Owen Jones (1809–74) and Henry Noel Humphreys (1810–79). However, neither of them was to design much for what had already become the standard type of cover, in cloth. Figure 16.2 shows the cover for *The Preacher* (Longman, 1849), which is moulded in wood. It contains an illuminated text by Owen Jones, who also designed the cover, though the three-dimensional pattern for stamping the cover was carved by WHR's father, William Gibbs Rogers.[6]

Both Jones and Humphreys became particularly associated with novel types of elaborate book cover which could only be executed under licence from patent holders. From 1846, Jones designed 'Relievo' covers, usually tan-coloured, on which a design in blind was impressed in deep relief in leather. From about 1845, Humphreys designed carton-pierre (also known as papier-mâché) covers, usually coloured black, for which a moulded design in blind was again created in deep relief.[7] Only a dozen or two designs for either type of cover were ever produced.

Figure 16.3 shows the carton-pierre cover for *The Coinage of the British Empire* by Noel Humphreys (Bogue, 1855), pierced and with a red paper underlay. The prominent HR

175

16.2 – The cover of *The Preacher*, 1849, stamped in wood according to a pattern designed by Owen Jones and carved by William Gibbs Rogers. Height 289mm.

16.3 – The cover of Noel Humphreys' *The Coinage of the British Empire*, 1855. The front and back panels have the same design in carton pierre. Height 255mm.

beneath the shield has been mistaken for the signature of W. Harry Rogers.[8] It actually represents Henricus Rex, the design being based on a sovereign of Henry VIII (Plate VI, No. 13 in the book).

JOHN LEIGHTON

The heyday for gilt cloth-bound books was in the 1850s and 1860s, by which time their designs had grown larger, more decorative and more diverse. The covers' power to attract the purchaser had been realised by the publisher, and their potential as a canvas had been realised by the artist. Though many designs were anonymous, some artists, like WHR, took to signing their cover designs.

John Leighton (1822–1912), an energetic scion of the prominent bookbinding Leighton family, designed book covers over the same period as WHR, from the late 1840s until the early 1870s, usually signing them with the letters JL. He was the only person whose designs for book covers exceeded those of WHR in quantity, though not in quality. His more formal work generally lacked WHR's graceful inventiveness and fine lines, as illustrated by *Pearls from the Poets* (1870), shown as Figure 16.4.[9] Lewis F. Day noted:[10]

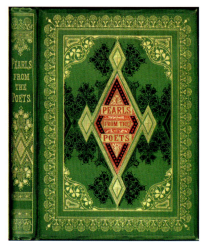

16.4 – The cover of *Pearls from the Poets* (1870), designed by John Leighton (signed JL on the front). Bound by Leighton Son and Hodge. Height 227mm.

> [Harry Rogers] was an excellent draughtsman too, in which respect he compares more than favourably with John Leighton,

Chapter Sixteen – Book Covers

his only competitor in designing for printers and bookbinders. ... John Leighton's drawing strikes one as hard-handed; there is an air of painstaking about it.

Where Leighton's talent did lie, however, was in his production of a seemingly endless variety of charming figural vignettes for the covers of numerous children's books. Using his pen-name of Luke Limner, he also produced a guide to designing in different styles for 'Artists and Art-Workmen', *Suggestions In Design* (Bogue, 1853), which to some extent anticipated Owen Jones's *Grammar of Ornament* (Day and Son, 1856) and was re-issued in a much enlarged form by Blackie in 1880.

ALBERT WARREN

Albert Henry Warren (1830–1911), a younger contemporary of WHR and John Leighton, designed about forty book covers, signing them with the letters AW. Warren did not start designing book covers until he had completed much of the preparation work for *The Grammar of Ornament* (1856), Owen Jones's famous compendium.[11] Warren often spread repetitive ornament over the whole surface of a book cover. Figure 16.5 shows one of his first designs, for *The Minstrel* by James Beattie (Routledge, 1858). On the left is the original artwork for his design, dated July 1857, with the design as executed on the right. In this revised design, the absolute height has been reduced and the absolute

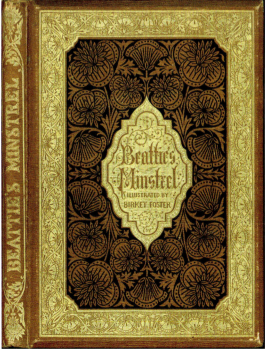

16.5 – The cover of James Beattie's *The Minstrel*, 1858, designed by Albert Warren. *Left:* Artwork, dated July 1857. Height of design 214mm. *Right:* The book, bound by W. Bone. Height of design 195mm, overall height 208mm.

177

dimensions of the lettering area slightly increased, which resulted in the removal of the foliage that originally surrounded the lettering area.

DANTE GABRIEL ROSSETTI

The designs of D.G. Rossetti (1828–82) for covering the books of his family and friends were few in number but invariably thoughtful. They ranged from the chaste minimalism of the cover for his own book, *The Early Italian Poets* (1861), to the elegant symbolism exemplified by Swinburne's *Atalanta in Calydon* (1865), and on to the exuberance of Hake's *Parables and Tales* (1872).[12]

WILLIAM RALSTON, H.G. WELLS AND TALWIN MORRIS

The Scotsman William Ralston (1841-1911) was identified by the author and Jane Brown as the designer of gilt bindings signed with a conjoined WR.[13] In WHR's lifetime, about forty book covers competently designed by Ralston appeared between 1866 and 1870, after which he became a comic artist at *Punch* and the *Graphic*. Figure 16.6 shows Quiz's *Sketches of Young Couples, Young Ladies, Young Gentlemen* (Cassell, Petter & Galpin [1869]).

Following WHR's death in 1873, the standard of design for ordinary trade bindings began to decline and was generally undistinguished from the mid-1870s to the mid-1890s. Jane Brown and the author have identified one of the leading lights of this era as H.G. Wells or, in full, Herbert Gustavus Wells (1838–1922). However, he rarely signed his work and has been overshadowed by his namesake H.G. Wells, the author Herbert George Wells (1866–1946).[14]

It was not until the last five years of the century that publishers' book covers reached artistic heights again, by way of another designer of genius. The Glasgow School influence of Charles Rennie Mackintosh (1868–1928) was channelled into book cover art primarily by his gifted disciple Talwin Morris (1865–1911).[15]

WILLIAM MORRIS AND PRIVATE PRESSES

The Aesthetic Movement which flourished in the latter decades of the nineteenth century ended up going in another direction in its search for the Book Beautiful (which had of course been WHR's speciality, *avant la lettre*). This was away from the trade binding and toward the exclusive Private Press, steered initially by the medieval enthusiasms of William Morris (1834–96). Stephen Calloway has observed, however, that it was the influence of Dante Gabriel Rossetti which soon came to predominate, for example in the work of Charles Ricketts (1866–1931).[16]

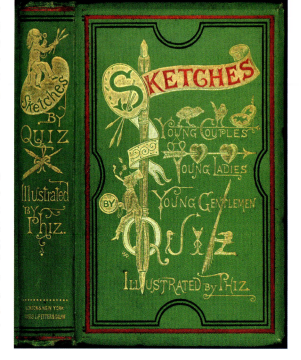

16.6 – The cover of Quiz's *Sketches* [1869], designed by William Ralston (signed WR on the front). Height 171mm.

The life of the gilt book cover as an important canvas for art came to an end with the economic austerity which swept in after the outbreak of war in 1914. In less than a hundred years it had transitioned from exciting discovery to dazzling achievements to slow decline and finally to obsolescence. In due course a colourful paper dust-wrapper would become the public face of the plain cloth beneath.

CHARACTERISTICS OF WHR'S DESIGNS FOR BOOK COVERS

Stamping out a design from gold leaf on to bookcloth using hand-cut brass blocks had a relatively brief life. As already noted, it began in 1832 and started to peter out in 1914. WHR created gold book cover designs for about twenty-five of these years, from 1848 to 1873. What is it about the WHR designs which makes his cloth book covers artistically the most distinguished ones produced during the whole period?

WHR appears to have been a quietly contemplative man, who thought deeply about his work but did not offer his views on design to the public between the covers of a book, unlike other designers such as Owen Jones, John Leighton and Lewis F. Day. However, from his scattered writings in journals, and from scrutiny of his quarter-century of book designs, it is clear that his masterly ability to create exquisite images – in this case via the unpromising technique of drawing for brass-cutters to make stamps for imprinting gold leaf on to cloth – relied on several resources. These included his scholarly study from an early age of historical artefacts; his unfailing and wide-ranging artistic imagination; and his appreciation of the limitations but also the opportunities offered by the techniques available to him.

Sometimes WHR can be seen to be imaginatively adapting a particular style. This is most notably the case with his use of Renaissance motifs such as grotesques, especially in the later 1860s for designs such as *182. Masterpieces of Italian Art 1868, 185. The World's Pictures 1869* and *186. Arundel Society Photographs 1869*.[17] But, in general, WHR's designs all bear a family resemblance to each other, rather than conforming to a particular historical style. The resemblance resides in recurring features of the designs, including their general elegance and imagination, their skilled draughtsmanship and their incorporation of particular stylised details. The delicacy of his execution allowed him to create cover designs that did not rely merely on the bold gilt lines encountered with other designers' works, but instead achieved a richer and more subtle overall effect, bringing alive the two-dimensional surface. A characteristic feature in this context is the interweaving of gilt lines as though they had a three-dimensional existence, with novel under-and-over patterns sustained in an apparently effortless way. Three further outstanding design features exhibited by WHR's work are as follows.

1. GLOBAL SYMMETRY AND LOCAL ASYMMETRY (GS-LA)

If one were to adopt a single phrase to describe many of WHR's designs, it could be 'modified classicism'. WHR was highly sensitive to classical factors of balance, restraint

 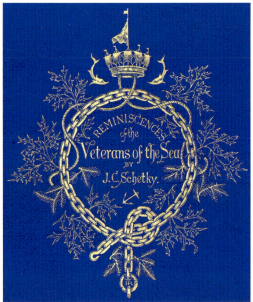

16.7 – Global Symmetry and Local Asymmetry within two cover designs by WHR.

and clear articulation, but combined these with an idiosyncratic repertoire of variations from the standard, neither baroque nor rococo, but instead a highly specific form of inflection in which classical symmetry is retained globally but subverted locally.

The clearest source of WHR's modified classicism is Grinling Gibbons, the hero of WHR's woodcarver father, William Gibbs Rogers. WHR's contemporary, Robert Hendrie, provided a highly concrete account of how Grinling Gibbons achieved this effect:[18]

> Gibbons had a peculiar manner of drawing and composing his subjects in his trophies and most of his drops; he appears to have made a rough draft of some general idea in outline only, then carefully to have drawn one side of his subject within this limit, to have then turned the paper over, and, tracing the outline, filled it up in keeping with the other side.

The compositions of WHR designs often have, like those of Grinling Gibbons, left–right symmetry in overall outline but asymmetry between the contents of the left and right envelopes. Example are provided by his designs for 7. *Pilgrimages 1850*, 90. *Birds and Beasts 1859* and 144. *The Book of Perfumes 1865* (all WHR designs mentioned here are illustrated in Appendix A).

There is extensive evidence of the importance to visual processing of the distinction between global and local.[19] The design principle often adopted by WHR and, before him, Grinling Gibbons can be called Global Symmetry and Local Asymmetry (*GS-LA* for short). *GS-LA* appears subjectively to offer the viewer a combination of calming redundancy, derived from overall symmetry, with exciting uniqueness, derived from the locally asymmetric detail. Figure 16.7 illustrates the *GS-LA* principle implemented by

WHR for both the *3. Drawing Room Table Book 1848* and the *157. Schetky's Reminiscences 1867* designs.

WHR's implicit adoption of the *GS-LA* principle is evident from the number of his designs, both for spines and for front covers, which expressed global symmetry across a vertical plane, with asymmetry between the details in the left and right sides, as already described. Occasionally, however, the global symmetry was across the horizontal plane, with vertical asymmetry, as in *155. Andersen's Household Stories 1866*.

The significance of WHR's use of *GS-LA* to a greater or lesser degree in many of his cover designs lies in the limitations imposed on the artist by gilt stamping of cloth, which offered little opportunity for subtleties, such as shading to add depth. Despite this, many contemporary designers employed pictorial realism of a necessarily stilted nature in their designs to convey a simple message or narrative. Other designs comprised abstract patterns which maintained strict symmetry at both local and global levels. This had the practical benefit that the designer needed to produce only one half (or even one quarter) of a cover design, with the balance requiring no further thought. However, the end result was a cover design which, however intricate and glittering its initial impact, contained little to engage the attention further. WHR's designs, on the other hand, were never pictorial. They often contained real objects – manmade or natural – but they were portrayed in a stylised way which caught their essence perfectly. In addition, the violation of local symmetry allowed WHR to give his book covers an extra dimension of subtlety and vitality, an invitation to the eye to linger on the composition, deepening the viewer's perceptions.

2. LATE GLOBAL ASYMMETRY

The primacy of *GS-LA* in WHR's designs for covers held for about twenty years, from his *7. Pilgrimages 1850* design to his *195. Fresh and Salt Water Tutors 1869* design. In the last five years of his life, WHR continued to design some book covers according to his *GS-LA* principle, including the series of exquisite botanical covers which he devised for William Robinson, the garden writer, such as *208. Alpine Flowers 1870*. However, he also started to design covers that excluded any form of reflectional symmetry, starting with *181. Ships and Sailors 1868*, and after 1869 such designs were in the majority.

In this later period, WHR's front cover's design is sometimes massed in the left and the upper regions, with the right and lower regions left unfilled, as with *218. The Brownies 1870* and *221. Streeter's Catalogue 1870*. It seems likely that WHR was responding at least in part to the growing influence of Japanese art, not in terms of the use of particular patterns or motifs but rather by exploring a new freedom of spatial segmentation. Japanese art received limited exposure at the 1862 International Exhibition in London, but a more extensive display at the 1867 Universal Exhibition in Paris created wide interest in artistic circles.[20] Another asymmetric innovation was the introduction of an oblique gilt bar on the spine. In designs such as those of *191. Many Happy Returns 1869* and *193. Montaigne's Essays 1869*, WHR introduced a prominent gilt lettering-bar in the shape of a parallelogram which he placed obliquely across the spine. For *196. Winter Sunbeams 1869*, he even placed the front cover's flamboyant lettering at the same angle as the spine's gilt bar.

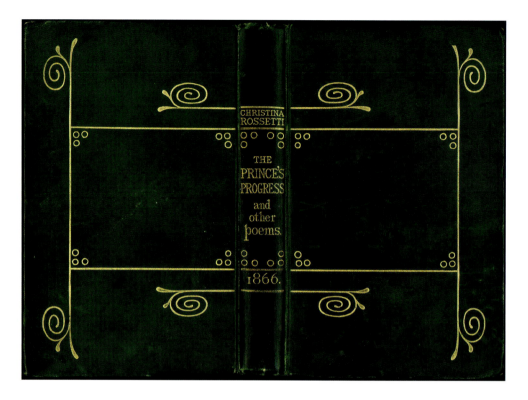

Another influence encouraging WHR in the direction of global asymmetry might have been the book covers designed by Dante Gabriel Rossetti (who was himself subject to Japanese influences, of course). Alastair Grieve has drawn attention to the presence of asymmetries in Rossetti's covers from the time of Christina Rossetti's *Goblin Market* (1862) onwards, at least in terms of their front covers. As an example, Figure 16.8 shows the cover design of Christina Rossetti's *The Prince's Progress* (1866), described by Grieve as resembling 'wrought-iron hinges found on medieval doors'.[21] However, though Rossetti's abstract front-cover designs eschewed a vertical plane of symmetry, they did retain a horizontal plane of symmetry, and if *The Prince's Progress* binding is viewed as a whole, including both front and back, the design is conservatively symmetrical.

The asymmetry of late WHR was thus more profound than that of Rossetti. As the designer already long practised in the subtle art of *GS-LA*, WHR was well placed to take the decisive step of abandoning altogether the constraints of symmetry which hitherto had been so widely observed in book cover design.

16.8 – The covers of Christina Rossetti's *The Prince's Progress*, 1866, designed by Dante Gabriel Rossetti. Bound by Burn. Height 17mm.

3. LETTERING

The inventiveness of WHR's lettering is another characteristic feature of his designs for book covers. WHR's lettering is sometimes based on gothic forms (black-letter) which historically have lent themselves to elaboration, as with *32. The Pilgrim Fathers 1853*,

175. Christian Lyrics 1868 and *240. Fairford Windows 1872*. More commonly, however, WHR's lettering is based on standard roman forms, as with *12. Art Journal Catalogue 1851, 75. Always Do Your Best 1859* and *231. Raffaelle Gallery 1871*. In another instance of inflected classicism, frequently each letter is provided with a centre emphasis, which could be a simple dash, as in *74. New Forest 1859*, or a ring, as with *190. Mansions of England 1869*, or a quatrefoil, as in *128. Life Portraits of Shakspeare 1864*. In addition, the occasional letter sprouts unpredictable but elegant and creative flourishes, as with *161. Routledge's British Poets 1867* or *224. Wood's Boy's Own Book 1870*. The letter S is particularly likely to fling serifs into the surrounding space, as with *197. Daisy's Companions 1869*. Standard lettering was thereby very often transmuted into a unique work of the imagination.

Occasionally WHR took the inflection of his lettering on book covers so far as to allow the embellished letters themselves to evoke pictorially the contents of the books. Crenelated letters featured for *36. Wonder Castle 1853* and icicled letters for *170. Ice-Peter 1868*, producing superbly evocative designs. *Ice-Peter* has the additional distinction of being part of WHR's introduction of the comic book to the anglophone world.[22] Figure 16.9 illustrates two aspects of WHR's lettering, centre emphasis in the *67. Light for the Path 1858* and pictorial adaptation in the *217. Peoples of the World 1870* designs.

Despite the brilliance of WHR's lettering, there have been very few attempts to emulate its joyous inventiveness. His only disciple in this area was Lewis F. Day (1845–1910), who in 1902 praised and illustrated several examples of lettering by WHR.[23] Day complained, however, that artistry in lettering had disappeared since WHR's time:[24] 'In modern days we seem to have lost sight of its artistic possibilities.'

An older contemporary of WHR's, Owen Jones, has also been singled out for his lettering, but in his case not necessarily in a good way. McLean said of one book that Owen Jones's letters[25] 'are frequently tortured into extreme illegibility'. A plausible rationale has been provided by Carol Hrvol Flores for Jones's lettering. Jones's wider theorising about the importance of

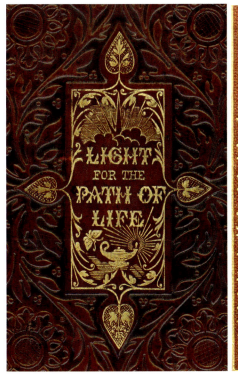
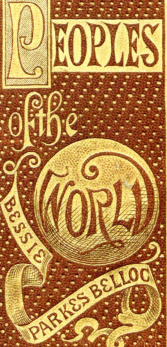

16.9 – Centre emphasis (*left*) and pictorial adaptation (*right*) within two cover designs by WHR.

active processes in perception led him to expect that the effort required to interpret his lettering would be experienced positively. Hrvol Flores attributed to Jones the belief that[26] 'a sense of pleasure and beauty results from viewing patterns that require a higher mental effort'.

WHR would probably not have disagreed with this sentiment in the abstract, but showed greater ability in practice at increasing letter complexity in a graceful and endlessly fertile way, and at judging where pleasing creativity would tip over into irritating illegibility.

FROM WHR DESIGNS TO THE PUBLISHED BOOKS

How many different designs for book covers by WHR were put into production by nineteenth-century edition-binders? Edition-binders were binding firms commissioned by publishers to put the same cover on either a whole edition or a substantial part of the edition. In 1985, Douglas Ball synthesised all that was known to that point about book covers bearing WHR designs, starting with the work of Sybille Pantazzi in 1961. Ball was able to list about forty books with WHR covers (together with some duplication and misattribution).[27] One of the covers misattributed to WHR by Pantazzi and Ball was Quiz's *Sketches*, designed by William Ralston and illustrated earlier as Figure 16.6.

By 2003, Edmund King had added a further twenty-five covers with designs by WHR, bringing the total number of known designs to about sixty-five.[28] In the present work, this number is almost quadrupled, with 244 cover designs by WHR identified and all but two illustrated, mostly for the first time.

In Appendix A, the gallery of WHR cover designs, each design is shown on the first book or journal on which it appeared, apart from a few exceptions. A considerable proportion of the designs were re-used on subsequent titles and a summary account of the extent of design re-use is included in Appendix C. A related issue is that of the longevity in use of WHR designs. Often they were current for only a year or two. A minority, however, were relatively long-lived, still being utilised into the twentieth century. The longest-lived of the gilt cloth covers was *123. County Families 1864*, which on its first appearance had bowled over at least one reviewer:[29] 'In its external aspect the volume is stupendously magnificent.'

After an erratic start, *County Families* settled down from 1870 into an annual edition, which continued to use essentially the same WHR cover design until it reached its final edition in 1920.

Even *County Families* was outlasted, however, by some of WHR's designs for the paper covers of periodicals. His very first such design, for *1. The Builder 1848*, remained in use until 1912. Other trade periodicals were equally conservative. WHR designs continued to be used well into the twentieth century by two journals founded by the six Morgan brothers. These were the *101. The Ironmonger 1861* and *100. Second Chemist and Druggist 1864* designs. The record for longevity however is held by a journal founded by William Reed, who married the Morgan brothers' only sister. This is for the *103. Second Grocer 1870* design. As late as 1960, nearly a century later, the masthead remained in use and still carried its original WHR monogram.

In the remainder of this chapter, six different aspects of the books shown in Appendix A are explored. The questions addressed are: First, who bound WHR's books? Second, what kind of contents did WHR's books have? Third, how many of WHR's books reached America? Fourth, how much was WHR paid? Fifth, is WHR the earliest known designer of a dust-jacket? And sixth, how rare are WHR's books now?

1. THE BINDERS WHO IMPLEMENTED WHR'S DESIGNS

The great majority of WHR's cover designs were realised in gilt on cloth. Altogether, 212 (87 per cent) of the 244 designs listed here appeared on British cloth bindings. The identities of the binders of these 212 publications are known in a surprisingly large number of cases because of the small binders' trade tickets which were often glued by the binder in the lower-left corner of a book's rear pastedown endpaper. As an example, the tickets used by the binder W. Bone are shown in Figure 18.2.

WHR's quarter-century of designing coincided with the heyday of edition binders' ticketing. It has been suggested by Douglas Ball that a fall-off in the extent of ticketing in the later 1870s may have reflected a fall-off in binder's pride in their work when the standard of design deteriorated. But even when ticketing was at its most frequent, Ball estimated that only roughly one book in fifteen (i.e. under 7 per cent) would bear a binder's ticket.[30] At that rate, one might expect that it would be possible for the binder to be identified for only about fourteen of the 212 WHR cloth bindings. In fact, however, the binder is identified in WHR's case for about ten times that number, 142 of the 212 WHR cloth designs, just over two-thirds (67 per cent) of the total. This high proportion might reflect both a raised prestige for books with WHR designs and also their binding by ambitious firms who were relatively assiduous at ticketing their books.

Who bound the 142 WHR cloth designs which have known binders? The overwhelming majority were bound by William Bone & Son of 76 Fleet Street (roughly a mile west of St Paul's Cathedral). Bone bound ninety-six of the WHR cloth designs, just over two-thirds (67.6 per cent) of the total number. Father and son Bone are discussed further in Chapter 18. The next most frequent binder was Westleys & Co. of Friar Street (about half a mile from Bone's, towards St Paul's Cathedral), but they bound only thirteen of the WHR cloth designs. The remaining thirty-three were bound by eight other London binders. In descending order of contributions they were as follows: Burn; A. W. Bain; Hanbury (Hanbury & Co., and Hanbury & Simpson); Leighton Son & Hodge; Eeles & Bell; Virtue (James S. Virtue, and Virtue & Co.); Straker & Son; and W. Greening. The one-third of WHR cloth designs whose binders are unknown must either be victims of haphazard ticketing or else were bound by firms who never ticketed, such as Kitcat.[31]

WHR's first cover designs were executed by the well-established firm of Westleys & Co. in 1848 and 1849, and in 1849 a couple of small WHR designs figure within the *Art Journal* series of 'Original Designs for Manufacturers'.[32] The accompanying text reflected WHR's ambition to introduce art and coherence into such designs:

These two designs are an attempt to introduce the Italian style of decoration to the purpose of bookbinding … These designs are a considerable improvement upon the unmeaning corners and centres so abundantly used by our binders, but we should like to see the idea still further extended. The entire side and back of a book should be expressly designed for it and made to harmonise with the subject of the work.

It was not until 1850 that Bone & Son executed a WHR cover design. At the Great Exhibition in 1851, however, it was Bone & Son rather than Westleys & Co. who exhibited design work by WHR. Both firms were awarded Prize Medals of the exhibition but, significantly, for almost opposite reasons.[33] On the one hand, Westleys & Co. was commended for a £75 leather binding (not designed by WHR) in a remarkably backhanded way:

The workmanship is highly meritorious, and proves that if work can be so well and elaborately executed, it is worthy of better designs.

On the other hand, W. Bone & Son was commended not for expensive but uninspired craftmanship in leather, but instead for inexpensive but excellent cloth covers:

Their specimens of binding attracted the attention of the Jury by the cheapness and general excellence of their cloth binding.

The *12. Art Journal Catalogue 1851*, recording the Great Exhibition, was itself published in a cover designed by WHR and bound by Bone, and symbolised the transfer of the role of binder of choice for WHR from Westleys to Bone. The cover design is also noteworthy as the first on a cloth volume to incorporate a WHR monogram, as was to become the norm subsequently. The relation between WHR and Bone continued to the end of WHR's life, the final WHR design bound by Bone & Son being that for *237. Magnet Stories 1872*.

2. THE GENRES WHICH RECEIVED WHR COVERS

A staple of publishing throughout the WHR period was the three-decker, or three-volume novel, and the listings of Victorian fiction compiled by Sadleir and by Wolff are full of such volumes.[34] Nevertheless the three-decker novel is a desert for the art of book covers. The only three-decker known to have a cover designed by WHR is *220. True to Herself 1870* by Frederick W. Robinson, a novel which ironically is absent from the listings of both Sadleir and Wolff. The genre of literature as a whole (novels and drama) is indeed only a relatively minor source of WHR covers. Instead, approximately three-quarters of all WHR cover designs appeared first on publications in five other categories. These are shown in Table 16.1.

Chapter Sixteen – Book Covers

TABLE 16.1
The five top categories of publication bearing covers designed by WHR, showing the percentage of all WHR cover designs which falls in each category.

Category	Incidence (%)
Children's	30
Poetry	15
Art	12
Topography	11
Periodicals	9

The remaining quarter of WHR cover designs appeared in relatively small numbers across half a dozen other types of book. In descending order of number of covers, these categories were literature, reference, religion, natural history, history and cooking.

It can be seen from Table 16.1 that just two categories, books for children and books of poetry, together provided the vehicles for almost half (45 per cent) of all WHR cover designs. Figure 16.10 illustrates these two categories with designs for a children's book, *228. Wood's Animal Traits 1872*, and a poetry book, *68. Gray's Poetical Works 1858* (in its late-1860s issue with coloured onlays). In the case of books for children, it was probably

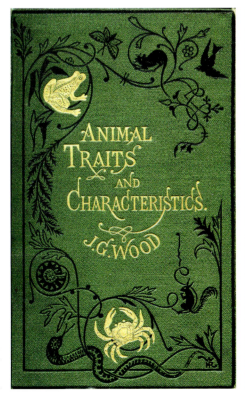
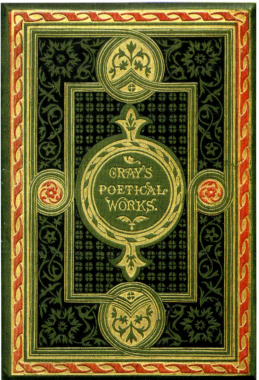

16.10 – The leading categories of books with WHR cover designs, children's and poetry.

187

hoped that intriguing gilt covers would hold out the promise of interesting interiors to children, even if they might not yet have been persuaded of the delights of reading. In the case of poetry books, an elegant cover was no doubt felt to provide an augury of the elevated aesthetic experience to be found inside. Of course, this reasoning could lead to disappointment if the reader found that the poetry itself did not live up to the expectations raised by the cover design. Thus the *Athenaeum* thought that WHR's cover design for *145. Edwy and Elgiva 1865* was 'perfection' but that unfortunately the poetry itself was 'wearisomely foolish'.[35] In a similar vein, James Orton, the author of *14. Excelsior 1851*, was irked by the prominence accorded by reviewers to its WHR cover design, stating that the editors of both the *Athenaeum* and the *Globe* had been 'moth-like attracted to the glittering cover'. Orton made this complaint in his follow-up volume *15. The Enthusiast 1852*.[36] Fortunately, though, Orton was happy to accept a second glittering cover by WHR for *The Enthusiast*.

For art books, as for poetry books, the presence of WHR cover designs will have signalled the aesthetic experience to be gained within. Topography books did not need to do so, but here the WHR cover probably served a second function (present also for poetry and art books) of signalling the high production values which had gone into the book's creation. These were of course associated with costliness, and this would have been particularly salient for gifts. Poetry, art and topography books were all highly acceptable forms of gift, since they implied that the recipient was an enlightened person who perused books for edification and refined pleasure. The centrality of gift-giving in book purchases during WHR's period is demonstrated by the ratcheting up in the level of book marketing which occurred each year from October to December – then, as now, in time to take advantage of gift-giving at Christmas and the New Year.

For periodicals, the last of the major categories of publication in Table 16.1, the driving forces were rather different. The wrappers of issues were mundanely printed in ink on paper, rather than impressively blocked in gold on cloth. Nevertheless, WHR applied his customarily detailed attention to designing attractive wrappers with titles whose lettering was idiosyncratic and yet harmonious, and, importantly, easy to read, the prime requirement for an item which needed to be plucked by the reader from other titles on display.

Contemporary reaction to WHR's rather stark wrapper for *168. The Broadway 1868* is informative in this respect. This monthly literary magazine was being re-launched after a poor first year. Its first issue had begun with an elaborate wrapper signed with a picture of a crane above a 'W', for the young Walter Crane (1845–1915). By the fifth issue the wrapper had been considerably simplified, losing its Crane signature en route. After the re-launch, the magazine *Fun* thought that the contents of *The Broadway* were as poor as ever, but admitted that the accompanying new wrapper was effective:[37]

> The new wrapper is telling, if not pleasing; it will catch the eye, as MR. HARRY ROGERS no doubt designed; his instructions probably being to that effect, for he can design admirably.

One WHR design for a periodical wrapper which certainly was found pleasing was that for *154. Belgravia 1866*, which remained in use for thirty years:[38]

> we ... must award the highest commendation to the ... exceedingly handsome cover, with its *unique* and artistically designed device.

3. WHR COVER DESIGNS IN THE USA

Outside the UK, it was the USA where WHR cover designs were most in evidence. According to title page evidence, fifty designs by WHR were used on the covers of USA publications, just over 20 per cent of the total 244 designs. The designs reached the USA in several different ways, which can be grouped into the authorised and the unauthorised. The authorised routes involved payments flowing from America to London, whereas the unauthorised routes did not. We first consider the authorised routes, which were the conduit for most cover designs by WHR reaching the USA.

One authorised route was for an American publisher to agree with a London publisher to purchase part of a title's London edition, which happened for fifteen designs. The London and American copies were then made alongside each other and were normally identical except for their title pages. The title pages destined for America usually replaced the London publisher's details with the American publisher's details, but sometimes merely added the American details to the London details. The earliest two cases exemplify this. American copies of *45. Poetry for Children 1854* replaced the London imprint of George Bell by the New York imprint of D. Appleton & Co., whereas American copies of the *52. Vicar of Wakefield Grolier 1855* merely added the New York imprint of Bangs, Brother, & Co. to the London imprint of Sampson Low.

The American issue could form a substantial portion of an edition. For *94. Bennett's Pilgrim's Progress 1860*, the Longman records show that a quarter of its 2,000 copies were sent to Appleton in New York; the cost of printing 500 title pages for the Appleton copies was shown as 11s.[39] Appleton was the most frequent adopter of this route, with seven imports of WHR designs, its last being *158. Two Centuries of Song 1867*. No other USA imprint had more than two such designs, the examples being shared out among Ticknor and Fields, Anson D.F. Randolph, J.B. Lippincott and Co., Scribner, Welford, and Co., and Roberts Brothers. The latest example was provided by Lippincott, for *238. Man in the Past 1872*.

An alternative authorised route was for UK publishers to open offices themselves in America, so that they could disseminate their own London-made books there. This occurred for twenty-nine designs, and was dominated by the twenty-five instances provided by Routledge from 1854 to 1872 (six of these designs were later Routledge editions of titles first published only in Britain in 1852 or 1853). The remainder came from Virtue and from Cassell, Petter & Galpin. In such cases, copies sold in America cannot be distinguished from copies sold in the UK unless they happen to have appropriate inscriptions.

A third authorised route to American publication of a cover design by WHR was for an American publisher to acquire the actual binding brasses (along with stereos of the contents) from the London publisher, to use for binding American copies of the title. This appears to have occurred for only one cover design by WHR, that for *95. Quarles' Emblems 1861*, which N. Tibbals and Co. of New York acquired from James Nisbet and Co. of London. The first issue of the Tibbals edition had the same binding as the Nisbet edition, except it omitted the front cover's blind stamping and rotated one of the six detachable roundels in the frame (so that the butterfly in the top roundel faced up instead of down); in later issues, Tibbals' front cover retained only the small circular design in the centre. Tibbals was so enamoured of the WHR cover for *Quarles* that it also copied the front cover's circle (complete with WHR monogram) and surrounding annulus in a new brass for their publication *Pictorial Life*, 1870, which also silently re-used the illustrations from *Quarles*.

Unauthorised borrowing of a British WHR cover in America started with a bang, with the frenzied copying of *7. Pilgrimages 1850* after it appeared in the *Art Journal* catalogue of the Great Exhibition. Figure 16.11 illustrates one early American adaptation of the *Pilgrimages* design (shown earlier as Figure 11.4), on Ik Marvel, *Reveries of a Bachelor* (NY: Charles Scribner, 1852).

Subsequently it fizzled out, however, with few further cases. Sever and Francis produced a close copy of *69. Gray's Poems 1858* which included an approximation of the gilt design on its front cover. Anson D.F. Randolph's copying of *218. The Brownies 1870* for their Golden Thread Series of children's books, which included titles such as *Fiddling Freddy*, may have been based upon either the UK or the authorised USA edition of *The Brownies* published by Roberts Brothers.

Finally, in three further cases WHR illustrations (rather than cover designs) were pressed into service in America in order to create new cover designs. One of these illustrations again came from the *Art Journal* catalogue of the Great Exhibition, and the other two came from WHR illustrations within *69. Gray's Poems 1858*.

16.11 – An American adaptation of a WHR book cover design exhibited by the bookbinder W. Bone at the Great Exhibition of 1851.

4. PAYMENTS FOR WHR COVER DESIGNS

For publishers, a cover design by WHR was a definite selling point, but how much were they prepared to pay WHR for it? First, some examples of publishers' advertisements mentioning WHR designs are given, followed by summaries of two cases in which WHR's fees are known. The first two publishers' advertisements are taken from *The Times* newspaper.

110. Divine Emblems 1863: 'elegantly bound in cloth super extra, the sides gilt to a design by Harry Rogers'.[40]

127. Woman in White 1864: 'Cheap edition of Mr. Wilkie Collins' celebrated novel. – This day, 2s. 6d., fancy boards, with designs by Harry Rogers, The Woman in White.'[41]

The third example shows a book in a WHR-designed cover attracting a 20 per cent premium over the cost of one in a plain cover:

193. Montaigne's Essays 1869: 'cloth 7s. 6d. Extra (Roger's design) [*sic*] 9s'.[42]

On fees, little is known about those paid to designers of covers, firstly because many publishers' records have been lost, and secondly because even surviving records usually do not itemise such fees separately. In two cases, however, the fees paid to WHR have been found, as follows.

86. Marriage Service 1859: For this publication, WHR designed both the cover and all the illustrations on each of its thirty-two pages. Details of the costs are in the Routledge archives.[43] Unfortunately, it is not entirely clear what its different components (dated 1 July 1859) refer to. The first entry seems to read 'Designing – Binding & illus's £118 10s', which probably represents a payment to an intermediary such as the Dalziel brothers. The next two lines probably record payments to WHR, namely, 'Brass Block Designs £5' and 'Artist for Designs £60'. The only other cost listed was for paper: '2 Reams Dbl Elepht. £21'. Finally, the costs in the entry were summed to £204 10s and divided by the edition size of 2,000, arriving at a figure of 2s 0½d per copy; it was sold at 7s 6d.

94. Bennett's Pilgrim's Progress 1860: WHR's contribution to this book was limited to designing the cover, and his payment for this is unambiguous in the Longman archives.[44] They record a payment of 5 guineas (£5 5s) to W.H. Rogers on 12 September 1859 for 'Design for back & side of cover'. It seems safe to take 5 guineas as the order of magnitude in general of WHR's fee for the design of a book cover.

5. EARLIEST DUST-JACKETS FOR WHR BOOKS

Although surviving dust-jackets (also called dust-wrappers) are common only from the twentieth century onwards, a sprinkling have survived from the nineteenth century.[45] Two of them appeared on book covers with designs by WHR, perhaps reflecting enhanced care being taken to protect his prestigious compositions.

94. Bennett's Pilgrim's Progress 1860: This is the earliest known illustrated dust-jacket, though the present location of its only surviving example is unknown.[46] John Carter reported the existence of a surviving dust-jacket in 1931, and at the time it was the earliest known dust-jacket of any description though, subsequently, earlier ones have been found.[47] The jacket was described as printed in red on grey paper and bore a copy of one of the illustrations from within the book – all of which had been drawn by WHR's close friend, C.H. Bennett. It can now be added here that the publisher's original note of the production of the dust-jacket has been found in the Longman archives, at the location already referred to in the preceding section.[48] It recorded the cost of 'envelopes' for the edition of 2,000 copies as £2 10s for the buff paper and £1 18s for printing it, which works out at just over a halfpenny each.

144. The Book of Perfumes 1865: Again, a sole surviving dust-jacket has been reported, in this case by Robin de Beaumont.[49] From the present perspective, it is even more interesting than the one on *94. Bennett's Pilgrim's Progress 1860*, because it is the only known dust-jacket to carry a design by WHR. Indeed, it appears to be the earliest dust-jacket in existence created by a known designer. The dust-jacket has the same design as the cloth cover which it protects, and thus bears a WHR signature on both its spine and front cover.

6. SURVIVAL OF COVERS WITH WHR DESIGNS

Finally, we turn to the issue of how many WHR covers survive to the present day. Most (but not all) publications with cover designs by WHR are scarce. The British copyright deposit libraries are the most likely places to find a particular cover designed by WHR, but even they have many gaps, due to two main causes.

Probably the largest area of gaps among WHR covers in copyright libraries is that of re-issued titles, where the later issue was given a new cover designed by WHR. Among a number of possible reasons for this, publishers might have been reluctant to deposit another set of copies, or libraries might have rejected their accession themselves on space grounds. A second large area of gaps in copyright libraries is that of paper or card wrappers for serials. This is because the wrappers were normally discarded when a run of the issues or parts was bound up as a single volume. This practice was standard both for libraries and for private owners. It is hard to believe that the removal of any trace of an attractive and informative part of the periodical was driven entirely by the customer. The hand-binder, on the other hand, could derive a useful supplementary income from the sale of accumulated 'waste' to paper merchants.

Occasionally titles were not deposited in the copyright libraries because they were entered at Stationers' Hall instead (e.g. *46. Little Susy 1854*) or circulated privately (e.g. *244. The Crèche Annual 1873*). Finally, some gaps have arisen from rebinding in library cloth, though this seems not to have occurred in the British copyright libraries on the scale seen in some other libraries.

Some publications with WHR covers are rare in absolute terms, generally absent both from library and bookseller holdings. In the case of *127. Woman in White 1864*, it is known from a newspaper advertisement (mentioned earlier in this chapter) that it was published with a cover design by WHR, and a design exists in the WHR archive at the V&A (see Appendix A), but no surviving copy has been traced. By contrast, some WHR covers are not rare, in the sense that they are widely distributed across institutional libraries and regularly become available in the antiquarian book market. One such is *144. The Book of Perfumes 1865*. Eugene Rimmel's work owes its present relative abundance to two factors: large sales and good preservation. With regard to sales, a relatively large number of copies of *The Book of Perfumes* must have been printed, with seven editions published between 1865 and 1871, in three different formats. Rimmel (1820–87), founder of the eponymous cosmetics firm, was highly adept at marketing and copies sometimes bear his presentation inscription. With regard to preservation, *The Book of Perfumes* must have benefited physically by being intended for the drawing room (mentioned in contemporary advertisements), and hence not subject to the rough treatment which, for example, a child's book might have received. Further, the academic value of the contents of the book has always been esteemed, enabling it to retain a readership and thus a viability both in commerce and for the librarian.[50] In particular, *The Book of Perfumes* is likely to have been one of the luckier

Chapter Sixteen – Book Covers

ones in avoiding being pulped in the twentieth century's two world wars.

For the Second World War, it has been reported that 60 million books were destroyed in a patriotic salvage operation in Britain during 1943 alone, subject only to a brief inspection to save books suitable for libraries or for the forces abroad.[51] Going back further to the First World War, a vivid account of triage for pulping has been provided by Ivor Armstrong Richards (1893–1979), then at the University of Cambridge, the pioneering literary theorist.[52] Richards recounted how he watched his entrepreneurial colleague Charles Kay Ogden (1889–1957) 'skim the cream from bulk purchases of pulp-worthy books' in order to stock his Cambridge bookshops with the cream, and to use the remainder for the paper ration needed for his *Cambridge Magazine*. No doubt *The Book of Perfumes* would have survived the cut but one fears that, at the time, many other publications with WHR covers would not have.

NOTES

1. Douglas Ball, *Victorian Publishers' Bindings* (Library Association, 1985), pp. 14-18.
2. A. Welby Pugin, *True principles of pointed or Christian architecture* (Weale, 1841).
3. It has been stated that the monogram reads AWNP, but this is not the case – it derives from A. Welby Pugin, the name on the title page. Clive Wainwright, 'Book design and production', in Paul Atterbury and Clive Wainwright (eds), *Pugin: A Gothic Passion* (New Haven, CT & London: Yale University Press and V&A, 1994), pp. 153-64; p. 154.
4. *Ibid.*, p. 161.
5. International Exhibition 1862. Official catalogue of the fine art department, p. 126. Class 38a, No. 2766.
6. *Art Journal*, 1849, p. 31.
7. Ball, *Victorian Publishers' Bindings, op. cit.*, pp. 45-6, 143-6.
8. Ruari McLean, *Victorian Book Design and Colour Printing* (Faber & Faber, 1963), Plate 25.
9. The 1870 edition of *Pearls from the Poets* used the same cover design as the 1860 first edition, but added a coloured onlay and replaced some gilt by black.
10. Lewis F. Day, in *British Art During Her Majesty's Reign* (J.S. Virtue, 1887), pp. 185-202; p. 189.
11. A reproduction of a 1902 painting of Albert Warren by his son, John Rosier Warren Warren [*sic*], bears the printed caption, 'Compiler of The Grammar of Ornament'.
12. Rossetti's cover designs have been extensively discussed by: Giles Barber, 'Rossetti, Ricketts, and some English publishers' bindings of the nineties', *The Library*, fifth series, Vol. 25, 1970, pp. 314-30; Alastair Grieve, 'Rossetti's applied art designs—2: Book-bindings', *The Burlington Magazine*, Vol. 115, 1973, pp. 79-84.
13. Gregory V. Jones and Jane E. Brown, 'Victorian binding designer WR: William Ralston (1841–1911), not William Harry Rogers', *The Book Collector*, Vol. 52, 2003, pp. 171-98.
14. Gregory V. Jones and Jane E. Brown, 'The other H.G. Wells: Henry Gustavus Wells (1838–1922), Victorian binding designer', *The Book Collector*, Vol. 62, 2013, pp. 436-45.
15. See especially Robert Gibbs, 'Talwin Morris again: Evaluation and collaboration', *Newsletter of the Charles Rennie Mackintosh Society (NCRMS)*, Nos 36 & 37 (unpaginated), 1984; Macintosh's book designs. *NCRMS*, No. 12 (unpaginated), 1976.
16. Stephen Calloway, 'The book beautiful', in Stephen Calloway and Lynn Federle Orr (eds), *The Cult of Beauty: The Victorian Avant-Garde 1860–1900* (V&A Publishing, 2011), pp. 252-5. See also Barber, 'Rossetti, Ricketts, and some English publishers' bindings of the nineties', pp. 323-30.
17. In the present and succeeding chapters, individual book cover designs by WHR are referred to by the design labels (e.g. *182. Masterpieces of Italian Art 1868*) which they are given in Appendix A, the gallery of book covers.
18. 'Wood sculpture', *Journal of Design,* 1850–51, Vol. 4, pp. 106-10 and 137-41; pp. 109-10. Hendrie was identified as the author by M. Digby Wyatt, *The Industrial Arts of the Nineteenth Century: A Series of Illustrations of the Choicest Specimens Produced by Every Nation, at the Great Exhibition of Works of Industry*, two volumes (Day & Son, 1851–3), Vol. 2, Plate CXXX text.
19. Christian Gerlack and Nicolas Poirel, 'Who's got the global advantage? Visual field differences in processing of global and local shape', *Cognition*, 2020, Vol. 195, No. 104131.
20. Stuart Durant, *Ornament: A Survey of Decoration since 1830* (Macdonald, 1986), pp. 163-4.
21. Grieve, 'Rossetti's applied art designs…', *op. cit.*, p. 83.
22. Gregory Jones and Jane Brown, 'Wilhelm Busch's merry thoughts: His early books in Britain and America', *Papers of the Bibliographical Society of America*, 2007, Vol. 101, pp. 167-204.
23. Lewis F. Day, *Lettering in Ornament* (B.T. Batsford, 1902), pp. 89, 118-19, 137, 140.
24. *Ibid.*, p. 8.
25. McLean, *Victorian Book Design and Colour Printing, op. cit.*, p. 129.
26. Carol A. Hrvol Flores, *Owen Jones: Design, Ornament, Architecture, and Theory in an Age in Transition* (New York: Rizzoli, 2006), p. 27.
27. Ball, *Victorian Publishers' Bindings, op. cit.*, pp. 155-8; Sybille Pantazzi, 'Four designers of English publishers' bindings, 1850–1880, and their signatures', *Papers of the Bibliographical Society of America*, 1961, Vol. 55, pp. 88-99.
28. Edmund M.B. King, *Victorian decorated trade bindings 1830–1880* (London: The British Library and Delaware: Oak Knoll, 2003), pp. 204-21; Edmund M.B. King, 'The book cover designs of William Harry Rogers', in *'For the love of the binding'. Studies in bookbinding history*

presented to Mirjam Foot (The British Library, 2000), pp. 319-28.

29. *Herald and Genealogist*, 1865, Vol. 2, p. 362.

30. Ball, *Victorian Publishers' Bindings, op. cit.*, p. 115.

31. *Ibid.*, p. 116.

32. W. Harry Rogers, 'Designs for book-covers', *Art Journal*, Vol. 11 = 1, April 1849, p. 126.

33. *Reports of the Juries* (1852), pp. 424, 451 and 453.

34. Michael Sadleir, *XIX Century Fiction: A Bibliographical Record Based on his Own Collection*, two vols (Constable [1951]); Robert Lee Wolff, *Nineteenth-century Fiction: A Bibliographical Catalogue Based on the Collection Formed by Robert Lee Wolff* (New York & London: Garland, 1981–6).

35. [John Westland Marston], *Athenaeum*, 18 March 1865, p. 384.

36. *Enthusiast*, 1852, p. 62.

37. *Fun*, 12 September 1868.

38. *Sporting Gazette*, 20 October 1866.

39. University of Reading Library, Special Collections, MS 1393: Longman Group Archive. Book D6 (Divide ledger; Index A7), p. 92; repeated in Impression Book 13 (Index H16), p 179.

40. *The Times*, 7 November 1863, p. 13.

41. *The Times*, 15 October 1864, p. 13.

42. 'Reprints Edited by Alex. Murray', the final page of *Hudibras* (Alex. Murray & Son, 1869).

43. Bodleian Microfilms of Publishers' Archives, MSS. Film, Routledge Publication Books Vol. 3, p. 455.

44. University of Reading Library, Special Collections, MS 1393: Longman Group Archive. Miscellaneous Publishing Expenses, Book A3 (Index C3), p. 174; repeated in Impression Book 13 (Index H16), p. 179.

45. Mark R. Godburn, *Nineteenth-century Dust-jackets* (Pinner: Private Libraries Association and New Castle, DE: Oak Knoll, 2016).

46. *Ibid.*, pp. 72 and 192.

47. G. Thomas Tanselle 'Book-jackets, blurbs, and bibliographers', *Library*, 1971, fifth series, Vol. 26, 91-134; pp. 92 and 118.

48. University of Reading Library, Special Collections, MS 1393, Longman's Impression Book 13 (Index H16), p. 179.

49. Robin de Beaumont, 'Nineteenth-century publishers' bindings 1820–1900: A brief survey from my shelves', *Private Library*, fourth series, Vol. 9, 1996, pp. 2-47; pp. 33-4, Figure 38.

50. Jisc Library Hub Discover indicates that more than twenty UK libraries hold this title.

51. Andrew Pettegree and Arthur der Weduwen, *The Library: A Fragile History* (Profile Books, 2021), p. 348.

52. I.A. Richards, co-author of the '"Meaning of Meaning"': Some recollections of C.K. Ogden', in P. Sargant Florence and J.R.L. Anderson (eds), *C.K. Ogden: A Collective Memoir* (Elek Pemberton, 1977), pp. 96-109; p. 98.

SEVENTEEN

Contemporary Owners

WHO WERE THE RECIPIENTS OF WHR's artistic endeavours? That is, what kind of person would possess objects designed by WHR? In the case of silver, only the affluent could aspire to ownership. But in the case of publications with WHR covers, the potential range of contemporary owners was much wider, given the low prices of some of the books and journals, and also their international distribution. Here we consider the contemporary evidence of ownership for fourteen books with covers designed by WHR, which together span both the social spectrum and the geographical world. As in Chapter 16, these books are referred to by the design labels which they are given in Appendix A.

The pinnacle of British society during WHR's professional life was of course occupied by Queen Victoria and (until his death in 1861) her consort, Prince Albert, and thus these two royal figures arise first.

1. GIFT FROM QUEEN VICTORIA

The *Court Circular* issued at Windsor on 26 December 1855 listed those attending the Queen's dinner party on Christmas Day.[1] One of these was Lady Caroline Barrington (1799–1875) and it transpires that, as a Christmas present, Victoria gave her a copy of *58. The Rhine 1856*, with WHR cover, inscribed warmly to her friend.[2] She was in effect the governess of the Queen's children. Lady Caroline Barrington held the post of Lady Superintendent to the Royal Family from 1850 until her death, when it was recorded that she had:[3]

> won the respect and esteem of the Queen and of the whole Royal Family, who now deeply lament the loss of one who was endeared to them by no ordinary ties of affection and gratitude.

Lady Caroline was a daughter of the 2nd Earl Grey (Prime Minister 1830–34), and the widow of a naval captain, the Hon. George Barrington, a younger son of the 5th Viscount Barrington.

2. GIFT FROM PRINCE ALBERT

In his role as President of the Society of Arts, Manufactures and Commerce, Prince Albert was the driving force responsible for the international triumph which became known as the Great Exhibition of 1851. To ensure that the implications of the exhibition for many different fields should be documented, Albert commissioned review lectures from twenty-four leading authorities and had these published in a pair of volumes the following year, *17. Lectures on the Great Exhibition 1852*, with WHR cover. Albert sent each contributor a copy of the published volumes, with a covering letter expressing his thanks. Underneath the printed letterhead of the 'Society of Arts, Manufactures, & Commerce, Adelphi, London', the body of the letter was in a scribal hand, but it was subscribed 'Albert / President' by the Prince himself.

3. SOLD BY A BOOK HAWKING ASSOCIATION

It would be heartening to be able to report that WHR's books were distributed uniformly across the social structures which fanned out below Victoria and Albert, but in practice their expense must have confined them largely to the upper and middle classes. In the present case, even what appears at first sight to be a welcome example of an explicitly humble provenance turns out upon examination to be something rather different.

The Norfolk Book Hawking Association was described as follows in a contemporary reference volume:[4]

> The Norfolk Book Hawking Association was established in 1855, for the sale throughout the county, by the agency of licensed hawkers, of bibles, prayer-books, tracts, and books and prints of a religious and instructive character. By its aid more than 21,000 such publications are annually disposed of, chiefly among farm labourers and servants. Its depôt is in the Upper close, and the Bishop is *president*, and the Rev. H. Howes and Mr. T. W. Hansell *central secretaries*.

A copy of a later edition, 1860, of *26. Evenings at Home 1852*, still with its WHR cover design, bears on the front free endpaper a promising embossed oval stamp: 'NORFOLK BOOK HAWKING ASSOCIATION'. The endpaper also bears a gift inscription, dated July 1862 from Aunt Henrietta to her namesake, Henrietta Louisa Howes.

Examination of census returns suggests that the recipient and purchaser of the book were probably a daughter and an unmarried sister, respectively, of Henry Howes, the Rector of Spixworth in Norfolk, who can presumably be identified with the Rev. H. Howes listed as one of the two secretaries of the Norfolk Book Hawking Association. Thus in this case at least, the promised 'farm labourers and servants' are disappointingly nowhere to be seen.

4. GIFT FROM A DUCHESS

Within the upper and middle classes who were the usual possessors of books with WHR covers, a number of different types of owner, and of route to ownership, can be distinguished. Some donors were socially only a notch or two below Victoria and Albert, as in the present instance.

A New Year's Day 1869 gift of *175. Christian Lyrics 1868* with WHR cover bears a simple inscription to a named son from his mother. But Algernon Malcolm Arthur Percy was a younger son of the 6th Duke of Northumberland, and so his mother was the Duchess. The seventeen-year-old Lord Algernon matriculated a fortnight later at Christ Church, Oxford.[5]

5. GIFT TO A MILLER'S SON

Other donors were of much more modest means. In 1874 Thomas Wyatt Appleford, always known as Wyatt, reached his ninth birthday in Coggeshall in Essex. He was a son of the miller at Abbey Mill, a water mill by the river Blackwater. For his birthday, he was given a copy of *239. Boy's Own Treasury 1872* with WHR cover, inscribed by his mother and father.

When Wyatt's father died in 1881, the mill failed to sell at auction.[6] Instead, his mother ran it until her death in 1904 and it then passed to Wyatt, who was the miller at Abbey Mill until his death in 1947, aged eighty-two. His Abbey Mill Cottage remained without mains water, electricity or sanitation, and he did not possess a radio. He was a well-known character, fishing and shooting, and observing the otters in their holt within sight of his house. There is an arcadian photograph of Wyatt and his dog in a punt, drawn up in front of huge, formerly pollarded willows and a few onlooking cattle.[7] It is a scene which could have been an illustration in Wyatt's own childhood copy of the *Boy's Own Treasury*.

6. GIFT FROM THE MASTER'S LODGE

A gift inscription on the half-title of a copy of *106. Domestic Life in Palestine 1862*, by WHR's own sister Mary Eliza Rogers, and with a cover by WHR, is from W.W. and E.F.A. of Trinity Lodge.

The donors' initials stand for William Whewell and Everina Frances Affleck. William Whewell was an eminent polymath and scientist – it was indeed Whewell who, in the early 1830s, had coined the word 'scientist'. Since 1841 he had been Master of Trinity College, Cambridge. Everina Frances Affleck was Lady Affleck, widow of Sir Gilbert Affleck and benefactor of All Saints' Church in Cambridge; her brother, Robert Leslie Ellis, was a fellow of Trinity. William Whewell and Lady Affleck, a widower and a widow, had married in 1858.

7. PRESENTED BY THE EDITOR

A particular case of the book as gift is the presentation copy, that is, a book presented by its author or editor. Presentation copies of the *12. Art Journal Catalogue 1851* with its WHR cover are unusual in that the editor, Samuel Carter Hall, had an extra presentation page printed and inserted before the normal preliminary pages. Figure 17.1 shows the elaborate '1851' frame for an inscription, signed with WHR monogram.

One copy was presented by Hall to G. Turner. This would have been the well-known

Chapter Seventeen – Contemporary Owners

17.1 – Design by WHR for the extra leaf in copies of the *Art Journal Catalogue 1851* to be presented by the editor. Width 177mm.

17.2 – Prize label from a ladies' college, on *Two Centuries of Song 1867*. Width 75mm.

journalist Godfrey Turner, whose occupation was given as 'Fine Art Reviewer' in the 1851 Census, and who was subsequently a mainstay of the *Daily Telegraph*, among other journals.

8. PRESENTED AS A SCHOOL PRIZE

Another special case of the book as a gift is the book as a prize. Many such books in this period were encased in the type of bland leather carapace, often with gilt institutional stamp on the front board, that is generally known as a Prize Binding. Some prizes, however, were in normal publishers' cloth. An example of the latter is a copy of *158. Two Centuries of Song 1867* with WHR cover, which was given as a prize by Tudor Hall Ladies' College in London. The recipient had shown marked industry and superior conduct.

Figure 17.2 shows part of the prize plate on the book's front free endpaper, with an engraving depicting ladies in crinolines on the lawns of Tudor College. The main house was demolished in the twentieth century.

9. OWNED BY AN EMPRESS

Simple indications of ownership such as book labels (*ex libris* plates) or book stamps provide less information about the acquisition of a book than do gift inscriptions. Allowing for that limitation, however, the same picture tends to emerge of an ownership which was heavily weighted towards the upper and middle classes, as this and the following example exemplify.

The title page of a copy of the 1882–3 edition of *244. The Crèche Annual 1873*, with cover by WHR, received a library stamp consisting of the legend *Farnbvrg Bibliotb* surrounding a bee.

The bee was a Napoleonic badge and the book belonged to the Empress Eugénie, who indeed is listed in the book as a donor that year of £3 to the Crèche charity. After the Second French Empire was brought to an end by the Franco-Prussian war, the erstwhile Emperor Napoleon III and Empress Eugénie lived in exile in Kent. Napoleon

199

died in 1873 and subsequently Eugénie moved to Farnborough in Hampshire, founding St Michael's Abbey there as a memorial to her late husband and son. She bought Farnborough Hill in 1880 and lived there until her death in 1920.

10. OWNED BY THE ARTIST

Birket Foster's copy of *56. Sabbath Bells 1856*, with cover by WHR, is identified by his printed book label on the front pastedown, giving his names both in full and as initials, together with the motto 'Persevere'.

The famous watercolourist and illustrator, Birket Foster (in full, Myles Birket Foster), imprinted on his viewers' minds an idealised view of the English countryside and its inhabitants. One of the earliest realisations of Foster's vision consisted of his illustrations for *Sabbath Bells*.

11. A NEW ZEALAND LIBRARY

Thus far, the examples of contemporary owners of books designed by WHR have been confined to Britain. How widely was ownership distributed across other countries? In the age of the internet it is possible to explore provenance worldwide. Three areas can be considered. First, such books were of course to be found in countries under direct British influence, constituents of what was then the British Empire. Second, there was a relatively small niche for them in continental Europe, restricted by the limited use there of the English language. Third, the United States of America was perhaps the most prominent overseas market for such books.

Considering first overseas countries under direct British influence, they imported unmodified copies of books with WHR covers, unlike the USA editions with replacement title pages.

In 1861 in New Zealand, a major gold rush started at the southern end of the South Island, near the Tuapeka river in Otago province. The small settlement of Lawrence became a centre for the gold miners during the boom years. Appropriately enough, at least one gold-stamped WHR binding was there. Figure 17.3 shows a printed label for the Cafe de Paris on the front pastedown of a volume in the deluxe series issue of Charles Dickens' *120. All the Year Round 1864*.

Joel Boulton opened his Cafe de Paris in December 1868, advertising it extensively in the *Tuapeka Times and Goldfields Reporter and Advertiser*.[8] The library was listed as the principal attraction:

> The library is replete with the most popular Works, Local and Home Papers, &c. / A separate room for ladies. / Chess, Draughts, &c

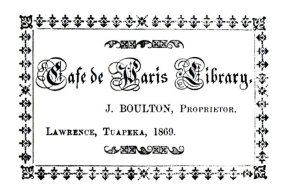

17.3 – Library label in a New Zealand gold rush town, on *All the Year Round 1864*. Width 68mm.

Chapter Seventeen – Contemporary Owners

12. GIFT FROM A SCULPTOR IN ROME

Turning now to ownership in continental Europe, a copy of *199. Deborah's Drawer 1871* with WHR cover bears on its front pastedown an oval bookseller's ticket that reads, 'Ermanno Loescher & Cia. Libreria Internationale / Roma / Corso 346-347'.

Facing this is an 1877 gift inscription to a daughter from her father. He was Shakspere Wood, an English sculptor and writer, who first visited Rome in 1851 and made it his home.

13. IMPORTED TO AMERICA

A book with Rimmel's *144. The Book of Perfumes 1865* cover by WHR was published in Philadelphia by Lippincott in 1866, according to its title page. An inscription indicates that it was given as a present in Montgomery, Alabama in 1868. The book also bears a binder's ticket of Bone & Son, showing that Lippincott had imported it from London.

14. HOME-GROWN IN AMERICA

A presentation copy of the Illustrated Edition of Ik Marvel's bestseller, *Reveries of a bachelor* (NY: Charles Scribner, 1852) is clothed with a version of the *7. Pilgrimages 1850* cover design by WHR (as shown in Figure 16.11). The spine carries a close copy of the original, while the front cover's gilt frame is a looser version of the original.

The proximal source of the WHR design will have been an engraving of the WHR design which appeared in the first instalment of the *Art Journal* catalogue of the Great Exhibition, in May 1851. This was widely distributed in America, with its wrapper bearing the publisher's address in New York as well as London, and priced (for Great Exhibition double-numbers) at $1.50 as well 5s. The author (Donald Grant Mitchell) has dated his inscription in New York as 28 November 1851, so Scribner was in the forefront of American publishers who surfed the wave of *Pilgrimages 1850* adoption.

These examples illustrate that books with WHR covers initially acquired in the United States tended to bear American imprints, whereas those acquired in other countries outside Britain bore standard London imprints.

NOTES

1. *The Times*, 27 December 1855, p. 7.
2. Although *The Rhine* bears on its title page the printed date 1856, it was reviewed by the *Athenaeum* on 8 December 1855
3. *Court Circular*, 28 April 1875.
4. William White, *History, Gazetteer and Directory of Norfolk*, third edition (Sheffield: William White; London: Simpkin Marshall, 1864), p. 223.
5. Joseph Foster, *Alumni Oxonienses: The Members of the University of Oxford, 1715–1886*, Vol. 3 (Oxford and London: James Parker, 1891).
6. This and other details are provided in Jane Greatorex, *Manors, Mills & Manuscripts Series: Coggeshall Abbey and Abbey Mill* [cover title] (Castle Hedingham, Essex: Jane Greatorex, 1999), pp. 53-61.
7. Reproduced by Greatorex, p. 55.
8. See paperspast.natlib.govt.nz

EIGHTEEN

Patrons

SOME OF WHR'S ARTISTIC OUTPUT was commissioned by private individuals, usually wealthy, and considered here first. After that, commissions are considered from professionals of more modest means, particularly publishers. They include some of the most interesting people animating the world of nineteenth-century publishing, who clearly admired WHR's art and acted as patrons for it.

PRIVATE PATRONS

DUDLEY COUTTS MARJORIBANKS

Dudley Coutts Marjoribanks (1820–94) fulfilled for WHR the classic role of a patron, directly soliciting artworks from him. Dudley was a son of Edward Marjoribanks, a wealthy partner in Coutts Bank. He served as an MP and added to his wealth by brewing. His successful career was rewarded by a baronetcy in 1866 and a peerage in 1881, when he became Lord Tweedmouth. Marjoribanks' London residence from 1854 was in Park Lane, where in due course he also bought the house next door, demolished them both, and in their place built Brook House, which he filled with his art collections.[1] Marjoribanks and WHR may have met through a shared interest in old pottery. They both appeared, for example, in Marryat's *Pottery* of 1857, Marjoribanks as an important contemporary collector and WHR by virtue of two of his drawings of majolica (one is reproduced here as Figure 7.3) that had appeared originally in the 1849 *Art Journal*.[2] The WHR archive of the V&A contains a number of designs for Dudley Coutts Marjoribanks, including scattered artwork for 'A Calendar of the Months' for 1852.[3] Elsewhere in the archive a design for a presentation plate bears the date 1866, so Marjoribanks was a long-term patron of WHR.[4] Other designs for Marjoribanks include what appears to be a book cover, an armorial incorporating monograms for DCM and IM (Dudley and his wife, Isabella) and a monogram for IM alone.[5]

  WHR's most important work for Dudley Coutts Marjoribanks was perhaps the creation from Soame Jenyns' *Disquisitions* [1782] of an artwork which was exhibited at the 1862 International Exhibition in London. Each page of the book was decorated by WHR with pen and ink, and the whole was then re-bound by M.M. Holloway in morocco with inlays, to WHR's design. Figure 11.11 shows the binding, as printed in colour lithography by

Chapter Eighteen – Patrons

Waring in 1863.[6] Holloway exhibited it at the London 1862 Exhibition, where he was awarded a Medal of the Exhibition 'For elegance of design and taste in finish'.[7]

Waring's brief accompanying description was confused and mistakenly referred to 'this very beautiful cover, designed by H. Shaw … to inclose a series of exquisite original etchings by Mr. H. Rogers'. Examination of a detailed contemporary review of Holloway's exhibits shows that Waring conflated two different volumes.[8] The review described

> 'Shaw's Decorative Arts of the Middle Ages,' elaborately tooled and inlaid, from a design by the Author, made expressly for the work

and

> 'Soame Jenyns' Disquisitions,' in a richly-inlaid Grolier style … from the design of W.H. Rogers.

A copy of Waring's image of the cover is present in the WHR archive in the V&A.[9] A pencilled inscription on the verso states that the cover was designed by WHR for an ornamented copy of Jenyns' *Disquisitions*, and gives the date of that as 1857.[10] The inscription's attribution of the entire artwork to WHR was confirmed when the *Disquisitions* appeared, nearly a century after its creation, as Lot 7 in a sale by Hodgson & Co. 'of finely bound books … sold by order of [a later] Lady Tweedmouth' on 11 November 1948. The catalogue stated that both 'the binding and the text-decoration' were signed by 'W.H. Rogers [1855]'. It was sold to a private buyer, and has not been traced further.[11]

SAMUEL DODD

Samuel Dodd was well-off but not rich, and lived a quiet life in the vicinity of Kentish Town Road, supported by his investments. His quiet life was a long one (born 20 June 1802, died aged ninety-two on 12 February 1895).[12] Dodd was interested in antiquities, and in 1853 donated an Iron Age coin to the British Museum.[13] He was a relation of the 'Mr. Dodd, of St. James's' who owned an enamel after Dürer which WHR mentioned in an 1848 article.[14] Dodd was a subscriber to privately printed archaeological works and lender to a provincial museum.[15]

Samuel Dodd appears to have commissioned WHR to enhance artistically the contents of a single copy of a volume in a manner similar to that carried out for Dudley Coutts Marjoribanks, though in Dodd's case the coverage was less thorough and the binding was left unchanged. The volume was a *Biblia Sacra* of 1581, printed in London by Henricus Middletonus. In 1865 it became Dodd's second donation to the British Museum, from which it passed to the British Library on its creation.[16]

ANGELA BURDETT-COUTTS

Commissions from private patrons, as opposed to professionals, were probably received by WHR most often via his father's wood-carving firm, for whom WHR was chief designer. Like Samuel Dodd, Angela Burdett-Coutts (1814–1906) reached the age of ninety-two years, but there any resemblance stopped. She was famous as the wealthiest woman in the country. Originally named Angela Burdett, she had had to add 'Coutts' in 1837 in order to

18.1 – Picture frame designed by WHR and carved in boxwood for Angela Burdett-Coutts, from the *Magazine of Art*, 1881. Image height 190mm.

inherit an estate of approximately £1.8 million derived originally from her grandfather, Thomas Coutts, the builder of Coutts Bank. She also became the most celebrated philanthropist of her time, funding innumerable charitable causes, and was created Baroness Burdett-Coutts in 1871.

As a friend of Queen Victoria, Burdett-Coutts would have been interested in emulating Victoria's commission of exquisite boxwood carvings designed by WHR. She decided upon a carved picture frame bearing the first line from Keats' *Endymion*, 'A thing of beauty is a joy forever', along with a carved roundel. Both objects were exhibited at the 1862 International Exhibition in London, and the Keats and roundel designs were engraved in its *Art Journal* catalogue, as described in Chapter 11.

The Keats line had been adopted as the motto for the Manchester Exhibition of Art Treasures in 1857, where Burdett-Coutts had exhibited, and the 1862 *Art Journal* catalogue explained that the frame was 'destined to hold that lady's testimonial' from Manchester (a certificate printed by Day & Son, lithographers to the Queen).

George Alfred Rogers, brother of WHR, was responsible for another display of the Burdett-Coutts picture frame (and also the Queen's cradle) in a large exhibition of wood-carving which he co-organised in 1880 at the Albert Hall. Figure 18.1 reproduces the illustration of the picture frame which he published when writing about the exhibition subsequently. He described the frame as:[17]

> in a somewhat mixed style, but very successful in result, being a combination of the more delicate Renaissance and natural flowers and foliage. It was designed by ... the late Mr. W. Harry Rogers, whose name will be known to those of our readers who have interested themselves in art-work during the last forty years, for he lent his facile pen and imaginative mind to almost every branch of art-manufacture.

G.A. Rogers was a drily humorous writer, and later in his account turned to what was inside the frame:

> This elaborate frame was made for a lithographic testimonial of thanks, a copy of which was forwarded to all contributors to the Manchester Fine Art Exhibition. We mention this to show how the art of wood-carving is appreciated in some parts of England, for it was lent some years since to a country exhibition, and was shown and entered in the catalogue as a 'Lithograph by Day,' the authorities probably not dreaming that the frame was worth over a hundred pounds, and the plate it contained comparatively nothing except as a memento of a great artistic display.

RALPH SNEYD

Another wealthy patron of wood-carving, representative of many others, was the landowner Ralph Sneyd (1793–1870) of Keele Hall in Staffordshire, who in the 1850s spent £80,000 replacing his old family pile with a more up-to-date pile, employing Anthony Salvin as architect.[18] William Gibbs Rogers was called in to provide, among other artefacts, carvings of fruit to occupy tall panels in the large (52 x 32 ft) drawing room, and also to solve what Sneyd perceived to be a problem with Salvin's ceiling of the room.[19] The coffered ceiling consisted of an array of large octagons, interspersed with smaller hexagons and crosses. Sneyd had very decided views on architecture, and the money to indulge them.[20] He first decided to have the fields within these three types of coffer painted bright blue, green and red, respectively, but then decided that the octagons' blue fields overpowered the others.[21]

As a result, Rogers was asked to provide designs for carvings with central bosses to occupy and tone down the thirty-two large blue octagons, which would also enhance the ceiling's overall richness. A letter survives from WHR to his father adding six more designs to those he had provided already, the additions comprising five symbolic designs (two for Kings of England and three relating to the meaning of 'Sneyd') and one abstract design.[22] In the end, Sneyd was presented with a scheme employing eleven different WHR designs – but opted instead for just two of WHR's non-symbolic designs to occupy alternating octagons.[23]

In Figure 2.6, referred to earlier, William Gibbs Rogers is shown holding one of these WHR-designed octagons for the drawing room of Keele Hall. Prior to mounting each panel within the ceiling's coffering, the flat part of each panel was painted blue and the relief carving was gilded. The overall effect is unorthodox but has been described as 'superb'.[24] The ceiling is still present in the mansion, which was acquired in the mid-twentieth century, along with part of its estate, from a later Ralph Sneyd in order to house the institution which became the University of Keele.

PROFESSIONAL PATRONS

Individuals such as Marjoribanks and Sneyd who commissioned one-off artworks from WHR for their private enjoyment were in a minority. More often the commissions came from manufacturers, who needed WHR's designs to maximise the attractiveness to potential purchasers of the artefacts they manufactured. Almost invariably, multiple copies would be produced from any single design, in order to benefit from the economies of scale which transformed manufacturing in the nineteenth century.

It would not be correct, however, to think of such artefacts as being churned out by machines in large numbers. In the mid-nineteenth century, many processes within, say, book production and silversmithing were still carried out by hand, and the numbers of copies of an artefact produced were usually relatively small. One and a half centuries later, it is often difficult to find more than a handful of surviving copies, and sometimes it has not been possible to locate even a single surviving copy of a WHR-designed artefact.

For book covers, the division of responsibility between the publisher and the bookbinder in commissioning designs from WHR seems to have been a flexible one. At one extreme, 'publisher commission', it is clear that the publisher Joseph Cundall was in direct contact with WHR and could discuss designs with him without an intermediary. At the other extreme, 'binder commission', it appears that when a vogue for small gilt roundels flourished in the late 1860s, WHR sold designs to several different bookbinders directly. In between these two extremes, there was probably 'binder mediation of publisher commission', where a publisher obtained a WHR design for a forthcoming book via a book-binder intermediary. For WHR designs, the go-to firm of bookbinders was W. Bone & Son of 76 Fleet Street (see Chapter 16). They presumably acted as, if not a patron, then at least as a mediator of publisher patronage.

WILLIAM THOMAS BONE

It was the 'Son' who was running W. Bone & Son in the period when they executed many of WHR's designs for book covers. According to contemporary records, the son was William Thomas Bone (1817–90) and he had been apprenticed as a bookbinder on 7 June 1831 to his father, William Bone (1794/5–1864). The father commenced bookbinding in the era of binding individual books in leather, but by the time his son commenced bookbinding the shift to cloth was well under way. As indicated in Chapter 16, edition-binding in cloth came in from the 1820s, and blocking the cloth in gold started in the early 1830s.

Father and son Bone soon became the partners in a bookbinding firm, which William Thomas Bone referred to in 1842 when he was a witness in a court case at the Old Bailey.[25] From about 1848, the firm started identifying much of their output with a small binder's ticket on the rear endpaper. Figure 18.2 shows the seven Bone signatures described by

Chapter Eighteen – Patrons

18.2 – The seven signatures of Bone & Son: A 1848–65, A1 (white instead of lemon) 1850, B 1857, C 1858–62, D 1865–9, E 1868–83, E1 (lilac instead of red) 1870. Widths: A and A1 18mm, B 40mm, C 21mm, D 17mm, E & E1 19mm.

Ball, together with their dates of use.[26] The six tickets are all found on books with covers designed by WHR, and on stylistic grounds the oval ticket C, used 1858–62, looks like a design by WHR.

By 1851, William Thomas Bone was running the firm. In the census of that year, he was living at 119 Portland Place North, Lambeth and his occupation was listed as 'Bookbinder / employs 70 men / 20 females'. His father was living at 4 Minerva Terrace, Islington and his occupation was listed simply as 'Bookbinder'. The father died in 1864 leaving an estate of more than £6,000. William Thomas Bone lived on until 1890, his final house being in Twickenham, and the firm of W. Bone & Son disappeared soon afterwards.

Since the flow of WHR covers executed by Bone & Son continued for more than twenty years, WHR and William Thomas Bone can be assumed to have been on good terms with each other. However, only one small piece of evidence hints at a warmer relation. This is an album in the WHR archive at the V&A, which is inscribed on the front pastedown, 'From W Bone / Feb. 1860', with WHR's signature added above it.[27]

We turn now to a group of people who acted as editors and authors, but for WHR primarily as publishers, and included two well-known married couples who acted jointly as patrons of WHR's work. The earliest to discover WHR were Mr and Mrs S.C. Hall, followed by Joseph Cundall. Later came Mr and Mrs S.O. Beeton and James Bertrand Payne (who ran Edward Moxon & Co.).

MR AND MRS S.C. HALL

Mr and Mrs S.C. Hall were influential early adopters of WHR's artwork. Samuel Carter Hall (1800–89) and Anna Maria Fielding (1800–81) were both born in Ireland but gravitated early on to London, where they met and in 1824 were married.[28] Both were prolific writers, and two of WHR's most lavish early book cover designs were for books by Anna Maria Hall, 3. *Drawing Room Table Book* 1848, and 7. *Pilgrimages* 1850.

Carter Hall's influence blossomed with that of the *Art Union* magazine (later the *Art*

207

Journal), which he edited from its first appearance in 1839 until 1880, and also became sole owner of in 1840. The magazine was the pioneer of art journalism in Britain and built up a healthy circulation in the 1840s, increasingly illustrating its pages with attractive but expensive engravings. As described in Chapter 7, many of these engravings reproduced WHR's drawings.

18.3 – The Rosery, residence of Anna Maria and Samuel Carter Hall, engraved as a letterhead, 1842. Image width 90mm.

From 1839 to 1849, the Halls lived in The Rosery in Old Brompton, Kensington, where WHR would surely have visited them. Thomas Moore called it a 'pretty little cottage', while Henry Vizetelly described it as the 'little doll's house' where he had attended a crowded reception for the Swedish Nightingale, Jenny Lind (1820–87).[29] Figure 18.3 shows its depiction on the Halls' letterhead, on an 1842 letter. The Survey of London reproduced a later ('about 1845') version of the same engraving but with the addition of a single-storey Gothic library on the east (left) side, and commented drily that this 'picturesque view … omits altogether the adjoining house to the west'.[30]

The way that the Halls presented their cottage was very much the same as the way in which they presented themselves, as an idealised view of the genuinely meritorious. Carter, in particular, was habitually self-righteous, which has led to a long-standing question as to whether he was the basis for the fictional hypocrite Pecksniff in Martin Chuzzlewit (1843–4) by Charles Dickens. Not really, a biographer has concluded after detailed consideration of the evidence.[31] Another review concluded that Carter attracted contemporary criticism in a number of quarters because his failings were more conspicuous than were his genuine positive qualities.[32] The Halls certainly had real merits as writers, generous hosts and, of particular relevance to WHR, patrons who did not stint production values in order to maximise profit.

During the 1840s, Carter Hall had had to dilute his ownership of the *Art Union / Art Journal* to fund the magazine's expansion. In 1851 came what was both a triumph and a disaster for Carter Hall, his *Art Journal* catalogue of the Great Exhibition. The catalogue itself was the triumph, with WHR's contributions instrumental in ensuring that the catalogue did justice to an event which captured the imagination of the world, as described in Chapter 11. The disaster was that the catalogue's lavish production values and competition from the official catalogue meant that sales, though extensive, did not cover the costs of production (see Chapter 9). Carter had to sell his remaining holding in the *Art Journal* to the publisher, George Virtue, who had become joint owner in 1848, and thereafter Carter was merely the paid editor of the magazine. Control passed to George's son, James Sprent Virtue, in 1855.[33]

Carter Hall still held one potential money-spinner, which was the permission Queen Victoria had granted him in 1851 to copy and then engrave (from the copies) many of the pictures of the Royal Collection. These would be published both in the *Art Journal* and as the four volumes of the *Royal Gallery of Art*, originally issued from 1854 in large-format Parts with cover design by WHR, *47. Royal Gallery Parts 1854*. Once again, however, the up-front costs of the lavish production overwhelmed Hall, plunging him into debt.[34] His horizons thereafter were narrowed, limiting WHR commissions to enhancing the *Art Journal* catalogues for the series of international expositions that followed the Great Exhibition.

JOSEPH CUNDALL

During a long career, Joseph Cundall (1818–95) produced a stream of artistic books for the discerning buyer. In 1841, the young Cundall took over the Juvenile Library at 12 Old Bond Street, and in 1843 became the publisher of the Home Treasury series of children's books instigated by the ubiquitous Henry Cole under his pseudonym Felix Summerly.[35] Also in 1843, Cole and Cundall launched the first printed Christmas card.[36] It was thus natural that when Cole moved on to the creation of Felix Summerly's Art-Manufactures from 1846, Joseph Cundall's premises became a principal retail outlet for Summerly's articles during their short period of production.

Cundall suffered a bankruptcy in about 1849 and moved to new premises, 21 Old Bond Street, with a partner who had also been bankrupted, H.M. Addey.[37] The Cundall & Addey partnership lasted only until the end of 1851. After that the imprint on books became Addey & Co., but the firm continued to reprint Cundall books and to publish new books which appear to have been put together by Cundall.[38] It was at this point that Cundall and WHR started a collaboration which was to last for the next twenty years, with Cundall commissioning designs from WHR for the covers of three books published by Addey in 1853, namely, *36. Wonder Castle 1853, 35. The Charm 1853* and *37. Sketches in Ultra-marine 1853*. Henry Markinfield Addey soon left the scene and in 1860 emigrated with William Newman, a *Punch* artist, to New York where together they started up an important comical magazine, *Momus*.[39]

The way that Cundall operated behind the scenes at Addey & Co. set a pattern for the future, firstly in providing regular commissions for WHR and secondly in keeping a low profile himself. Sometimes Cundall's name did appear in a book as publisher or in some other capacity (e.g. as editor), but at other times his involvement is known only by an oblique route. A good example of this pattern is provided by *182. Masterpieces of Italian Art 1868*. Neither the 1868 first edition nor the later 1870 edition bears any hint of the involvement of Cundall but, in between, the preface of the 1868 'second edition' is signed 'J.C.' Although all three editions are bound in an identical cover designed by

WHR, only the middle edition allows us to infer that Cundall was the patron.

Apart from commissioning many cover designs from WHR, Cundall also commissioned designs for the contents of a number of books, including WHR's extensive suites of embellishments to the poetical works of Edgar Allan Poe and of Robert Burns, both 1858. An indication of the personal interactions which must have occurred between Cundall and WHR is provided by the JC monograms which WHR created for Cundall. An early printed one appeared in *56. Sabbath Bells 1856* (Figure 13.1), and a Cundall family scrapbook contained a manuscript sheet of six more extensive monograms and crests for Joseph Cundall, though Cundall appears not to have used these in print.[40]

MR AND MRS S.O. BEETON

If Joseph Cundall catered for the discerning art-lover, the Beetons aimed their publications at a much wider population, centred on the emerging middle classes. Samuel Orchart Beeton (1831–77) and Isabella Mary Mayson (1836–65) were married in 1856.[41] Samuel had entered publishing in 1852 with a bang, producing one of the British editions of Harriet Beecher Stowe's bestselling *Uncle Tom's Cabin* and also starting up a successful magazine, the *Englishwoman's Domestic Magazine*. After their marriage, Samuel and Isabella worked hard as a team, and from 1859 to 1861 S.O. Beeton published in parts *The Book of Household Management* by Mrs Isabella Beeton, the book which was to immortalise her.

Sales of *The Book of Household Management* took off from the start and, thus encouraged, from the early 1860s the Beetons greatly upped their production values, chasing ever more sales. From 1863 they commissioned WHR to create striking cloth and paper covers for a number of their books and magazines. WHR was, for example, the largest contributor of binding designs to Beeton's 'Boy's Own Library', such as *116. Beeton's Robinson Crusoe 1864*. Their lavish gilt covers, larger format and extensive illustrations, often in colour, raised the bar for the appearance of children's books intended for wide circulation.

The flowering of the Beeton books was cut short all too quickly. Tragically, Isabella died in 1865 aged only twenty-eight years, days after giving birth. Her story has been told in several biographies.[42] Samuel's finances hit the buffers the following year, and the outcome was that a rival publisher, Ward, Lock and Tyler, took over his Beeton brand name, most of the existing Beeton titles (including *The Book of Household Management*), and all of Beeton's future publishing activities. Production values sank back down and commissions for WHR from Samuel dried up after 1866, apart from two small cover designs in 1870 (*213. Beeton's Modern Men and Women 1870* and *214. Beeton's Bible Dictionary 1870*).

Mrs Beeton's *Dictionary of Every-Day Cookery* was published with covers by WHR for both its paper-covered twelve-part issue (completed 1 March 1865), *134. Mrs Beeton's Everyday Cookery Wrapper 1864* and, for its cloth-covered book issue, *135. Mrs Beeton's Everyday Cookery Cloth 1865*, with just time for Samuel to add a leaf to the final part (and to the book) mourning the tragic passing of Isabella on 6 February 1865. It was entitled 'Usque ad Finem' (i.e. 'To the very end'), and commenced:

> Her hand has lost its cunning – the firm, true hand that wrote these *formulæ*, and penned the information contained in this little book. Cold in the silent tomb lie the once nimble, useful fingers … .

The view has been expressed that Isabella was quickly forgotten, but this seems mistaken. It has been claimed that:[43]

> After 1865 the 'Usque Ad Finem' obituary was quietly dispensed with, never to appear again in any of the publications with which she had been associated.

But, in fact, editions of this book up to at least the sixty-first thousand of *c.* 1872 did include the Usque ad Finem tribute. Similarly, it has been claimed that, when S.O. Beeton himself died in 1877:[44]

> The fact that Isabella had written a book that, over the next twenty-five years, would make her name live in history and eclipse that of Sam's would have astounded everyone who gathered around the musty Norwood grave in June 1877, including Jerrold and Dowty.

However, on the contrary, those gathering to mourn Sam, including his colleagues Jerrold and Dowty, would have been fully aware for years of the unprecedented fame of Isabella's *Book of Household Management*, 1861. As the 'Christmas, 1870' list of Ward, Lock and Tyler put it:

> The Best Book in the World for English Families, At Home, Abroad, in British Colonies, India, or in the United States. Original Volume, 146th Thousand. New Edition, 30th Thousand. Total, 176,000. … As a Wedding Gift, Birthday Book, or Presentation Volume at any Period of the Year, or upon any Anniversary whatever, Mrs. Beeton's Household Management is entitled to the very first place.

JAMES BERTRAND PAYNE

James Bertrand Payne (1833–98) was both more shadowy and more shady than the other publishers considered here. Payne was shadowy because he was not a publisher in his own right, but instead managed the firm of Edward Moxon and Co. from 1864, on behalf of Emma and Arthur Moxon (Edward's widow and his son, who was a minor). He was shady because he soon started to behave less as the manager and more as the owner of the Moxon firm. After a few years the firm collapsed and a claim by Emma Moxon of fraud by Payne was upheld.[45] Sitting in the Court of Chancery for Moxon *v* Payne, the Lords Justices of Appeal observed:[46]

> The obtaining of property by means of undue influence had always been treated in this court as a fraud of the gravest character.

When Payne first took control in 1864, the Moxon firm had for years been publishing poetry in an austere format, unillustrated and with plain covers. Payne decided to break into the gift-book market, where premium prices were paid by purchasers but publishers could conversely incur heavy costs for illustrations and more interesting bindings. Eventually, as analysed by Jim Cheshire, losses made on Gustave Doré illustrations for Tennyson appear to have been instrumental in the collapse of the firm. At the start of Payne's regime, however, he succeeded in commissioning several leading artists to produce elegant gilt bindings for

Moxon books: Dante Gabriel Rossetti for Swinburne's *Atalanta in Calydon* (1865), WHR for Tilston's *145. Edwy and Elgiva 1865*, and Arthur Hughes for Tennyson's *Enoch Arden* (1866). For the latter two titles, Payne introduced a new way of crediting not only the artist but also himself. The title page verso of *Edwy and Elgiva* extends the traditional listing of the printer there with:

> the cover from a design by W. Harry Rogers; the book produced under the superintendence of [JBP monogram in a shield].

With regard to Rossetti's design for *Atalanta*, Swinburne's biographer Edmund Gosse stated that:[47]

> Bertrand Payne, who was now responsible for the firm of Moxon, believed that the only hope of success which the poem offered lay in the beauty of its appearance, and accordingly no pains were spared to adorn the ivory-white sides of the buckram cover with mystic golden spheres.

Payne's fears about *Atalanta* turned out to be unfounded, and he probably had much deeper misgivings about *Edwy and Elgiva*, whose poetry was duly slammed by the *Athenaeum*:[48]

> *Edwy and Elgiva: a Tragedy*, by Thomas Tilston, B.A. (Moxon & Co.), does unusual credit to the binder and printer. … Its surface is perfection; would that we could say half as much of its substance!

Snatching whatever comfort he could from such comments, Payne adopted WHR as his favourite designer. WHR's circular gilt 'E M & Co' motif on the front cover of *Edwy and Elgiva* appeared on much of Moxon's output, and Payne commissioned several further cover designs from WHR. Many of these clothed the works of Martin Tupper, including the range of formats in which his famous bestseller *Proverbial Philosophy* was packaged, starting with *147. Pocket Proverbial Philosophy 1865*. The public appetite for *Proverbial Philosophy* was at last becoming sated, but Payne's refreshment of the Tupper brand by packaging it in attractive new WHR covers managed to squeeze out yet further sales.

WHR's commissions from J. Bertrand Payne started a couple of years after his commissions from the Beetons, but likewise were unexpectedly ended by external forces after a period of only about three years. Finding stable patronage for artistic designs among the publishers was no easy task for WHR.

NOTES

1. F.H.W. Sheppard (ed.), *Survey of London: Volume 40, the Grosvenor Estate in Mayfair, Part 2 (The Buildings)*, (1980), pp. 264–89.
2. Joseph Marryat, *A History of Pottery and Porcelain, Mediaeval and Modern*, second edition (John Murray, 1857), pp. 26, 76, 438.
3. Rough sketches are at V&A E694.101–1998. Worked-up sketches are at E694.52,53,54,55–1998. More detailed drawings, which WHR annotated for Marjoribanks, are at E693.73-1998 and E693.74-1998; the latter includes the date 1852.

4. V&A E694.5-1998.

5. These are V&A E694.9-1998, E694.7-1998 and E694.8-1998, respectively.

6. J.B. Waring, *Masterpieces of Industrial Art & Sculpture at the International Exhibition*, 1862, three volumes (Day & Son, 1863), Plate 206.

7. *Reports of the Juries* (1863), Class 28, p. 12.

8. *Bookseller*, Vol. 53, 31 May 1862, p. 322.

9. V&A E693.190-1998.

10. The inscription refers to 'Sir Dudley' and hence must have been made between 1866 and 1881, following Marjoribank's baronetcy and before his peerage.

11. *Book-auction Records*, Vol. 46 (London and New York: Stevens & Stiles, 1950), p. 269.

12. *The Times,* 14 February 1895.

13. BM 1853,0507.1.

14. W. Harry Rogers, 'On the history of enamelling', *Journal of the British Archaeological Association*, Vol. 3, 1848, 280-96; p. 292. This was James Dodd, of 31 St James's Street.

15. Charles Roach Smith, *Collectanea antiqua*, Vol. 4, 1857, p. 226; Charles Roach Smith, *Illustrations of Roman London* (1859), p. 173; *Wiltshire Archaeological and Natural History Magazine*, Vol. 6, 1860, p. 260.

16. BL, Western Manuscripts, Add MS 26751.

17. George Alfred Rogers, 'Wood-carving.—I & II', *Magazine of Art*, Vol. 4, 1881, pp. 120-24, 226-32; pp. 227-8, 231.

18. J.M. Kolbert, *Keele Hall: A Victorian Country House* (University of Keele, 1986), pp. 3, 10, 52.

19. *Ibid.*, p. 45.

20. David Spring, 'Ralph Sneyd: Tory country gentleman', *Bulletin of the John Rylands Library*, Vol. 38, 1956, pp. 535-55; pp. 544-5.

21. Kolbert, *Keele Hall, op. cit.*, p. 40.

22. Dated 12 November 1862; National Art Library's Special Collections, V&A number MSL/1985/4.

23. Kolbert, *Keele Hall, op. cit.*, p. 40 & Plate 20.

24. *Ibid.*, p. 41.

25. oldbaileyonline.org
Case 1326. An employee of the printers of *Chamber's Edinburgh Journal*, Bradbury and Evans, had stolen a hundred copies. He was sentenced to transportation for seven years.

26. Douglas Ball, *Victorian Publishers' Bindings* (Library Association, 1985), pp. 172-3. The embossed B (W. BONE & SON, BINDERS) does not appear on any WHR covers, and is known only from Routledge's Ainsworth titles.

27. V&A E851-1998.

28. Peter Mandler, 'Hall [née Fielding], Anna Maria (1800–1881)' and 'Hall, Samuel Carter (1800–1889)', *Oxford Dictionary of National Biography* (2004).

29. See Maureen Keane, *Mrs. S.C. Hall: A Literary Biography* (Gerrard's Cross: Colin Smythe, 1997), p. 199.

30. Hermione Hobhouse (ed.), 'Hereford Square area: The Day estate', in *Survey of London*, Volume 42, 1986, pp. 158-67, Plate 65c.

31. Hazel Morris, *Hand, Head and Heart: Samuel Carter Hall and the Art Journal* (Norwich: Michael Russell, 2002), pp. 52-61.

32. Jeremy Maas, 'S.C. Hall and the Art Journal', *Connoisseur*, 1976, Vol. 191, pp. 206-09.

33. S.C. Hall, *Retrospect of a Long Life: From 1815 to 1883*, two volumes (Richard Bentley & Son, 1883), Vol. 1, p. 380; G.C. Boase, revised by J.P. Hopson, 'Virtue, James Sprent (1829–1892)', *Oxford Dictionary of National Biography* (2004).

34. Morris, *Hand, Head and Heart, op. cit.*, pp. 100-08.

35. Ruari McLean, *Joseph Cundall: A Victorian Publisher* (Pinner: Private Libraries Association, 1976), p. 4.

36. *Ibid.*, p. 12.

37. *Ibid.*, p. 22.

38. *Ibid.*, p. 75.

39. Jane E. Brown and Richard Samuel West, *William Newman: A Victorian Cartoonist in London and New York* (Easthampton, MA: Periodyssey Press, 2008), pp. 31-2, 37-45.

40. The sheet was reproduced by McLean in his *Cundall*, p. 92.

41. Janette Ryan, 'Beeton [née Mayson], Isabella Mary (1836–1865)' and Margaret Beetham, 'Beeton, Samuel Orchart (1831–1877)', *Oxford Dictionary of National Biography* (2004).

42. Most recently, by Kathryn Hughes, *The Short Life & Long Times of Mrs Beeton* (Fourth Estate, 2005).

43. *Ibid.*, p. 384.

44. *Ibid.*, p. 382.

45. Jim Cheshire, 'The fall of the house of Moxon: James Bertrand Payne and the illustrated *Idylls of the King*', *Victorian Poetry*, 2012, pp. 50, 67-90; pp. 67-9, 88.

46. *The Times*, 13 June 1873, p. 12, Law Report.

47. Edmund Gosse, *The Life of Algernon Charles Swinburne* (Macmillan, 1917), p. 107.

48. *Athenaeum*, 18 March 1865, p. 384.

Appendices

APPENDIX A
Gallery of Book Covers

IN THIS GALLERY OF BOOK COVERS, 244 book cover designs by William Harry Rogers known to have been put into production as publishers' bindings or wrappers are described and (in all but two cases) illustrated. Each WHR binding design is shown on an actual publication, usually the book on which it first appeared. Spine and front cover are shown as the two standard components of binding design. In a very few instances, the back cover bears a further design of interest, in which case it is shown as well.

The entry for each design in the gallery takes the following form. It starts with its design label, printed in red for clarity, such as *25. Great Cities 1852*. The label gives first the design's *number* in the sequence here of WHR cover designs; second, its *name*; and third, its *date*. These three elements have been arrived at as follows.

DESIGN LABEL: NUMBER

Designs are numbered primarily in the order of year of first use. Within a year, the allocation of numbers aims primarily at grouping similar designs or repeated publishers, rather than arranging by calendar date of publishing. In addition, numbering by year is overridden in the case of closely related designs (e.g. from a publisher's series) that were issued over more than one year, in which case later designs in the series are brought forward to join earlier ones.

DESIGN LABEL: NAME

The design's name is usually taken (often in shortened form) from the title (and sometimes the author) of the first publication to bear the design. Occasionally a further descriptor has to be added to distinguish between two different designs by WHR for the same book contents. Two extra terms are also occasionally added where relevant. First, the term '(Re-issued)' means that the WHR design appeared on an issue of a book which was later than the date on its title page. Second, the term '(Modified)' means that a WHR design taken from inside a book has been modified, without WHR's involvement, for use on a cover in America.

DESIGN LABEL: DATE

The date assigned to each design is the date of the first publication to bear that design. If the publication has a date on its title page, then that is used.[1] If the publication is not dated

Appendix A – Gallery of Book Covers

on the title page, then its year is deduced from other sources, such as contemporary reviews or advertisements.

Each design label is followed by a description which again focuses on the publication on which WHR's cover design first appeared. Each description has five elements. The first four elements are always given in the same order, in the first paragraph.

1. TITLE PAGE

Standard title page information is given: author, title, publisher, year. If the year is not printed on the title page, it is shown here in square brackets. Unless indicated otherwise, the place of publication is London.

2. ATTRIBUTION

The reason for attributing the design to WHR is given. For the great majority of designs, the reason is that it includes a WHR monogram as signature. If it does, it is indicated whether the signature is on the spine, the front cover or both. For unsigned designs, one or more of the following objective pieces of evidence is usually given: WHR is identified as the designer within the book; WHR is identified as the designer within a contemporary advertisement; the unsigned cover design is the same as a printed design which is signed by WHR; or the design is present in the WHR archive at the V&A. Finally, for a very small number of unsigned designs, the attribution is made because of high overlap with known WHR designs in terms of author, publisher, binder and style.

3. BINDER (IF KNOWN)

If the binder's name is known (usually from the presence of a binder's ticket), then it is given. If the name is not known, no mention is made of the binder.

4. SIZE

The final information in the first paragraph of each entry is the front cover's height in millimetres. Traditional indications of size, such as 'quarto', are not used because they really refer to page imposition (for nineteenth-century books of limited significance), and provide only an indirect suggestion of size.

5. COMMENTARY

A second paragraph contains a short commentary on the design or the publication on which it appears.

1. The Builder 1848
The Builder. This design was used from 1 January 1848 (Issue 256, Volume 6) until 1912. The masthead is signed WHR. 342mm.

This design occurred on the first of the outer, unnumbered pages of each issue, which carried advertisements. They enclosed the inner, numbered editorial pages. When the issues were bound up, the outer pages were usually discarded.

2. The Town 1848
Leigh Hunt, The town; its memorable characters and events, two volumes (Smith, Elder, 1848). It is stated internally (Vol. 1, p. xii) that the cover is designed by WHR. Bound by Westleys. 206mm.

Internal attribution of the cover designer, as here, is rare, though Smith, Elder did make a similar internal attribution that year for another Leigh Hunt title (this was for the cover by Owen Jones of *A Jar of Honey from Mount Hybla*). Publishers soon realised that internal attribution was a problem if they later wanted to have those pages bound up in a different, cheaper cover.

3. Drawing Room Table Book 1848
Mrs S.C. Hall (ed.), The drawing room table book (George Virtue [1848]). The spine lettering matches the engraved title page, which is signed WHR. Bound by Westleys. 296mm.

This was the first of several cover designs by WHR for Mrs S.C. Hall or her husband, who are discussed in Chapter 18 (although she was born as Anna Maria Fielding, her publications style her as Mrs S.C. Hall). The book appeared at the end of 1848 with *1849* on its cover (but not inside), and was advertised in *The Times* on Christmas Day, 1848, as 'beautifully bound'. Later copies have the cover date removed.

4. Seven Lamps 1849
John Ruskin, The seven lamps of architecture (Smith, Elder, 1849). WHR was thanked in the book by Ruskin for designing its cover (Note 14 on p. 204, cited on p. 133). Bound by Westleys. 265mm.

In this celebrated work, Ruskin identified his seven lamps by the chapter headings Sacrifice, Truth, Power, Beauty, Life, Memory and Obedience. These are rendered on the cover (whether by Ruskin or by WHR) by Latin terms not present in the text: Religio, Fides, Auctoritas, Observantia, Spiritus, Memoria and Obedienta. WHR's dramatic design is unique (at least for the period) in relying on variation solely in surface level and texture, with lettering and figures not marked in gold or colour but instead emerging in relief.

5. Stones of Venice 1851
John Ruskin, The stones of Venice, three volumes (Smith, Elder, 1851–3). The cover design is attributed to WHR because the volumes have the same author, publisher and binder as the previous design, with characteristic WHR lettering and asymmetries. Bound by Westleys. 268mm.

On the cover of this major work, the stylised vine blind stamping is a free adaptation, with no repetitions, of Ruskin's capital with thistle-like leaves (Vol. 2, Plate VIII, Fig. 15, p. 130) and exemplifies WHR's globally symmetric, locally asymmetric, (*GS-LA*) design principle.

6. Vernon Gallery 1850
S.C. Hall (ed.), The Vernon gallery of British art, four vols (George Virtue, 1850–54). When this design first appeared on the Vernon Gallery, blocked in gilt, it was unsigned but later the original version signed by WHR appeared on paper covers printed for Germany, as shown: Europäische Galerie. Auswahl der berühmtesten Gemälde. London: G. Virtue & Leipzig: G. H. Friedlein, 1858. Bound by Virtue. 384mm.

The *Europäische Galerie* consisted of two series of annual collections of engravings, one for paintings and one for sculptures, and was published from 1852.

7. Pilgrimages 1850
Mrs S.C. Hall, Pilgrimages to English shrines (Arthur Hall, Virtue, 1850). Also second series, 1853. The design was unsigned until an expanded spine was created for *8. Combined Pilgrimages 1853*. Bound by Bone. 224mm.

WHR's design was exhibited at the Great Exhibition in 1851 and illustrated in its *Art Journal* catalogue (p. 39), but without any lettering and hence not previously identified as used on *Pilgrimages 1850*. Illustrated as Figure 11.4 is one of a few copies in morocco rather than cloth. The binding firm of Bone was to become by far the most frequent executant of WHR's designs for covers, as discussed in Chapters 16 and 18.

8. Combined Pilgrimages 1853
Mrs S.C. Hall, Pilgrimages to English shrines, new edition (Arthur Hall, Virtue, 1853). Contains both series. The new spine is signed WHR. Bound by Bone. 224mm.

The price came down from 16s for each of the two individual books ('morocco elegant', as illustrated in Figure 11.4, was 24s) to a guinea (21s) for the combined volume.

9. Colville Family 1853
Frank E. Smedley, The fortunes of the Colville family (George Hoby, 1853). The design is unsigned but so similar to that of *Pilgrimages* 1850 that, given that both books were bound by Westleys (and that Hall, Virtue were on the point of succeeding Hoby as publisher of both) it must be by WHR. Bound by Westleys. 179mm.

The story had been serialised in *Sharpe's London Magazine*, which Smedley edited.

Appendix A – Gallery of Book Covers

1

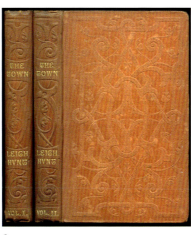
2

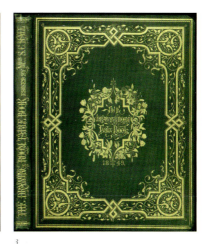
3

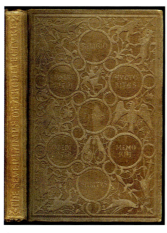
4

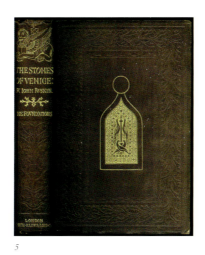
5

6

7

8

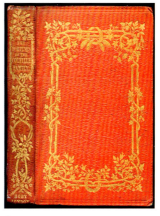
9

William Harry Rogers – Victorian Book Designer and Star of the Great Exhibition

10

11

12

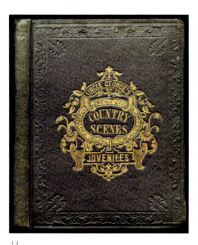
13

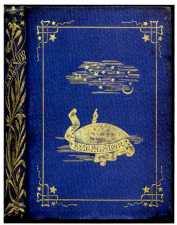
14

16

10. *Pipe of Repose* 1851
Robert Ferguson, The pipe of repose, second edition (John Ollivier, 1851). The spine design is unsigned but known to be by WHR because a proof on cloth is present in the V&A WHR archive, E693.178-1998. 173mm.

Shown here is a later use of the spine design (with a circular gilt device added at the base), on *Poems, by Edward Hind* (Houlston and Stoneman, 1853). The title on the V&A proof is *Oracles from the British Poets*. The *Oracles* compilation by James Smith had four editions between 1849 and 1865, but none of them appears to have used this design.

11. *Art Journal* 1851
The Art Journal, new series, Vol. 3 (London and New York: George Virtue, 1851). Used until 1858. The spine and front cover are signed WHR. Bound by James S. Virtue. 337mm.

This design appeared on quarter-morocco deluxe bindings of volumes of the *Art Journal*, in the period 1851 to 1858. It was only in 1851 that the WHR signature started to appear on gilt bindings. There are a few cases in which the title page dates for gilt bindings signed by WHR are earlier than 1851, but these are in fact late bind-ups of earlier sheets, as will be pointed out in the course of some later entries.

12. *Art Journal Catalogue* 1851
The Art Journal illustrated catalogue, The industry of all nations 1851 (George Virtue, 1851). The front cover is signed WHR. Bound by Bone. 338mm.

The catalogue is the finest published legacy of the Great Exhibition. WHR's central role in the catalogue is traced

Appendix A – Gallery of Book Covers

in Chapter 11. The WHR cover design was used not only on cloth but also – uniquely for WHR designs – on deluxe copies in both morocco and calf. Cloth copies for presentation have an additional printed leaf designed by WHR (see Figure 17.1).

13. *Science of the Exhibition (Modified) 1851*
Uncle George's Juveniles (New York: Leavitt & Allen, 1853). This is an American modification of WHR's design for *The science of the exhibition* in the *Art Journal Catalogue 1851* (p. I★, shown in Figure 11.7). 148mm.

Leavitt and Allen made a habit of borrowing London designs for their book covers, deploying designs by Albert Warren and William Ralston as well. The present design was used for at least ten of the titles in their Uncle George series, all anonymous.

14. *Excelsior 1851*
Alastor [James Orton], 'Excelsior;' or, the realms of poesy (privately printed, 1851). Also: 'Excelsior' or the realms of poesie (Pickering, 1852), which is shown here. The 1852 spine is signed WHR (and replaced a blank 1851 spine). Bound by Bone. 198mm.

Ruari McLean, a student of WHR's images, called this 'A very peculiar design'.[2] The striking front cover does, however, reflect Orton's view of the poet as 'He whose finger is ever pointed to the hopeful Heavens' (1852, p. 101).

15. *The Enthusiast 1852*
James Orton, The enthusiast or the straying angel a poem (Pickering, 1852). The front cover is signed WHR, with a linked back-cover design. Bound by Bone. 196mm.

This book is exceptional for WHR in that he designed a back cover for it – a snapped lily – which was not merely a repeat of the front one. Orton was clearly an enthusiast for WHR's imagery, but was conflicted about the attention it received. His final chapter addressed critical reactions to his previous book, *Excelsior*. He was proud that 'The cover of Excelsior has been almost universally admired, and that by some of the best judges of taste in England' but miffed that '[the editor of 'The Globe'] like the 'Athenaeum' editor, is moth-like attracted to the glittering cover of the book' rather than to its contents (pp. 59, 62).

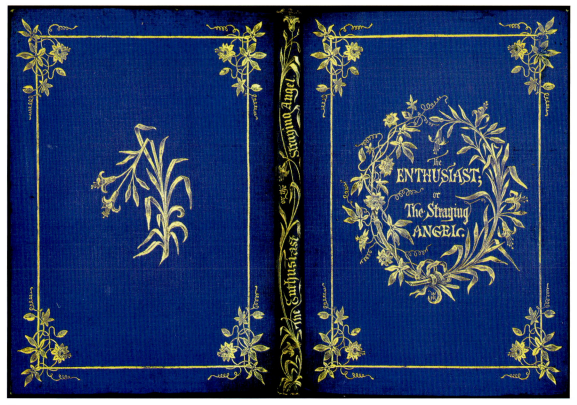

15

17

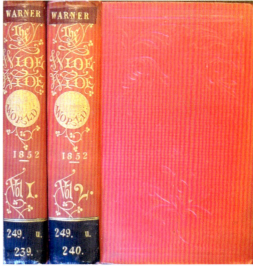

18

16. Sharpe's London Magazine 1852
Mrs S.C. Hall (ed.), Sharpe's London Magazine (Virtue, Hall and Virtue). The front cover is signed WHR. 259mm.

When Mrs S.C. Hall took over the editing of this monthly magazine, her first issue in July 1852 started a new series, with a new wrapper design by WHR. Though the design continued in use until at least 1866, surviving copies are scarce, since wrappers for periodicals were customarily discarded when their contents were gathered into a bound volume.

17. Lectures on the Great Exhibition 1852
Lectures on the results of the Great Exhibition of 1851, delivered … at the suggestion of H.R.H. Prince Albert (Bogue, 1852; second series, 1853). The front cover is signed WHR in blind. Bound by Bone. 196mm.

Prince Albert commissioned these two volumes of reviews in his capacity as President of the Society of Arts, Manufactures and Commerce, instigators of the Great Exhibition.

18. Wide Wide World 1852
The wide, wide world; or, the early history of Ellen Montgomery, edited by a clergyman of the Church of England, two volumes (Sampson Low, 1852). The front cover is signed WHR. Bound by Bone. 175mm.

A number of British publishers rushed out editions of this American bestseller by Susan Warner (writing as Elizabeth Wetherill). Sampson Low and Routledge are the two publishers who occurs most frequently in the present gallery of WHR covers.

The Bodleian Libraries, University of Oxford, (OC) 249 u.239 (v.1) & (OC) 249 u.240 (v.2).

19. Peter Parley's Walks 1852
Peter Parley's walks in the country (Tegg, 1852). The spine only is by WHR, and signed. 177mm.

In the first half of the 1850s, binders occasionally experimented with the use of multicoloured cloth, either striped or else marbled – the copy shown uses blue cloth marbled with red and black.

20. Holiday Book 1852
A holiday book for Christmas and the New Year (Ingram, Cooke [1852]). The spine and front cover are signed WHR. Bound by Bone. 419mm.

This copy lacks its upper spine, but is the only copy found (an issue with paper-covered boards seems more common). The wreath on the front cover was re-used subsequently on the covers of some other large books, most notably on remainder copies of the 1856 first edition of the famous *Grammar of Ornament* of Owen Jones.

21. Cooke's Rome (Re-issued) 1852
Rome, and its surrounding scenery; illustrated … by W.B. Cooke (Tilt, 1840). Only the wreath is by WHR, and signed. Bound by Bone. 281mm.

Although dated 1840 on the title page, this is a re-issue which was advertised in 1852 by Tilt's successor, David Bogue, and bears a Bone binder's ticket which came into use only in 1848.

Appendix A – Gallery of Book Covers

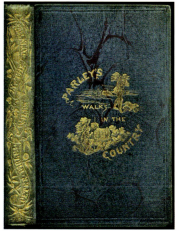
19

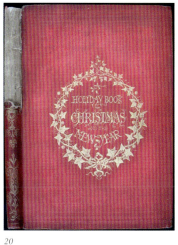
20

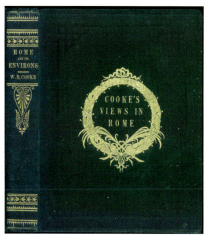
21

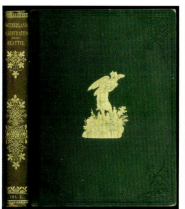
22

23

24

22. Beattie's Switzerland (Re-issued) 1852
William Beattie. Switzerland. Illustrated … by W.H. Bartlett, two volumes (George Virtue) [c. 1852]. Only the spine is by WHR and, unusually, is signed by letters in line rather than a monogram: W.H.R. Bound by James S. Virtue. 279mm.

This is a later issue of a title first published in 1836. Its WHR cover was available either in cloth or, as shown here, in quarter-morocco.

23. Longfellow's Works 1852
The poetical works of Henry Wadsworth Longfellow, with illustrations by John Gilbert (Routledge, 1852). Also: The prose works …, 1853. The spine and front cover are signed WHR. Bound by Bone. 169mm.

The block for this front cover's gilt design was re-used fifteen years later on the back cover of *Heber's Hymns*, 1867, in blind. This back cover could be taken to suggest that Heber's gilt spine and front cover (signed W) were also by WHR. However, Heber's gilt front cover is actually a slight modification of its engraved title page by T. Kennedy, carried out perhaps by the engraver of the new block.

24. Swiss Family Robinson 1852
The Swiss family Robinson, a new edition (Routledge, 1852). The spine and front cover are signed WHR. 169mm.

This copy lacks its top-left spine, but is the only copy found. The spine is signed not with a monogram but by letters in line: W H R (as found also on *22. Beattie's Switzerland (Re-issued) 1852*).

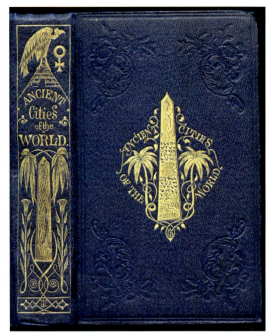

25

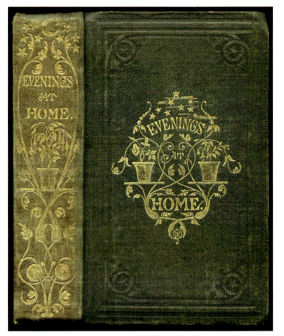

26

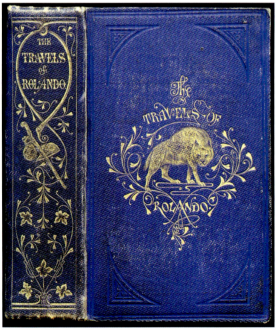

27

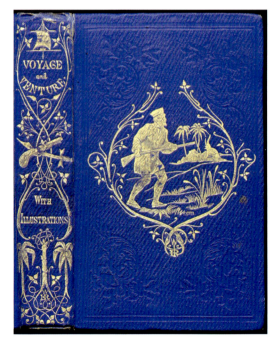

28

Appendix A – Gallery of Book Covers

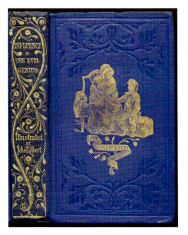 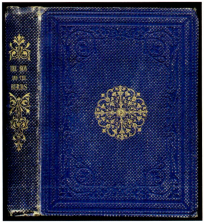 

29   *30*   *32*

25. Great Cities 1852
Theodore Alois Buckley, The great cities of the ancient world (Routledge, 1852). The spine and front cover are signed WHR. Bound by Bone. 175mm.

George Routledge issued the contents of this book also in a different cover, designed by John Leighton. Twin bindings of this kind occurred also for Routledge's *Swiss Family Robinson 1852*, *Evenings at Home 1852*, and *Travels of Rolando 1853*. Presumably Routledge felt that prospective purchasers would enjoy being able to choose between two different designs for each of these titles.

26. Evenings at Home 1852
Dr Aikin and Mrs Barbauld, Evenings at home (Routledge, 1852). The spine and front cover are signed WHR. Bound by Bone. 169mm.

As with adjoining Routledge titles, the WHR cover design carried on in use throughout the 1850s, in this case for issues dated 1853, 1855, 1858 and 1860.

27. Travels of Rolando 1853
Travels of Rolando (Routledge, 1853). The spine and front cover are signed WHR. Bound by Bone. 176mm.

The two letterings of *Rolando* are both characteristic of WHR, centre-emphasised on the spine and inventive on the front cover.

28. Voyage and Venture 1853
Voyage and venture (Routledge, 1853). The spine and front cover are signed WHR; the pictorial scene is not by WHR. Bound by Bone. 174mm.

WHR generally avoided simple pictorial representation, and the scene on the front cover comes from an illustration in the book.

29. Influence 1853
Influence; or, the evil genius (Routledge, 1853). The spine and front cover are signed WHR; the pictorial scene is not by WHR. Bound by Bone. 175mm.

This title is one of the few in this gallery to have its contents recorded by Wolff.[3] Wolff described some objective features of his books' bindings, but did not embark on their designers.

30. Boy and the Birds (Re-issued) 1853
Emily Taylor, The boy and the birds, third edition (Yorke Clarke, 1848). The spine only is by WHR, and signed. Bound by Hanbury. 139mm.

This is a re-issue by Virtue, who took over the title in 1853; one copy with the WHR cover has Virtue advertisements dated 1859.

31. Pictures from Sicily 1853
[W.H. Bartlett], Pictures from Sicily (Hall, Virtue, 1853). The spine is signed WHR. Bound by Westleys. 260mm.

Although WHR's lettering is very free, he always took great care to ensure that gilt tendrils (here gathering in knot-like groups) cross each other in meaningful over-and-under sequences.

32. The Pilgrim Fathers 1853
W.H. Bartlett, The pilgrim fathers (Hall, Virtue, 1853). The spine is signed WHR. Bound by Westleys. 260mm.

This design harks back to WHR's Ruskin designs for Westleys in its emphasis on blind stamping, with even his monogram blind stamped at the base of the spine.

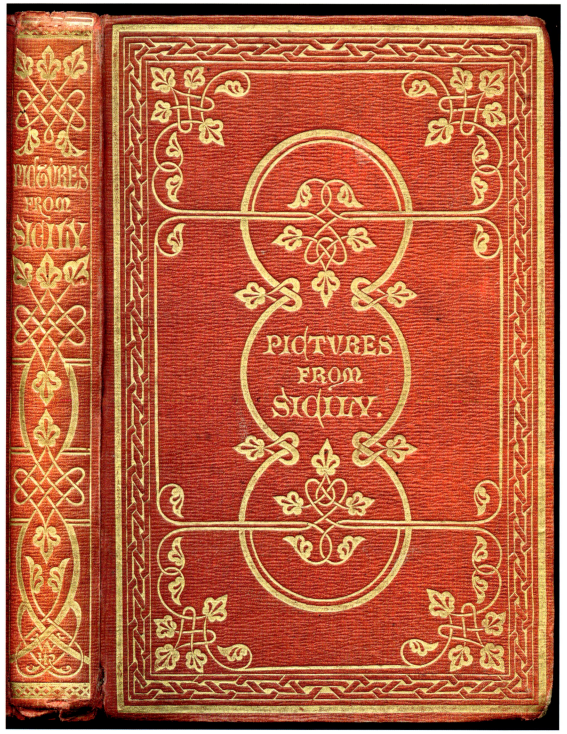
31

Appendix A – Gallery of Book Covers

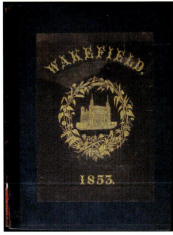
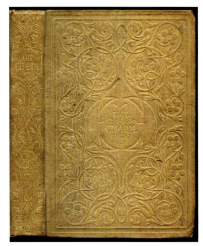

33 *34* *35*

33. Castile and Andalucia 1853
Lady Louisa Tenison, Castile and Andalucia (Bentley, 1853). Artwork for the plaited border (shared with *31. Pictures from Sicily 1853*) is in the V&A WHR archive, E694.30-1998, and all else is characteristic of WHR. Bound by Westleys. 292mm.

WHR would have enjoyed the opportunity to create three different As for the single word ANDALUCIA.

34. Views in Wakefield 1853
Revd. T. Kilby, Views in Wakefield (published by the author). Only the wreath, which is signed, is assuredly by WHR. 551mm.

At 551 x 406 mm, the boards are among the largest with a WHR design.

35. The Charm 1853
The charm, a book for boys and girls (London: Addey; Edinburgh: Menzies; Dublin: M'Glashan, 1853). The spine is signed WHR. Bound by Bone. 201mm.

This is the cover for binding up a year's copies of a monthly magazine edited by Joseph Cundall. Cundall, who had recently been in partnership with Addey as publishers, often commissioned designs from WHR in the following years.

36. Wonder Castle 1853
A.L. Frere, Wonder Castle: A structure of seven stories (Addey, 1853). The spine is signed WHR. 190mm.

As with *19. Peter Parley's Walks 1852*, the copy shown uses marbled cloth. In its striking design, the castle is evoked synecdochically by its battlemented initial.

37. Sketches in Ultra-marine 1853
James Hannay, Sketches in ultra-marine, two vols (Addey, 1853). Re-issued as two-volumes-in-one (London & NY: Routledge, 1854) with the same cover design (the copy shown has received some crude repairs). The spine and front cover are signed WHR. Bound by Burn. 206mm.

The hyphen added within *ultra-marine* on the title page must have been intended to convey amusingly that the contents of the book relate to the extreme doings of mariners. The binder, however, seems to have thought it was merely a misspelling of ultramarine (as referring to the blue of the sea) and hence removed the hyphen, and with it the joke.

38. Women of Israel 1853
Grace Aguilar, The women of Israel, third edition, two vols (Groombridge, 1853). The wreath only is certainly by WHR, and signed. Bound by Westleys. 177mm.

Between 1859 and 1866, Groombridge re-issued all its Aguilar titles in covers uniform with *The Women of Israel 1853*. These covers were, however, made by a new binding firm. Their engraver made a copy of the wreath and replaced its WHR monogram by GL, presumably the engraver's own initials. Meanwhile the original block was used for the covers of several other titles, such as *Passing thoughts in sonnet stanzas*, 1854.

39. Flagg's Venice 1853
Edmund Flagg, Venice, the city of the sea, in two volumes (London: Sampson Low; New York: Scribner, 1853). The spine combines two WHR designs: the upper is in the V&A WHR archive, E693.182-1998; the lower is part of the *42. Illustrated London Library 1853* design (shown later). Bound by Bone. 200mm.

William Harry Rogers – Victorian Book Designer and Star of the Great Exhibition

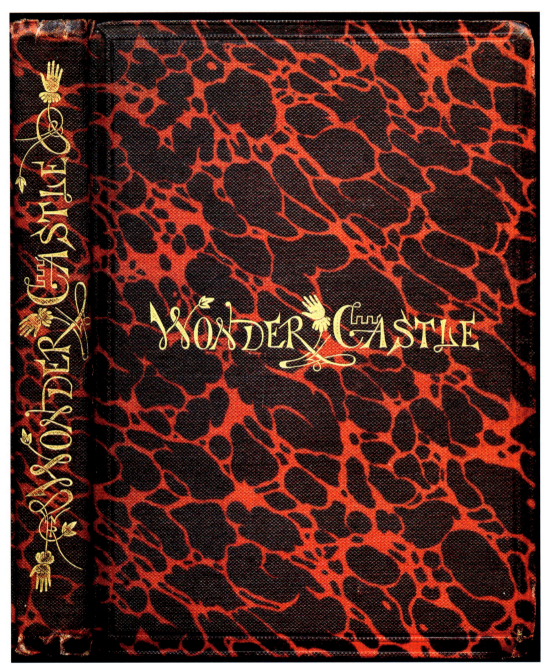

36

Appendix A – Gallery of Book Covers

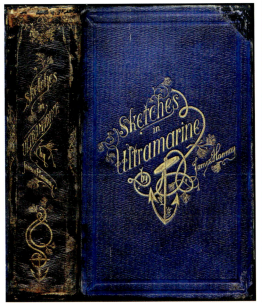

37

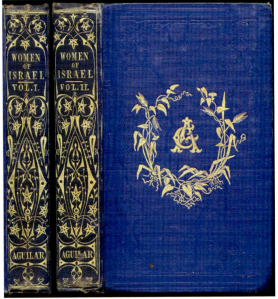

38

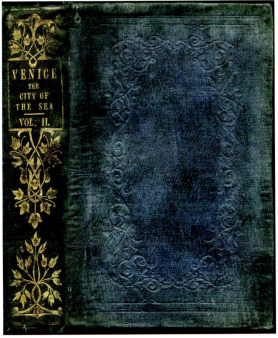

39

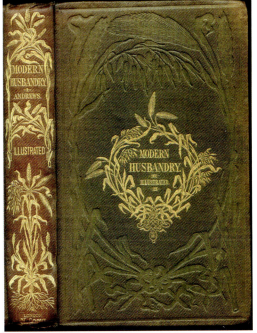

40

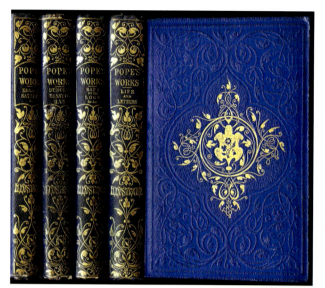
41

42

The paper and typography show the contents to have been printed in the USA, then bound in London. Sampson Low had an active specialism in importing American books into Britain.

40. Modern Husbandry 1853
G.H. Andrews, Modern husbandry (Cooke, 1853). The spine and front cover are signed WHR. Bound by Bone. 230mm.

This binding is signed with a record number of five WHR monograms: once in gilt on the spine, once in gilt and once in blind on the front cover, and twice in blind on the back cover (which repeats the front entirely in blind).

41. National Illustrated Library 1853
This extra gilt cover was introduced as a uniform binding for volumes in the *National Illustrated Library* (*NIL*) in 1853, when it was published by Nathaniel Cooke (NC monogram on spine). The spine and front cover are signed WHR. Bound by Bone. 191mm.

The *NIL* commenced in 1851, issuing monthly volumes with gilt spines for 2s 6d each. The optional WHR cover (with all page edges gilt) raised the cost to 3s 6d each. It was in use in the period 1853–4, both for new titles and for the *NIL* back-catalogue. After ownership changes at the *NIL*, the WHR cover was reintroduced in 1856, but this time bound by Leighton Son & Hodge. It copied the Bone design closely, except it replaced the WHR monograms on the spine and front cover by perfunctory ornaments. Altogether the WHR design appeared on thirty-two titles, more than any other design in the gallery, and it was also later re-used in part on nine titles unrelated to the *NIL*. Shown here are the four volumes of the Alexander Pope title, published 1853–4.

42. Illustrated London Library 1853
This extra gilt cover was introduced as a uniform binding for volumes in the *Illustrated London Library* (*ILL*) in 1853. The spine and front cover are signed WHR. Bound by Bone. 220mm.

The *ILL* was a companion to the *NIL* (the previous design), with a standard cost of 6s instead of 2s 6d per volume. It comprised many fewer titles, and only three of them have been seen in this WHR premium binding. The illustration shows that the spine was blocked in gilt using an assemblage of three engraved brasses, with the middle brass appearing in different orientations on two copies of the same title.

43. Beautiful Birds 1854
John Cotton, edited by Robert Tyas, Beautiful birds, three volumes (Houlston and Stoneman, 1854, 1855 and 1856). Only the front cover's frame is by WHR, and signed. Bound by Bone. 169mm.

Re-uses of this design include Mrs. R. Lee's *Playing at settlers*, 1855.

44. Lives of the Queens 1854
Agnes Strickland, Lives of the queens of England, fourth edition, eight volumes (Hurst and Blackett in succession to

Appendix A – Gallery of Book Covers

43

44

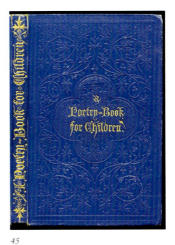
45

46

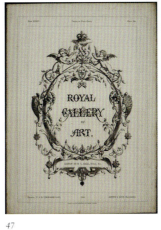
47

48

Henry Colburn, 1854). The spine is signed WHR; the gilt crown is not by WHR, but is from an earlier cover. Bound by Westleys. 204mm.

Another design with extensive blind stamping (including the WHR monogram) executed by Westleys.

45. Poetry for Children 1854
A poetry book for children (London: George Bell, 1854 or New York: D. Appleton & Co., 1854). The spine is signed WHR. 179mm.

The Preface is signed J.C., for Joseph Cundall. This is the first book in the gallery which exists in separate British and American editions, both printed and bound in London, and differing only in their title page publisher entries.

46. Little Susy 1854
Little Susy's six birthdays by her Aunt Susan (for Cundall by Sampson Low, 1854). The front cover is signed WHR (the copy illustrated has a replacement spine). Bound by Bone. 151mm.

Unusually this book was entered at Stationers' Hall (verso of title page) to secure copyright, rather than being deposited with the Copyright Libraries.

47. Royal Gallery Parts 1854
S.C. Hall (ed.), The royal gallery of art ancient and modern (London: Colnaghi; Manchester: Agnew, 1854–60). The front wrapper is signed WHR. 454mm.

This was a lavish production for which S.C. Hall was permitted to engrave pictures from the Royal Collection. Few people could afford the forty-eight parts at 12s each.

231

49 *50* *51*

Hazel Morris has documented Hall's strenuous efforts to find subscribers for the series. He had incurred substantial costs in having the paintings first copied and then engraved from the copies, and got into serious financial difficulties at this period.[4]

48. Royal Gallery Volumes 1855
The royal gallery of art, ancient and modern, four volumes (London: Colnaghi; Manchester: Agnew [1855] – [1860]). The front cover is signed WHR. Bound by Bone. 455mm.

This copy lacks its lower spine. The cost of the set was £30, which was roughly a year's pay for an agricultural labourer at the time. It has been estimated that in 1851 such pay averaged 9s 7d per week, or approximately £25 per year.[5]

49. Tytler from Royal Gallery 1854
Sarah Tytler, Life of her most gracious majesty the Queen, two volumes (J. S. Virtue, [1884]). 322mm.

Tytler's title was issued as a serial in fifteen parts or five divisions, both of which bore the printed cover shown. The cover was an adaptation of the engraved title page, signed WHR, produced thirty years earlier for the Royal Gallery of Art.

50. History for Boys 1855
John G. Edgar, History for boys or annals of the nations of modern Europe (Bogue, 1855). The spine is signed WHR. Bound by Bone. 175mm.

The Crimean War was in progress at this time, and the design includes devices of the United Kingdom, France and the Ottoman Empire, who were in alliance.

51. Waikna 1855
Samuel A. Bard, Waikna; or, adventures on the Mosquito Shore (Sampson Low, 1855). The front cover is signed WHR in blind. Bound by Bone. 213mm.

This is another set of American sheets given a WHR cover in London. The additional engraved title page lists New York: Harper & Bros first, and Sampson Low second.

52. Vicar of Wakefield Grolier 1855
Oliver Goldsmith, The Vicar of Wakefield (published for Cundall by Sampson Low, 1855. Also: London: Sampson Low and New York: Bangs, Brother, & Co., 1855). The spine is signed WHR. Bound by Bone. 207mm.

This is an essay in the grolieresque, with interlaced geometric shapes as found in bindings made for Jean Grolier in the sixteenth century. It was available in a US as well as a British edition, and in morocco (as shown here) as well as cloth.

53. Vicar of Wakefield Foliage 1855
Oliver Goldsmith, The Vicar of Wakefield (published for Cundall by Sampson Low, 1855). The spine and front cover are signed WHR. Bound by Bone. 201mm.

This book has the same contents as the preceding one, but with a binding in WHR's *GS-LA* mode (globally symmetric, locally asymmetric). This was the first time that two different WHR designs were used in parallel. The publisher's aim was presumably to increase the chance of a purchaser liking at least one of the book's bindings (as with the Routledge pairings of WHR and Leighton designs, considered under *25. Great Cities 1852*).

54. In Honorem 1856
In honorem, Songs of the brave (Sampson Low, 1856). The front cover is signed WHR. Bound by Bone. 203mm.

The title on the cover, *Songs of the Brave*, was intended to catch the martial mood prevailing during the Crimean War, which had commenced in 1853. However, by the time the book appeared in May 1856, the war had just ended.

Appendix A – Gallery of Book Covers

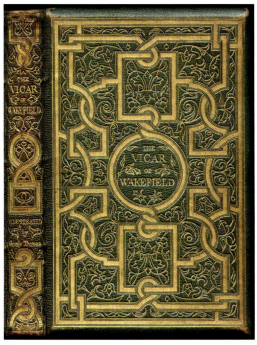

52

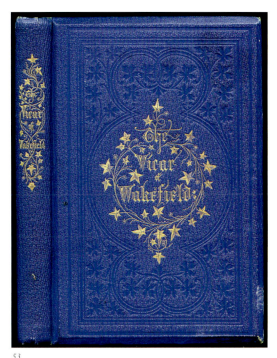

53

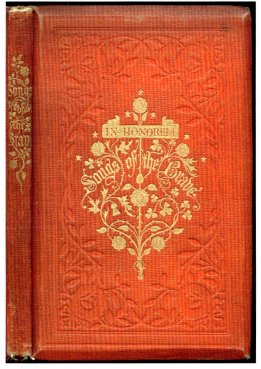

54

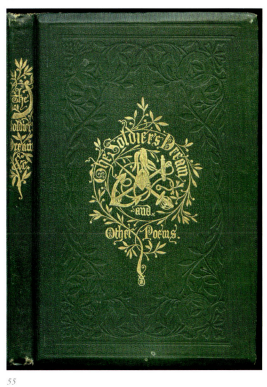

55

233

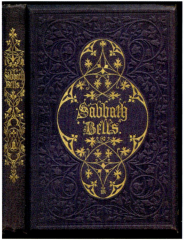  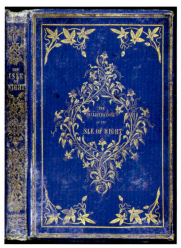

56   57   59

55. Soldier's Dream 1856
Songs of the brave, The soldier's dream, and other poems and odes (Sampson Low, 1856). The front cover is signed WHR. Bound by Bone. 203mm.

The preceding book was re-issued at the end of 1856 with a new title page and more pacific title on the cover, *The Soldier's Dream*.

56. Sabbath Bells 1856
Sabbath bells chimed by the poets (Bell and Daldy, 1856). The spine and front cover are signed WHR. Bound by Bone. 232mm.

The front cover sees WHR playing with a gilt frame composed of one large and two small circles, with their intersected arcs replaced by stylised tendrils, continuing the exploration he made with three equal-sized circles for *31. Pictures from Sicily 1853*.

57. Hemming's Designs 1859
S. Hemming, Designs for villas, parsonages, and other houses (Thompson [1859]). The front cover is signed WHR. 380mm.

Here WHR has encased the design shown for *56. Sabbath Bells 1856* within a harmonious outer border to render it suitable for larger books, the only occasion on which he augmented one of his existing designs in this way.

58. The Rhine 1856
Henry Mayhew, The Rhine and its picturesque scenery (London: Bogue; Paris: Mandeville; New York: Bangs, Brother, 1856. Also, Upper Rhine: Routledge, 1858). The spine and front cover are signed WHR. Bound by Bone. 241mm.

The first leaf inside credits WHR with the binding design, and names the riparian states whose arms mingle with other motifs. Queen Victoria gave copies of the book to her intimates for Christmas 1855 (see Chapter 17).

59. Isle of Wight 1857
Illustrations of the Isle of Wight, from original drawings by Leitch [et al], third edition (Ryde: James Briddon, 1857). The wreath is signed WHR (the spine was re-used from *7. Pilgrimages 1850*). Bound by Bone. 276mm.

The binders, Bone, must have decided that this was a suitable wreath for local publishers in fashionable resorts, because they re-used it for Mrs. F.P. Gwynne's *The Tenby Souvenir*, published there by R. Mason in 1863.

60. Fielding and Smollett 1857
This was a uniform edition of three titles each from two eighteenth-century writers, Fielding and Smollett (London & NY: Routledge, 1857); shown here is Smollett's *The Adventures of Peregrine Pickle*. The front cover is signed WHR in blind. Bound by Burn. 186mm.

All six volumes in this uniform edition were illustrated by Hablot K. Browne, better known as Phiz, who at this time was approaching the end of his reign as the illustrator most favoured by Charles Dickens.

61. Pic-nic Papers 1857
Charles Dickens (ed.), The pic-nic papers (Ward and Lock [1857]). The spine is signed WHR. Bound by Burn. 196mm.

WHR's monogram under the publisher's name is easily overlooked, with the very wide arms of his W surmounting a squeezed HR.

Appendix A – Gallery of Book Covers

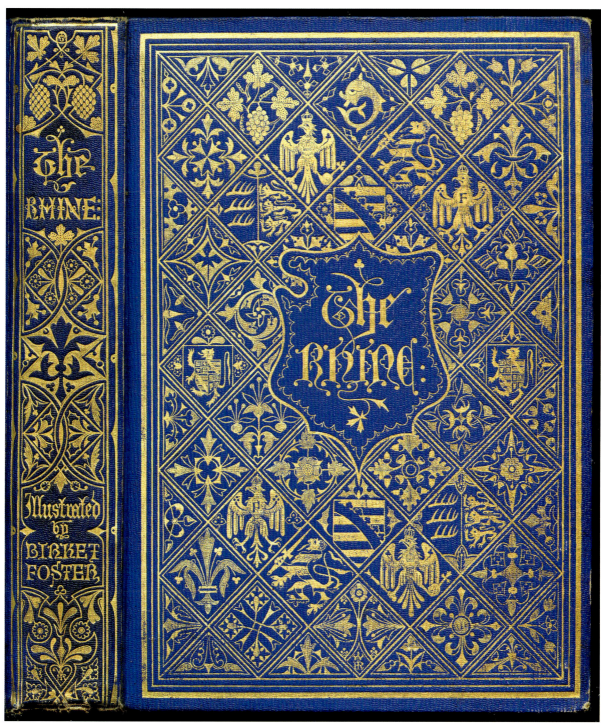

60 61 62

64 65 66

62. Little Lychetts 1857
The little Lychetts, by the author of 'The head of the family' (London and New York: Routledge [1857]). The front cover is signed WHR. 191mm.

This is one of the stories from *The Charm 1853* (it was divided between the 1854 and 1855 volumes). At first sight it looks like a yellowback, a cheap binding with boards covered in yellow paper bearing a printed design. However, it is an *imitation* of a yellowback with the design printed on cloth, not paper. The logic of imitating a cheaper binding was dubious, and cloth yellowbacks seem to be confined to the year 1857 and to the publishers Routledge and also J. and C. Brown.

63. Great Wonders 1857
Arthur C. Wigan, The great wonders of the world from the Pyramids to the Crystal Palace (London and New York: Routledge [1857]). The front cover is signed WHR. 191mm.

This is a companion to the preceding item, deriving from *The Charm* and bound as a cloth yellowback. Though it has been seen (the cover features the Sphinx), no copy has been found to illustrate.

64. Routledge's American Poets 1857
The 'American Poets' series included Oliver Wendell Holmes (illustrated here) and at least two other titles with this uniform cover (Routledge, 1857 onwards). Artwork for the front cover's gilt roundel is in the V&A WHR archive,

Appendix A – Gallery of Book Covers

67   68   69

70   71   72

part of E694.118-1998, verso. Bound by Straker (according to the artwork). 134mm.

The artwork originally had crossed quill pens above the oil lamp, but a kind of speech bubble has been added showing a crescent moon and stars to replace the quills, as in the gilt blocking. This might have been at the request of Straker, or it might be an unusual case of second thoughts by WHR.

65. Mrs Smith's Cookery 1858
Mrs [Ann] Smith, Practical and economical cookery (Chapman and Hall, 1858). The front cover is signed WHR. 199mm.

The engraver has omitted the horizontal bar of the H in WHR's monogram, suggesting that WHR's ever-changing elaborations of his monogram meant that sometimes even the engraver of the binding brass could not parse it correctly.

66. Historical Charades 1858
[Julia Charlotte Maitland] Historical acting charades; or, amusements for winter evenings, new edition (Griffith and Farran, 1858). The spine is signed WHR. 176mm.

The design's copious holly and sprig of mistletoe confirm it is aimed at the Christmas season.

67. Light for the Path 1858
Light for the path of life (Griffith & Farran [1858]). The front cover is signed WHR. Bound by Bone. 188mm.

This refined mixture of blocking in gilt and blind houses one of Samuel Stanesby's works of colourful printing in the manner of an illuminated manuscript.

237

73   74   75

76   77   78

68. Gray's Poetical Works 1858
The poetical works of Thomas Gray (Sampson Low [1858]). The spine is signed WHR in blind. Bound by Bone. 156mm.

WHR enriched the interior as well as the exterior of this book. In the later 1860s, Bickers and Son issued some copies with the front cover bearing coloured onlays and with stamping in blind replaced by gilt and black, as shown in Figure 16.10. At about the same time, John Camden Hotten was advertising the book as 'A perfect gem. It is perhaps the most elegant little volume of the kind produced in the present century.'

69. Gray's Poems 1858
The poetical works of Thomas Gray (Sampson Low [1858]). The front cover is signed WHR. 155mm.

This book has the same contents as the preceding one, but their bindings have only the front cover's blind stamping in common, and this one is much scarcer. A close copy of this binding (and the contents, which retained the same title) was published by Sever and Francis in Cambridge, Massachusetts, with the WHR monogram replaced by 'S&F'.

70. Gray's Wreath (Modified) 1858
[Horace E. Scudder] Dream children, by the author of 'Seven little people and their friends' (Cambridge, MA: Sever and Francis [1864]). 166mm.

Having published a copy of 69. Gray's Poems 1858 (see preceding entry), Sever and Francis borrowed from WHR further by adapting his wreath (p. 44) for this book cover.

Appendix A – Gallery of Book Covers

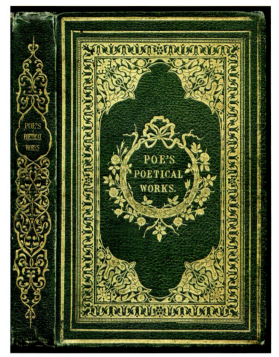

79

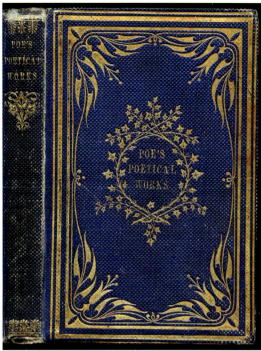

80

71. Gray's SPQR (Modified) 1858

Ballads by Amelia B. Edwards (New York: Carleton [1865]). The front has been adapted from a WHR design. Bound by Geo. W. Alexander of New York (ticket). 158mm.

Carleton joined in the borrowing from *68. Gray's Poetical Works 1858* by adapting one of WHR's designs (p. 88) for this cover, replacing WHR's SPQR (i.e. Senatus Populusque Romanus) by BALLADS.

72. Pastoral Poems 1858

William Wordsworth, Pastoral poems (Sampson Low, 1858 or New York: Appleton [c. 1861]). The spine is signed WHR. Bound by Bone. 201mm.

The WHR monogram at the base of the spine gilt is unusually minute.

73. Children's Bible 1858

M[eredith] J[ohnes]. The children's Bible picture book (Bell and Daldy, 1858 or New York: Appleton, 1861). The front cover is signed WHR. Bound by Bone. 174mm.

This is the first of twenty-two children's titles in similar format published for Joseph Cundall by Bell and Daldy and by Sampson Low in the period 1858–62. Of these, the present entry and the following five entries are signed by WHR, all of which have trademark globally symmetric, locally asymmetric (*GS-LA*) compositions in gilt on their front covers, in the present case featuring passion flowers.

74. New Forest 1859

Harriet Myrtle, A visit to the New Forest (Sampson Low, 1859). The front cover is signed WHR. Bound by Bone. 176mm.

The gilt designs are composed of oak foliage and acorns, which also feature in the blind stamping.

75. Always Do Your Best 1859

Harriet Myrtle. Always do your best, and Lizzie Lindsay (Sampson Low, 1859). The front cover is signed WHR. Bound by Bone. 176mm.

The gilt design is now composed of strawberry foliage and fruit, while the oak blind stamping is retained from the preceding book.

76. Home Treasury 1859

The home treasury of old story books (Sampson Low, 1859). The front cover is signed WHR. Bound by Bone. 175mm.

The gilt composition on the front cover is articulated by a rambling rose, with a harebell at its base.

239

81 *82* *83*

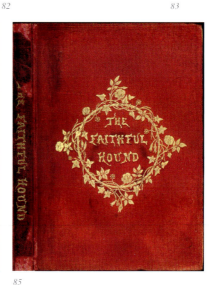

84 *85*

77. Children's Fable Book 1860
The children's picture fable book (Sampson Low, 1860 or Boston, MA: Ticknor and Fields, 1860). The front cover is signed WHR. Bound by Bone. 175mm.

The front cover's gilt alludes to one of the book's fables, of the Fox and the Crow (and the latter's piece of cheese), here separated by much oak.

78. Children's Book of Birds 1860
The children's picture book of birds (Sampson Low, 1860). The front cover is signed WHR. Bound by Bone. 175mm.

The gilt on the front cover features a perching songbird with a swallow whizzing by.

79. Poe & Goldsmith 1859
This design was used for: The poetical works of (a) Edgar Allan Poe, and (b) Oliver Goldsmith (both titles were issued both by Kent, 1859, and by J. and C. Brown [1858]). Only the front cover's wreath is certainly by WHR and signed. Bound by Bone. 188mm.

These two titles appeared in an extraordinary diversity of bindings. Both titles were issued by both publishers in numerous non-WHR cover designs, including six others for both the J. and C. Brown and the Kent issues of Goldsmith.

Appendix A – Gallery of Book Covers

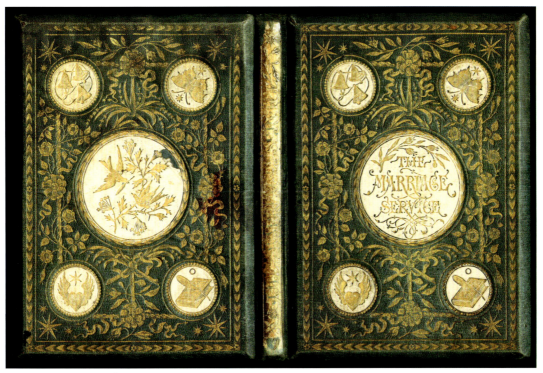

86

80. *Poe Ivy Wreath* 1859
The poetical works of Edgar Allan Poe (Kent, 1859). Only the front cover's wreath is certainly by WHR and signed. 188mm.

This design covers the same contents as the preceding design, but is much scarcer. Uniquely, the three letters in the normal WHR monogram have become detached from each other, forming a triangle amid a tangle of ivy shoots.

81. *Relics of Genius* 1859
T.P. Grinsted, Relics of genius (Kent, 1859). The spine and front cover are signed WHR. Bound by Bone. 181mm.

Exceptionally, the base of the spine is signed not only by WHR as designer but also by EE, perhaps referring to Edmund Evans, although his firm is generally associated with the execution of wood engravings rather than of binding brasses.

82. *Miles Standish* 1859
Henry Wadsworth Longfellow, The courtship of Miles Standish, and other poems (Kent, 1859). The front cover is signed WHR. Bound by Bone. 210mm.

This book is also found in a non-WHR cover, bound by Burn.

83. *Charlie and Ernest* 1859
M. Betham-Edwards, Charlie and Ernest or play and work (Edinburgh: Edmonston and Douglas, 1859). The wreath is signed WHR. Bound by Burn. 178mm.

The book is indicative of the unexpectedly close relation between a minor Edinburgh publisher and a major London binder. The following year, 1860, Burn introduced a range of denominated binder's tickets, which bore the correct postage rate for each book to which they were affixed. Jane Brown and the author have discovered that Edmonston and Douglas were the only large-scale adopters of Burn's ingenious scheme, which consequently folded in 1864.[6]

84. *Home for the Holidays* 1859
[Joseph Cundall], Home for the holidays, by the editor of 'The Playmate' (James Nelson, 1859). The front cover is signed WHR. Bound by Burn. 228mm.

This book is a re-issue of the same title published with card covers by Cundall and Bogue in 1848. The WHR design appeared also on two other remainder issues which bore misleadingly early title page dates: (a) T. Adolphus Trollope, A summer in Brittany [two volumes in one] (Colburn, 1840 – but in fact Bohn, 1860); (b) [Bürger], Leonora, trans. by Julia M. Cameron (Longman, 1847 – but in fact Willis and Sotheran, 1861).

241

85. Faithful Hound 1859

The faithful hound: A true tale for children, by E.T. (Griffith and Farran, 1859). The front cover is signed WHR. Bound by Bone. 194mm.

The title page of the first edition states that it was issued on behalf of Great Ormond Street Hospital for Sick Children. The second edition of 1863 drops this and reveals the author as Lady [Emily] Thomas, while keeping the cover unchanged.

86. Marriage Service 1859

The marriage service, illustrated by W. Harry Rogers (Routledge, Warne, and Routledge [1859]). The front and back covers are signed WHR, with different central onlays. Bound by Bone. 150mm.

One of only two occasions on which WHR designed a back cover that differed from the front cover (the other was *15. The Enthusiast 1852*), in this case in terms only of the design of its central circular onlay. By 1864 the contents by WHR had been taken over by Dean & Son, who were still advertising his designs in 1888 in the *Athenaeum* (pp. 484–5).

87. Poets of the West 1859

The poets of the west (Sampson Low, 1859). The front cover is signed WHR. Bound by Bone. 221mm.

There is a variant cover in which the spine's gilt foliage has been extended downwards for another 20mm, unbalancing the design. The extra gilt may have been aimed at the American market, because the following year Sampson Low was joined on the title page by Anson D.F. Randolph of New York, and to the extra gilt spine was added the wholesale replacement of the front cover's stamping in blind by its stamping in gilt.

88. The Hamlet 1859

Thomas Warton. The hamlet, an ode written in Whichwood Forest (Sampson Low, 1859). The front cover is signed WHR. 239mm.

This book was originally issued in the striking combination of red morocco spine and dark green paper-covered boards. Nowadays this would be called a quarter-binding, but at the time it was advertised as 'half morocco'. In a later issue, the WHR design was used on a standard cloth cover instead.

89. L'Allegro 1859

John Milton, L'Allegro (Sampson Low, 1859). The spine is signed WHR. Bound by Bone. 201mm.

The spine and front cover designs are essentially symmetric, apart from their lettering, giving this design a relatively prosaic appearance.

90. Birds and Beasts 1859

A picture book of birds and beasts for young people (Sampson Low, 1859). The front cover is signed WHR. Bound by Bone. 265mm.

The charming cover disguises a crude bind-up of two titles (one on birds, the other on beasts) issued in paper-covered boards the previous year and still retaining their individual 1858 title pages.

91. Poets of England and America 1860

Poets of England and America (London: Hamilton, Adams; Liverpool: Howell, 1860). Only the front cover's central frame is certainly by WHR and signed. Bound by Bone. 173mm.

This cover design was used on the 1860 and 1861 editions of this work, which Edward Howell of Liverpool first issued in 1853.

92. Wightwick's Hints 1860

George Wightwick. Hints to young architects, second issue (Lockwood, 1860). Contains 1871 advertisements. The spine is signed WHR. Bound by Bone. 208mm.

Though only the lower of the spine's two main gilt motifs is signed, the upper one is probably also by WHR. Bone perhaps commissioned such motifs not for any specific title but instead for general use.

93. Merchant of Venice 1860

William Shakspeare, The most excellent historie of the merchant of Venice (Sampson Low, 1860 or New York: Appleton, 1860). The front cover is signed WHR. Bound by Leighton Son & Hodge. 231mm.

The book was 'handsomely bound in Venetian ornamented cloth', according to Sampson Low's catalogue dated 1 November 1860. The contents include WHR designs symbolising the drama throughout. The editor was Joseph Cundall (evidenced by WHR's monogram for JC) who bowdlerised the text: 'In offering an illustrated edition of one of Shakspeare's immortal plays as a gift-book for families, the editor has considered it to be his duty to omit a few lines, which, in the present age, might be thought objectionable.'

94. Bennett's Pilgrim's Progress 1860

Bunyan's pilgrim's progress with illustrations by Charles Bennett (Longman, 1860 or New York: Appleton, 1860). The front cover is signed WHR. Bound by Westleys. 213mm.

This design bears some resemblance to that for *5. Stones of Venice 1851*, also bound by Westleys, in terms of its panels of highly stylised and deeply blind stamped vine juxtaposed with gilt emblems, such as a pilgrim's cockleshell on the present spine.

Appendix A – Gallery of Book Covers

87

88

89

90

91

92

93

94

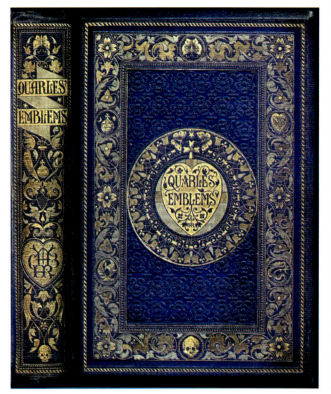

95

96

95. Quarles' Emblems 1861
Quarles' emblems, illustrated by Charles Bennett and W. Harry Rogers (Nisbet, 1861 or New York: Tibbals [c. 1865]). The front cover is signed WHR. Bound by Leighton Son & Hodge. 227mm.

As with the preceding book, WHR worked here with his close friend C.H. Bennett, this time sharing the illustrations with him, and placing a joint monogram on the spine. The covers of the copies published by Tibbals in New York appear to have been made from blocks shipped over from London. This was exceptional because books with WHR bindings for American publishers were normally made entirely in London, as with the copies of the two preceding titles published by D. Appleton and Co. of New York.

96. Quarles' in Carton Pierre 1861
Quarles' emblems, illustrated by Charles Bennett and W. Harry Rogers. Nisbet 1861 on title page, but this later issue in carton pierre boards was by Charles Griffin. A design first used for *Sentiments and Similes of William Shakespeare*, 1857, was modified by WHR. Bound by Leighton Son & Hodge. 226mm.

Charles Griffin, who specialised in attractively repackaging remainder books, advertised *Quarles' Emblems* in 1866 as 'handsomely bound, price 12s. ... A few copies of this work, magnificently bound in antique carved oak, price 21s.' The boards were in fact made in a mould, not carved.

97. Virtue's Holy Bible 1861
The Holy Bible, with commentary by Jamieson and Bickersteth (London and New York: James S. Virtue [1861–5]. In thirteen and a half divisions or forty and a half parts, for two volumes. The front cover is signed WHR. 382mm.

WHR managed to create strikingly original versions of the traditional emblems for the four evangelists (left to right, upper then lower: Matthew, Mark, Luke and John).

98. Picturesque Selections 1861
Picturesque selections: Drawn on stone by J.D. Harding. Kent, and Winsor and Newton [1861]. The V&A WHR archive has an album bearing a variant of this cover design,

Appendix A – Gallery of Book Covers

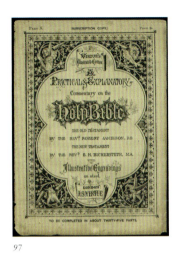

97

98

99

100

101

102

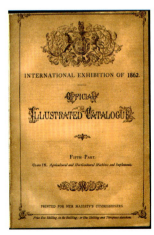

103

104

105

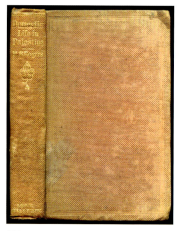 106

 107

 108

E1135.54-1998. Bound by Bone (the album is ticketed). 574mm.

With boards measuring 574 x 440 mm, this is the largest book bearing a WHR design. The boards are even larger for the large-paper issue of *190. Mansions of England 1869*, but that is really a portfolio rather than a book.

99. First Chemist and Druggist 1861
The Chemist and Druggist, a monthly trade circular, published [for Morgan Brothers] by Firth, 1861. The masthead is signed WHR; used for Vols 2-4, 1861–3. 208mm.

This design was later used on the title page of annual bound volumes of the journal. The founding editor of *The Chemist and Druggist* was WHR's friend, John Cargill Brough. The journal was started in 1859 by six brothers from the Morgan family. Three years earlier they had founded the industrial company which for many years was known as Morgan Crucible.

100. Second Chemist and Druggist 1864
The Chemist and Druggist, a monthly trade journal (Firth, 1864; Canning, c. 1866). The masthead is signed WHR; used from Vol. 5, 1864, until at least 1916. 266mm.

This new design was introduced when the journal's format was enlarged in 1864. WHR also provided a variety of internal headers and emblematical section headings for the enlarged journal.

101. The Ironmonger 1861
The Ironmonger and Metal Trades Advertiser, published for the Proprietors [c. 1861]. The masthead is signed WHR; used until at least 1898. 255mm.

This journal was also started by the Morgan Brothers in 1859. The design is probably contemporary with 99. *First Chemist and Druggist 1861*, although the earliest copy seen is 1874.

102. First Grocer 1862
The Grocer: A weekly trade circular [William Reed], 1862. The masthead is signed WHR; used for Vols 1-2, 1862 only. 262mm.

The six Morgan Brothers had one sister, Mary Anne Morgan. She married William Reed, who emulated the brothers in starting up a pair of long-lived journals that were given memorable covers by WHR. The first editor was WHR's friend at the Savage Club, Gustave Strauss.[7] In the centenary issue of the *Grocer* in 1962, Morgan Brothers (Publishers) Ltd took out a full-page advertisement to congratulate its publisher, still William Reed Ltd.
© The British Library Board 0 LOU.TD27 (5/7/1862) page 1.

103. Second Grocer 1870
The Grocer: A weekly trade circular [William Reed], [c. 1870]. After a period with an anonymous masthead, this new one signed by WHR was introduced by 1870, remaining in use until 1960. 271mm.

WHR's first cover for the *Grocer* had met with some resistance from subscribers, who suggested to the editor he should adopt 'the figure of Britannia gracefully seated on a sugar-cask, and wielding the trident, surrounded by bags and bales of merchandise' (11 January 1862, p. 24). The editor patiently explained that he did not want a 'hackneyed' design and that WHR had, in fact, included 'the tea, coffee and spice trees, and the sugar-cane'. Nevertheless, this second, more compact design was subsequently commissioned from WHR.
© The British Library Board 0 LOU.TD27 (1/1/1870) page 1.

Appendix A – Gallery of Book Covers

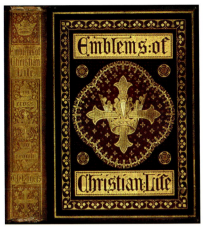

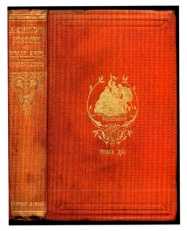

109   *110*   *111*

104. The Wine Trade Review 1864
The Wine Trade Review (Henry S. Simpson, 1864). The masthead is signed WHR, used from Vol. 3, July 1864, until at least 1940. 285mm.

This Reed title started as a supplement to the *Grocer* in 1863, becoming an independent publication the next year. The masthead continued to bear its WHR signature until at least 1940, latterly with the amplified title of the *Wine and Spirit Trade Review*.

105. Official Exhibition Catalogue 1862
International Exhibition of 1862, Official illustrated catalogue, Her Majesty's Commissioners, [cover title only], thirteen parts. The front cover is signed WHR, with proofs of its various components in the V&A WHR archive, E851-1998, pp. 36, 40, 45 and 52. 255mm.

The set of parts covered Classes 1 to 36 of the Exhibition, which together comprised the British Division of the Industrial Department. Their contents were also gathered (along with a 'Concise History') into two substantial cloth-bound volumes with a similar title, but ditching the word 'Official' on their title pages; two further uniform volumes dealt with exhibits from overseas. The fate of WHR's design for the cloth bindings is dealt with in Chapter 9.

106. Domestic Life in Palestine 1862
Mary Eliza Rogers, Domestic life in Palestine (Bell and Daldy, 1862). The spine is signed WHR. Bound by Bone. 203mm.

Mary Eliza Rogers, sister of WHR, had immersed herself in Palestine life while visiting another brother, Edward Thomas Rogers. The following year there was a second edition of her detailed account, revised and enlarged, which retained its WHR cover.

107. Spiritual Conceits 1862
Spiritual conceits, extracted from the writings of the Fathers, the old English poets, &c., and illustrated by W. Harry Rogers (Griffith and Farran, 1862). The spine is signed WHR. Bound by Bone. 208mm.

A livre d'artiste which here has a chapter to itself, Chapter 12. WHR was responsible for designing the book's interior and exterior and selecting its texts.

108. Spiritual Conceits in Leather 1862
Spiritual conceits (Griffith and Farran, 1862). The cross-and-crown motif is a smaller version of the cloth cover iconography. 206mm.

Contemporary advertisements listed the 'cloth elegant' binding option (i.e. the preceding entry) at one guinea (£1 1s) and a plain 'morocco antique' binding option at one and a half guineas (£1 11s 6d). The present design was a third option in 'calf extra' at an intermediate price (£1 7s).

109. Emblems of Christian Life 1870
Emblems of Christian life, illustrated by W. Harry Rogers, from the writings of the Fathers, the old English poets, &c. (Griffith and Farran [1870]). The spine is signed WHR. 208mm.

This is a re-issue of *Spiritual Conceits 1862* with a new title page and a binding bearing new WHR title-panels, with front-cover blocking in black (for most copies) instead of in blind.

110. Divine Emblems 1863
John Bunyan, Divine emblems, or, temporal things spiritualised, &c. (Bickers [1863]). The front cover is signed WHR. Bound by Bone. 171mm.

Due to an engraving error, the signature on the front

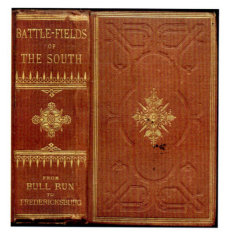

112

113

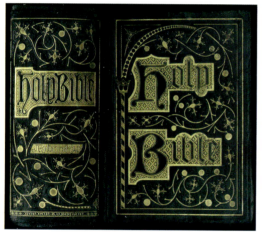

114

115

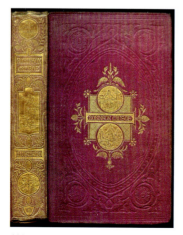

116

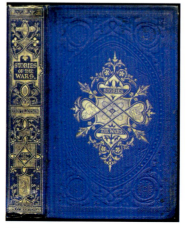

117

119

Appendix A – Gallery of Book Covers

cover reads W/HB rather than W/HR. An advertisement in *The Times* (7 November 1863, p. 13) nevertheless confirmed WHR: 'elegantly bound in cloth super extra, the sides gilt to a design by Harry Rogers'.

111. Child's History of England 1863
Charles Dickens, A child's history of England, new edition (Chapman and Hall, 1863). Only the front cover is by WHR and signed. 195mm.

Unusually for a cloth-covered book with a WHR gilt design, the price was displayed on the cover. A later issue dated 1868 was unchanged, except that the price on the cover was reduced from 7s 6d to 6s.

112. Battle-fields of the South 1863
Battle-fields of the South, from Bull Run to Fredericksburg, by an English combatant [two volumes in one] (Smith, Elder, 1863). Only the front cover's gilt design is known to be by WHR; artwork is present in the V&A WHR archive, part of E694.119-1998 verso. 194mm.

The original issue, in two volumes also dated 1863, had relatively plain covers.

113. Our Own Fireside 1863
Charles Bullock (ed.), Our Own Fireside (Macintosh. Part 1, October 1863). The front cover is signed WHR. 251mm.

By 1872, this journal's wrappers were printed with a non-WHR design. © The British Library Board 0 PP.357.C Front cover.

114. Beeton's Holy Bible 1863
The Holy Bible (Beeton [1863]). The spine is signed WHR. 283mm.

This is one of only two WHR designs where the expansive width of the spine is of a comparable order of magnitude to the width of the covers, making for an unwieldy book in practice. The other such book was *123. County Families 1864*, the following year.

115. Curiosities of Savage Life 1863
James Greenwood, Curiosities of savage life [two series] (Beeton, 1863–4). The spine is signed WHR. Bound by Bone. 223mm.

In 1863, Samuel Beeton introduced adventure books for boys which had higher production values than their predecessors. His books were larger and clothed in lavish gilt covers commissioned from leading designers. By 1866, Beeton had formalised the series as his 'Boy's Own Library'. Four further covers which WHR designed for the Library are listed next.

116. Beeton's Robinson Crusoe 1864
Daniel De Foe, The adventures of Robinson Crusoe, tenth edition (Beeton, 1864). The spine and front cover are signed WHR. Bound by Bone. 223mm.

This is another member of Beeton's 'Boy's Own Library'. As well as the Library's five cover designs by WHR, there were four by Robert Dudley and one by Albert Warren.

117. Stories of the Wars 1865
John Tillotson, Stories of the wars, 1574–1658 (Beeton, 1865). The spine and front cover are signed WHR. Bound by Bone. 222mm.

This book was re-issued two years later with a title page that gave the publisher as S.O. Beeton, 1867. No other example of a Beeton 1867 imprint appears to be known, because Beeton lost control of his remaining publications to Ward, Lock and Tyler in 1866 (having already sold some to Warne).

118. Silas the Conjurer 1866
James Greenwood, Silas the conjurer (Beeton [1866]). The spine and front cover are signed WHR. 220mm.

The skull-based cover design is strikingly macabre.

119. Runnymede 1866
J.G. Edgar, Runnymede and Lincoln Fair (Beeton [1866]). The front cover is signed WHR. 220mm.

Relatively unusually, the lettering on the spine and cover is reverse-blocked. That is, letter shapes were formed by excavated areas of the binding brass, rather than by intact areas as usual, yielding cloth-coloured letters instead of gilt letters.

120. All The Year Round 1864
All The Year Round, a weekly journal, conducted by Charles Dickens, Vols 1 (1859) to 20 (1868). The spine and front cover are signed WHR. Bound by Bone. 247mm.

Following on from WHR's *111. Child's History of England 1863*, this was his second design for Charles Dickens. It was introduced in 1864 as a more luxurious option for the journal's ten back-volumes and remained an option for the ten volumes published subsequently, priced at 6s per volume instead of the 5s 6d for ordinary cloth (*Athenaeum*, 9 January 1864, p. 68).

121. Ran Away to Sea 1864
[Mayne Reid], Ran away to sea: An autobiography for boys (London and New York: Routledge, Warne, and Routledge, 1864). The spine is signed WHR. Bound by Bone. 175mm.

The author's name was omitted from the title page, but included on the spine.

122. Effie's Friends 1864
[Lady Augusta Noel], Effie's friends (Nisbet, 1864). The spine and front cover are signed WHR. Bound by Leighton Son and Hodge. 185mm.

The book was re-issued with title pages bearing the

249

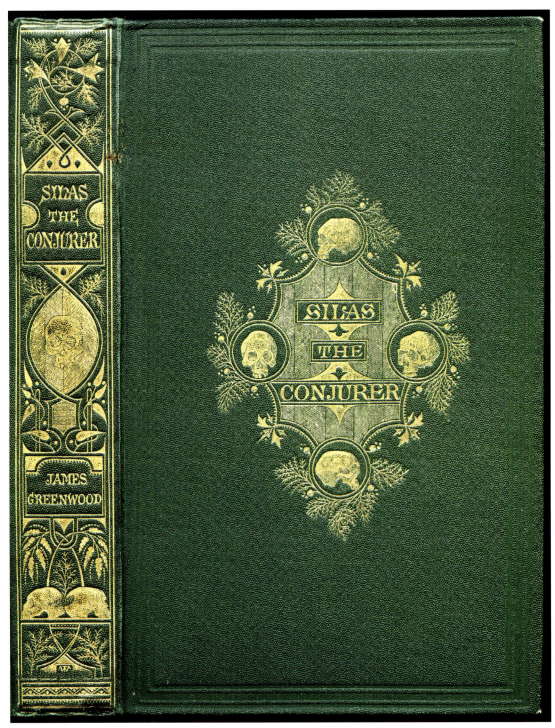

118

Appendix A – Gallery of Book Covers

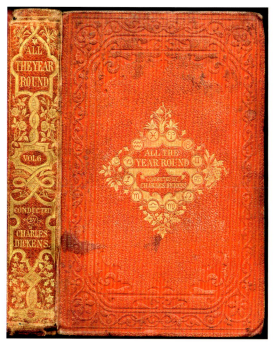

120

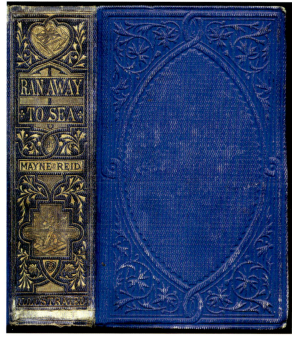

121

dates 1865, 1866, 1870 and 1875, all with the WHR cover, but none with any indication of being a later issue, leading subsequently to some confusion over the date of the first edition.

123. County Families 1864
Edward Walford, The county families of the United Kingdom, second edition (Hardwicke, 1864). The spine and front cover are signed WHR, from the second edition until the final, sixtieth in 1920. Bound by Bone. 268mm.

The first edition of this title, in 1860, was in a plain, non-WHR cover. WHR's cover design was used for all the many subsequent editions. Publication was initially erratic – 1864 second edition, 1865 third, 1868 fourth, 1870 fifth and 1871 sixth. It then became annual and numbered itself accordingly, commencing with an 1872 twelfth edition which quietly suppressed the five potential editions from seventh to eleventh.

124. Illustrated London News Christmas 1864
Illustrated London News, Christmas Supplement, 24 December 1864. The masthead is signed. 426mm.

The signature is W/HRogers, in the usual triangular arrangement of the three capitals, but on this occasion spelling out the surname in full.

125. The Mausoleum 1864
Amraphel. [Vol.1:] The mausoleum … [Vol 2:] English and French miscellany … (Marchant Singer, 1864). Only the spine is certainly by WHR and signed. Bound by Bone. 228mm.

This book comprises two volumes bound in one, with separate title pages and pagination.

126. Christmas Carol 1864
'Christ was born on Christmas Day.' A carol, with illustrations by John A. Hows (Sampson Low, 1864). The front cover is signed WHR. Bound by Bone. 235mm.

Printed in New York by C.A. Alvord, according to the title page verso. This is the only known occasion on which WHR created a cover with a specific title (as opposed to a generic design) to be used for the London binding of sheets which had been printed in America.

127. Woman in White 1864
Wilkie Collins, The woman in white (Sampson Low, 1864). The cover is not illustrated here because no copy has been traced, but the cover of this secondary edition was advertised as being designed by WHR (*The Times*, 15 October 1864, p. 13) and there is WHR artwork for the spine in the V&A WHR archive, E694.36-1998.

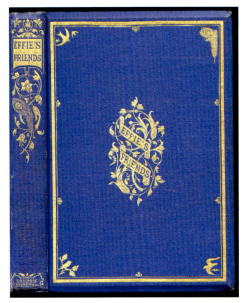

122

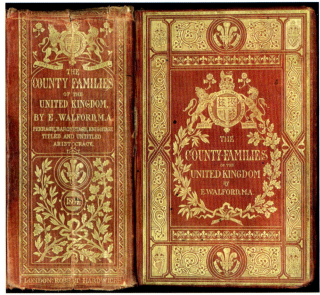

123

128. *Life Portraits of Shakspeare 1864*
J. Hain Friswell, Life portraits of William Shakspeare (Sampson Low, 1864). The front cover is signed WHR. Bound by Bone. 228mm.

This book was issued as ordinary and augmented copies. The augmented copies (as shown here) contained an extra chapter on Shakspeare's Will, with photographs.

129. *Works of Shakespeare 1864*
The works of William Shakespeare edited … by Charles and Mary Cowden Clarke, four vols (Bickers, 1864). The spine and front cover are signed WHR. Bound by Bone. 235mm.

Bickers also published in 1864 a one-volume edition which used the same front cover but a non-WHR spine. The same covers were used for later issues of both the four-volume and one-volume works. Illustrations were added to the 1876 and 1892 issues of the four-volume set, and its spine title amplified accordingly to 'The Boydell Shakespeare'.

130. *Shakspeare Memorial Wrapper 1864*
[Mary Eliza Rogers], Shakspeare memorial (Beeton, 1864). The front cover is signed WHR. 384mm.

The third Shakespeare title with a WHR cover to be published in 1864, the tercentenary of the playwright's birth. Mary Eliza Rogers is not mentioned in the book, but was identified as author by Samuel Timmins, as reported in Justin Winsor's bibliography of Halliwell-Phillipps (1881, p. 24). A mangled attribution appeared later in Jaggard's Shakespeare bibliography (1911, p. 591). The title page repeated WHR's wrapper and he also made other contributions to the contents.

131. *Shakspeare Memorial Cloth 1864*
[Mary Eliza Rogers], Shakspeare memorial (Beeton, 1864). Unsigned but can be attributed to WHR in view of the preceding paper-covered issue, the elegant lettering, the presence of Bone the binder, and the existence of some copies with wooden panels carved doubtlessly by his father's firm. Bound by Bone. 385mm.

Jaggard (as cited in the preceding entry) recorded a copy with carvings from Herne's Oak (mentioned also in Chapter 10). For the copy illustrated, only the lowest of three carved panels remains attached.

132. *Musical Mélange 1864*
A musical mélange (Beeton, 1864). Issued as an adjunct to the January 1864 double-number of the Englishwoman's Domestic Magazine. The front cover is signed WHR. 273mm.

Beeton issued another musical mélange in January 1865, advertised in *The Times* as 'in a handsomely engraved wrapper', but it is not known if the 1864 wrapper was re-used.

Appendix A – Gallery of Book Covers

124

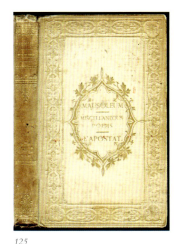

125

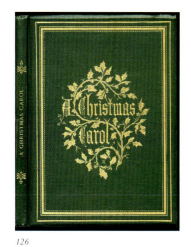

126

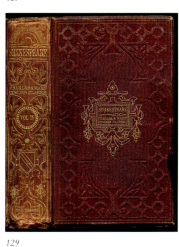

129

130

132

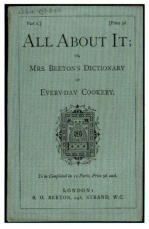

134

253

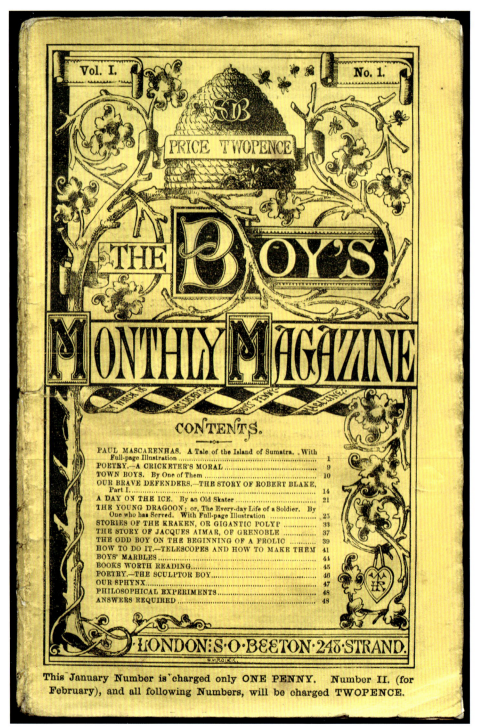

133

Appendix A – Gallery of Book Covers

135   136   137

133. Boy's Monthly Magazine 1864
The Boy's Monthly Magazine (Beeton, 1864). The front cover is signed WHR; used until at least the end of the second annual volume. 221mm.

The price was only tuppence, reduced for the first issue to a penny. An indication of the economy of scale which made such prices conceivable was provided in an album of Beeton material seen at auction, where 100,000 copies of the first issue were said to have been printed. Of course, only a tiny proportion of those wrappers have survived to the present.

134. Mrs Beeton's Everyday Cookery Wrapper 1864
[Cover title:] All about it; or, Mrs. Beeton's dictionary of every-day cookery, twelve monthly parts (Beeton [1864–5]). The front cover is signed WHR. 199mm.

The *Dictionary of Every-Day Cookery* was the smaller sibling of Mrs Beeton's celebrated *Book of Household Management*, which had first appeared in book-form in 1861. Tragically, Isabella Mary Beeton died on 6 February 1865, aged only twenty-eight years. The final part was scheduled for 1 March 1865, allowing just enough time for her husband, Samuel Orchart Beeton, to add a lament for her passing, as described in Chapter 18.

Reproduced by kind permission of the Syndics of Cambridge University Library. 1864.7.202.

135. Mrs Beeton's Everyday Cookery Cloth 1865
The 'All about it' books. Mrs.Beeton's dictionary of every-day cookery (Beeton, 1865). The spine and front cover are signed WHR. 193mm.

Two variants of the design appeared in 1865, as shown. One had 'Practical Illustrations' at the base of the spine and 'With Many Illustrations' at the foot of the front cover. The second variant had 'Published at the Sign of the Beehive' in both positions and was retained for later editions.

136. Payn's People 1865
[James Payn]. People, places, and things, by the author of 'Lost Sir Massingberd' (Beeton, 1865). The spine is signed WHR, but it is not his title or author lettering. 194mm.

This design is clearly an adaptation of the previous one, for a much narrower spine (20mm instead of 32mm between gilt rules).

137. Young Englishwoman Monthly Wrapper 1865
The Young Englishwoman (Beeton, 1865). Monthly parts contained four or five weekly issues. The masthead is signed WHR; used 1865–6. 313mm.

Ward, Lock and Tyler took over from Beeton as publisher during the course of the fourth half-yearly volume, which was completed in December 1866, and re-launched it in a new format (and no WHR) after that.

138. Young Englishwoman Cloth 1865
The Young Englishwoman [half-yearly volume] (Beeton, 1865). The front cover is signed WHR; used 1865–6. 312mm.

A completely new cover for binding the re-launched magazine from 1867 was signed by WR, that is, William Ralston.

139. Parables from Nature 1865
Mrs Alfred Gatty, Parables from nature, With notes on the natural history; and illustrations by C.W. Cope [etc] (Bell and Daldy, 1865). The spine and front cover are signed WHR. Bound by Bone. 227mm.

There was a plethora of editions of this title. This book is the illustrated issue of the first two series (of four) of parables, here shown bound in publisher's morocco, as opposed to the basic cloth.

255

William Harry Rogers – Victorian Book Designer and Star of the Great Exhibition

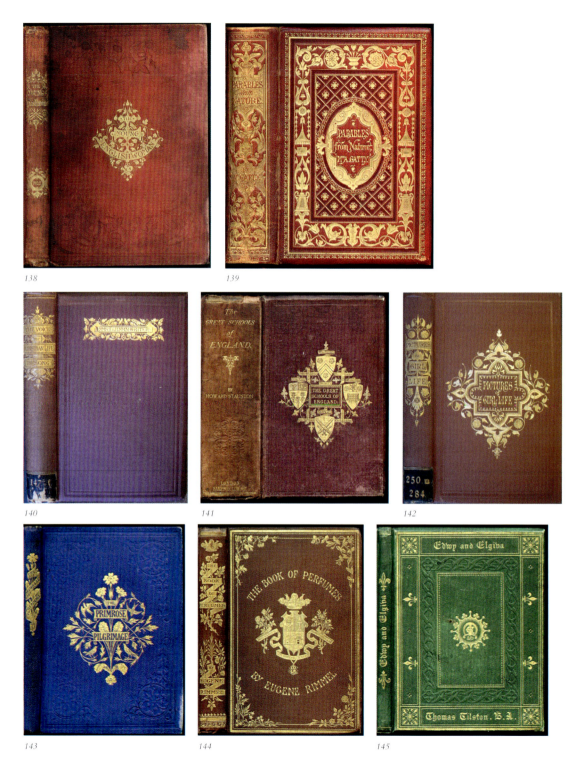

138

139

140

141

142

143

144

145

256

Appendix A – Gallery of Book Covers

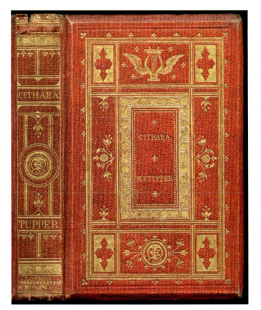

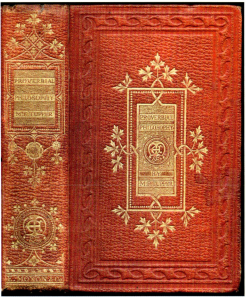

146

147

140. *Voice of Christian Life in Song 1865*
[Elizabeth Charles], The voice of Christian life in song; or, hymns and hymn-writers of many lands and ages, second edition (Nisbet, 1865). The front cover is signed WHR. Bound by Westleys. 197mm.

The book also contains four designs signed by WHR. The Bodleian Libraries, University of Oxford, (OC) 147 f.21.

141. *Great Schools 1865*
Howard Staunton, The great schools of England (Sampson Low, 1865). Only the front is by WHR and signed. Bound by Bone. 208mm.

The author was the famous chess-player who in 1843 won the match often viewed as the first world championship, and later gave his name to the Staunton chess pieces which became the standard design.

142. *Pictures of Girl Life 1865*
Catherine Augusta Howell, Pictures of girl life (Griffith and Farran, 1865). The spine and front cover are signed WHR. 175mm.

Even in an apparently symmetric design like this, WHR took care to follow a consistent under-and-over clockwise path for the front cover's elaborated gilt rectangle, so that the design in fact has no true vertical or horizontal plane of symmetry and, rather, conforms to WHR's enlivening *GS-LA* principle of global symmetry, local asymmetry. The Bodleian Libraries, University of Oxford, (OC) 250 m.284.

143. *Primrose Pilgrimage 1865*
M. Betham Edwards, The primrose pilgrimage (Griffith and Farran, 1865). The front cover is signed WHR. Bound by Bone. 187mm.

Again, a typical example of WHR's *GS-LA* principle, the apparent left-right symmetry of the front cover's gilt design dissolving on closer examination.

144. *The Book of Perfumes 1865*
Eugene Rimmel, The book of perfumes (Chapman & Hall, 1865, or Philadelphia: Lippincott, 1866). The spine and front cover are signed WHR. Bound by Bone. 206mm.

Shown here is the echt WHR cover design, with a different perfumed plant in each corner of the front cover. Rimmel, a pioneer of marketing, managed to double the price of his book from 5s to 10s 6d with a large-paper 'Drawing-Room Edition' whose cover replaced WHR's four plants by a thick gilt frame, and then doubled it again to £1 1s for 'Rich Copies' bound in moiré silk, with a non-WHR wreath on the front cover.

145. *Edwy and Elgiva 1865*
Thomas Tilston, Edwy and Elgiva; a tragedy (Moxon, 1865). The cover design is credited to WHR on the title page verso. 214mm.

This unusual location for crediting WHR's design was adopted briefly by J. Bertrand Payne, who had taken over the running of the Moxon firm and is described more fully in Chapter 18.

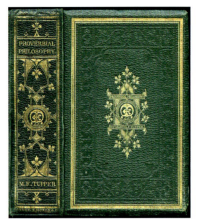 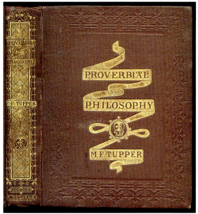 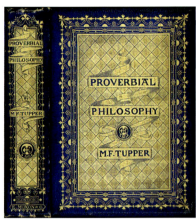

148   *149*   *150*

146. Cithara 1865
Cithara: A selection from the lyrics of Martin F. Tupper (Virtue Brothers, 1863, but issued by Moxon, 1865). The binding designer was advertised as WHR in Moxon's December 1865 'List of Books'. Bound by Hanbury & Simpson. 187mm.

The binding shows that Virtue's unbound sheets had passed to Moxon, who is credited on spine and front cover ('E M & Co' in a roundel). This is the first of five designs created by WHR for the works of Martin Tupper. The other four, listed next, were devoted to different editions of his bestseller, *Proverbial Philosophy*.

147. Pocket Proverbial Philosophy 1865
Martin F. Tupper, Proverbial philosophy: Hundred-and-fifteenth thousand (Moxon, 1865). The first of four WHR designs for this title. The front cover is signed WHR. Bound by Hanbury & Simpson. 153mm.

This book was described in Moxon's December 1865 listing as 'Pocket Edition. 18mo'. It derived from the hundred-and-tenth thousand produced in 1864 by the title's previous publisher, Hatchard, as their smaller-format edition.

148. Library Proverbial Philosophy 1865
Martin F. Tupper, Proverbial philosophy: Thirty-ninth edition (Moxon, 1865). Binding designer advertised as WHR. 187mm.

This was listed by Moxon in December 1865 as 'Library Edition, post 8vo'. It derived from Hatchard's larger-format 1863 edition, which also identified itself as the thirty-ninth edition. All three of the Tupper books considered thus far contain the residual sheets which Moxon had bought up from Tupper's previous publishers. For the following two editions, J. Bertand Payne re-launched the *Proverbial Philosophy* title and hiked up its prices.

149. Bijou Proverbial Philosophy 1866
Martin F. Tupper, Proverbial philosophy: [Bijou Edition.] Two hundredth thousand (Moxon, 1866). The unusual title punctuation is original. The design is a smaller version of the next one, which is signed WHR. 158mm.

The figure of 200,000 copies is suspect, in view of the 115,000 copies listed in the Pocket Edition the previous year. Perhaps the publisher incorporated a guesstimate of the title's pirated sales in America, which were indeed substantial. The 200,000 was however taken at face value in Altick's influential account of the Victorian reader.[8] It was unchanged when a new Bijou Edition appeared in 1870 (with the same WHR cover), consistent with it being a notional figure.

150. Illustrated Proverbial Philosophy 1867
Martin F. Tupper, Proverbial philosophy (the first and second series), illustrated, a new edition (Moxon, 1867). The spine is signed WHR. Bound by Hanbury & Simpson. 227mm.

The gilt diaper pattern of the Bijou Edition's spine has been expanded here (with small WHR signature shoehorned in at the very base) and extended to the front cover.

151. Funny Fables 1866
Funny fables for little folks. By the most eminent writers of all ages and countries, with sixteen illustrations by Grandville (Charles Griffin, 1866). Only the spine design is certainly by WHR, and signed. Bound by Bone. 186mm.

This book is not related to one published by Frances

Appendix A – *Gallery of Book Covers*

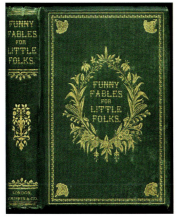 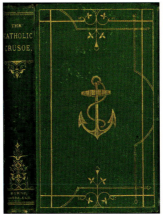 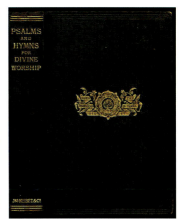

151 152 153

Freeling Broderip in 1860 with the same main title (i.e. Funny fables for little folks). Instead Griffin appears to have resuscitated Tilt's 1839 edition of Grandville's fables.

152. The Catholic Crusoe 1866
W. H. Anderdon, The Catholic Crusoe; adventures of Owen Evans (Burns, Oates, [*c.* 1866]). Only the spine is by WHR and signed. 171mm.

The binder has mistakenly inverted the block for the gilt design on the lower spine, and hence the WHR signature appears inverted at the top of the lower spine's gilt.

153. Psalms and Hymns 1866
Psalms and hymns for divine worship (Nisbet, 1866). The front cover's design is unsigned but is the same as that on the title page, where it is signed WHR. 175mm.

The Preface states that the volume was prepared by members of the Presbyterian Church in England. The annulus in the centre of the design encloses a burning bush and bears the legend Nec Tamen Consumebatur ('Nor yet was it consumed').

154. Belgravia 1866
Belgravia: A London Magazine, conducted by M.E. Braddon (Warwick House, 1866). The front wrapper is signed WHR, and continued in use until at least 1895. 226mm.

The *Belgravia Annual*, published each Christmas, had the same WHR cover design, but was printed in red and blue.

155. Andersen's Household Stories 1866
Hans Christian Andersen's stories for the household, trans. by H.W. Dulcken, with … illustrations by A.W. Bayes (Routledge, 1866). The spine and front cover are signed WHR. 200mm.

This is the first WHR design to use black as well as gilt blocking, in an integrated design. It includes elements from the stories, such as the Hardy Tin Soldier (with only one leg).

156. Grimm's Household Stories 1866
Household stories collected by the Brothers Grimm, with … illustrations by E.H. Wehnert, new edition (London and New York: Routledge [*c.* 1866]). The spine and front cover are signed WHR. Bound by W. Greening. 198mm.

This companion design again includes elements from the stories, such as the Three Brothers – the lowest panel of the spine alludes to a fencing-master, a farrier and a barber.

157. Schetky's Reminiscences 1867
Reminiscences of the veterans of the sea, a series of photographs … from the professional works of J.C. Schetky (Cundall and Fleming, 1867). The front cover is signed WHR. 443mm.

John Christian Schetky (1778–1874) had been a marine painter since early in the century, and the veterans in this impressively produced volume are naval warships.

158. Two Centuries of Song 1867
Walter Thornbury (ed.), Two centuries of song (Sampson Low, 1867 or New York: Appleton, 1867). The spine is signed WHR. Bound by Burn. 235mm.

As signalled by the fitting of a brass clasp to the binding, no expense was spared in the production of this book. Years later, Sampson Low's business partner, Edward Marston, referred to the cost in awed tones:[9] 'Among the many other finely illustrated books produced by us was a volume edited by Walter Thornbury, entitled "Two Centuries of Song." On the production of this work we expended over £2,000.'

259

William Harry Rogers – Victorian Book Designer and Star of the Great Exhibition

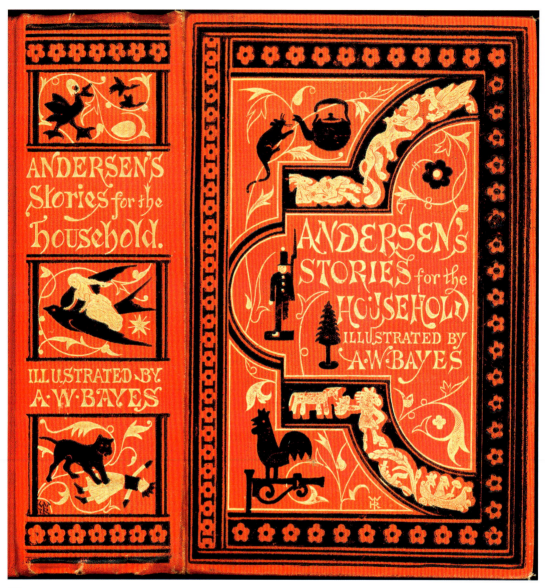

155

159. Leigh Hunt's Sonnets 1867
Leigh Hunt and S. Adams Lee (eds), The book of the sonnet, two vols (Sampson Low, 1867). Only the front cover's gilt motif is certainly by WHR and signed. Bound by Bone. 184mm.

The dedication page refers to 'the surviving editor', Leigh Hunt having died in 1859.

160. Savage Club Papers 1867
Andrew Halliday (ed.), The Savage-Club papers (Tinsley Brothers, 1868; also second series, 1869). Only the front cover was designed by WHR, and signed. 176mm.

WHR's engraved title page for the 1867 first edition was pressed into service for a yellowback issue the following year. For the copy shown here, the spine and front cover have been preserved separately.

Appendix A – Gallery of Book Covers

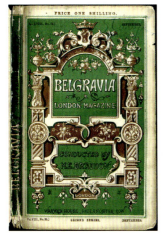
154

156

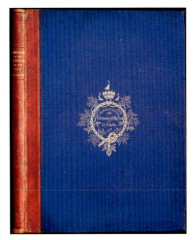
157

158

159

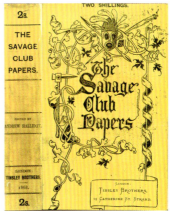
160

161. Routledge's British Poets 1867
This design for the British Poets series was a premium option used on at least four members of the series (London and New York: Routledge, 1867), including 'The poetical works of William Cowper', illustrated here. The front cover is signed WHR. 167mm.

Colourfulness was ensured by affixing three coloured-paper onlays on both spine and front cover (and then blocking over them in gilt). In a curious episode, the cover design was re-used a decade later for a similar series published by Nimmo in Edinburgh, but using re-engraved blocks which for some reason removed the 'W' from the WHR signature.

162. Piedmont and Italy (Re-issue) 1868
Dudley Costello, Piedmont and Italy, from the Alps to the Tiber [two volumes in one] (London and New York: James S. Virtue, 1861; but later issue [c. 1868]). Only the spine's palmette motif is certainly by WHR and signed. 278mm.

Given the book's subtitle, its front cover's citation of Palermo, Bourbon and Naples, all to be found south of the Tiber, was stretching a point.

163. Student and Intellectual Observer 1868
The Student and Intellectual Observer of Science, Literature and Art (Groombridge, Vol. 1, 1868). The spine is signed WHR; the journal and this cover continued until at least Volume 5. Bound by Bone. 235mm.

A plainer (and no doubt cheaper) non-WHR publisher's cover was also used in parallel for the bound volumes.

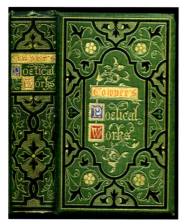

161

162

163

164

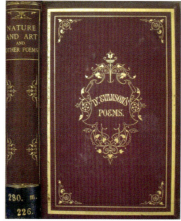

165

166

167

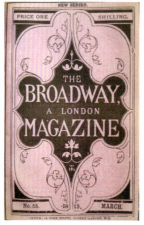

168

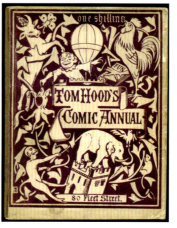

169

Appendix A – Gallery of Book Covers

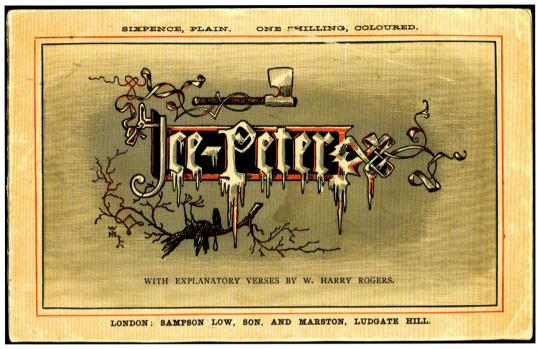

170

164. Climbing the Hill 1868
[Matilda Anne Planché, later Mackarness], Climbing the hill, by the author of 'A trap to catch a sunbeam' (Groombridge, 1868). The front cover is signed WHR. Bound by Bone. 183mm.

Unlike the preceding design, for example, the present blocks could in principle be used for a wide range of titles.

165. Nature and Art 1868
Richard Tonson Evanson, Nature and art; or, reminiscences of the international exhibition, opened in London on May the first, 1862. A poem; with occasional verses, and elegiac stanzas (Hunt, 1868). The front cover is signed WHR. Bound by Bone. 184 x 120mm.

Another general-purpose gilt frame, this time with matching corners. The Bodleian Libraries, University of Oxford, (OC) 280 m.226.

166. Printing Types 1868
Specimen of printing types, borders, ornaments, &c, octavo edition (Sheffield and London: Stephenson, Blake [c. 1868]). Only the front's frame is by WHR, and signed. Bound by Bone. The design also appeared [c. 1868] on the Scrap Book shown here. 218mm.

This is no less than the fourth (and final) WHR design to be pressed into service as a gilt frame for the front cover title of a scrap album. The three other designs used for this purpose were those for *41. National Illustrated Library 1853*, *89. L'Allegro 1859* and *164. Climbing the Hill 1868*.

167. Murby's School Books 1868
Francis Young (ed.), Sixth excelsior reader (Murby, 1876). The front cover is signed WHR. 154mm.

Thomas Murby was a musician who moved into educational and technical publishing. He may have been introduced to WHR by the Beetons, having edited *Beeton's Musical Album for 1866*. This design first appeared as an engraved title page for Murby's Excelsior books in 1868.

168. The Broadway 1868
The Broadway: A London magazine, new series, No. 1 (Routledge, September 1868). The front cover is signed WHR and was used until the journal closed in about 1873. 208mm.

The Broadway was started in September 1867, aimed at both London and New York. It was not successful, and Routledge re-launched it in September 1868, aimed only at London, and with a wrapper by WHR. The Bodleian Libraries, University of Oxford, Per. 2705 e.271. Books 604417852.

171

172

173

169. Hood's Comic Annual 1868
Tom Hood's comic annual for 1868 (Fun Office [1868]). The front cover is signed WHR. The following years were forward-dated, starting with '1870'. 208mm.

This boisterous design was used (with slight modifications) until the final annual in 1893. Tom Hood died in 1874, and 'Tom' was removed from the title from 1877 onwards.

170. Ice-Peter 1868
Ice-Peter, with explanatory verses by W. Harry Rogers (Sampson Low [1868]). The cover is signed WHR. 154 (x 254) mm.

This is the first of four comic picture-stories by Wilhelm Busch, which were also published in a four-in-one format as *A Bushel of Merry-thoughts 1868*. The latter is advertised on each story's back cover, crediting Busch and WHR. WHR presented Busch's work for the first time to a British audience, providing designs which included four engraved title pages that doubled as covers, as well as descriptive verses.

171. Sugar-bread 1868
Sugar-bread, with explanatory verses by W. Harry Rogers (Sampson Low, 1868). The cover is unsigned. 154mm.

This story, unlike the other three, also has a printed title page (with date): The disobedient children who stole sugar-bread. Told in pictures by Wilhelm Busch, and in verse by W. Harry Rogers.

172. Cat and Mouse 1868
Cat and mouse, with explanatory verses by W. Harry Rogers (Sampson Low [1868]). The cover is signed WHR. 154mm.

The three stories Ice-Peter, Sugar-bread, and Cat and Mouse all derived from Busch's *Bilderpossen*, 1864 – respectively, *Der Eispeter*, *Hansel und Gretel*, and *Katze und Maus*.[10] The Bodleian Libraries, University of Oxford, Opie PP 280.

173. Naughty Boys of Corinth 1868
The naughty boys of Corinth, with explanatory verses by W. Harry Rogers (Sampson Low [1868]). The cover is unsigned. 154mm.

This story derived from *Diogenes und die bösen Buben von Korinth*, which had appeared in *Fliegende Blätter* in 1861.

174. A Bushel of Merry-thoughts 1868
A bushel of merry-thoughts by Wilhelm Busch, described and ornamented by Harry Rogers (Sampson Low, 1868). The front cover is signed WHR. Bound by Bone. 165 (x 250) mm.

This book contains the four preceding items. WHR's cover design wittily evokes Busch by depicting a 'c' slung between the 's' and 'h' of Bushel. The other elements do not relate directly to the contents of the book, with the exception of the ogre and the girl in plaits, who both derive from 'Sugar-bread'. The cover is described inside the book by a nonsense verse in rhyming couplets (absent in some copies):

OUR COVER.
A BUSHEL OF MERRY THOUGHTS—over they go!
  Just look on our book-cover,—isn't it so?
  The basket's upset, and you'll find, when you've been to it,
  More fun than you'd think ever *could* be got into it.
  Young chicks and jugged hare tumble out in a group
  For the ogre, as soon as he's finished his soup;
  And next, over-head, comes a dear little girl,

Appendix A – Gallery of Book Covers

174

That the Marquis of Cobweb claws up by the curl,
As she, pretty darling, is teaching to fly
The unlikeliest bird ever hatched in a stye.
But now starts an animal stranger than any—
A lobster, with claws and enormous antennae,
Who makes his own salad (he's grown so obedient),
Tho' he knows his own body's its choicest ingredient.
And lastly comes galloping out in a flurry,
(It's hunger, I think, that induces such hurry),
In the loudest of trowsers that ever were built,
A roe-buck that's given up wearing the kilt.
That's all, little friends, so I'll bid you adieu,
With a bumper for Busch, and good wishes for you.
W.H.R.

175. *Christian Lyrics 1868*

Christian lyrics (Sampson Low, 1868 or New York: Scribner, Welford). The front cover is signed WHR. Bound by Bone. 220mm.

The American publication by Scribner, Welford, and Co. has been found with the WHR design not only on cloth (complete with Bone ticket) but also on morocco, whereas it has been found only on cloth for the Sampson Low, Son, and Marston publication. A similar pattern has been found for some other designs (e.g. *72. Pastoral Poems 1858* and *94. Bennett's Pilgrim's Progress 1860*) and perhaps reflected a greater American willingness to pay a premium for deluxe bindings.

176. *Helps's Las Casas 1868*

Arthur Helps, The life of Las Casas, 'The Apostle of the Indies' (Bell and Daldy, 1868). Artwork for the front's gilt design is in the V&A WHR archive, part of E694.119-1998, recto. Bound by Burn. 195mm.

The copy illustrated was presented by the author to Bessy Helps, his wife, and other copies bear a different, non-WHR design. The WHR design appeared again in blind on titles in Griffith and Farran's Favourite Library, c. 1870.

177. *Lyra Sacra Americana 1868*

Charles Dexter Cleveland (ed.), Lyra sacra americana: or, gems from American sacred poetry (Sampson Low, 1868). Artwork is in the V&A WHR archive. Bound by Burn. 157mm.

This is the first of four designs for small gilt roundels where artwork exists on the same page in the V&A WHR archive, E694.118-1998, recto. This roundel depicts two trumpets crossing behind a lyre, whose sides are shaped like swans' necks.

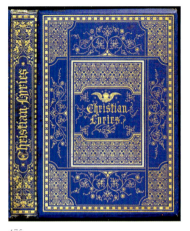

175 *176* *177*

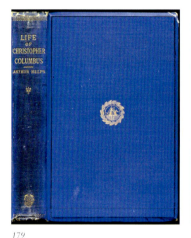
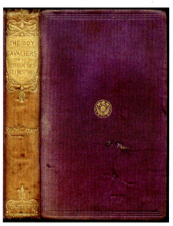

178 *179* *180*

178. Under the Rose 1868
H.G. Keene, Under the rose: Poems written chiefly in India (Bell and Daldy, 1868). Artwork is in the V&A WHR archive. 168mm.

The roundel depicts a trumpet, a lily and a lyre, with their tops respectively on the left, in the centre, and on the right.

179. Helps's Columbus 1869
Arthur Helps, The life of Columbus, the discover of America (Bell and Daldy, 1869). Artwork is in the V&A WHR archive. Bound by Eeles & Bell (written on the artwork). 195mm.

The roundel depicts a sailing ship within a wreath of seaweed. The second edition (same year as the first) had the same cover.

180. Boy Cavaliers 1869
H.C. Adams, The boy cavaliers (London and New York: Routledge, 1869). Artwork is in the V&A WHR archive. Bound by Straker (written on the artwork). 168mm.

This fourth and final roundel depicts a circular shield surmounted by a helmet, with two types of mace crossing behind it.

181. Ships and Sailors 1868
C.C. Cotterill and E.D. Little, Ships and sailors ancient and modern (Seeley, 1868). The front cover is signed WHR. 191mm.

This dramatic design was also used for two other Seeley titles, in 1868 and in 1870. It was WHR's first radically asymmetric design, with an absence of symmetry at not only the local level but at the global level as well.

Appendix A – Gallery of Book Covers

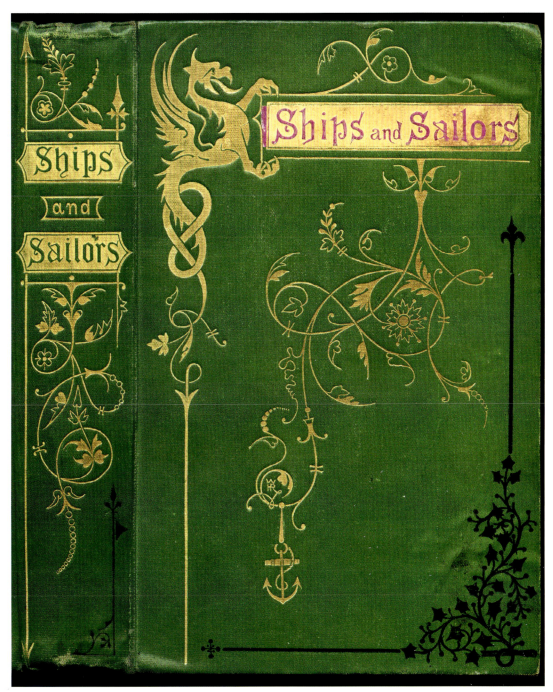

181

William Harry Rogers – Victorian Book Designer and Star of the Great Exhibition

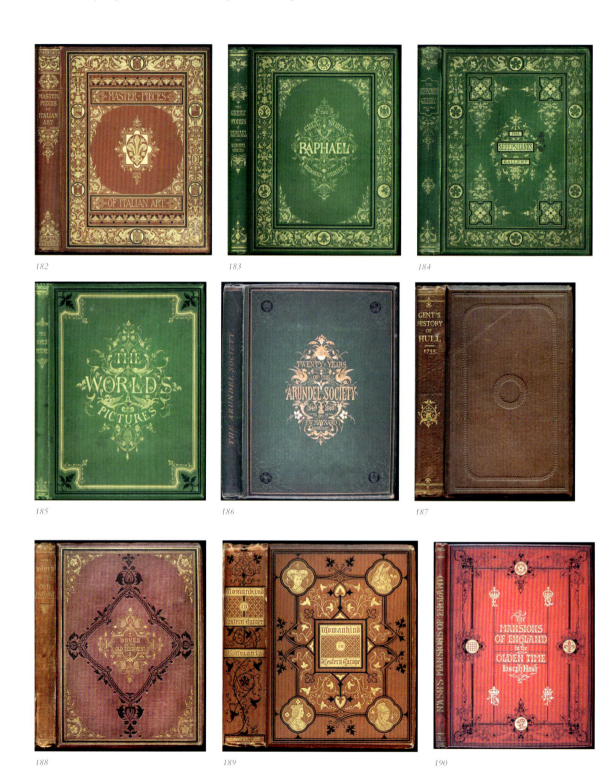

182 *183* *184*

185 *186* *187*

188 *189* *190*

Appendix A – Gallery of Book Covers

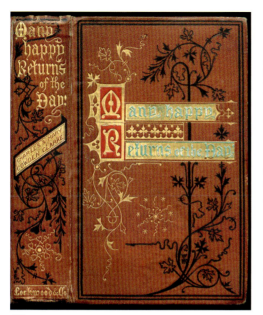
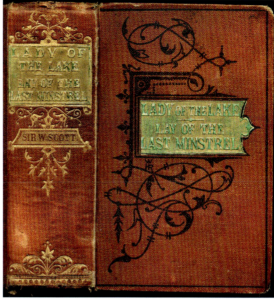

191

192

182. Masterpieces of Italian Art 1868
Masterpieces of Italian art, twenty-six photographs (London: Bell and Daldy; Cambridge (England): Deighton, Bell, 1868). The spine and front cover (both the Florentine fleur-de-lys and the outer frame) are signed WHR. Bound by Eeles & Bell. 283mm.

The six small discs in the front cover's outer frame portray Italian coats of arms. The discs were engraved on separate brasses so that they could be replaced by more appropriate designs for other titles. The frame was re-used in conjunction with two other WHR designs which are illustrated next, as well as with other, non-WHR designs (see Appendix C).

183. Great Works of Raphael 1869
Joseph Cundall (ed.), The great works of Raphael Sanzio of Urbino, twenty-six photographs, second series (London: Bell and Daldy; Cambridge: Deighton, Bell, 1869). The front cover's motif (and its frame re-used from preceding Masterpieces) are signed WHR. Bound by Eeles & Bell. 283mm.

The cover's 'Madonna Series' does not occur inside the book, and in some copies has been replaced by a more prosaic 'Second Series'. The frame's six discs have been replaced by new WHR designs. For the first series, the present cover was not used until its fourth (and final) edition in 1870.

184. Sheepshanks Gallery 1870
The Sheepshanks gallery, a series of twenty pictures …

Reproduced in permanent tint by the Autotype process (Bell and Daldy, 1870). The spine and front cover are signed WHR, inherited from *Masterpieces of Italian Art 1868* with cognate additions. Bound by Eeles & Bell. 281mm.

The frame's six discs all have the same cinquefoil design. The title page of some copies replaces 'Autotype' by 'Woodbury', reflecting the turmoil at the time in creating permanent photographs.

185. The World's Pictures 1869
The world's pictures, a series of photographs of the fifteen most celebrated paintings in the world (Bell and Daldy; Cundall and Fleming, 1869). The front cover is signed WHR. 283mm.

The photography was recorded in Helmut Gernsheim's valuable census of early photography.[11] He stated that it had been preceded by an 1860 edition, but no trace of this has been found, though there was a later 1872 edition which used the same cover.

186. Arundel Society Photographs 1869
Frederic W. Maynard, Descriptive notice of the drawings and publications of the Arundel Society, from 1849 to 1868 inclusive; illustrated by photographs of all the publications (Nichols, 1869). The front cover is signed WHR. 380mm.

As with the preceding cover, WHR used grotesques to bring an element of fantasy to even his most elegant designs.

269

193 *194*

187. *History of Hull* 1869
Gent's history of Hull … re-printed in fac-simile of the original of 1735 (Hull: Peck, 1869). The spine is signed WHR. Bound by Bone. 229mm.

A large-paper issue had the same cover design, but WHR's gilt vignette looked lost in its tall spine.

188. *Women of the Old Testament* 1869
The women of the Old Testament … With twelve photographs (Seeley, 1869). The front cover is signed WHR. 212mm.

Over the period 1866 to 1873, Seeley, Jackson, and Halliday issued seven other titles in a similar format, each illustrated with twelve photographs, but none of these others had a cover designed by WHR.

189. *Womankind in Western Europe* 1869
Thomas Wright, Womankind in Western Europe (Groombridge, 1869). The spine is signed WHR. Bound by Bone. 214mm.

During the later 1860s, the availability of blocking in black alongside blocking in gold allowed WHR to introduce a further element of dramatic contrast. Here he played with the figure/ground distinction, with black appearing as ground on the front cover, but as figure on the spine.

190. *Mansions of England* 1869
Joseph Nash, The mansions of England in the olden time, re-edited by J. Corbet Anderson, four vols (Sotheran, 1869–72). The front cover is signed WHR. 378mm.

Also issued as four volumes in two, with the same front cover. In addition, for 16 guineas rather than the basic 6 guineas there was an issue with the constituent lithographs hand-coloured and on large mounts, and housed in four book-like portfolios, each quarter-bound in calf and with the WHR gilt title blocked on its front cover. Their dimensions of 586 x 461 mm make them the largest of all WHR covers.

191. *Many Happy Returns* 1869
Charles and Mary Cowden Clarke, 'Many happy returns of the day!', new edition (Lockwood [1869]). The spine and front cover are signed WHR. Bound by Bone. 182 mm.

In this all-singing, all-dancing design with colourful onlays and gilt amoebae, WHR even introduced a slanting author panel on the spine.

192. *Lady of the Lake* 1869
Sir Walter Scott, The lady of the lake, The lay of the last minstrel [two separately paginated books in one] (Liverpool: Howell, 1869). The front cover is signed WHR. Bound by Bone. 124mm.

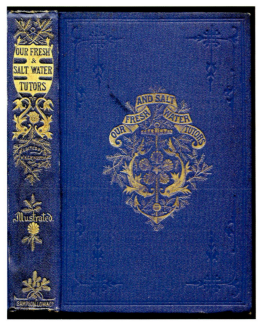

195

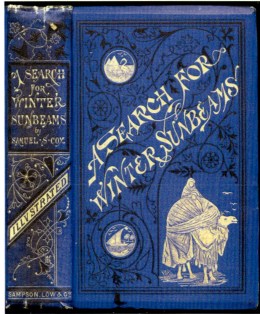

196

In a reversal of the normal progression, the front cover's blocking in black was instead blocked in gilt on a later book, Thomas Carter's *Curiosities of War*, second edition [1871].

193. Montaigne's Essays 1869
All the essays of Michael Seigneur de Montaigne: … Made English by Charles Cotton, third edition (Alex. Murray, 1869). The spine and front cover are signed WHR. Bound by Bain. 186mm.

Here WHR accommodates the slanting spine panel by daringly unbalancing the neighbouring semicircles and other elements.

194. Church Seasons 1869
Alexander H. Grant, The church seasons historically and poetically illustrated (Hogg, [1869]). The spine and front cover are signed WHR. Bound by Bain. 190mm.

The present spine and the preceding spine differ from each other, but both harmonise with the same front cover, suggesting that WHR designed all three components for the binder, A.W. Bain, at the same time.

195. Fresh and Salt Water Tutors 1869
W.H.G. Kingston (ed.), Our fresh and salt water tutors (Sampson Low, 1869). The front cover is signed WHR. Bound by Bone. 173mm.

Despite WHR's late exploration of total asymmetry, he did not abandon his *GS-LA* idiom of global symmetry, local asymmetry, as in this marine example.

196. Winter Sunbeams 1869
Samuel S. Cox, Search for winter sunbeams in the Riviera, Corsica, Algiers, and Spain (London: Sampson Low; New York: Appleton, 1869). The spine and front cover are signed WHR. Bound by Bone. 217mm.

Appropriately enough, the author, who was a member of the US Congress, was known as 'Sunset' Cox. When Appleton alone published the book in New York in 1870, the new non-WHR cover included copies of the two WHR roundels.

197. Daisy's Companions 1869
Daisy's companions, by the author of 'Grandmamma's nest' (Bell and Daldy [1869]). The front cover is signed WHR. 139mm.

This is the first of three diminutive books by Eleanor Grace O'Reilly with WHR designs, which are grouped together here.

198. Doll World 1872
Mrs Robert O'Reilly, Doll world (Bell and Daldy, 1872).

William Harry Rogers – Victorian Book Designer and Star of the Great Exhibition

197 *198* *199*

200 *201*

202 *203 and 204*

Appendix A – Gallery of Book Covers

The front cover is a partial re-use of a WHR design, with other elements characteristic of WHR. 140mm.

The design in black on the front cover comes from *197. Daisy's Companions 1869*, but turned upside-down and consequently with its bird-cage and its WHR signature removed.

199. Deborah's Drawer 1871
Eleanor Grace O'Reilly, Deborah's drawer (Bell and Daldy, 1871). The spine and front cover are signed WHR. 141mm.

After WHR's death, the cover of a fourth O'Reilly title re-used the present design's blocking in black, complete with its WHR signatures, but amplified by another hand and hence not illustrated here. This was Mrs Robert O'Reilly, Giles's minority (Bell, 1874).

200. Andersen's Tales in Two Volumes 1869
A pair of volumes with uniform bindings: (a) Andersen's tales for children (Bell & Daldy, 1869); (b) Fairy tales and sketches by Hans Christian Andersen (Bell and Daldy, 1870). The front covers are signed WHR. Bound by Burn. 198mm.

Despite their non-uniform titles, these two volumes have uniform drop-head titles, namely, (a) Andersen's Tales and (b) Andersen's Tales. Second Series. There are a couple of oddities about the covers of these volumes. The first oddity is that the three roundels for Volume (a) are not by WHR but instead were parachuted in from the non-WHR cover of an 1866 edition of the book; the roundels on Volume (b) are also not by WHR. Further, the roundels on both spines appear to have landed on top of the lower halves of WHR signatures. The second oddity is that the central WHR signature on each front cover is absent in some copies, which appear to be later issues from about 1871. Later editions with the same cover design, starting with one for Volume (b) in 1872, all lack the WHR signatures. The motivation of the binder, Burn, in removing the signatures is unclear, but a Machiavellian possibility would be that Burn did not want to publicise WHR because he was mainly associated with a rival binder, Bone. Certainly, at about this time Burn bound a number of other covers which were in the style of WHR but were not signed by him (and hence have not been included here).

201. Andersen's Fairy Tales Abstract 1869
Hans Christian Andersen, Tales and fairy stories, trans. Madame de Chatelain, new edition (London and New York: Routledge [1869]). The front cover is signed WHR. Bound by Bone. 166mm.

The contents of this book had appeared in Routledge editions since 1852. This undated issue with a new, abstract cover design has an advertisement at the back for *Routledge's Every Boy's Annual for 1870*.

202. Andersen's Fairy Tales Figural 1872
Hans Christian Andersen, Tales and fairy stories, trans. Madame de Chatelain, new edition (London and New York: Routledge [1872]). Unsigned but artwork for the front cover is in the V&A WHR archive, E694.19-1998. 166mm.

In the V&A artwork for this late, figural design by WHR, the bottom-right corner of the design bears his signature, which the unknown binder removed. This undated issue has an advertisement at the back for the *Young Gentleman's Magazine*, which stated that, 'Part XII., the First Part of the New Volume, appeared on the 28th of November, 1872.'

203. Great Army Battles 1869
The great battles of the British army, a new edition (London and New York: Routledge, [1869]). The spine and front cover are signed WHR. Bound by Bone. 191mm.

This is the first of four titles on a military theme which share the same front cover design (with three coloured onlays) but have different spines (each with one onlay). It is also the only title to have been found to bear a Bone binder's ticket (but the common front cover means that the other titles must also have been bound by Bone). The present book is an extended version of the same title by Charles MacFarlane, 1853; it was subsequently credited to Charles R. Low.

204. Great Sieges 1871
The great sieges of history, a new edition (London and New York: Routledge [1871]). The spine and front cover are signed WHR. Bound by Bone. 192mm.

The present book is an extended edition of the same title published by William Robson, 1858 (the Preface of the present book is initialled W.R.).

205. Great Navy Battles 1872
Charles R. Low, The great battles of the British navy (London and New York: Routledge [1872]). Only the front cover is signed WHR, but the spine is also characteristic of WHR. Bound by Bone. 192mm.

The British Library dates the book as [1873], but the 1872 *English Catalogue of Books* gave its date of publication as October 1872, a few months before WHR's death.

206. Great Commanders 1872
G.P.R. James, Memoirs of great commanders, a new edition. London and New York: Routledge [1872]). The spine and front cover are signed WHR. Bound by Bone. 192mm.

According to the *English Catalogue of Books*, this book also appeared in October 1872. Subsequently, its spine design formed the basis for a fifth military title with uniform front cover, namely, James Grant's *British Heroes in Foreign Wars* [1873]; the spine modification was not by WHR, however.

273

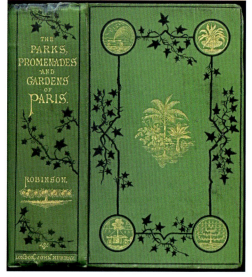

205 and 206   *207*

208   *209*   *210*

207. Parks of Paris 1869
W. Robinson, The parks, promenades & gardens of Paris (John Murray, 1869). Unsigned, but there is a proof on cloth in the V&A WHR archive, E693.184-1998. Bound by Bone. 232mm.

This is the first of five WHR designs for the works of William Robinson, the garden writer, which appeared from 1869 to 1872 and are grouped together here. The present front cover's central vignette (with palm tree) was re-used on a sixth Robinson title: The subtropical garden (John Murray, 1871).

208. Alpine Flowers 1870
W. Robinson, Alpine flowers for English gardens (John Murray, 1870). The spine and front cover are signed WHR. Bound by Bone. 205mm.

The design allies botanic accuracy with elegant artifice. The signature under the author's name on the spine extends the boundaries of disguise for the WHR monogram.

Appendix A – Gallery of Book Covers

211

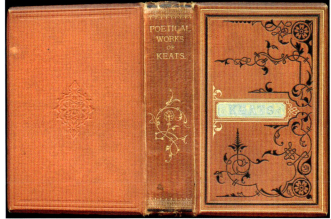
212

213

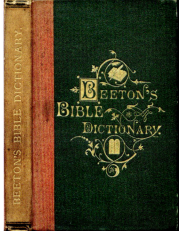
214

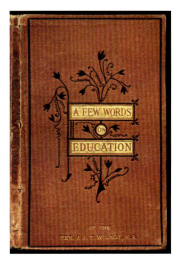
215

209. Hardy Flowers 1871
W. Robinson, Hardy flowers (Warne, 1871). Unsigned but has the same author and binder as the two preceding entries together with characteristic WHR lettering and botanising. Bound by Bone. 196mm.

As with Alpine Flowers, the front cover design well exemplifies the principle of global symmetry, local asymmetry, not only in the gilt centre but even in what appear to be two bordering plants of Lilium regale, expressed in blind.

210. The Garden Wrapper 1871
The Garden: An illustrated weekly journal, founded and conducted by William Robinson, November 1871. Unsigned, but artwork for the masthead is in the V&A WHR archive, E694.18-1998. 284mm.

As with the very first entry here, *1. The Builder* 1848, the WHR masthead occurred at the start of the outer, unnumbered pages of each issue, which carried advertisements. When the issues were bound up, normal practice was to discard the outer pages.

211. The Garden Cloth 1872
The Garden: An illustrated weekly journal, Volume 1, 1872. The front cover is signed WHR. 284mm.

This is one of WHR's last designs (it featured in the advertising pages of the *Garden* from 27 July 1872). It was used for the first eight volumes of the journal, after which it was replaced by an anonymous, relatively plain design.

275

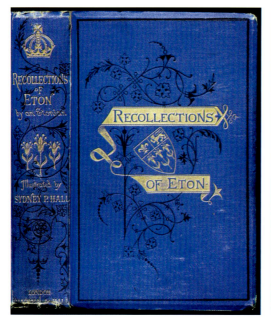
216

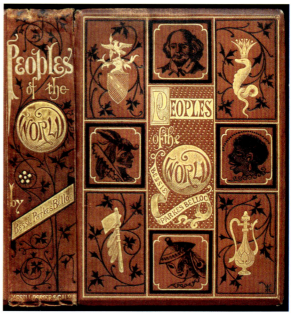
217

212. Keats' Poetical Works (Re-issued) 1870
The poetical works of John Keats (Moxon, 1866; but later issue [1870]). Artwork for the blind-stamped motif on the back cover is in the V&A WHR archive, E694.24-1998; the front cover and spine, though unsigned, are also in the style of WHR. Bound by Bone. 204mm.

A copy of this book carries a scarce binder's ticket (Ball 17E1) known only from 1870, belying the title page's 1866.

213. Beeton's Modern Men and Women 1870
Beeton's modern men and women (Ward, Lock and Tyler [1870]). The front cover is signed WHR. Bound by Bain. 175mm.

This and the following design are throwbacks to the period 1863 to 1866, when several S.O. Beeton publications received WHR covers, before Beeton lost control of his publishing. Presumably he persuaded Ward, Lock and Tyler to commission designs from WHR for two of the 'S.O. Beeton's National Reference Books' which he compiled for them.

214. Beeton's Bible Dictionary 1870
Beeton's Bible dictionary (Ward, Lock and Tyler [1870]). The front cover is signed WHR. Bound by Bain. 179mm.

This and the preceding title were issued for 1s 6d in ordinary cloth (as shown for *213. Beeton's Modern Men and Women 1870*) or for 2s in what was called half-bound (nowadays called quarter-bound), as shown here, with red cloth spine and green cloth boards.

215. Wilmot's Education 1870
J.J.T. Wilmot, A few words on education, fifth edition (Hunt, 1870). The front cover is signed WHR. 160mm.

The publisher advertised this book (in the *Educational Times* for 1870) as 'Handsomely bound in limp cloth, gilt'.

216. Recollections of Eton 1870
Recollections of Eton. By an Etonian (Chapman and Hall, 1870). The front cover is signed WHR. 210mm.

WHR's design deploys Etonian motifs such as three lilies, but overall seems dutiful rather than inspired.

217. Peoples of the World 1870
Bessie Parkes-Belloc, Peoples of the world (London and New York: Cassell [1870]). The front cover is signed WHR. Bound by Straker. 183mm.

The design has a lively overall effect, though the interpretation of its components seems not always clear.

218. The Brownies 1870
Juliana Horatia Ewing, The brownies and other tales (Bell and Daldy, 1870; also, Boston: Roberts Brothers and London: Bell and Daldy, 1871). The front cover is signed WHR. 188mm.

Appendix A – Gallery of Book Covers

218

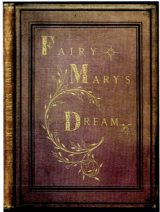
219

220

221

222

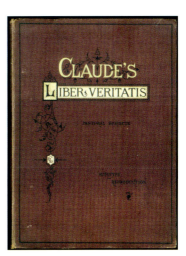
223

This design remained in use on successive editions until 1892. In the (undeclared) second London edition of 1871, the date on the Dedication page was inappropriately updated from 1870 to 1871, thus matching the title page, so that it has sometimes been mistaken for a first edition.

219. Fairy Mary's Dream 1870
A.F.L., Fairy Mary's dream (Groombridge, 1870). The front cover is signed WHR. Bound by Westleys. 257mm.

This is a relatively spare design, though it has been viewed by Edmund King as more balanced than other, more elaborate ones.[12]

220. True to Herself 1870
Frederick W. Robinson, author of 'Anne Judge, spinster,' … etc. True to herself. A romance, in three volumes (Sampson Low, 1870). The front covers are signed WHR. Bound by Bone. 194mm.

This is the only known design by WHR for a three-decker, the classic format for Victorian novels. Wolff recorded fifteen titles by this author, but not the present title.[13] Sadleir had no titles by this author.

221. Streeter's Catalogue 1870
E.W. Streeter, Catalogue, with designs and prices, of diamond ornaments [etc.] (London [1870]). The front cover is signed WHR. 194mm.

Illustrated here is the seventh edition [c. 1871]. Edwin Streeter raced through the editions of his catalogue, his business thereby rapidly assuming the air of a venerable

277

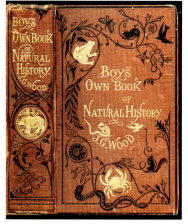

224

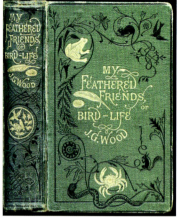

225

226

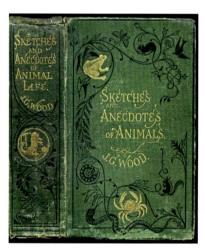

227

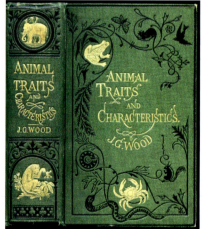

228

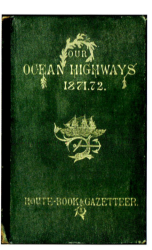

229

establishment (consistent with the mock-antique cover title, Ye Catalogue of Designs, &c.). The sixtieth edition (still with WHR cover) was reached in about 1885. The hype worked, so much so that Streeter entered fiction as the go-to jeweller for valuing the diamonds found in Rider Haggard's *King Solomon's Mines* (1886), p. 318.

222. Liber Studiorum 1870
Turner's liber studiorum reproduced in autotype from the original etchings, three volumes (Autotype, and Cundall and Fleming, 1870–71). The front cover is signed WHR. 379mm.

WHR's cover design was also used for the portfolios (quarter-bound in morocco) in which students at the Government's Schools of Art were presented with a dozen Turner autotypes as a prize, in the period 1872–8. Over the period 1876 to 1894 the scheme was generalised to at least nine other areas of art for which prints were presented as prizes in WHR portfolios, with adapted titling.

223. Liber Veritatis 1872
Claude's liber veritatis reproduced in autotype from selected etchings by Richard Earlom, three volumes (Autotype, 1872). The front cover is signed WHR. 376mm.

Such a dark cloth was chosen by the binder that it is difficult to make out the designs and lettering in black.

Appendix A – *Gallery of Book Covers*

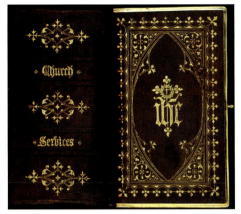
230

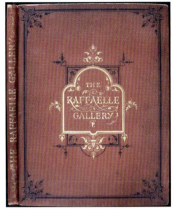
231

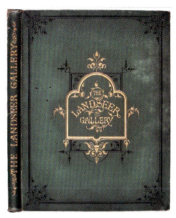
232

224. *Wood's Boy's Own Book 1870*
J.G. Wood, The boy's own book of natural history (London and New York: Routledge, [1870]). The spine and front cover are signed WHR. 165mm.

This is the first of five titles by the Rev. J.G. Wood with a partly uniform design, but individualised gilt lettering and roundels. A sixth title, the Rev. Charles Williams's *Dogs and their ways* (Routledge [1873]), shared the uniform parts but its crude titles and roundel were not by WHR and hence are not illustrated.

225. *Wood's My Feathered Friends 1870*
J.G. Wood, My feathered friends (London and New York: Routledge [1870]). The spine and front cover are signed WHR. 167mm.

All the titles are also found with two different configurations of rearranged spine designs. In the first spine modification [c. 1872], the positions of title and roundel were swapped, so that the WHR roundel was above the title, and furthermore the black blocking at the bottom (with its WHR signature) was replaced by a non-WHR gilt vignette. In the second spine modification [c. 1873], the positions in the first modification of the WHR roundel and the non-WHR vignette were swapped, so that the non-WHR vignette became on top, with the WHR roundel at the bottom.

226. *Wood's White's Selborne 1871*
Gilbert White, The natural history of Selborne, with additional notes by J.G. Wood (London and New York: Routledge [1871]). The spine and front cover are signed WHR. 167mm.

This book and the following two have dated prefaces in the range 1853 to 1855, accompanied by undated title pages, which can suggest to the unwary that these books were issued nearly twenty years before their actual appearances.

227. *Wood's Sketches and Anecdotes 1872*
J.G. Wood, Sketches and anecdotes of animal life, new edition (London and New York: Routledge [1872]). The spine and front cover are signed WHR. 166mm.

The next entry is a continuation of the present volume, with subtitle: Sketches & anecdotes of animal life. Second series.

228. *Wood's Animal Traits 1872*
J. G. Wood, Animal traits & characteristics, a new edition (London and New York: Routledge [1872]). The front cover is signed WHR. 167mm.

This title has not been found with the original uniform spine design, only with the first spine modification (as here) and the second spine modification. It is not known whether the title exists in the original uniform format.

229. *Our Ocean Highways 1871*
J. Maurice Dempsey and William Hughes (eds), Our ocean highways (Stanford, 1871). The front cover is signed WHR. 190mm.

The whimsical cover and the preface (p. v) refer to this as the volume for 1871–2, rather than the title page's 1871. There was a previous edition in 1870 which had a non-WHR cover.

230. *Courtier's Church Services 1871*
The book of common prayer ... Together with the Proper lessons (Courtier, 1871), 'Bourgeois 32mo'. The front cover's configuration of sacred symbols resembles a sketch in the V&A WHR archive, E694.106-1998 (though without the legend 'Hallelujah'). 129mm.

279

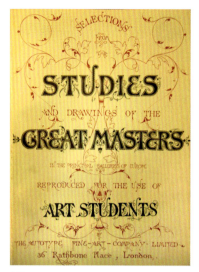 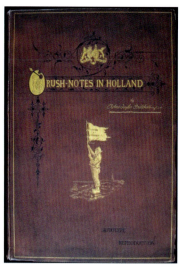 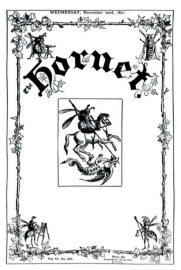

233   234   235

As usual, the binding title for a combination of works of this type was Church Services. Another Courtier copy bears the same cover configuration but has even smaller font [1872], 'Ruby 32mo'. It has the smallest of all WHR covers, 101 × 64 mm.

231. Raffaelle Gallery 1871
The Raffaelle Gallery, A series of twenty autotype reproductions (Bell and Daldy; Cundall and Fleming, 1871). The front cover is signed WHR. 372mm.

Some copies of this book declare twenty-two autotypes on the title page, instead of twenty.

232. Landseer Gallery 1871
The Landseer Gallery, A series of twenty autotype reproductions (Bell and Daldy; Cundall and Fleming, 1871). The front cover is signed WHR twice. 375mm.

As with its preceding companion, *Raffaelle Gallery 1871*, some copies declare twenty-two autotypes on the title page. The cover differs from the Raffaelle only in its titling, with the front cover's title block wholly new and separately signed WHR.

233. Great Masters 1871
Selections from the studies and drawings of the great masters. Autotype [c. 1871]. Part 1 [to 8]. The front wrapper is signed WHR. 375mm.

The same wrapper was used as the title page of a book containing all eight Parts, with binding title: Studies from the great masters. The title page is shown here, and omits the number and price which are included on an individual Part's wrapper. The Bodleian Libraries, University of Oxford, 913 Aut.

234. Brush-notes in Holland 1871
Robert Taylor Pritchett, Brush-notes in Holland, generally known as ink pots (Autotype [1871]). The front cover is signed WHR; blank spine. 559mm.

This book of autotype reproductions of Pritchett's paintings is dedicated to the Queen of the Netherlands, whose arms are included at the top of the front cover. The same year, a companion work was published, entitled: *Brush-notes in Paris. Paris 1871, being the reign of the Commune*. Its cover is a modification of the present one, replacing the Netherlands arms by tricolours with the cap of liberty, and removing the windswept figure holding aloft the motto of Zeeland. Pritchett was commissioned by Queen Victoria to paint a record of many of her public events. The Royal Collection Trust's copy of Paris 1871 is the only institutional holding that has been located.

235. The Hornet 1871
The Hornet (Frederick Arnold, 1871). The front cover is signed WHRogers. 296mm.

This weekly magazine first appeared in 1866 with the alliterative title of the Hornsey Hornet, dropping the 'Hornsey' the following year, and was much concerned with the administration of the City of London. The known range of the amusing WHR wrapper is 1871 to 1873. It includes five anthropomorphic hornets, which are writing (upper left) or drawing (lower left), and acting as a judge (upper right) or as a town-crier (lower right); in

Appendix A – Gallery of Book Covers

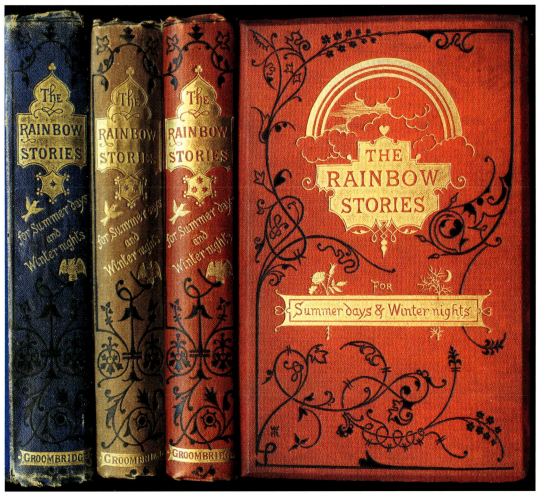

236

the centre, a hornet St George is slaying a dragon labelled 'abuses'. It is the only WHR cover design whose publisher intermingled it with an array of advertisements. To show WHR's design more clearly, these have been blanked out in the illustration.

236. *Rainbow Stories 1871*
The rainbow stories for summer days and winter nights (Groombridge, three volumes, [1871] – [1872]). The front cover is signed WHR. Bound by Bone. 188mm.

The only indication that each book provides of its volume number is the number of asterisks shown on its title page and its spine (i.e. ★, ★★, or ★★★). Several colours of cloth were employed, appropriately for volumes with the name Rainbow Stories.

237. *Magnet Stories 1872*
The magnet stories for summer days and winter nights (Groombridge, eight volumes, [1872]). The front cover is signed WHR. Bound by Bone. 170mm.

This was the cheaper companion of the Rainbow Stories, at 2s 6d per volume instead of 3s 6d. Using the same system of numbering by asterisks, it can be seen here that by Volumes 6 to 8, asterisk congestion sets in.

281

William Harry Rogers – Victorian Book Designer and Star of the Great Exhibition

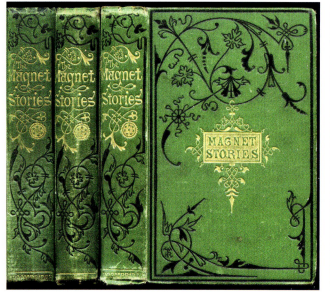

237

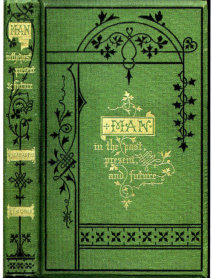

238

239

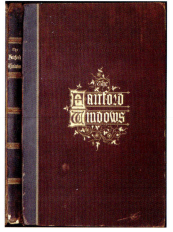

240

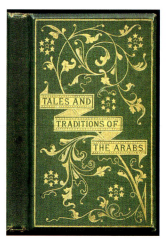

241

Appendix A – Gallery of Book Covers

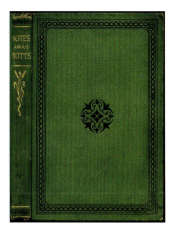  

242   243   244

238. Man in the Past 1872
Dr L. Büchner, Man in the past, present and future, trans. by W.S. Dallas (Asher, 1872, either alone or with the addition of Philadelphia: Lippincott). The front cover is signed WHR. Bound by Bain. 225mm.

This was *Die Stellung des Menschen in der Natur in Vergangheit, Geganwart und Zukunft* (1869), by the German Darwinian Ludwig Büchner, translated by the Assistant Secretary of the London Geological Society. It was an interesting departure for such a book to receive a cover by WHR, who did not however live to repeat the experiment.

239. Boy's Own Treasury 1872
The boy's own treasury of sports and pastimes, by J.G. Wood, J.H. Pepper, Bennett, Miller, and others (London and New York: Routledge [1872]); a later issue of this title. The front cover is signed WHR. 178mm.

The bold use of simplified lettering and zigzag spine titling again suggests a new direction in which WHR's work might have developed, if it had not been cut short.

240. Fairford Windows 1872
James Gerald Joyce, The Fairford windows (Arundel Society, 1872). The front cover is signed WHR. 572mm.

This massive account of the medieval stained-glass windows in the parish church at Fairford, Gloucestershire, was given a front cover title design by WHR that was appropriately substantial in scale.

241. Traditions of the Arabs 1873
J. Brown, Tales and traditions of the Arabs (Elliot Stock [1873]). The front cover is signed WHR. 167mm.

The Preface is dated 'January, 1873' and WHR died on 19 January 1873, so this may have been his last completed design.

242. Notes about Notts 1873
Cornelius Brown, Notes about Notts (Nottingham: Forman, 1874). Artwork for the front's central motif only is present in the V&A WHR archive at E694.22-1998. 188mm.

This is the first of three cover designs by WHR which are known only from their posthumous appearances over the period 1874 to 1878. They are listed here as 1873 designs, but each of them could be earlier than this.

243. Grimm's Goblins 1873
Grimm's goblins (Meek, 1877). Only the front cover's cartouche is by WHR, and signed. 216mm.

This is a late re-issue of Grimm's household stories, translated from the Kinder und Haus Marchen by E. Taylor, with Cruikshank's illustrations.

244. The Crèche Annual 1873
Marie Hilton, The Crèche annual, seventh year (Morgan & Scott, 1877–8; used until at least the twelfth year). The front cover is signed WHR. 142mm.

Prior to this seventh year, the annual reports on The Crèche children's home issued in calf bore a different, non-WHR design. The WHR design was used subsequently on the calf issues until at least the twelfth year. In that twelfth year, the WHR design appeared on a morocco as well as a calf issue. Again, no prior use of this WHR design has been found and it is therefore allotted a nominal 1873 date.

283

NOTES

1. Whether or not forward-dating has occurred is ignored. An example of forward-dating would be the publisher giving a title page date of 1859 to a book actually published in November 1858, to enhance its chance of success in the Christmas market of 1859 as well as 1858.
2. Ruari McLean, *Victorian Publishers' Book-bindings in Cloth and Leather* (Gordon Fraser, 1974), p. 46.
3. Robert Lee Wolff, *Nineteenth-century Fiction*, five volumes (New York: Garland, 1981–6), No. 5573.
4. Hazel Morris, *Hand, Head and Heart: Samuel Carter Hall and the Art Journal* (Norwich: Michael Russell, 2002), pp. 100-103, 106-107.
5. Arthur L. Bowley, *Wages in the United Kingdom in the Nineteenth Century* (Cambridge University Press, 1900), table of nominal weekly wages of agricultural labourers.
6. Gregory V. Jones and Jane E. Brown, 'Bound for Edinburgh: Burn's denominated tickets of 1860', *Book Collector*, 2004, Vol. 53, pp. 525-32. Further findings have been made at Princeton: Robert J. Milevski, 'More on "Burn's denominated tickets of 1860"', *Book Collector*, 2013, Vol. 62, pp. 348-51.
7. [Gustave L.M. Strauss], *Reminiscences of an Old Bohemian*, new edition (Tinsley Brothers, 1883), p. 112.
8. Richard D. Altick, *The English Common Reader: A Social History of the Mass Reading Public, 1800–1900*, second edition (Columbus, OH: Ohio State University Press, 1998), p. 387.
9. E. Marston, *After Work: Fragments from the Workshop of an Old Publisher* (London: William Heinemann and New York: Charles Scribner's Sons, 1904), p. 102.
10. Gregory Jones and Jane Brown, 'Wilhelm Busch's merry thoughts: His early books in Britain and America', *Papers of the Bibliographical Society of America*, 2007, Vol. 101, pp. 167-204; see pp. 177-80.
11. Helmut Gernsheim, *Incunabula of British Photographic Literature* (London and Berkeley, CA: Scolar Press, 1984), No. 127.
12. Edmund M.B. King, 'The book cover designs of William Harry Rogers', in *'For the love of the binding'. Studies in bookbinding history presented to Mirjam Foot* (The British Library, 2000), pp. 319-28; p. 321.
13. Robert Lee Wolff, *Nineteenth-century Fiction*, five volumes (New York: Garland, 1981–6), Nos 5929-5943.

APPENDIX B

Paris

As described in Chapter 3, George Isaacs wrote a short memoir of life with WHR in Paris in 1844, when they were both aged nineteen. Here his memoir is reproduced in full.[1] Figure B.1, after Jean Béraud, chronicler of the Belle Époque, is anachronistic but it includes a view of the Bibliothèque Mazarine (to the left of the portico), as referred to in Chapter 3.

HOW WE FARED WHEN HARD-UP IN PARIS

B.1 – 'A Gust of Wind', after Jean Béraud, published as a supplement to the Pictorial World, 8 July 1886. Width 455mm.

For about six months of the year 1844, Harry R— and myself lived in Paris, Rue de Bussi No. 15, *au cinquieme*. For about a fortnight we starved there; when I say starved, I mean that we went short of food, had no certainty of a meal from day to day, and were obliged to resort to strange devices to prolong existence.

Harry R— was an artist; I had no profession; but shared with him an enthusiasm for art, a great passion for antique remains, and some taste for literature. We also had a taste for masquerades, dances at the Barrieres, billiards, punch, and pastry lunches. We had neither of us reached the age of twenty.

Harry's income was a precarious one. He received from time to time a five-pound note from England, and made some few francs a week out of commissions from the booksellers. I had more assured resources; about £125 a year, from house property—and £100 saved from the rents of two previous years.

We had, however, a common purse, and resided together, in a suite of rooms, as I have said before, in the Rue de Bussi, on the fifth floor.

With ordinary prudence, we could have very well managed, on our united means, to avoid the embarrassments I am about to relate. But lovers of art and literature, of masquerades and pastry lunches, are not always prudent at the age of nineteen. We certainly were not.

When I left England, I took £60 with me—leaving £40 in the hands of my father, who also undertook to collect my rents—and remit, when advised. We both agreed, that, as a young man could live very joyously in Paris—where amusements were cheap—on 250 francs a month, I should not require a remittance for six months. Six weeks after that calculation, I was without a *sous*.

The Pastry Lunches—the little suppers of four—the excursions (also of four) to Versailles, Montmartre, and other suburban shows—did not alone effect this result: no—it was my ungovernable passion for old china, silver chasings, quaint enamels, ivory carvings, and illuminated MSS., that finished me off: nearly £40 were absorbed in these treasures.

After borrowing 30 francs from our landlady, I wrote home, but, not feeling inclined to reveal the exact state of my finances, I merely stated that I had laid out a large proportion of the cash I had taken with me in antiquities, and should require a remittance soon, as it might prove inconvenient to be straitened in funds in a foreign country. To this letter I received no reply—and the joint funds of Harry R— & Co. were only three half-pence. Harry R— was a philosopher: 'Where shall we dine to-day?' he asked.

I, also, was a philosopher, and replied, 'Wherever dinners are to be obtained without money.'

'Good,' returned Harry, 'they are to be so obtained to-day.'

I did not object—I merely questioned 'how?'

'I shall dine at the Restaurant, and forget my purse; you can dine at the Café, and leave your purse at home,' was the reply.

Decidedly Harry had great administrative talents. We dined—he at the Restaurant, where previously we had both dined daily; I at the Café, where, until then, we had both occasionally lunched.

We supped that night on bread and mulled *vin ordinaire*; having a stock of the latter in our cupboard, and a monthly account with the baker.

The next morning, Harry announced that we were out of coffee and sugar—'we must see about breakfast,' he said, 'what do you think of bread and *vin ordinaire*?'

I replied, 'I should prefer coffee, and had no partiality for dry bread.'

Harry shrugged his shoulders, and asked ironically, 'Could you not suggest cream cheese, a few anchovies, or a slice of ham?'

'Why not?' said I, with a sudden inspiration—'here are three half-pence.'

'And then?' asked Harry.

'And then,' repeated I, seizing from the *secretaire* a brand new fourpenny piece (which Harry had imported specially for a young lady, who had a taste for numismatics)— 'here is what will pass for a half-franc;' and I hammered the four-penny into the semblance of that coin with the landlady's bronze inkstand.

Harry was half inclined to be angry; but coffee, cream cheese, and butter mollified him.

The passing the battered four-penny as a five-penny was hardly legitimate, as a commercial transaction, but we were, as I have before stated, philosophers, and argued that if the grocer was content to receive the coin as a half-franc, he would pass it again as such, and as it would, therefore, obtain currency, it was, in point of fact, as good as a half-franc.

No dinner that day; mulled wine and bread for supper.

Mulled wine and bread for breakfast next day: to the post-office—no letter; wrote home for a remittance, in more urgent terms, than hitherto. Mulled wine and bread for dinner and supper.

Next morning, intensely hungry, and somewhat griped—Harry, wistfully regarding my collection of rarities,— 'We can't starve while we have these,' he remarked, at length.

I pointed out to him, that his observation was illogical. We could not feed off them, and *might*, therefore, starve while we had them.

'We can sell them,' he said.

Surprise, for a moment, struck me dumb: were the pangs of hunger driving Harry mad, that he, an artist, and an antiquary, should suggest such an outrage. When I recovered speech, I briefly stated, I would see him — further first; 'things were not so desperate as that came to.'

'Am I a chameleon, then,' inquired Harry, warmly, 'that things are not desperate?—Can I live on air?—Have I a wooden interior, that sour wine has no effect on?—What am I—a beast or a cask?'

'You *were* a philosopher,' I replied, reproachfully.

'One can be a philosopher on a full stomach,' he sadly returned; 'my philosophy will come back after I shall have dined.'

'Then, *we will dine*,' I cried; 'come to the pastrycook's, and leave the means with me.'

'*A la bonne heure*,' exclaimed Harry, once more radiant, ' you have an idea then.'

I had.

Monsieur Legros, where we used, in happier times, to lunch on patties and curaçao, received us with bows and smiles; 'he was afraid "Milords" had departed from Paris; he was enchanted it was not so; with what could he do us pleasure; he had invented a new patty of an extreme merit; would we honour him by tasting?'

Harry looked a ravenous 'yes,' but I checked him, with a glance.

'You are an *artist*, Monsieur Legros.'

The fat pastry-cook bowed, and smiled; 'he would permit himself to say he had his small talents.'

'Great talents,' I cried, with energy; '*même la genie*; undoubted genius, Monsieur Legros.'

Monsieur Legros bowed and smiled again; 'he felt distinguished by "Milord's" approval.' Now, for the *coup de main*.

'I have determined,' I proceeded, 'to entrust you with a commission of the highest importance' (more bows and smiles), 'to-day is my birth-day; we have friends to dine with us' (bows and smiles, still), 'we desire to *fête* them with a novelty, something *magnifique*' (fat *pâtissier* excited), 'at five o'clock you must have ready an English plum-pudding.'

The pastry-cook turned pale; he murmured something faintly, and leaned on the counter.

Of this I took no notice, but continued, 'No one but a man of the most profound skill could attempt so great an enterprise! No one but Monsieur Legros can accomplish it!'

The pastry-cook's excitement was here intense; 'he had never made a 'plom-poudin;' with blushes, he confessed he did not know of what it was composed. *Comment faire*, then. Is the 'plom-poudin' of necessity?—would anything else do? Anything but the 'plom poudin' (and Monsieur Legros waved his hands with dignity), and—*c'etait une affaire accompli.*'

Harry looked at me inquiringly. I shook my head. What to us, in our dire necessity, were the elegant trifles—the light paste, and flimsy creams of a French *pâtissier.*

'Monsieur Legros,' I resumed, with solemnity, 'it must be done.' 'Monsieur Legros,' I cried, 'you shall do, it: I, myself, will give you the secret of the combination, as I had it from the Duke of Wellington.'

'*Allons,*' gasped the chief, with a sigh of relief, '*voyons*—let us see?'

At 5 o'clock, that evening, the pastry-cook's boy left with our landlady a plum-pudding, weighing eight pounds; as we could not be disturbed, he left it without payment.

For days we lived on that pudding, and the thin Bordeaux wine: plum-pudding hot—plum-pudding cold— plum-pudding fried—plum-pudding devilled—until the very smell of it was hateful,—to eat it, impossible. Starvation, with its haggard eyes, was staring us in the face. I had again written home, but without avail.

I was sitting, gazing gloomily at the fire (it was the winter season), wondering what was to be the end of this, and whether I should, at length, be forced to sacrifice my dearly cherished art-treasures, when Harry, who had been dining on a sniff at the restaurants, returned, smiling.

'The landlady has got potatoes,' he whispered.

'What then,' I muttered cynically. 'The landlady has got potatoes! Well, the landlady will eat them!'

'We have pudding—we have wine—we have brandy,' said Harry.

I shuddered. 'Do I not smell them?' I asked, bitterly; 'wherever I go, do they not haunt me, and make me sick?'

'We will get rid of the pudding, and some of the brandy, and wine to-night,' said Harry, mysteriously, 'and we will have potatoes.'

He revealed his design, and I smiled.

That night, the landlady, after tea, paid us a visit, by invitation. She ate pudding—she drank wine—she did not disdain to empty tumblers of stiff grog, which she pronounced to be a noble invention, doing the English nation honour.

We borrowed sugar from her, as we had forgotten to get any from the grocer, and made the grog hot, strong, and sweet.

The landlady, who was more than old enough to be our mother, did not affect coyness; she was not afraid of her reputation suffering in our society; so she stayed late, sang sentimental songs in a cracked voice, chatted of her youthful days, and ate more pudding, and drank more grog.

The hour had arrived, and Harry artfully led the conversation into a discussion on the relative merits of the French and English cookery, apropos of the pudding.

'You may say what you please, Madam,' I exclaimed, 'in favour of your *cuisine*, but the English is far in advance of it.'

Madam denied this, with emphasis, and Harry gallantly supported her. 'You talk nonsense,' he said to me.

'Nonsense, or not,' I cried, with simulated warmth, 'give me the plain, wholesome, sensible food of English homes: why, you cannot even get a potato properly served in France!'

Harry, indignantly, disputed this: he enumerated at least twenty delicious dishes made of potatoes by French cooks.

'Where,' I inquired, with a sardonic grin, 'is the Frenchman, or French woman either, who can correctly roast a potato in the ashes?'

Harry admitted that might be the case; but Madam would not—no, for the honour of France, she would roast potatoes, then and there, at our fire.

When the landlady, returning with an apron full of large murphies, proceeded to lay them on the embers, raked in front of our fire, joy lit up the haggard faces of the two conspirators.

The landlady went to bed before the potatoes were cooked; she said the pudding had not agreed with her, and she staggered somewhat. The grog could not have made her ill?—oh, no! *Harry and I ate the potatoes.*

They helped us on over the next day, on the evening of which, no remittance having arrived, I submitted to part with a choice gold ring, set with an antique gem.

'Delavigne, of the Palais Royal,' I said to Harry, 'has over and over again offered l00 francs for it. He is constantly worrying me for it. If the worst comes to the worst, take his offer, but endeavour to arrange with him, to hold it for a fortnight, so that I may re-purchase for a 50 francs' profit; previously, however, see if you can pledge it at the Mont de Piété for 40 or 50 francs. While you go on this commission, to-morrow morning, I will order breakfast at the Café de France.'

I remember that morning well. It was extremely cold; snow had fallen during the night, and was then falling; it was the bitterest day of the severest winter that had been known in Paris for many years. We were, nevertheless, in high spirits. The prospects of a good breakfast made the weather, and the gem I was about to sacrifice, of little moment.

Harry went on his mission; I went on mine.

I ordered chocolate, coffee, a beef-steak, cold fowl, hot rolls, eggs, and a bottle of Chateau-Lafitte [*sic* – for Lafite], and I regaled on those generous provisions. I should, perhaps, in courtesy, have waited for Harry's return, prior to breakfasting, but he was a long time gone.

Would he have waited for me after what we had gone through? Do famished men stand on ceremonies? When he should have returned, could he not also order delicacies, and regale on them unmolested? So I reasoned, as I luxuriously leaned back on a velvet couch, and smoked a cigarette.

Harry at length arrived; snow was on his whiskers, in his ears, and covered his apparel. He appeared as if wrapped in the fur of the white polar bear; his pinched and blue face alone of his person being visible.

I shouted for chocolate, more coffee, more everything.

'Hold,' whispered Harry, with a ghastly leer, 'I have no money.'

'No money,' I reiterated, turning pale; 'have you, then, lost the ring?'

No; he had not lost the ring; the superintendent at the Mont-de-Piété had taken it, and was about to advance the money required, when a sudden suspicion seemed to seize him.

'Your passport, if you please,' he said to Harry.

'*La voila*,' repeated my unfortunate friend.

The official glanced rapidly over it. 'You are under age,' he at length said, 'you cannot legally dispose of this article.—Profound regret, Monsieur, but you cannot reclaim it until you are accompanied by a respectable householder to vouch for your right to it.'

How I got out of that Café, leaving my cane and gloves on the marble table, I cannot describe; what excuse I made to the waiter I cannot remember; I only know that my brain whirled, and a sudden panic took me, and that I did not breathe freely until I gained my domicile.

There, to my inexpressible pleasure, I found my father, who had just arrived in Paris; and Harry and I returned to the Café with a full purse and a contented mind.

The next evening we gave a party. Our guests were my father, our landlady, the grocer and his wife, the pastry-cook, accompanied by two pretty daughters, and the wife of the *cafétièr* [*sic* – for *cafétier*] (he himself could not come). We had round games, romps, dances, songs, and supper, after which, over a bowl of punch, I related, amidst much laughter these adventures, truthfully as they are written here; saving, that out of courtesy to an elderly lady, I did not mention how the pudding disagreed with one of those present.

NOTES

1. George Isaacs, *Rhyme and Prose; and, a Burlesque, and its History* (Melbourne: Clarson, Shallard, & Co., 1865), pp. 23–33.

APPENDIX C

Cover Design Re-use and Materials

THE PURPOSE IN ASSEMBLING a considerable number of publications that bear designs by WHR has been the study of the designs themselves, as discussed in Chapter 16. However, these publications also allow two issues in the field of bibliography, rather than that of design as such, to be addressed here. First, to what extent were blocks bearing WHR designs re-used in whole or in part for later covers? Second, how prevalent were publishers' bindings in leather rather than cloth? The answers to these questions cannot be definitive, since other relevant instances may turn up in the future. Further, there will always be an issue regarding the extent to which results for covers by WHR can be extrapolated to other types of cover. Despite these caveats, however, it seems useful to explore the incidence of cover design re-use and of leather rather than cloth as material for publishers' bindings.

1. RE-USE OF COVER DESIGNS

Douglas Ball appears to be the only writer to have raised the issue of the re-use of binding designs. Ball concluded, however, that the task of investigating re-use was too difficult to attempt in general:[1]

> The extent of re-use of blocks is hard to substantiate and the work involved in recording and comparison of bindings to do so would be excessive.

Nevertheless, the extent of re-use in the limited case of WHR cover designs has been estimated. By a *re-use* is meant the appearance of the design in whole or in part on a different title, which is not part of a single, uniform series. Thus the uniform titles within, for example, the *161. Routledge's British Poets 1867* series are not categorised as re-uses. As a corollary, when a design was re-used to clothe a uniform series of titles, that is counted as only a single re-use. Further, the three WHR cover designs existing only as unauthorised borrowings by American publishers from London illustrations have been excluded as unrepresentative of re-use.

For the remaining 241 designs, the full distribution of known re-uses is shown in Table C.1. From this it can be seen that the proportion of all designs which are known to have been re-used at least once is surprisingly high, amounting to about 31 per cent. The design with the most number of unrelated re-uses (namely, nine) was *41. National Illustrated Library 1853.*

TABLE C.1

The number of re-uses of each cover design by WHR varied from 0 to 9; the table shows the number of different cover designs by WHR observed at each level of re-use.

Number of re-uses	Number of designs
0	166
1	36
2	20
3	8
4	5
5	4
6	0
7	1
8	0
9	1

The present discovery of quite extensive re-use of old blocks implies that it was possible for the binder to retrieve an old block with an appropriate design from among a mass of inappropriate blocks, though the system or systems which allowed this to be achieved do not appear to have been described at the time. Darley described how an example of each new case (i.e. cover) which the binder Burn produced was stored for reference in dusty racks in a cellar at their factory under the care of a single custodian, but does not say anything about the corresponding blocks.[2]

Most re-uses appear to have been opportunistic and unplanned. However, WHR's occasional use of small, detachable roundels within designs was probably intended explicitly to assist re-use, because new roundels could be tailored to a new title. A good example of this deliberate provision for recycling is provided by *182. Masterpieces of Italian Art 1868.* Figure C.1 shows the original, together with three re-uses of its frame. For the *Wagner Festival*, for example, three of the frame's roundels evoked Wagner himself (top), The Flying Dutchman (upper left) and Lohengrin (upper right).

2. INCIDENCE OF PUBLISHERS' LEATHER BINDINGS

Hardback books bearing WHR designs usually appeared with cloth covers. However, this was not the only material and a surprisingly large number of publishers' covers bearing WHR designs appeared as leatherbound books, either as a deluxe alternative to a cloth cover or as the sole binding option. In all, about forty WHR designs appeared on leatherbound books (occasionally as re-uses of the WHR blocks, rather than on their original title).

The deluxe copies were usually medium-sized books bound in full leather. The use of leather greatly increased the cost of a book. Standard sources, such as the *English Catalogue*

C.1 – Masterpieces of Italian Art, 1868, with three re-uses of its WHR frame, showing variation across titles in the frame's six roundels: The Rhyme of the Duchess May, 1873; Men of Mark, 1876; Wagner Festival, 1877. Height 560mm.

Appendix C – Cover Design Re-use and Materials

of Books, rarely mention deluxe copies. However, as an example, *158. Two Centuries of Song 1867* was priced at one guinea in cloth, but at two guineas in leather, according to a listing by its publisher (Sampson Low) in *175. Christian Lyrics 1868*. The leather used for WHR covers was usually morocco, although deluxe copies of *12. Art Journal Catalogue 1851* were issued in full calf as well as in full morocco, and *244. The Crèche Annual 1873* was conversely usually bound in calf but also found in morocco.

Books which appeared only in leatherbound format, on the other hand, were usually large volumes whose heavy boards needed a stronger bridge between them and the spine than could be provided by cloth. This need for functionality rather than luxury was usually met by giving such books only a quarter-binding (spine only) or occasionally a half-binding (spine and corners) in leather.

NOTES

1. Douglas Ball, *Victorian Publishers' Bindings* (Library Association, 1985), pp. 69, 71–2; p. 72.
2. Lionel S. Darley, *Bookbinding Then and Now: A Survey of the First Hundred and Seventy-eight Years of James Burn & Company* (Faber and Faber, 1959), pp. 64–5.

APPENDIX D

Kate Rogers and Others

I**N THIS LAST CHAPTER, THE ACHIEVEMENTS** and associates of some descendants of WHR mentioned in Chapter 2 are considered. There was a notable echo of WHR's artistic world in his daughters, Kate and Isabel Rogers. Kate was the elder, but still only eleven years old when WHR died in 1873. The sisters would nevertheless have retained some memories of their father and his activities from before his death, and these would certainly have been kept alive and added to by his sister Mary Eliza, who took them in, and his brother George Alfred, both of whom were great admirers of WHR's work and artists in their own right. Kate Ruskin Coughtrie, eldest grandchild of WHR and niece of Kate and Isabel Rogers, is also discussed, as are William Hyde, husband of Kate Rogers, and the Rogers' family friends Hannah and Arthur Barlow.

Kate and Isabel both became professional artists within the Art Pottery movement. The Rogers family had already played an important role in the earliest development of this movement by introducing into the Doulton firm, pioneers of Art Pottery, members of the Barlow family that included the celebrated artist, Hannah Barlow.

THE ROGERS AND BARLOW FAMILIES

Art Pottery developed in the late 1860s from the collaboration of John Sparkes, director of the Lambeth College of Art, and Henry Doulton, owner of the eponymous firm of stoneware manufacturers in Lambeth. When Sparkes came to write an early history of the movement in 1874, the artist to whom he gave pride of place was Hannah Barlow. Sparkes recounted that it had been Mary Eliza Rogers, WHR's sister, who had introduced Hannah to him in 1868:[1]

> The artist who has given to the new ware one of its strongest characters is Miss Hannah B. Barlow. She was introduced to me some six years ago, by Miss Rogers, a lady who has written a most charming little work on 'Domestic Life in Palestine,' and the daughter of Mr. Rogers, the well-known wood-carver. An artist herself, she had an artist's quickness to perceive that her young friend, Miss Barlow, was destined to do good work in art. Miss Barlow's …

etched out figures are, so to speak, instantaneous photographs of the animals. She possesses a certain Japanese faculty of representing the largest amount of fact in the fewest lines.

Hannah's brother, Arthur Barlow, was a successful artist at Doulton as well. In his 1874 article, John Sparkes also described his work:

> Another artist, whose skill has done very much for the ware I am describing, is Mr. Arthur B. Barlow. He has taken an entirely different line from that followed by his sister. His ornament is original – a flowing, tumbling wealth of vegetable form wreaths around … The occasional use of a gouge, or carver's chisel, or other carving tool, gives frequent evidence of what resources are his.

In Arthur's case, it was WHR's father who had helped develop his art. Arthur was physically disabled by an injury to his hip (and was to die at the age of thirty-four in 1879), but had taken up wood carving at his doctor's suggestion. His carving had flourished with the help of William Gibbs Rogers, who enlisted the support of John Ruskin, and this had enabled Arthur also to join Doulton as an artist.[2] WHR's father warmly inscribed a carte-de-visite portrait of himself to Hannah and Arthur's mother, 'Mrs Barlow from her old friend W G Rogers'.[3]

KATE ROGERS

Kate Rogers exhibited a 'Japanese Plaque' at the 1880 Art Pottery Exhibition of Howell & James in Regent Street, when she was aged eighteen or nineteen. In view of the friendship between the Rogers and Barlow families, it is not surprising that the artistic talents of Kate Rogers, and later Isabel Rogers, propelled them in the direction of Doulton's art pottery, and Kate's signature as an art painter has been found on Doulton pottery from 1881. The work of Kate and Isabel at Doulton has been widely appreciated both at the time and subsequently.[4]

Kate specialised in painting plants, and had a bold impressionistic technique that contrasted with her father's refined elegance. Figure D.1 shows a pair of vases she painted which nevertheless exhibit compositionally that same tension between balanced global and unruly local elements which her father and grandfather had inherited from Grinling Gibbons. In the 1880s and early 1890s, many splendid items from Doulton's Faience, Impasto and Carrara ranges carried her KR monogram.[5]

Kate established a reputation for her painting beyond art pottery, and the *Journal of Decorative Art* commissioned a series of flower studies from her. These were first published as four large coloured lithographs in each of Volumes 8 (1888) and 9 (1889). In 1890, the eight plates were re-issued separately in a portfolio entitled *Flower Studies after Originals by Miss Kate Rogers*. On 30 April 1895, however, Kate Rogers married another successful artist, William Hyde, and at that point had no option within contemporary society but to give up her career.

WILLIAM HYDE

D.1 – Pair of vases painted with brambles by Kate Rogers for the Faience range of Doulton Lambeth art pottery, c. 1885. Height 270mm.

Kate's partner, and WHR's posthumous son-in-law, William Hyde (born 2 October 1857), produced atmospheric pictures of both pastoral and London scenes. Hyde was a collaborator of Ford Madox Hueffer (1873–1939), the writer who later changed his name to Ford Madox Ford, and of Edward Garnett (1868–1937), the literary critic. The diary for this period of one of Edward Garnett's unmarried sisters, Olive Garnett (1871–1958), has been published.[6] It is clear from the diary that Olive was an admirer of William Hyde, and this no doubt coloured her less than sisterly account of Kate and Isabel. On 14 October 1894, she spent the evening with them and several other people, afterwards telling her diary that:

> One of the Miss Rogers is betrothed to Mr. Hyde; both girls seemed commonplace, slightly vulgar & plain. It was a pleasant evening.

Upon marrying, Kate and William Hyde moved to Shere, a picturesque village in Surrey, and no longer moved in London's artistic circles. As the twentieth century unfolded, William Hyde's work fell out of fashion and, as a result, William and Kate and their children eked out a life of relative poverty in Shere on the proceeds of William's sparse commissions, until his death on 28 August 1925. Kate died on 26 November 1942.

Decades later, at the start of the 1980s, there was a revival of interest in Kate Rogers and William Hyde, when works of theirs which had remained within their family were sold for the benefit of a surviving daughter, via two exhibitions.[7] More recently, the pictures of William Hyde are again receiving serious critical attention, after years of relative neglect.[8]

ISABEL ROGERS

Isabel Rogers followed her sister into the Doulton establishment at Lambeth, but did not become a mainstay of art pottery in the way that Kate did. Isabel's relatively small oeuvre bears little resemblance to that of Kate, her designs being formal and non-floral.

Figure D.2 shows a jug by Isabel (signed with her IR monogram) which is unusual both technically and iconographically. The technique is true sgraffito, a brown ground having been covered in white slip, which has then been partially removed by the artist in order to create the design. The design itself is in classicist style, with motifs such as putti operating a waterwheel, dolphins and tridents, and here the Renaissance-inspired thread of her father's artistic heritage may be discerned.

After Doulton, Isabel Rogers moved to the Royal School of Art Needlework, the 1921 census recording her as an 'Art worker' there and living in Chelsea. In retirement, Isabel joined Kate at Shere, and it was there that she died on 13 January 1951.

KATE RUSKIN COUGHTRIE

Finally, we turn to Kate Ruskin Coughtrie, the first grandchild of William Harry and Mary Ann Rogers, born in Hong Kong on 7 March 1873. She was the daughter of their eldest child Mary Eliza Rogers – who was usually called Isa to differentiate her from her aunt of the same name – and her husband, James Billington Coughtrie.

The Coughtries returned from Hong Kong in the late 1890s, and the 1901 census found Isa and James living in London with six daughters and two sons, aged from twenty-seven (Kate Ruskin) to thirteen (Celia Lucilla), all born in Hong Kong. Three of the daughters – Kate, Phyllis and Constance – exhibited

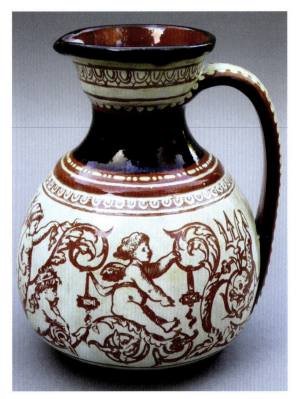

D.2 – A jug decorated in true sgraffito by Isabel Rogers for Doulton Lambeth art pottery, *c.* 1890. Height 180mm.

Appendix D – Kate Rogers and Others

work at the Woman's Exhibition at Earl's Court in 1900, for which the catalogue listed them as sharing one of the St Paul's Studios for artists in West Kensington.[9] Their father James continued to be respected in artistic circles. Thus, a report of the funeral of the artist Frederic Shields mentioned among the mourners only William Rossetti and James Coughtrie.[10] James died on 17 April 1920 in Acton, followed some years later by Isa on 10 June 1934 in Ealing.

D.3 – Kate Ruskin Coughtrie in an allegorical tableau created by the atelier of Reinhold Begas in Berlin, 1897. Miss Cate [*sic*] Coughtrie is Third Victory. Image width 125mm.

Between Hong Kong and London, Isa Coughtrie had taken the children to live in Kassel in Germany, where Kate and two other sisters had been drawn into the artistic life of the imperial summer residence, Schloss Wilhelmshöhe. Kate Ruskin Coughtrie was in the atelier of Professor Reinhold Begas (1831–1911) who dominated public sculpture in Berlin in the late nineteenth century, creating, for example, the national monuments to Bismarck and to Wilhelm I.[11] In 1897, members of the atelier put together a celebration of his career which featured a living tableau of the allegorical figures which abounded in his sculptures. Figure D.3 reproduces a photograph of the tableau, in which the Third Victory (with head close to the seaweed dangling from Neptune's trident) was identified in the caption as Kate Coughtrie.[12]

When Kate Ruskin Coughtrie moved on to London, she practised both as a painter and as a sculptor, associating with the famous, although she never became famous herself. We catch glimpses of Kate in the autobiography of Brian Sewell (1931–2015), the

299

iconoclastic art critic.[13] Sewell recalled that his mother had been 'taken on' by Kate Ruskin Coughtrie, who had taught her to paint 'moderately well' and to sculpt figures in terracotta. Kate had also introduced her to Walter Sickert (1860–1942) and to residual members of the short-lived Omega Workshops which had been set up in 1913 by Roger Fry (1866–1934) and other members of the Bloomsbury Group. Sewell lamented that Kate Ruskin Coughtrie has nevertheless been 'omitted from all works of reference'. Much of Kate's life and career remains obscure, but at some point she moved to Scotland, where she died on 26 February 1968.

Kate Ruskin Coughtrie's most successful work was perhaps her *Remembrance*, which Sewell recalled in his autobiography having seen in 1966, while he was on the road for Christie's. It shows a mourning woman amid a group of wreaths under a cartouche with a lapidary inscription commemorating the fallen in the First World War. It was exhibited at the Summer Exhibition of the Royal Academy in 1917, where it was bought for 100 guineas;[14] a high-quality art print was made of the painting by the Fine Art Publishing Company.

NOTES

1. John Sparkes, 'On some recent inventions and applications of Lambeth stoneware, terra cotta, and other pottery for internal and external decorations', *Journal of the Society of Arts*, 1874, pp. *22*, 557-68; p. 562. An edited version of this article also appeared in *The Builder*, 1874, pp. *32*, 390-91.
2. *Memoire* [*sic*] *of Arthur Bolton Barlow by his Mother* (privately printed, 1879), p. 16. Cited by Peter Rose, 'The life and work of Hannah Barlow, in *Hannah Barlow: A Doulton Artist* (Richard Dennis, 1985), pp. 4–38; p. 9.
3. Reproduced by Rose, *ibid.*, p. 10.
4. Desmond Eyles (rev. Louise Irvine), *The Doulton Lambeth Wares* (Richard Dennis, 2002). The works of Kate and Isabel Rogers are illustrated on pp. 142, 150 and 184, and their monograms shown on p. 318.
5. Confusingly, there were also two unrelated Rogers sisters at Doulton, Martha and Edith. Their brother, Mark Rogers Jr (a woodcarver, adding to the confusion), married a third Doulton painter, Mary Mitchell.
6. Barry C. Johnson (ed.), *Olive & Stepniak, the Bloomsbury Diary of Olive Garnett 1893–1895* (Birmingham: Bartletts Press, 1993), p. 126.
7. The catalogues of the two exhibitions were: John Charlish (Introduction), *Kate Rogers and William Hyde, Exhibition 14 November – 19 December*

1980, Bedford Way Gallery, London; Auriol Earle (Foreword), *Two Victorian Artists from Shere: Kate Rogers 1861–1942, William Hyde 1859–1925, 2–30 January 1982*, Guildford House Gallery, Guildford.
8. Jerrold Norththrop Moore, *The Green Fuse: Pastoral Vision in English Art, 1820–2000* (Woodbridge: Antique Collectors' Club, 2007) – the first and second chapters deal with Samuel Palmer and William Hyde, respectively; Simon Knowles, 'Railway visions: William Hyde's re-imagining of London as a networked space', *London Journal*, 2017, Vol. 42, pp. 291-310.
9. Imre Kiralfy (Director-General), *Woman's Exhibition 1900: Fine Art, Historical, and General Catalogue* (Spottiswoode & Co., 1900), p. 232.
10. *The Times*, 3 March 1911.
11. Alfred Gotthold Meyer, *Reinhold Begas* (Bielefeld & Leipzig: Velhagen & Klasing, 1901).
12. The photograph of the tableau appeared in *Velhagen & Klasings Monatshefte*, 1901–02, Band 1, p. 510.
13. Brian Sewell, *Outsider – Always Almost: Never Quite. An autobiography* (Quartet Books Ltd, 2011), pp. 3-4, 332.
14. T.A. Ingram, *The New Hazell Annual and Almanack for the Year 1918* (Henry Frowde and Oxford University Press, 1918), p. 733.

Index of Titles for Books and Journals with WHR Covers

Entries in Appendix A are indicated by page numbers in bold. Illustrations have page numbers in italic.

Adventures of Robinson Crusoe, The 210, *248, 249*
All The Year Round 200, *200*, 249, *251*
Alpine flowers for English gardens 181, 274, *274*
Always do your best, and Lizzie Lindsay 183, *238, 239*
American Poets (Routledge) 236, *236-7*
Andersen's stories for the household 181, 259, *260*
Andersen's tales for children 272, *273*
Animal traits & characteristics 187, *187*, 278, *279*
Art Journal illustrated catalogue, The 118-128, 183, 186, 190, 198-9, *199*, 208, **220**, 220-1, *294*
Art Journal, The 220, *220*
Arundel Society, from 1849 to 1868, The 179, **268**, *269*
Ballads by Amelia B. Edwards 237, *239*
Battle-fields of the South 248, *249*
Beautiful birds 230, *231*
Beeton's Bible dictionary 210, 275, *276*
Beeton's modern men and women 210, 275, *276*
Belgravia 189, 259, *261*
Book of common prayer, The *279*, 279-80
Book of perfumes, The 157, 180, 192–3, 201, *256, 257*
Book of the sonnet, The 260, *261*

Boy and the birds, The 225, *225*
Boy cavaliers, The 266, *266*
Boy's Monthly Magazine, The 254, *255*
Boy's own book of natural history, The 183, **278**, *279*
Boy's own treasury of sports and pastimes, The 198, **282**, *283*
British Poets (Routledge) 183, 261, *262*
Broadway: A London magazine, The 188, 262, *263*
Brownies and other tales, The 181, 190, **276-7**, *277*
Brush-notes in Holland 280, *280*
Builder, The 184, **218**, *219*
Bushel of merry-thoughts, A 158, *158*, **264-5**, *265*
Castile and Andalucia 227, *227*
Cat and mouse 264, *264*
Catholic Crusoe, The 259, *259*
Charlie and Ernest or play and work 240, *241*
Charm, a book for boys and girls, The 209, **227**, *227*
Chemist and Druggist, The 155, 184, **245**, *246*
Children's Bible picture-book, The 238, *239*
Children's picture fable-book, The 238, *240*
Children's picture-book of birds, The 238, *240*
Child's history of England, A 247, *249*
Christ was born on Christmas Day. A carol 251, *253*
Christian lyrics 183, 198, 265, *266*
Church seasons, The 270, *271*
Cithara 257, *258*
Claude's liber veritatis 277, *278*

301

Climbing the hill *262*, 263
County families of the United Kingdom, The 184, 251, *252*
Courtship of Miles Standish, The *240*, 241
Crèche annual, The 192, 199–200, 283, *283*, 294
Curiosities of savage life *248*, 249
Daisy's companions 183, 271, *272*
Deborah's drawer 201, *272*, 273
Designs for villas, parsonages, and other houses 234, *234*
Divine emblems 190, 247, *247*, 249
Doll world 271-2, *272*
Domestic life in Palestine 198, *246*, 247
Drawing room table book, The 149, *180*, 181, 207, 218, *219*
Dream children *237*, 238
Edwy and Elgiva; a tragedy 188, 212, *256*, 257
Effie's friends 156, 249, 251, *252*
Emblems of Christian life 145-7, 247, *247*
Enthusiast or the straying angel, The 188, 221, *221*
Evenings at home 197, *224*, 225
Excelsior; or, the realms of poesy 188, *220*, 221
Fairford windows, The 183, *282*, 283
Fairy Mary's dream 277, *277*
Fairy tales and sketches by Andersen 272, 273
Faithful hound, The *240*, 242
Few words on education, A *275*, 276
Fielding titles 234, *236*
Fortunes of the Colville family, The 218, *219*
Funny fables for little folks 258-9, *259*
Garden, The *274*, 275, *275*
Gent's history of Hull in fac-simile 268, *270*
Great battles of the British army, The *272*, 273
Great battles of the British navy, The 273, *274*
Great cities of the ancient world, The *224*, 225
Great schools of England, The *256*, 257
Great sieges of history, The *272*, 273
Great wonders of the world, The 236
Great works of Raphael Sanzio, The *268*, 269
Grimm's goblins 283, *283*
Grocer, The 155, 184, *245*, 246
Hamlet, The 242, *243*
Hardy flowers *274*, 275

Hints to young architects 242, *243*
Historical acting charades *236*, 237
History for boys 232, *232*
Holiday book for Christmas, A 222, *223*
Holy Bible, The (Beeton) *248*, 249
Holy Bible, The (Virtue) 244, *245*
Home for the holidays *240*, 241
Home treasury of old story books, The 151, *238*, 239
Hornet, The *280*, 280-1
Household stories collected by the Brothers Grimm 259, *261*
Ice-Peter 183, *263*, 264
Illustrated London Library 230, *230*
Illustrated London News, Christmas Supplement 251, *253*
Illustrations of the Isle of Wight 234, *234*
In honorem. Songs of the brave 232, *233*
Influence; or, the evil genius 225, *225*
Ironmonger and Metal Trades Advertiser, The 184, *245*, 246
Lady of the lake, The *269*, 270-1
L'Allegro 242, *243*
Landseer gallery, The *279*, 280
Lectures on the results of the Great Exhibition 197, 222, *222*
Life of Columbus, The 266, *266*
Life of her most gracious majesty the Queen 232, *232*
Life of Las Casas, The 265, *266*
Life portraits of William Shakspeare 183, 252, *253*
Light for the path of life 183, *183*, 237, *237*
Little Lychetts, The 236, *236*
Little Susy's six birthdays 192, 231, *231*
Lives of the queens of England 230-1, *231*
Lyra sacra americana 265, *266*
Magnet stories, The 186, 281, *282*
Man in the past, present and future 189, *282*, 283
Mansions of England in the olden time, The 183, *268*, 270
Many happy returns of the day! 181, *269*, 270
Marriage service, The 151, 151, 153, 191, *241*, 242
Masterpieces of Italian art 179, 209–10, *268*, 269, 292, 293
Mausoleum, The 251, *253*

Memoirs of great commanders 273, *274*
Merchant of Venice, The 153, 242, *243*
Modern husbandry *229*, 230
Montaigne's essays 181, 191, *270*, 271
Mrs. Beeton's dictionary of every-day cookery 210–1, **255**, *255*
Murby's Excelsior books *262*, 263
Musical mélange, A 252, *253*
My feathered friends *278*, 279
National Illustrated Library 230, *230*, 292
Natural history of Selborne, The *278*, 279
Nature and art; or, reminiscences *262*, 263
Naughty boys of Corinth, The 264, *264*
Notes about Notts 283, *283*
Official illustrated catalogue, 1862 Exhibition 104, 155, *245*, 247
Our fresh and salt water tutors 181, 271, *271*
Our ocean highways *278*, 279
Our Own Fireside *248*, 249
Parables from nature 255, *256*
Parks, promenades & gardens of Paris, The 274, *274*
Pastoral poems 237, *239*
People, places, and things 255, *255*
Peoples of the world 183, 276, *276*
Peter Parley's walks in the country 222, *223*
Pic-nic papers, The 234, *236*
Picture book of birds and beasts, A 180, 242, *243*
Pictures from Sicily 225, *226*
Pictures of girl life *256*, 257
Picturesque selections 244, *245*, 246
Piedmont and Italy 261, *262*
Pilgrim fathers, The 182, 225, *225*
Pilgrimages to English shrines 74, 180, *122*, 123, 181, 190, 201, 207, *218*, 219
Pilgrim's progress 189, 191, 242, *243*
Pipe of repose, The 220, *220*
Poetical works of Edgar Allan Poe, The *239*, 240, 241
Poetical works of John Keats, The 275, *276*
Poetical works of Longfellow, The 223, *223*
Poetical works of Oliver Goldsmith, The *239*, 240
Poetical works of Thomas Gray, The 150–1, *150*, 187, *187*, 190, *237*, 238
Poetry book for children, A 189, 231, *231*
Poets of England and America 242, *243*

Poets of the west, The 242, *243*
Practical and economical cookery *236*, 237
Primrose pilgrimage, The *256*, 257
Proverbial philosophy 212, 257, 258, *258*, 294
Psalms and hymns for divine worship 158, 259, *259*
Quarles' emblems 28, *29*, 30, 146, 153, *154*, 155, 190, **244**, *244*
Raffaelle gallery, The 183, *279*, 280
Rainbow stories, The 281, *281*
Ran away to sea 249, *251*
Recollections of Eton 276, *276*
Relics of genius *240*, 241
Reminiscences of the veterans of the sea *180*, 181, **259**, *261*
Rhine and its picturesque scenery, The 196, 234, *235*
Rome, and its surrounding scenery 222, *223*
Royal gallery of art, The 150, 209, *231*, 231-2
Sabbath bells chimed by the poets 150, *150*, 200, 210, 234, *234*
Savage-Club papers, The 158, 260, *261*
Search for winter sunbeams 181, 271, *271*
Selections from the studies of the great masters 280, *280*
Seven lamps of architecture, The 218, *219*
Shakspeare memorial 156, 252, *253*
Sharpe's London Magazine *220*, 222
Sheepshanks gallery, The *268*, 269
Ships and sailors ancient and modern 181, 266, *267*
Silas the conjurer 249, *250*
Sketches and anecdotes of animal life *278*, 279
Sketches in ultra-marine 209, 227, *229*
Smollett titles 234, *236*
Songs of the brave. The soldier's dream *233*, 234
Specimen of printing types *262*, 263
Spiritual conceits 139-147, *246*, 247
Stones of Venice, The 218, *219*
Stories of the wars *248*, 249
Streeter's catalogue 181, *277*, 277-8
Student and Intellectual Observer, The 261, *262*
Sugar-bread 264, *264*
Swiss family Robinson, The 223, *223*

Switzerland. Illustrated by Bartlett 223, *223*
Tales and fairy stories *272,* 273
Tales and traditions of the Arabs *282,* 283
Tom Hood's comic annual *262,* 264
Town, The 218, *219*
Travels of Rolando *224,* 225
True to herself. A romance 186, 277, *277*
Turner's liber studiorum *277,* 278
Two centuries of song 189, 199, *199,* 259, *261*
Uncle George's Juveniles *220,* 221
Under the rose 266, *266*
Venice, the city of the sea 227, *229,* 230
Vernon gallery of British art, The 129, 150,
    218, *219*
Vicar of Wakefield, The 189, 232, *233*
Views in Wakefield 227, *227*
Visit to the New Forest, A 183, *238,* 239
Voice of Christian life in song, The *256,* 257
Voyage and venture *224,* 225
Waikna; or, adventures on the Mosquito
    Shore 232, *232*
Wide, wide world, The 222, *222*
Wine Trade Review, The 156, *245,* 247
Woman in white, The 190, 192, **251**
Womankind in Western Europe *268,* 270
Women of Israel, The 227, *229*
Women of the Old Testament, The *268,* 270
Wonder Castle 183, 209, 227, *228*
Works of William Shakespeare, The 252, *253*
World's pictures, The 179, *268,* 269
Young Englishwoman, The 157, 157, **255,**
    255, 256

Index

Italic numbers indicate illustrations.
William Harry Rogers is abbreviated to WHR.

A

Abney Park cemetery, London 27, 33–4, *33*
Addey, Henry Markinfield 209
Albert, Prince 72, 110, 197
Albert Institute of Design 12–13
album covers 121–2, *121*
All About Shakespeare 65, **65**
altar-cloth 122
Alton Towers, Staffordshire 110
antiquarian collections 21, 22, 24
antiquarianism 41–2, 44
Appleton & Co 189
architectural college
 see Freemasons of the Church
art books 187, 188
art history 38
Art Journal/Art Union 69–79
 articles by WHR 75, 78
 caddy spoon 82
 campaign against Sir Henry Cole 98–9, 100, 101–2
 capital letters 64, 72
 card backs 161, *162*
 cradle for Queen Victoria 74, 107–9, *109*
 exhibitions covered by 77–8, 102
 'Finis' design 79
 Freemasons of the Church 56–7
 goldsmith's work, illustrations of 78
 introduction to 14
 jewellery *168*, 169
 letterheads 44–5, *44*, 79
 Limoges enamel, project to recreate 70
 masthead 74, 75
 Original Designs for Manufacturers 64, 65, 72–3, *73*, 76–7, 78, 79, 185–6
 ownership 207–8, 209
 picture frame 204
 silver designs 91–2
 Spiritual Conceits, review of 144
 on William Gibbs Rogers 23–4, 70–1, 72
 wood-carving designs 70, 71–2
Art Journal/Art Union catalogues
 Dublin Exhibition (1853) 128–30, *129*
 Great Exhibition (1851) 14, 102–3, 119–28, *120–3*, *125*, *127*, 186, 198–9, 208–9
 London Exhibition (1862) 131–3, *132*, *134*
 London Exhibition (1871) 135
 London Exhibition (1872) 135–6, *136*, 170, *170*, 172, *172*
 Paris Exhibition (1855) 130–1, *130*
 Paris Exhibition (1867) 133, 135
Art Pictorial and Industrial 170, 171
Art Pottery 295, 296, *297–8*, 298
asymmetry, in book cover design 181–2, *182*
Athenaeum 82, 83, 144, 188
Atkin, Henry 84
auction sales 37–8, 44
Australia
 George Isaacs emigrates to 25, 42, 44
 other emigrants to 26–7

B

Ball, Douglas 184, 185, 291
Barclay, G.
 Monograms 152, 153

305

Thirty varieties of the monogram 160
Barlow, Arthur 296
Barlow, Hannah 295–6
Barry, Charles 130
Bartholomew, Alfred 14, 51, 52, 53
Beeton, Isabella 210–11
   Mrs Beeton's Dictionary of Everyday Cookery
      210–11
Beeton, Samuel Orchart 210–11
Beeton's Annual; a book for the young 157
Beeton's Christmas Annual 156
Beeton's Great Book of Poetry 160
Beeton's Musical Album for 1866 157
Beeton's Robinson Crusoe 210
Begas, Reinhold 299
Belgravia 189
Bennett, Charles Henry 27–8, *29*, 30, 153, 191
Benson, J.W. 133
Bernal, Ralph 28, 52, 75–6
Betjeman, John 146–7
Bible cover 123
Biblia Sacra 203
Bickersteth, Rev. E., *A Companion to the Holy
   Communion 159*, 160
Billings, Robert William 51, 78
binder's tickets 206–7, *207*
Birbeck, Richard 20
Bone, William 133, 185, 186
Bone, William Thomas 206–7, *207*
Book-buyer's Guide 163
book covers 174–93
   19th century methods and designs 174–9,
      175–8
   binders 184–5, *207*
   covers by WHR in the USA 189–90, *190*
   covers by WHR, number of 184
   covers by WHR, survival of 192–3
   designed by Henry Fitzcook 65, *65*
   designed by Mary Eliza Rogers 135, *136*
   dust jackets 191–2
   genres 186–9
   in the Dublin Exhibition (1853) 129
   in the Great Exhibition (1851) 122–3, *122*,
      124, 125, *125*, 186
   in the London Exhibition (1862) 133, *134*
   introduction to 16–17, *17*
   lettering 182–4, *183*
   payments to WHR 190–1

   from Stowe, drawn by WHR 57, *57*
   symmetry and asymmetry in the designs of
      WHR 179–82, *180*
   *covers by WHR are illustrated in Appendix A,
      216-84, and separately indexed, 301-4*
book hawking 197
book interiors
   Dublin Exhibition (1853) catalogue 129–30
   Great Exhibition (1851) catalogue 125–6, *127*
   Paris Exhibition (1855) catalogue 130–1, *130*
   see also illustrations
book plates 199–200
bookbinders 184–5, 206–7, *207*
bookbinding 174, 292, 294
Boy's Book of Ballads 155
Boy's Own Magazine 156
bracelet 172, *172*
brackets 71, 72, 129, *129*
Bray, Anna Eliza 88
bread platters 100
bridles 122, 129
Briggs, Asa 84–5
British Archaeological Association 41–2
British Museum 41, 42, 44, 76
Broadhead & Atkin 84
Broadhead, Roger 84
brooch 24–5, *25*, 48, *48*
Brough brothers 28
Builder, The 50–61
   articles by WHR 40, *40*, *46*, 52, 53, 54,
      56, 57, *57*, 59
   campaign against Sir Henry Cole 99, 100
   church interiors 58–9, *58*, 60–1, *60*
   Freemasons of the Church *43*, 50–1, 53,
      56–7, 57–8, 59–60
   Great Exhibition 59–60
   illuminated letters by WHR *47*, 52
   illustrations by WHR 53–4, *55*, *57*
   introduction to 13
   letterhead 61, *61*
   masthead by WHR 54
   monograms of WHR 46, *46*–7, *47*
   wood-carving, discussion of 113–16
Burdett-Coutts, Angela 203–5, *204*
Burges, William 10, 88
Burn, William 21
Burns, Robert, *Poems and Songs* 151
Bury, Shirley 82, 97, 101, 168

C

caddy spoons 81–5, *82*, 124
Calloway, Stephen 178
capital letters 64, 72
carriage door handle 76, 77
Carter, John 191
carton-pierre book covers 175–6, *176*
Cartouche and Spiral tableware 91, *91*
caskets 133, 136
ceramics
   Art Pottery 295, 296, *297–8*, 298
   majolica 75, *75*
   porcelain 70
Chamberlain, Walter 51, 70
Chamberlains 83
chandelier 131–2, *132*
Chandler, Louise, *Evaline, Madelon, and Other Poems* 153
Charity, or Rich Figure design 91–3, *92*
chatelain-head 123, *123*
Cheshire, Jim 211
children's books 32, 187–8, *187*
Children's Pilgrim's Progress 153
Child's Play 151
church interiors 58–9, *58*, 60–1, *60*
claret-jugs 132–3
Claudet, A. 130
Cole, Sir Henry 96–105
   effect of campaign by WHR 101–2
   Great Exhibition of 1851 97
   Joseph Cundall and 209
   other exhibitions 119
   reform of design and 15
   Society of Arts and 97
   Summerly's Art-Manufactures 81
   WHR and 96–7
   WHR campaign against 97–101
collections of antiquities 21, 22, 24
college of architecture *see* Freemasons of the Church
copyright 88
copyright libraries 192
Coughtrie, James Billington 32–3, 298, 299
Coughtrie, Kate Ruskin (granddau.) 33, 298, 299–300, *299*
Coughtrie, Mary Eliza (Isa), (née Rogers, dau.) 25, 30, 32, 33, 145, 298, 299

court actions 63, 65, 66
Cowper, William, *John Gilpin* 66–7, *67*
cradle for Queen Victoria 106–16
   announcement of 74
   carving of 111–16
   denounced by John Henry Newman 110–11
   design of 106–9, *107*, *109*, 128
   introduction to 13–14
   mythological iconography 108–9, *109*, 111
   response of Queen Victoria 110
Cressy and Poictiers 157
Culme, John 90
cultural restitution 76
Cundall, Joseph 104–5, *150*, 209–10

D

Daily News 144
Dalziel, George 126
Darley, Lionel S. 292
Day, Lewis F. 10, 12, 155, 172, 176–7, 183
De La Rue 161
designs for manufacturers
   see Original Designs for Manufacturers
Dickens, Charles 103
   Martin Chuzzlewit 208
Divine and Moral Songs for Children 66
Dobson, Austin 146
Dobson & Pearce 132–3
Dodd, Samuel 203
door-knockers 40, *40*
Dorothea, sculpture 101, *101*
Doulton, Henry 295
Dover, Kent 19
Dresser, Christopher 10
Dublin Exhibition (1853) 128–30, *129*
dust jackets 191–2

E

education in design 101–2
Edward Moxon & Co 211
emblems 139, 143, 144, 146
Emblems of Christian Life 145–6, *147*
emigration *see* Australia
enamelling 41–2
engraving a rainbow 126, *127*

etui 76
Evans, J.W. and J.S. *120*, 121–2
Examiner 144
Express 83

F

fire-irons 64, *64*
First World War 193
Fitzcook, Henry 25, 63–7, *64–5, 67*, 72, 98, 150
flatware *see* tableware
Flores, Carol Hrvol 183–4
foliage, designs featuring *73, 74, 82, 82*
Fourdrinier, Hunt & Co. 162, 167
frames 131
Franks, Sir Augustus Wollaston 42
freemasonry 51–2
Freemasons of the Church *43*, 50–1, 53, 56–7, 57–8, 59–60
French, George Russell 57–8, 59
Friswell, J. Hain, *The Gentle Life* 157
Fun 188

G

Garnett, Olive 297
gas lamps *see* chandelier
Gellatly family 21, 27, 33, *33*
Gibbons, Grinling 14, 20, *20*, 180
gift-giving 188, 196, 197–8
glass 124, 129, 132–3
Global Symmetry and Local Asymmetry (*GS-LA*) 14, 179–82, *180*
Godwin, George 14, 53, 58, 60, 61
goldsmith's work, illustrations of 78
Gombrich, Sir Ernst 103
Goodall & Son 161
Gosse, Edmund 212
graphotype process 66
Great Exhibition (1851)
    catalogues 14, 102–3, 119–28, *120–3, 125, 127*, 186, 198–9, 208–9
    cradle for Queen Victoria 106–7
    exhibits of WHR 119–24, *120–3*
    Freemasons of the Church and 59–60
    introduction to 10, *11*, 12, 15
    key 44

silver 84, 89, 90–1
    Sir Henry Cole and 97
Greenwood, James, *Reminiscences of a raven* 157
Grieve, Alastair 182
Griffith, William Pettit 53, 56
Grosart, Alexander 155
Groves, J.B. 31
Gruel of Paris 124

H

Hall, Anna Maria (Mrs S.C. Hall) 64, 207–9
    The Drawing Room Table Book 149, 207, 218, *219*
    The Old Governess, a Story 149–50
    Pilgrimages to English Shrines *122*, 123, 190, 201, 207, 218, *219*
Hall, Samuel Carter 14, 69, 99, 102–3, 207–9
    The Royal Gallery of Art Ancient and Modern 150, 209, 231–2, *231*
    The Vernon Gallery of British Art 150, 218, *219*
Handley-Read, Charles 129
Hansom, Joseph 50
Harford, Harry 21–2
Harrison, T. 122
Harrow & Son 131–2, *132*
Hendrie, Robert 180
Herne's Oak 112
Hesperus, The 38
Higgins, Francis 85–6, *85*, 88, 89–91, *89*, 91–2, *91–2*, 93, 121, 129
Hill, Rosemary 21
Hirst, Damien, *Bilotti Paintings* 147
Holloway, M.M. 133, *134*, 202–3
Hong Kong 32, 34, 298
Howell & James 168, 170–2, *170, 172*
Humphreys, Henry Noel 175–6
Hunt, Joseph *see* Joseph Hunt & Sons
Hunt, William Holman 66
Hunt & Roskell 86–7, *87*
Hyde, William 297–8

I

illuminated letters *47*, 52
illustrated books 146
Illustrated London News (*ILN*) 41, 65, 82, 93, *94*, 132–3

illustrations 15–16, 149–60
  early (1844–57) 149–50, *150*
  main (1858–62) 150–1, *150–2*, 153, *154*, 155–6, *156*
  late (1863–70) 156–8, *157–9*, 160
  in *The Builder* 53–4, *55*, 57, *57*
  see also Art Journal/Art Union catalogues; Original Designs for Manufacturers; *Spiritual Conceits*
Institute of the Fine Arts and Art-Unions 70
invitation *43*
ironwork 40, *40*, 52
Isaacs, Emily Georgina 25, 44
Isaacs, George 37–45
  emigrates to Australia 25, 42, 44
  enamelling, interest in 41–2
  family background 37–8
  France, visits to 42
  friendship with WHR 24, 42
  Hesperus, editor of 38
  ironwork owned by 52
  Paris trip 38–41 *see also* Appendix B
Isaacs, Marion (née Lane) 25, 44
Isaacs, Samuel 37

J

Japanese art 181
Jaques, John *see* John Jaques & Son
Jenyns, Soame, *Disquisitions* *134*, 202–3
jewellery 168–72, *169*
  brooch 24–5, *25*, 48, *48*
  lockets 170–1, *170*
  marriage bracelet 172, *172*
  rings 41–2
Jewitt, Llewellynn 163
John Jaques & Son 166, *166*
Johnson, Martha (grandmother) 27
Johnson, Mary (mother) 21, 22, 30, 33
Jones, Owen 10, 12, 74, 161, 175, *176*, 183–4
Jonquet, Adolphe 12
Joseph Hunt & Sons 162–4, *164–5*
Journal of Decorative Art 296
journals 184, 187, 188–9, 192

K

Keele Hall, Staffordshire *31*, 205–6
Kellner of Nuremberg 124
Kensington Palace 20
keys 44, 123–4
King, Edmund M.B. 16, 184
Knüttel style *122*, 123

L

Ladies' Guild 129
Ladies, The 170–1, 172
Lady's Newspaper 99, 150
Lambert, Miss, *Church Needlework* 149
Lane, Marion 25, 44
Lansdale, Mary Ann 24–5, 34
leatherbound books 292, 294
Leighton, John 16, 176–7, *176*
letterheads 44–5, *44*, 61, *61*, 79
letters *47*, 52, 64, 72, 182–4, *183*
libraries 200
Limoges enamel 70
linen cloth 121
Literary Churchman 145
lockets 170–1, *170*
London Exhibition (1871) 135
London Exhibition (1872) 135–6, *136*, 170, *170*, 172, *172*
London International Exhibition (1862)
  Art Journal/Art Union catalogue 131–3, *132*, *134*
  official catalogue 104–5, 155–6, *156*, 245, 247
London locations linked to WHR
  Abney Park cemetery 27, 33–4, *33*
  Bow 23–4, 31, 34
  Carlisle House, Soho 25–6, *26*
  Chalk Farm Road 34
  Marylebone 32
  Soho 21, 22, 23–4, *23*, 30, 31
  St Pancras 27
  West Brompton 60–1, *60*
  Wimbledon 27
Lothair Crystal 76
Lyra consolationis 157–8, *158*

M

Mackintosh, Charles Rennie 178
Magazine of Art 111
magic lantern slides 66–7, *67*
majolica 75, *75*
manufacturing methods 90
Marjoribanks, Dudley Coutts 133, *134*, 202–3
Marvel, Ik, *Reveries of a bachelor* 201
masthead 54, *74, 75*
match-boxes 100–1
McDermott, Edward, *The Merrie Days of England* 151
McLauchlan, David 20
McLean, Ruari 146, 150, 183
Middlesex Hospital Benefaction book 93–4, *94*
Millais, Sir John Everett 139
missal cover 129
monograms 46–9, *46–8, 150*, 210
Moore, Thomas, *Poetry and Pictures* 151
Moral Emblems 139–40
Morel, Jean-Valentin 168, *169*
Morning Post 143
Morris, Talwin 178
Morris, William 178
mottos 44–5
Moxon, Edward 211
Moxon Tennyson 139
Murby, Thomas 158, *262*, 263
Murray, John VI (Jock) 146–7
Murray, John G. 146
mythological iconography 108–9, *109*, 111

N

Newman, John Henry 110–11
Norfolk Book Hawking Association 197
novels 186
Number One 38–9

O

Ogden, Charles Kay 193
Once a Week 153
Original Designs for Manufacturers 64, 65, 72–3, *73*, 76–7, *78, 79*, 185–6
Ornamental Designs Act (1842) 88–9

Ornamental Elizabethan tableware 86–90, *87, 89*
Orton, James 188

P

Pantazzi, Sybille 16
paper, writing 162, 167
papier-mâché
    book covers 175–6, *176*
    furniture 66
Parables (Millais) 139
Parables from Nature 139
Paris Exhibition (1855) 130–1, *130*
Paris Exhibition (1867) 133, 135
Paris, France
    other visits 42
    WHR and George Isaacs visit 24, 38–41, *40*
      see also Appendix B
patrons 202–12
    private *31, 134*, 202–6
    professional 206–12, *207*
Payne, James Bertrand 211–12
Penny, J. 122, 129
periodicals 184, 187, 188–9, 192
Perry, William 112, 115
Pevsner, Nikolaus 13, 19, 66, 123
Pickford, Ian 90, 91
picture frames 133, 204, *204*
plated metal 84
playing cards 161–4, *162–6, 166*
poetry books 187, *187*, 188
porcelain 70
Pre-Raphaelite Brotherhood 10, 139
    see also Rossetti, Dante Gabriel
presentation copies 198–9, *199*
prizes 199, *199*
Publishers' Weekly of New York 162
Pugin, Augustus 10, 175
    True Principles 175, *175*
pulping of books 193

Q

Quarles' Emblems 146, 153, *154*, 155, 190, 244, *244*

R

rainbow, engraving of 126, *127*
Ralston, William 16, 178, *178*
re-used designs 149, 166, 190, 291–2
Redgrave, Richard 99, *99*
religion 145
reliquary 44
Reliquary 163
Renaissance style 13–14, 54, 56, 71, 108, 126, 128
Reynolds & Sons 164, *165*
Richards, Ivor Armstrong 193
Richardsons of Derby 129
Ricketts, Charles 178
rings 41–2
Robertson Brooman & Co 88–9
Rogers, Arthur (son) 27, 32
Rogers, Charles Bennett (son) 32, 34
Rogers, Edward Thomas (brother) 21, 30, 34
Rogers, Emily (dau.) 27, 34
Rogers, Frederick Horace (brother) 21, 26–7
Rogers, George Alfred (brother)
    on cradle for Queen Victoria 111, 115
    death 34
    family background 21, 22–3, 24
    picture frame 204–5
    on WHR 115–16
    on wood-carving 113–14
    wood-carving career 31, 32
    wood carvings by 132, 135, 136
Rogers, Isabel (dau.) 32, 34, 145, 298
Rogers, Kate (dau.) 27, 34, 145, 296, *297*, 298
Rogers, Mary Ann (née Lansdale, wife) 24–5, 34
Rogers, Mary Eliza (Isa), (dau.) *see* Coughtrie, Mary Eliza (Isa)
Rogers, Mary Eliza (sister) 21, 22, 33, 34
    book cover designed by 135, *136*
    Domestic Life in Palestine 198, *246*, 247
    and Hannah Barlow 295
    Shakspeare Memorial 156, 252, *253*
Rogers, Mary (née Johnson, mother) 21, 22, 30, 33
Rogers, Sydney (son) 27–8, 32
Rogers, William Gibbs (father)
    antiquarianism 38
    Art Journal and 23–4, 70–1, 72
    and Arthur Barlow 296

and college of architects 51
cradle for Queen Victoria 74, 110, 111–12, 114
death 34
family background 19–21, 25–6, 30, 31, *31*
wood carvings 13, 14, 120–1, *120*, 128–9, *129*, 130, 131, 133
work at Keele Hall *31*, 205–6
Rogers, William Harry (WHR)
    childhood 22–3
    death 33
    early career 23–5, 27
    family background 19–22, 25–7
    financial issues 30–1
    introduction to 10, 12–13
    lifestyle 28
    marriage 24–5
    poems 22, 24, 27
    religion and 145
Rossetti, Christina, *The Prince's Progress* 182, *182*
Rossetti, Dante Gabriel 178, 182, *182*, 212
roundels 78
Routledge 189
Rowley, Charles 133
Royal Collection 209
Royal Society of Arts *see* Society of Arts
Royal Worcester 70
Ruskin, John 16
    The Seven Lamps of Architecture 54

S

salt cellar 120–1, *120*, 131
Saul, Jane 31, 33
Savage Club 28, 30, 32–3
school prizes 199, *199*
Second World War 193
Sewell, Brian 299–300
signatures *see* monograms
silver by WHR 81–95
    caddy spoon 81–5, *82*
    Cartouche and Spiral tableware 91, *91*
    Charity, or Rich Figure design 91–3, *92*
    Dublin Exhibition (1853) 129
    Great Exhibition (1851) 84, 89, 90–1, 121
    introduction to 13
    manufacturing methods 90

Middlesex Hospital Benefaction book
93–4, *94*
Ornamental Elizabethan tableware 86–90,
87, *89*
sugar tongs 85–6, *85*
silver-plating 84
Smith, Benjamin 82
Sneyd, Ralph *31*, 205–6
Society of Arts
exhibition of British Manufactures …
(1848) 82, 98
Sir Henry Cole and 97, 98, 99, 101
Sparkes, John 295, 296
Spiritual Conceits 139–47, *140*
concepts, examples of 141–2, *142–3*
construction 141
contemporary works 139–40
new edition 145–6
reception of 143–4, 146–7
religion and WHR 145
St Eustace Head Reliquary 44
St Mary The Boltons, West Brompton, London
60–1, *60*
St Mary's church, Ware, Hertfordshire
58–9, *58*
Stannus, Hugh 12, 74
Stationers' Hall 192
stationery 162, 167
stereoscope stand 130
Stothard, Thomas 88
Strauss, Gustave 33
sugar tongs 85–6, *85*
Summerly, Felix *see* Cole, Sir Henry
Summerly's Art-Manufactures 81–3
survival of covers with WHR designs 192–3
Swain, Joseph 31, 141
symmetry, in book cover design 179–82, *180*

T

tableware 86–90, *87*, *89*, 91, *91*
teapot 98–9, *99*
Thornhill, Walter 123, *123*
three-volume novels 186
Timbs, John 94
toad stones 42
topography books 187, 188
Train, The 28
tuberculosis 30, 33

U

United States of America 189–90, 201

V

Vanity Fair 102
Victoria, Queen 110, 196
see also cradle for Queen Victoria

W

Wainwright, Clive 21, 175
Wallis, Thomas Wilkinson 112–14, *113*, 116
Ware, Hertfordshire 58–9, *58*
Waring, J.B. *134*, 202–3
Warren, Albert Henry 177–8, *177*
wars, impact on survival of covers 193
Weir, Harrison 162, *163*
Wells, Herbert Gustavus 178
Westleys & Co. 185, 186
White, Gleeson 146
Whittingham, Charles 141
William Bone & Son 133, 185, 186, 206–7, *207*
wood-carving working practices 114–16
wood carvings
designs by WHR 70, 71–2, *120*, 120–1, 128–9, *129*, 131, 133, 135, 203–6, *204*
by George Alfred Rogers 132, 135, 136
by William Gibbs Rogers 13, 14, 120–1, *120*, 128–9, *129*, 130, 131, 133
see also cradle for Queen Victoria
Worcester porcelain 70
Wornum, Ralph 101, 123, 126, 128
writing papers 162, 167